Religion and Touch

Religion and the Senses
Series Editor: Graham Harvey, The Open University, UK

Everyday and/or vernacular religions are now at the cutting edge of the study of religions. The agenda of Religious Studies as well as that of other disciplines which overlap in some aspects with the study of religion (e.g. Classics, History, Sociology, Anthropology and [in some places] Philosophy) has been revitalised by this focus on lived reality. This resonates with the growing interest in materiality and embodiment which have both provoked 'turns' in academic debate and teaching. Criticisms, however, have been levelled against the ways in which 'materiality' does not always engage with materials (stuff) and 'embodiment' sometimes suggests the priority of some interiority (mind, agency, etc.).

The proposed series aims to push further the project of placing lived, material and bodily religion at the definitive centre of studies of religion(s). It will do this by foregrounding bodily sensation and material practice as religion (rather than expressions, experiences or representations of something prior to bodies, acts and things). It develops the interdisciplinary conversation encouraged by Paul Stoller's *Sensuous Scholarship* (1997) and, especially, presents and promotes research about real-life religion approached through performative and materialist methods, as illustrated by, e.g., Manuel Vasquez's *More than Belief* (2011) and Graham Harvey's *Food, Sex and Strangers* (2013).

Published:

Sensual Religion: Religion and the Five Senses
Edited by Graham Harvey and Jessica Hughes

Religion and Senses of Place
Edited by Graham Harvey and Opinderjit Takhar

Religion and Sight
Edited by Louise Child and Aaron Rosen

Forthcoming:

Religion and Senses of Humour
Edited by Stephen E. Gregg

Religion and Touch

Edited by
Christina Welch and Amy R. Whitehead

SHEFFIELD UK   BRISTOL CT

Published by Equinox Publishing Ltd.
UK: Office 415, The Workstation, 15 Paternoster Row, Sheffield, South Yorkshire S1 2BX
USA: ISD, 70 Enterprise Drive, Bristol, CT 06010

www.equinoxpub.com

First published 2021

© Christina Welch, Amy R. Whitehead and contributors 2021

All rights reserved. No part of this publication may be reproduced or transmitted in any form or by any means, electronic or mechanical, including photocopying, recording or any information storage or retrieval system, without prior permission in writing from the publishers.

British Library Cataloguing-in-Publication Data
A catalogue record for this book is available from the British Library.
ISBN-13 978 1 80050 032 7 (hardback)
         978 1 80050 033 4 (paperback)
         978 1 80050 034 1 (ePDF)
         978 1 80050 112 6 (ePub)

Library of Congress Cataloging-in-Publication Data

Names: Welch, Christina, editor. | Whitehead, Amy, editor.
Title: Religion and touch / edited by Christina Welch and Amy R. Whitehead.
Description: Sheffield, South Yorkshire ; Bristol, CT : Equinox Publishing Ltd, 2021. | Series: Religion and the senses | Includes bibliographical references and index. | Summary: "The volume argues that touch is not only an intrinsic part of religion but the principal facilitating medium through which religion, religious encounters and performances take place. The diverse contexts presented here signal how investigations that centralise the body and the senses can produce nuanced, culturally specific knowledges and allow for the development of new definitions for lived religion. By placing both 'body' and the sense of touch at the centre of investigations, the volume asserts that material practice and bodily sensation are lived religion"-- Provided by publisher.
Identifiers: LCCN 2021009219 (print) | LCCN 2021009220 (ebook) | ISBN 9781800500327 (hardback) | ISBN 9781800500334 (paperback) | ISBN 9781800500341 (epdf) | ISBN 9781800501126 (epub)
Subjects: LCSH: Human body--Religious aspects. | Touch--Religious aspects. | Senses and sensation--Religious aspects.
Classification: LCC BL65.B63 R45 2021 (print) | LCC BL65.B63 (ebook) | DDC 204/.2--dc23
LC record available at https://lccn.loc.gov/2021009219
LC ebook record available at https://lccn.loc.gov/2021009220

Typeset by S.J.I. Services, New Delhi, India

Contents

List of Figures vii

Acknowledgements viii

Series Foreword ix
    Graham Harvey

Introduction: Religion and Sense of Touch 1
    Christina Welch and Amy R. Whitehead

PART I Reciprocity and Knowing: Being in Touch with Things

1   Tattooing Ritual and the Management of Touch in Polynesia 25
    Sébastien Galliot

2   Touching Deities: Offerings, Energies and the Notion of Touch in Guyanese Hinduism 51
    Sinah Theres Kloß

3   Accommodating Crisis: Exploring the Dynamics of Touch and Material Devotion in Alcalá de los Gazules 67
    Gabriel Bayarri and Amy R. Whitehead

4   The Heathen Lyre: On Religion, Music and Touch 93
    Andy Letcher

5 Being There: Anglo-Indian Roots Tourism Experiences 114
   Robyn Andrews

PART II Crafting Devotion: Ritual Labour

6 The Senses and Their Absences in Balinese and Tamil Hinduism 137
   Graeme MacRae

7 Death Doulas and Coffin Clubs: Exploring Touch and the
   End of Life 154
   Suzi Garrod and Bronwyn Russell

8 Touch and Other Senses: Feeling the Truth in Basket Divination 175
   Sónia Silva

PART III Touch, Ritual Efficacy and Communication

9 'I am broken, I am remade. And I am held tightly through all
   that comes between.' —BDSM and Religioning on the Edge 195
   Alison Robertson

10 Religion, Touch and Death: Ritual and the Human Corpse 214
    Christina Welch

11 Immersive Hugging as a Ritual Act 236
    Michael Houseman

12 Handling Things Unseen: Tactile Aspects of the Christian Faith 253
    George D. Chryssides

Index 276

List of Figures

1.1	Samoan men displaying *pe'a*	34
1.2	Samoan women displaying *malu*	35
1.3	The apprentice's hand below holds in place the tattoing tool that is being made by the *tufuga* using his hands and feet	37
1.4	Making a tattooing needle	38
1.5	Stretching the skin for a tattoo	39
1.6	Applying pressure to the hand of the initiate	40
1.7	Applying pressure to the head, and fanning the initiate	41
1.8	Washing the skin at the end of a tattooing session	42
1.9	The *tufuga* applies egg-white on the head of an initiate	43
1.10	An assistant anoints the tattooed body with a mixture of coconut oil and turmeric powder	44
2.1	Hindus touching shoulders and forming a ritual unit during *puja*	54
3.1	Image of the Virgin of Alcalá in her shrine	69
3.2	The Virgin's mantle	71
3.3	The shrine souvenir shop	76
3.4	Local artists' picture of the Virgin to protect every house from the Coronavirus	80
3.5	Advertisement for face masks created by the Brotherhood of the Virgin, published on Facebook	82
3.6	Detail showing the mask with the image of the Virgin	82

3.7 and

3.8 Visit of the Virgin to Alcalá in 1929 and in 1949, praying for rain 88

3.9 Photograph sent by a village resident in which one can see banners of the Virgin displayed on balconies 89

5.1 Two sisters in Saint Paul's Anglican Cathedral in Calcutta, standing on the same spot their great-grandparents had stood when they married 124

5.2 The sisters trace their fingers along the lines in the register recording the marriage of their great-grandparents 126

5.3 Record books of a church in Northeast India 131

Acknowledgements

We would like to thank the contributors to this collection for their hard work. We are also grateful for the encouragement of Professor Graham Harvey.

Series Foreword

GRAHAM HARVEY

Religion is sensual because it is corporeal and earthy. Religion is something that people (always bodies) do in the world (always physical). It is seen, heard, tasted, smelled and touched and often involves senses of place, decency, awe, humour, value and honour. These and other senses work together (although not always successfully), and they are integral to corporeality and to engagement with the world. Some of our experiences privilege particular senses—as when we close our eyes to better appreciate music. The sensual impact of religious activities can be staged to employ or heighten one sense at a time, perhaps allowing incense or singing to take a lead. Or they can work together as when the burning of incense coincides with the ringing of bells to direct attention. There are myriad ramifications. This series engages with a wide range of such matters.

It is true that some religions make the physical senses a battleground: encouraging the suppression of bodily senses and desires in favour of 'more spiritual' leanings. In doing so, they do not contradict the assertion that religion is sensual but, rather, they evidence it. Progress in seeking putatively non-material gains or experiences, or of seeking mystical and transcendent states, may be recognised by degrees of success in restraining the more everyday senses. If these senses are not restrained, they may be trained to serve 'more elevated' purposes. Paying attention to the feeling of inward and outward breathing to initiate mindfulness does not negate sensuality but employs it. The banning of music creates alternative sonic environments (e.g. of silence or spoken words) that are deemed suitable to the feel of some ways of being religious. Similarly, quasi-cyborg interactions in online and virtual religion do not challenge the sensuality of religious activities but are conducted through the touch of keyboards, sight of screens and hearing of digital sounds. Examples could be multiplied.

This series has deep foundations in approaches to religion which emphasise the everyday, practice or performance, materiality, embodiment and affect. It owes much to the scholarship of religion and gender which brings into sharp focus the importance of attending to lived realities and refuses to waft away the stench of patriarchal power dynamics. *Religion and the Senses* begins with the assumption that religion is something people do. For some people, this 'doing of religion' is especially about cognition: the encouragement of correct believing or correct understanding. These activities have been emphasised by scholars as well as religious practitioners in most publications about religion. However, religion is as much about the preparation, eating and waste-management of the foods people eat or avoid as it is about the putative meanings of food-rules. Communities are made by eating together, sharing appropriate foods at appropriate times, and equally by avoiding inappropriate foods and those who eat them. They may be riven by the wearing of the wrong costume or by visual or auditory attention to inappropriate media. Religious conflicts can be less about differences of belief than about the censorial setting apart of sensory worlds.

Religion and the Senses builds on these relatively familiar perspectives on lived religion. However, the series is more than summative of existing knowledge. It seeks to advance the cutting edge of debates. It is provocative because it engages with the sensuality of religion on the understanding that religion is *fully* sensual, corporeal and earthy. It pushes further an existing project in which religious senses largely serve to enhance appreciation of the lived reality of religions. Great advances in understanding and analysing religion have been made. However, just as debates about 'materiality' have not always engaged with materials (stuff) and those about 'embodiment' have sometimes suggested the priority of some interiority (mind, agency, etc.), so those about religion and the senses have sometimes suggested that 'religion' exists before and apart from senses. In the books which comprise *Religion and the Senses*, religion will be pursued as something that is not merely represented by or expressed in sensual data (e.g. arts and acts), but is a matter of bodies moving through the world. Attending to sensuality does not (merely) add colour and drama to our views of religion(s). It is not only about the vignettes that introduce our debates. Religion is the smelling, tasting, touching, hearing and seeing of the world in particular ways. We need to attend to everything from bodily affects to trained enculturation (not to evoke a nature/culture dualism but to indicate a rich diversity of topics) in order to understand how sensual religion propels people in their daily and ritual negotiations with life.

This foreword has made use of the conventional idea that there are five senses, albeit with some recognition that these can or must work together (sometimes conflictually). However, the series is not restricted to discussion of those five senses or their synaesthetic interactions. These are our entry points, our 'starting from where we are' places. The journey towards a richer and fuller sense of religion will entail a much wider notion of senses. It will require us to explore senses of place, decorum, decency, value, health/well-being, the uncanny, humour, honour and others. These 'extra' senses provide even greater possibilities for considering movement, relationships, interactions, locations and other matters.

Some of these 'senses' might make more immediate sense than others—e.g. sense of place is a relatively familiar theme in discussing religious locations and commitments. Sense of value encourages consideration of religion and economic systems (e.g. capitalist, gift, votive and sacrificial economies), charity or philanthropy, and of ultimate versus putatively lesser 'needs' or concerns. Sense of decorum might bring discussions of religion and costume into dialogue with discussions of religious discipline and deportment (e.g. stipulations that elders should not run, children should be silent, women should be humble). Sense of honour can generate acts of violence against perceived wrong-doers as well as celebration of specific practices. The sense of the uncanny brings us face-to-face with the worlds of possession and ghosts, with feelings of unease or dread that may require the employment of religious specialists. In contrast with sense of place perhaps the sense of the uncanny is about dislocation and un-ease in the presence of the unknown, unexpected or unwelcome. As these presences are sometimes faced with edgy trickster tales, they provide an additional reason (if we needed it) to immerse ourselves in the sense of humour. If nothing else, jokes told within a religion (about that religion or about others) are revelatory of what is truly at the heart of that lifeway. Reiterating the synaesthetic and corporeal nature of all the senses, perhaps these religious jokes sometimes provoke throaty chortles or 'belly laughs'. Engaging with these many and varied, but usually interacting senses will require authors and readers to confront a broad spectrum of religious acts and ideas, some more edgy or contested than others.

There are, in short, many good reasons for studying religion and the senses, including the assertion made by this foreword (and contested both by some religionists and by perhaps within some of the following chapters) that religion is fully and definitively sensual, corporeal and worldly. This series takes up the project of the 'turns' to lived religion, everyday religion, materiality, gender, embodiment and performance. By sustained focus on the senses—perhaps mediating mechanisms between our bodies and our world—we will gain a greatly improved sense of what religion is and what religious people do.

Graham Harvey is Professor of Religious Studies at The Open University. His research largely concerns the rituals and protocols through which Indigenous and other communities engage with the larger-than-human world. These contribute to a focus on material- and lived-religion. His recent teaching related work has involved a focus on foodways and associated 'purity' practices. His publications include *Food, Sex and Strangers: Understanding Religion as Everyday Life* (2013) and *Animism: Respecting the Living World* (2nd edition 2017). He is editor of the Equinox series 'Religion and the Senses' and the Routledge series 'Vitality of Indigenous Religions'.

Introduction: Religion and Sense of Touch

CHRISTINA WELCH AND AMY R. WHITEHEAD

Religion is, at its very root, a sensual and often tactile affair. From genuflections, prayer, dance and eating, to tattooing, wearing certain garments or objects, lighting candles and performing other rituals, religions of all descriptions involve regular bodily commitments. The five bodily senses, however, are so much a part of daily, or mundane, life that until recently they have been underprivileged in the academic Study of Religions which has tended to focus more on the rules, taboos, constraints, movements and traditions that govern physical actions. This has resulted in entire corpuses of lived, sensually engaged, bodily and performed religious knowledges being, apart from a few exceptions, largely overlooked. The objective of this edited collection has been to creatively seize upon the rich opportunities left open to us by this general oversight. Forming part of a larger, ongoing project that explores religion and the senses through 'each sense' (while recognising that the senses are in a continual state of interplay), contributors to this volume have isolated the 'sense of touch' from the general sensorium as a particular 'sense tool' through which to creatively innovate and operationalise concepts, theories and methods.

At the onset of the development of this project, we approached potential contributors, asking them to think about the roles of touch in different forms of religion. We prompted that we were looking for contributions that deal with touch, not as metaphor, but as a real (rather than symbolic) action. Looking to move away from the dualistic ideas of representation that have dominated the field since its inception, we suggested that authors might contribute work based on touch and sensuality, sex, abstinence, taboos, ritual efficacy, which hands we use and when to touch, hierarchies of touch, tattooing, crafting, and the 'touchy' subject of inappropriate touch in religion, given we now live in the wake of numerous sexual abuse scandals that sadly span a good number of religions (old and new). We were happy to hear how contributors might interpret the theme of touch using their existing research, and what followed has resulted in an extraordinary realisation of academic creativity. Thus, experimentally, we have brought the provocative 'sense of touch' into critical conversation with a range of diverse examples drawn from different religious traditions and spiritual lifeways in locations and communities from Africa, South America, Polynesia, Europe, and South and Southeast Asia. The diverse contexts presented here bear on larger questions that signal how investigations that centralise the body can inspire the inclusion of sensually religious 'body knowledges', widening scopes of inquiry and debate that will, in particular, enrich the emergent fields of lived, sensual and material religion.

LIVED, MATERIAL, SENSUAL RELIGION

In different ways, contributors to this volume explore how the sense of touch is not only an intrinsic part of religion, but the principal facilitating medium through which religion, religious encounters and performances take place. This falls in line with advances in recent scholarship that have generated a general move away from emphasis on metaphysics, and into different realms of inquiry that include vernacular or 'lived' religion, ritual and performance, the 'material turn' (or 'turn to things') in the Study of Religions, and now the 'sensory turn'. These different turns in the Study of Religions have one thing in common, they are all interested in what ordinary religionists 'do' and how their religions are expressed, every day, from the ground up. After all, as Birgit Meyer et al. tell us, 'religion happens materially' (2010: 209), or to paraphrase Peter Bräunlein, we need to think religion through things (2016). Material religion is therefore a key component of these discussions, and since the body is nothing if not living matter, then this includes the bodily senses. In fact, all religious practices require that the people doing the practising are living, breathing, 'doing' beings who are invariably entangled in and with their worlds. Lived religion is not, nor ever has been, dualistic. It is materialist, performative, tactile and inherently sensual.

But what does it mean to define religion through the senses, and more specifically, through the sense of touch? And what can exploring the sense of touch in religion offer scholarship that is not being offered already by those who are dealing with religion and the senses generally? One of the primary advances being proposed here is that religion is evidenced through that which we can see religionists doing with their hands. Emphasising touch (as with the other senses found in this larger senses project) requests that we stop privileging belief, metaphysics, text and the supernatural, and understand religion *as it is*, as we can see, smell, taste, hear and touch it.

However, for many, but by no means all, traditional Western (broadly understood) scholars of religions and/or theologians, religions are not meant to be understood through things, or as inherently tactile or tangible, and deities are not to be known through the touch of human hands. In Protestant Christianity, for example, God is transcendent, and believers are often meant to behold their divine with their souls or perceive God in their minds (a difficult concept for those with aphantasia). Colleen McDannell (1995: 5) tells us:

> [Calvin] maintained that humanity comes close to God only in our souls because God is a spirit. 'Since God has no similarity to those shapes by means of which people attempt to represent him,' he wrote in his *Institutes of the Christian Religion*, 'then all attempts to depict him are an impudent affront... to his majesty and glory.' Divinity, the wholly other and sacred, should not be brought into the profane world of bodies and art.

The perceived distance between the realm of God and the profane realm of humans (and their visible religious statues and other art) by Protestant Reformers such as Martin Luther, Ulrich Zwingli and John Calvin led to their avowal that genuine Christianity is a religion of 'hearing' instead of 'seeing'. Indeed, religious objects and images were a perceived threat. David Chidester says: 'As the Protestant Reformation developed, genuine Christian religion came to be defined by the reformers as an ongoing war against idols' (2000: 348). Here, though, touch, particularly when it comes to religious images, is contested and Protestants, like all religionists, engage with their religious worlds through a variety of touch-oriented mediums; it is an inevitability of being human and having skin and it is also an inevitability of being religious.

Marleen de Witte askes: 'What is touch in religion? And what does it do? What role do hands, skin, and the nervous system play in evoking a sense of the supernatural?' (2015: 263). When belief is made real and physical in the world through the material, whether through crafting objects or crafting ways of engaging with those objects, the metaphysical assumption of religion can be reimagined. This is not to say that belief, the supernatural or ideas have no place in religion. S. Brent Plate makes a pertinent point to this effect. He writes (sic): '*The senses are the media of the body*, the channels through which understanding occurs. The senses do not merely influence cognition but *become* the thought itself. Beliefs, and conceptions of supernatural/transcendent higher powers, are not possible to be disentangled from sense perceptions, nor from the media in which religious conceptions occur' (2012: 173). Building on Plate's argument, we can however, understand how sense perceptions are prioritised depending on the religious context in question. Regarding touch, we can also answer de Witte's questions with the assertion that religion is a 'fully bodied' (as opposed to 'embodied') and sensual affair that is mediated primarily through the sense of touch, where individual perceptions of the supernatural and its evocation are difficult to measure. But for the sake of addressing a scholarly imbalance that has regularly demonstrated favour for that which cannot be physically touched, we can begin by presupposing the equal significances of the physical and material, the tangible and immanent.

Indeed, thinking about sense hierarchies and priorities, as the contributors to this volume demonstrate, in some cases the physical and the sensual take precedence over abstract notions of categories such as belief. Examples of such cases can be found on the edge of what is considered 'religion' where other phenomena exist which push the boundaries of the common usage of the term but can still be considered 'religious' when the term is broadly conceived. So, whilst traditional tattooing may be understood as an artistic practice, preparing the dead for burial or cremation might be understood in practical terms, and Bondage, Domination, Sadism and Masochism (BDSM) is often comprehended as only a hedonistic hobby, these touch-centric activities can be placed into the realms of the sacred; they are typically replete with potency, have associated rituals that reek of meaning and/or are deeply spiritually significant to those involved. For that matter, sensual religion is so relational that whilst its primacy often varies from religious context to religious context, the physical and the material are a constant and consistent lived reality among all of them. Building on Plate (2012), and as the chapters in this volume illustrate, religion is a volatile and entangled phenomenon.

Anthropologists have, however, been producing scholarship about the roles of the senses in culture generally for the past few decades (see Constance Classen and David Howes 2006; Sarah Pink 2009; Tim Ingold 2011). Yet for scholars in the Study of Religions, the senses continue to offer somewhat uncharted territory to be explored. Exceptions include (but are not limited to) Birgit Meyer and Jojada Verrips' (2008) conception of the senses as an analytical tool-set for the Study of Religions, and the work of the before-mentioned S. Brent Plate (2012). Graham Harvey and Jessica Hughes' (2018) edited collection *Sensual Religion: Religion and the Five Senses* is particularly pertinent to the objectives of this edited collection in that the contributors address each sense from two perspectives, contemporary and historical, to better inform the practice of the study of religion, and two chapters are dedicated to the sense of 'touch' (Hughes 2018; Whitehead 2018). Marleen de Witte (2015) also explores the sense of 'touch' in religion specifically. Whether through inquiries originating in Anthropology or the Study of Religions (or a combination of the two), the significance and centrality of 'touch' is an emerging contender for analysis in the field.

Acts of touch not only have the ability to shape and craft religious things and direct attention, they also defy the elite Western analytical and cultural constructs that keep their significances muted, contained and reflective of Western Christian, predominantly Protestant, discourses. Significantly, and since religious gestures of 'touch' are mostly relegated to the category of 'symbolic', defining religion through the senses requires that we de-colonise notions of symbolism and representation in order to allow for *more than* approaches. As many of the chapters in this volume demonstrate, not all acts of touch are understood to be symbolic for the diverse peoples engaged thus. The dualistic nature of Enlightenment modernity bore concepts that have determined an imperial course in the academy whereby religious gestures and objects are treated not only as 'other than', but 'lesser than' that which they supposedly refer to. This can be understood as a legacy of Plato's ideal forms, and it is a discursive model that often deters academics and practitioners alike from engaging fully with the rich opportunities available through understanding religion as sensually involved and performed in a variety of cultural contexts. Taking seriously the sensory, religious worlds of others means not relegating their practices and objects to modern statuses of representation or symbolism, or comparing their cosmological or religious frameworks with Western ones.

Contributors to this volume, then, ask us to re-think religion sensually. They ask us to question the prized and privileged epistemologies that make up familiar discourses of 'agency', 'representation', 'symbolism', 'metaphor' and even 'embodiment'; all of which emphasise some degree of separation from the physical world. The bodily senses and the Other are brought into conversation in each of the chapters here, but it is the sense of touch that dictates the shape of the volatile, reciprocal and rather complex dynamic. Common and overlapping themes among the contributions include how touch mediates direct physical (often deliberate) contact between physical bodies (human and other than human) and the things that are crafted, blessed, related with, engaged with or worn. Understanding touch as the vehicle to alternative forms of knowledge-making in specific religious contexts is the driving force behind the contributions to this collection. Further themes are concerned with reciprocal touch, and also its opposite, touching an inanimate object such as a coffin, or a corpse which is no longer alive and thus cannot physically touch back. What follows in the chapters are evidences that imply a *more than* approach, e.g. touch is more than symbolic, more than metaphorical and more than representational. By placing both 'body' and the 'sense of touch' at the centre of investigations, we assert that material practice and bodily sensation *are* lived religion.

PART I: RECIPROCITY AND KNOWING

The sense of touch can be distinguished from the other senses because whilst all other senses can be functionally inactive through various permanent disabilities or temporary illness and our lives continue, our sense of touch only becomes inactive when we physically die; when, in essence, the neural transmitters that sense our world stop firing in our brains (Abraira and Ginty 2013). Touch is also our prime sense, in that our skin, the medium through which we touch and are touched, is our largest organ. Further, touch affects change in a way our other senses do not; when we touch, we leave a physical trace of ourselves on the other (be it person or object). If we touch an object, say a religious artefact, we leave our unique fingerprint behind along with our unique bacterial signature (Fierer et al. 2010), and given we write this in the time of Covid-19, we also leave behind on everything we touch a potentially deadly virus. By touching, we leave a trace of ourselves on whatever and whoever we physically interact with.

Touch is also unique because it is typically reciprocal. When we touch things, we are usually touched in return. This is especially the case when we consider touch and religion, for often artefacts and objects that in everyday life may be understood as 'inanimate' can be perceived as alive, sentient and/or sensitive. In this way, we generate reciprocal, sensual knowledges. By this we mean that we can know through our fingers, or indeed even through our lips which are another part of our body that we often use to 'touch'; as Plate argues, 'the skinscape' plays an 'active role' in the 'construction of body, self, other, world, as well as social-sacred space' (2012: 164). Touch then is not just generative but also determinative. However, our skinscape is made up of distinct types of skin, including glabrous, that is non-hairy skin, as well as skin that is covered in hair. Our glabrous skin, such as on our palms to our fingertips, helps us understand texture and shape, whilst our hairy skin, which makes up around 90%, is more concerned with touch that evokes an emotional response (Zimmerman, Bai and Ginty 2014: 1). Skin then is complex and central to touch, and being in touch with things and people, enables us to know and consequently construct our worlds, for touch facilitates body knowledges and acknowledges resonances.

Skin, and its mediation of being in continual touch with the world, provides us with an interesting angle on the sense of touch for religion, and fine-tunes us into our knowledge-making faculties that go beyond immediate cognition and into 'other' ways of knowing. For example, in religions and religious life-ways there are sensory hierarchies, rules, boundaries, taboos, notions of pollution and regulations concerning skin and touch, the physical practices of which visually communicate that certain traditions are taking place. In Aotearoa New Zealand, for Maori, it is *tapu* (Maori code for things dangerous, restricted or forbidden) for a person or thing to touch another person's head, as the head is the most sacred part of the body. If the head gets touched (including by one's own hands), a number of ritual procedures have to be carried out until the *tapu* state is transformed back into *noa* (being free from restriction, safe or everyday; the opposite of *tapu*). Objects can also carry levels of *tapu* that must be cleared by priests before the objects can be touched again. Also highly ritualised and dealing with issues of *tapu* are Maori tattoos, or *tā moko*. These visually provide real and tangible evidences that speak to complex social systems about *mana* (authority, prestige, presence), place and social standing or status.

Sébastien Galliot's chapter 'Tattooing Ritual and the Management of Touch in Polynesia' (Ch. 1), turns the dynamics of representation and symbolism on their head, arguing that scholarly literature has typically confined tattooing to discourses concerning politics and identity, and/or it has been relegated to focus on technique, skill or pain. In light of this, he makes a theoretical advance to 'touch and religion' by arguing that tattooing as a practice should not be subordinated to language or ideas about mental representation, symbolism or metaphor, but that it is essential to look at the way the body itself perceives the tattooing process to understand how bodily perception could substantiate representations rather than the opposite. In his practice-centred approach to the ritual of Samoan tattooing, Galliot demonstrates that the effect of the tattoo is fully mediated by the skinscape of the person being tattooed, and by the touch of the tattooer and their team. Handmade tools and tactile knowledge craft designs that, through the stillness and movements of bodies, produce culture and religion that are embedded within the skin. Touch here is central, not just in the marking of the body, but also in the permanent effects of this marking, for tattooed skin perceives touch differently from non-tattooed skin.

Whilst Galliot demonstrates how tattooed skin outwardly demonstrates the permanent results of a specific type of traditional touch in Samoa (that of the tattooer), Sinah Theres Kloß (Ch. 2) asks us to consider the role of touch in relation to cloth and clothing in Guyanese Hinduism. Here, whilst the touch of the cloth is impermeant, through exchanging cloth and clothing, the essence of one person is transferred to the other, resulting in a form of intimate mutual touch. This is most potent in regard to the gifting of cloth to a *murti* (an avatar of a Hindu deity) where it becomes *prasadam*; consecrated or imbued (for want of better terms) with the spiritual essence of that *murti*. A piece of cloth or clothing can also gain auspicious energy by touching it to a *murti* and as such it becomes a personal ritual representation of that *murti*. Clothing can also be used to keep transnational connections between home and diasporic communities, and thus exchanging cloth and clothing establishes and reinforces distant relationships. However, as with any relationship, there is always the creation of a complex social hierarchy between the gifter and receiver. As Kloß points out, this is particularly the case when gifting cloth to a *murti* as any clothing given to a *murti* by a human is considered *juthaa* (inherently polluting to the *murti*). However, any clothing touched by a *murti* cannot be conceived of as inherently dirty or polluting (*juthaa*) as the energy of the deity is sacred, and therefore any *murti*-touched cloth or clothing must be treated appropriately. The touch of the *murti* is central, therefore, to the status of the material.

The absence of touching also speaks volumes about taboos, parameters and hierarchies. In some religious traditions only certain designated people, or people of only one gender, are permitted to touch. The Greek Orthodox Church comes to mind here as only male priests are allowed into the sanctuary and to touch the sacred artefacts; unless one is the female cleaner who wipes away the dust to ensure the precious items are fit for the sanctified male hands that pick them up. Physical, sensual engagement with particularly potent objects expresses the deepest passions, and having something physical 'to do' is, in many cases, essential to generate and keep beliefs and faith 'going'. To regulate the touching of 'things' that matter most to devotees, they are displayed in such a place, or cordoned off in such a way, that prohibits physical interactions. As Louise Tythacott argues, this can be both in religious spaces as well as in museums (2017: 116). Limiting access to only the chosen few not only regulates who can touch but when and where touch occurs (Classen and Howes 2006); as such, some 'objects' that are meant to be touched are firmly placed away from human hands, for instance Hopi and Zuni Kachina which can be found in many a museum, whilst others are handled by those whose touch may, in the originating culture, be deemed inappropriate (Welch 2014: 184).

The general 'do not touch' conservation ethos of museums, where touch is very much regulated, can often be in stark contrast to the religious ritual use of devotional artefacts (Buggeln, Paine and Plate 2017). In the increasingly rare cases where touching precious and protected religious objects is encouraged, religious objects, such as devotionals and the spaces they inhabit, are designed and displayed to be ritually utilised on both everyday and more highly ritualised occasions. Gabriel Bayarri and Amy Whitehead's chapter about the role of touch in the Andalusian Marian shrine at Alcalá (Ch. 3) explores this, arguing that the shrine's popularity in the region is based on the fact that devotees can physically interact with their Virgin by carrying out the ritual performance of placing her protective mantle over their heads. In this way, devotees can be 'in touch' with the Virgin in an intimate physical setting; thus, the divisions that conceptually separate object (statue) from subject (Virgin) dissolve allowing for the generation and emergence of her personhood through the ritual act. The popularity and primacy of this touch-oriented ritual resonates throughout the village; it has even been found when devotees cannot be in her presence, such as during the Coronavirus pandemic.

Explorations into religions and the sense of touch can be further enhanced through use of James G. Frazer's notion of contagious magic. The idea that things that were once in touch with, or formed part of, a person, place or thing retain an essence or remnant of their original can help frame discussions about how, for example, things that have been in touch with the shrine of the Virgin of Alcalá carry a kind of potency once they have been purchased and taken away. In this way, the significance of how religious materialities facilitate 'remaining in touch' can be seen in how the Virgin is accommodated in the homes of the villagers through Virgin-devotionals that are displayed on home altars, on walls and on ceramic plaques by the doors of houses. The dynamics of religious artefacts in sensory hierarchies can also be considered through the example of how Catholic relics are classified. Catholic canonical structures organise the power of 'being in touch' in terms of power and potency. There are, for example, three classes of sacred relics: a first-class relic is part of saint's body (bone, hair); a second-class relic is an article of clothing or some other artefact that had been in touch with, or used, by the saint; and a third-class relic is an object that has been touched to a first- or second-class relic. Following the paths of these objects and their 'object-biographies', the twice-removed relic loses strength the further it gets away from the original source. Comparable with the case of Kloß's as well as Bayarri and Whitehead's chapters, things being in touch with other things can carry a kind of 'charge', a potency or a power, the relationships with which help us reimagine religious artefacts as dynamic and relational, along with the ritual engagements and the role of touch in religious knowledge-making.

Building on this, as religious touch communicates and creates knowledges, then, it can also assist in the building of enduring relationships with objects and places, such that being 'in touch' creates and generates relationships with things, objects and places. This relation-making of touch enables us to discuss how acts of physical 'touch' indicate personhood and can be considered a form of animism (the newer usage, see Harvey 2005). This theme is picked up in two of the chapters found in this collection: the before-mentioned chapter by Bayarri and Whitehead (Ch. 3) on the Virgin of Alcalá, and the next chapter by Andy Letcher (Ch. 4). Letcher explores the sense of touch in religion through an auto-ethnographic account of his processual attempts to learn to play the lyre (a replicated 5th century CE, six-stringed instrument from Trossingen, South Germany). By drawing on his own experience, he centres the notion that only through a 'careful examination of the context of the musicking' can an instrument be understood as more than 'just a physical device used to make a sound'. Indeed he argues that any instrument that makes a sound (even if that is a laptop) is more than just a physical thing, as it has cultural associations and rootedness, and these can give certain instruments a personhood. Letcher gives the example of the *ngombi* harp as a case in point, as for the Bwiti people of East Africa, not only is a *ngombi* harp a person, but it is a gendered person and as such, playing involves not just touch, but intimate touch. With instruments understood as having personhood he argues that if they lie unused, they die, and museums can therefore be understood as mausoleums displaying instrument-shells that speak of their lived vibrant past as part of, and often essential to, a community. Unless instruments are played, touched as they were designed to be, they cannot live. The living personhood then of musical instruments is not purely in their form, but in the intimate touch-based relationship between the instrument and the player.

Touch-based relationships are also central to understanding one's place in the world, and being in touch with ancestral 'place' is illustrated in Robyn Andrews' 'Being There: Anglo-Indian Roots Tourism Experiences' (Ch. 5) where she examines an aspect of the growing phenomenon typically termed 'Roots Tourism'. Andrews' focus is on Anglo-Indians returning to India to explore their family roots; to get back in touch with their ancestry. Family history information is more accessible than ever, and also more popular, with DNA analysis allowing for genealogical tracing and technology-enhanced searches providing access to digitised archives. As Andrews has found, Anglo-Indian expectations and reflections of roots tourism ventures are more than a 'getting in touch with the past experience'. These journeys on which they encounter significant material objects and places linked to ancestors resemble pilgrimages for roots tourists, like sacred journeys for those needing to physically touch things in the spaces where they are potent. In effect, in order to feel fully in touch with their past, roots tourists need to be physically in touch with it too.

Whilst the importance of touch includes being in-touch (such as roots tourism), and/or touching to bring life or be in touch with life-enhancing power (such as playing an instrument or venerating the Virgin), it is important to highlight that touch can also be polluting. The damaging nature of inappropriate touch has been brought to the fore in recent years through numerous sexual abuse scandals, from paedophile priests in the Christian Church to sexually abusive new religious 'cult' leaders and the sex-slave scandals in Indian temples (Paul 2014); sadly not all forms of religious touch are good. Given we are writing this in the time of the 2020 Covid-19 pandemic, even what was once innocent touch can be accidentally contaminating and as such prayer halls globally have either closed, or opened with strict socially-distancing measures that include an absence of touch. But in times of death and disease, religion and its devotional practices are understood to offer a form of personal protection. Home altars and shrines, plaques and icons, rosaries and votive offerings allow the religious practitioner to be in touch with the object of their devotion or protective spirit. Understanding the significance of religious material cultures and the dynamics of temporal and physical relating during Covid-19, and how presence and touch are accommodated in a time of a social pandemic crisis, is a subject for scholars to come. But it is interesting for us, that we are producing a book on religion and touch at a time when touch can be dangerous to the point of transmitting a potentially lethal virus, and yet touch is a sense that is central to being fully human; if one cannot feel, if one has no working central nervous system, then one is devoid of life. Touch is crucial, we touch and are touched, and make and are made through this most vital of senses. These aspects of touch inform Part II of this volume.

PART II: CRAFTING, RITUAL AND CREATIVITY

Considering touch in religions allows us to re-centre our thinking on human actions and interactions, to focus on relationality and to consider religious objects and artefacts as more than just conduits to being in touch with the divine or spiritual other, for these items too are made by human hands. Without 'touch', religion cannot be crafted, or made. This practicality does not exclude other senses. They interface, interplay, generate, all at the same time. Yet in terms of practicality, religion cannot 'happen' without a variety of forms of touch. Temples, churches, cathedrals, mosques, synagogues, gurdwaras and other sites of veneration would not be built if there were no hands to carry out the labour. Altars would not be maintained, and specially configured gifts and offerings would not be made if human hands were not involved. Religious statues, musical instruments, incense, scrolls, special foods and other 'things' would not be crafted or prepared without human hands. In other words, touch is the primary facilitator of all religious materiality and activity. In Christian cosmologies, 'the divine' is set apart from this 'mortal coil'. Theologically, it is not meant to be touched, handled or known physically. That would, in fact, soil it or make it profane. However, if we read between the lines and consider, for example, the ways that, say, the Abrahamic religions with their transcendent God are lived by people on the ground, then we can see quite clearly that all of the senses are deeply involved with religious activities, and that even an abstract concept such as belief involves touch.

Religions then are essentially sensual, and hands and lips in particular are central to our lived connection with all things religious. Take contemporary Judaism. Any and every Torah scroll (Sefer Torah) is written by hand on parchment, but the scroll once finished should not be touched by human hands, which over time would damage the expensive text that contains the words of G-d. Instead of using a finger (part of one's hand) to keep place when cantillating (ritually reading) from the Torah scroll, a *yad* (Hebrew: יד literally 'hand') is used. When the scroll is taken from its housing (the Ark), and paraded before the synagogue or temple congregation, hands reach out to touch the scroll coverings, often lips kiss the fingers that then touch the Torah mantle. Further, Judaism is replete with festivals that involve food, much of which is eaten by hand, and all of which is made by hand (even if today, sometimes hands just turn on the food mixers). Homemade food is handmade food, and the love and attention that goes into producing the very sustenance of life is often undervalued, especially in Western academia which has until very recently been male and public space dominated, and concerned with less domestic and 'mundane' matters. And yet touch as a sense takes us to the very heart of the mundane, for as we note, even the most sacred of objects was once crafted by human hands. As Graham Harvey (2013) has argued, religion everywhere is all about everyday life: food, sex, relationships with others (including other than human others) and with objects crafted with care.

In many religions, the human nature of crafting is signified by the deliberate inclusion of a fault; the deliberate design error in Islamic art and architecture is there to remind us that only Allah is perfect, and imperfections are deliberately woven into traditional Navajo (Diné) blankets. Because it is believed the spirit of the Navajo artist entwines part of themselves into the cloth, the pattern includes a flaw in the border design that allows the spirit of the weaver to exit the blanket, separating them from any harmful thoughts the blanket may come into contact with once in use. Further, because weaving resonates closely with spiritual concepts, rituals and myths, traditionally it is the crafting of the blanket, replete with meaningful symbols, where the Navajo (Diné) people 'experience beauty'; it is for them 'in creating and expressing, not in preserving and possessing' where the significance lies (Thomas in M'Closkey 2004).

Sometimes, as with Navajo blankets, the significance of something is not always clear to the outsider and this is the topic that Graeme MacRae explores in his chapter on the deeply sensory and sensual Hindu temple exchanges in Bali (Ch. 6). Here rituals are described as a feast for the senses, with sights, sounds and smells that delight, for these are the senses favoured by the gods. But what of touch? Touch is present in these rituals but because of concerns over purity and pollution, it is typically related to the background. This chapter, however, in taking a 'between the lines' exploration of temple rituals in Tamil Nadu, reveals the political-economic realities that are often obscured by the usual focus on the ritual feasts. In Bali, an often academically marginalised corner of the Hindu world, touch, both ordinary touch and the subtle extrasensory 'touch' that occurs in *darshan*—the central moment in ritual devotions—speaks to, and of, people-making through life-cycle rituals: cementing ancestral connections at birth, the coming of age transitioning to a full and proper human, and finally cremation which sends this full and proper (now dead) human back to the land of the ancestors, for the cycle of reincarnation to start once more.

Touch and death is a topic explored by Suzi Garrod and Bronwyn Russell (Ch. 7), although in a Western context often described (possibly misdescribed) as death-denying. Garrod examines the role of touch at life's end through her work as a death doula in England. Through anonymised case studies, she explores how holistic therapeutic touch at end-of-life helps provide spiritual, emotional and practical support to both the dying and their caregivers. Russell meanwhile explores the phenomenon of coffin clubs in Aotearoa New Zealand. Here, everyday, individuals face the reality that they will at some stage die by making and decorating the box (coffin) they will be buried or cremated in. In this chapter, the two writers theorise their own intimate relationships with mortality through the use of touch, the physical care and comfort of the dying (Garrod) and the practicalities of manufacturing a coffin (Russell), but the chapter also centres the role of touch as a form of communication, and crucial in communication.

Sónia Silva (Ch. 8) also explores the connection between touch and communication in her chapter on basket divination, a technique found in the southern fringes of Central Africa. Through her exploration of touch, Silva highlights how the distant senses of sight and hearing work together with the near and affective senses of touch, kinaesthesia and pain. Basket divination exemplifies the value of synergy, co-sensing, intersensoriality and synaesthesia in religious practice where 'Zambia, Angola and the Democratic Republic of the Congo share borders'. Additionally it shows that spiritual truths are not only seen in the form of material symbols and heard as words, but are also felt with the hands, the moving body and the aching heart. Basket divination challenges any definition of religiosity that denies the senses, the body and material religion a key role in its performance. The role that touch plays in communication is deepened further in Part III which focuses on the ritual efficacy of touch.

PART III: TOUCH, RITUAL EFFICACY AND COMMUNICATION

Using our fingertips to know our worlds is as natural as breathing. After all, it is human to want to feel things with our hands, and this is no different in religious contexts. But our sense of touch does not work alone. Take a moment and imagine yourself at one of the many religious locations in India, such as the Golden Temple in Amritsar, the most sacred of places for the Sikhs; the Jama Masjid in Old Delhi, one of the largest mosques in India; or visiting one of the many Buddhist temples in Bodh Gaya. What might you see, smell or hear? What might you be expected to do? Each place teems with pilgrims and tourists alike, whilst beggars and street vendors vie for your attention before you make your way inside each site. Each sacred space, a haven from the everyday bustle of the outside world, would have its own rituals and etiquette. In the Sri Harmandir Sahib Gurdwara you would see hundreds of people communally eating with their hands the vegetarian food, blessed by prayer, that is served to all as part of Sikh practice of *langar*; in the Masjid-i Jehan Numa you might see men doing *wudu*, the purification ritual of their hands, arms, feet and face before performing *salat* (the physical, mental and spiritual act of Islamic worship) in the prayer hall. The multiple temples in Bodh Gaya may be different in style both inside and out, but in each will be handmade offerings to the Buddha, and monks (possibly nuns too) will be seen moving their fingers over their *mala* of 108 prayer beads. Or maybe you find yourself in one of the many Hindu temples that line the banks of the River Ganga in the city of Varanasi. Here you would be hit with powerful wafts of heady incense, combined with the smells of woodsmoke from the many cremation pyres, the pungency of human sweat and the excrement from the sacred cows that wander the narrow hot and humid streets. You would hear the ringing of bells, the resonance of which signals to the divine that a body is ready to venerate and receive blessings. Temple etiquette would suggest that you put your hands together, fingertips touching, so that you greet others (including the deity) appropriately using the traditional Indian salutation, 'namaste' (in yogic practice, each finger is said to produce a certain energy). In instances such as these, all the senses will undoubtedly be engaged in an orchestral overload of colour, sound, movement and smell. But you would also notice how touch is a commonality, for touch relays, expresses and communicates. It is a prime conveyer of ideas, intentions, purposes and beliefs.

We all touch. We are compelled, like moths drawn to flames, to touch that which we want to know through our bodies. When we go to buy objects, we necessarily handle them. We want to touch things, to feel textures, to engage with the world around us; indeed, touch is one of the first things a baby does in reaching out to feel the warmth of its mother, and children routinely touch to gain understanding (how many parents have not warned their child that putting a hand into a flame is not very sensible!). Understanding religion through the senses is vital in comprehending everyday lived practice; we may use sight to glean knowledge from ancient texts and contemporary textbooks alike, and as such we often assume the eyes are our first point of engagement with other religions, but we turn the pages of those texts with our fingers. We read about, and look at pictures and films of people doing religion, but we rarely step back to think that these people are doing things, touching things, often with their hands but sometimes with their lips. Touch as a sense, it seems, is so taken for granted in religion that we rarely explore it in its religious domain. But the way one touches, and moves one's hands or lips to touch, says a lot about religious norms.

This next chapter (Ch. 9) pushes at the norms of religious practice, as Alison Robertson explores religioning on the edge by exploring touch in relation to BDSM (Bondage, Domination, Sadism and Masochism). Touching and being touched is the foundation of most BDSM practice, as sensations are deliberately created by one person for another. Many of the sensations involved could be categorised as pain, and many of the techniques used to create the sensations themselves, and the scenes built upon them, could be said to carry significant physical and/or emotional risks. Factors like these, as well as other sensory and situational elements and the emotional weight attached to the activities, contribute to the synaesthetic whole that is BDSM 'play', resulting in a multivalent experience of an 'other' world. Through ethnographic fieldwork, Robertson unpacks this otherworld experience in relation to the concept of spiritual edgework, theorising how this otherworld is co-constructed through an iterative and relational process of sensation and response to form a counter-pleasure; an action that transgresses what is understood as a socio-cultural norm of pleasureability. And touch is central to this counter-pleasure, and BDSM play.

Desiring touch, and desiring to touch something or someone, is an act we typically associate with pleasure, even if that is socio-normally transgressive pleasure and only pleasurable for some people, such as those who engage in BDSM. But some things we touch or allow to touch us are not associated with any sort of physical pleasure, and indeed can be related to religious penance, or acts of spiritual strength. Examples of the former would include the Opus Dei wearing of a cilice that for two hours each day cuts into the wearer's thigh as a form of corporeal mortification to remind them of, and join them with, the suffering of Christ; and the Shi'a Muslim self-flagellation ritual of Tabir (or Talwar / Zanjeer / Qama Zani depending on geographical location), a blood-letting ritual performed as an act of mourning for the death of Husayn ibn Ali, the younger grandson of Muhammad (PBUH), who was killed along with his children, close relatives and companions at Karbala (61 AH / 680 CE). Another such ritual is the Sun Dance of the Great Plains tribes of North America, where men pierce their breasts or the flesh above their shoulder blades, and suspend themselves in an act of extreme endurance. Participation in such a rite can be engaged in after having survived a crisis, or because a dream or vision indicated it was necessary, but aside from personal motivations, bringing oneself into contact with Wakan Tanka, the embodiment of spiritual power, is often enough. There is a political element to this ritual and other spiritual practices; the Sun Dance was prohibited in 1884 by colonial powers and re-established as part of the Red Power movement.

Whilst some forms of touch, such as those noted above, deliberately bring pain, others can bring a sense of revolution. But if to touch is to understand, then sometimes we do need to touch that which nauseates, and no more so is that the case than when dealing with the dead. The disposal of a human corpse is something that every society must do, and that is the subject of the chapter by Christina Welch (Ch. 10). Welch explores a wide variety of ways that religions and spiritual lifeways have dealt with, and continue to deal with, dead bodies: from the 'secret' Chevra Kadisha societies of Judaism where the deceased is ritually washed by members of the community before burial, to the passing over of the corpse to professional corpse-bearers in Zoroastrianism whose job it is to mitigate the corruption associated with the lifeless flesh. But what constitutes the dead is not only the intact fleshy recently-deceased body, but also parts separated from a body as in the case of the victims of terror acts, decomposing corpses of the long dead or skeletal remains. All of these are dealt with religiously in various contexts, but each involves the intimate handling of a person, or parts of a person, who no longer lives. Touching the deceased can bring out feelings of disgust in the living, and as well as being potentially spiritually polluting, a dead body can cause disease; as such it is no surprise that touching the dead is universally rife with ritual.

The notion that touch is a generator of different types of religious knowledges is one of the contributions to wider academic knowledge that this book makes, no matter how personally distasteful or socially problematic some types of touch might be. But most forms of touch are unproblematic, and the chapter by Michael Houseman (Ch. 11) focuses on hugging, a form of touch that is socially normative; or has been until the 2020 Covid-19 global pandemic forced the world to avoid forms of physical contact with anyone outside one's own 'safe social bubble'.

Houseman's chapter explores the interactive workings of immersive hugging through the lens of ritual. Immersive hugging is a hug done with attentiveness that extends beyond the usual social norms of close personal contact. With a spiritual, therapeutic ethos, immersive hugging, although very long, is not an act that demonstrates an established close personal relationship nor does it suggest one might follow. Drawing on ethnographic fieldwork and other illustrative material, Houseman identifies eight recurrent features in ritualised immersive hugs in order to speculate about what is at stake in their performance, and performance Houseman argues, is crucial to the act. In exploring immersive hugging as a public spiritual ritual act, Houseman sheds light on the importance of understanding touch in context, and demonstrates how by breaking the usual formal etiquette of hugging, immersive hugging as ritual complicates notions of intimacy and self-awareness.

The final chapter also explores the performance of touch but with a focus on those aspects that are more usually found in present-day expressions of the Christian faith: devotional, healing, initiatory and metaphorical touch. George Chryssides in 'Handling Things Unseen: Tactile Aspects of the Christian Faith' (Ch. 12) draws on the many and varied aspects of the Christian faith concerned with touch. Touch here can serve to demonstrate friendship, to maintain tradition and to make the invisible visible. The Eucharistic bread and wine is a tactile anticipation of the future heavenly banquet which has not yet been made available to Christ's followers. Roman Catholic popular piety employs sacramentals—objects such as holy water, crucifixes, medallions, rosaries and scapulars—which can be used for devotional or protective purposes. But some Christian objects are not available for touching, either because they are too sacred or damageable, or because they have been lost through time. Further, the liturgical calendar provides occasion for the use of tactile phenomena: the distribution of chrism oil, the imposition of ash on Ash Wednesday, foot washing on Maundy Thursday, veneration of the cross on Good Friday and the lighting of the Paschal Candle at Easter. Touch also features in initiation rites, notably baptism, confirmation and ordination, and the presentation of tactile objects to the candidates is an accompanying practice. With the advent of the Internet, online rituals have given rise to some experimentation with substitutes for direct physical contact, and when Covid-19 prevented many Christians from physically assembling, some Anglican churches have revived the practice of 'spiritual communion' in lieu of the more usual physical tactile form of the sacrament; in essence, Chryssides argues that touch is central to lived Christian practice.

CONCLUSION

Plate says: 'By focusing on the vital role that the sensual body plays in human experiences of the world, we are able to investigate religious traditions in ways that complement and expand traditional approaches to religion' (2012: 162). Contributions to this collection have done just that. They have brought new, fresh and innovative ideas about how utilising the sense of touch can advance debates about sensually engaged religion. In taking a bottom-up approach to studying touch in religions, we are able to glean an abundance of possibilities that are visibly evidenced through practitioners' performances. As the chapters demonstrate, touch is not privileged, highlighted or avoided to the same degree across the board but the roles of touch, as well as its absence, speak volumes about religious phenomena broadly. Although this volume has been unable to engage with the full range of touch-oriented religious activities that exist in the world, the contributors have provided exemplary case studies that signal new areas, approaches and methods for future research. We hope that this book provides a catalyst for such studies.

BIBLIOGRAPHY

Abraira, Victoria E. and David D. Ginty. 2013. 'The Sensory Neurons of Touch'. *Neuron* 79 (4): 618 –639. https://doi.org/10.1016/j.neuron.2013.07.051

Bräunlein, Peter J. 2016. 'Thinking Religion through Things: Reflections on the Material Turn in the Scientific Study of Religion/s'. *Method and Theory in the Study of Religion* 28: 365-399. https://doi.org/10.1163/15700682-12341364

Buggeln, Gretchen, Crispin Paine and S. Brent Plate (eds.). 2017. *Religion in Museums: Global and Multidisciplinary Perspectives.* London: Bloomsbury.

Chidester, David. 2000. *Christianity: A Global History.* London: Penguin Books.

Classen, Constance and David Howes. 2006. 'The Museum as Sensescape: Western Sensibilities and Indigenous Artifacts'. In Elizabeth Edwards, Chris Golden and Ruth B. Philis (eds.), *Sensible Objects: Colonialism, Museums and Material Culture*, 199-222. London: Bloomsbury. https://doi.org/10.4324/9781003086611-11

de Witte, Marleen. 2015. 'Touch'. In S. Brent Plate (ed.), *Key Terms in Material Religion*, 261-266. London: Bloomsbury.

Durkheim, Emile. 1982 [1895]. *The Rules of Sociological Method and Selected Texts on Sociology and Its Method.* Steven Lukes (ed.), W.D. Halls (trans.). New York: Free Press.

Fierer, Noah, Christian L. Lauber, Nick Zhou, Daniel McDonald, Elizabeth K. Costello and Rob Knight. 2010. 'Forensic Identification using Skin Bacterial Communities'. *Proceedings of the National Academy of Sciences of the United States of America* April 6, 107 (4): 6477-6481. https://doi.org/10.1073/pnas.1000162107

Harvey, Graham. 2005. *Animism: Respecting the Living World.* London: Hurst & Company.

Harvey, Graham. 2013. *Food, Sex and Strangers: Understanding Religion and Everyday Life.* New York: Routledge. https://doi.org/10.4324/9781315729572

Harvey, Graham and Jessica Hughes (eds.). 2018. *Sensual Religion: Religion and the Five Senses.* Sheffield and Bristol: Equinox.

Hughes, Jessica. 2018. 'The Texture of the Gift: Religious Touching in the Greco-Roman World'. In Harvey and Hughes (eds.), *Sensual Religion*, 191–214.

Ingold, Tim. 2011. *Being Alive: Essays on Movement, Knowledge and Description.* Oxford: Routledge. https://doi.org/10.4324/9780203818336

McDannell, Colleen. 1995. *Material Christianity: Religion and Popular Culture in America.* Newhaven and London: Yale University Press.

M'Closkey, Kathy. 2004. 'Towards and Understanding of Navajo Aesthetics'. *SEE: Semiotics, Evolution, Energy* 4 (1). http://see.library.utoronto.ca/SEED/Vol4-1/M%27Closkey.htm

Meyer, Birgit and Jojada Verrips 2008. 'Aesthetics'. In David Morgan (ed.), *Key Words in Religion, Media and Culture*, 20–30. New York: Routledge.

Meyer, Birgit, David Morgan, Crispin Paine and S. Brent Plate. 2010. 'The Origin and Mission of Material Religion'. *Religion* 40 (3): 207–211. https://doi.org/10.1016/j.religion.2010.01.010

Paul, Stella. 2014. 'India's "Temple Slaves" Struggle to Break Free'. *Inter Press Service* 22 June 2014. http://www.ipsnews.net/2014/06/indias-temple-slaves-struggle-to-break-free/

Pink, Sarah. 2009. *Doing Sensory Ethnography.* London: Sage. https://doi.org/10.4135/9781446249383

Plate, S. Brent. 2012. 'The Skin of Religion: Aesthetic Mediations of the Sacred'. *Crosscurrents* 62 (2): 162–180. https://doi.org/10.1111/j.1939-3881.2012.00228.x

Tythacott, Louise. 2017. 'Curating the Sacred: Exhibiting Buddhism at the World Museum Liverpool'. *Buddhist Studies Review* 34 (1): 115–133. https://doi.org/10.1558/bsrv.29020

Welch, Christina. 2014. 'Religion and Culture: Religious Artifacts as T-shirts, Toys and Museum Exhibits'. In Paul Hedges (ed.), *Controversies in Contemporary Religion: Volume 2: Debates in the Public Square and Ethical Issues*, 177–212. Oxford: Praeger.

Whitehead, Amy. 2018. 'Touching, Crafting, Knowing: Religious Artefacts and the Fetish within Animism'. In Harvey and Hughes (eds.), *Sensual Religion*, 215–236.

Zimmerman, Amanda, Ling Bai and David D. Ginty. 2014. 'The Gentle Touch Receptors of Mammalian Skin'. *Science* 21: 346 (6212): 950–954. https://doi.org/10.1126/science.1254229

Christina Welch, PhD, is an interdisciplinary neurodiverse scholar and Reader in Theology, Religion and Philosophy at the University of Winchester (UK), where she leads a Master's degree in Death, Religion and Culture. Her main research interests focus around the intersections between religion, and visual and material culture and her work in this area includes late-medieval cadaver sculptures, religion and erotic death imagery, and the role of Christianity in colonial visual representations. She is currently co-authoring a book on the materialities of Caribbean religion.

Amy R. Whitehead is a Senior Lecturer in Social Anthropology at Massey University in Aotearoa New Zealand. An Anthropologist of Religion/Religious Studies scholar, she is the author of *Religious Statues and Personhood: Testing the Role of Materiality* (2013), as well as several journal articles and chapters for edited volumes. Amy's primary areas of research concern the material and performance cultures of religions, the 'turn to things' in the Study of Religions, the development of new approaches to animism and 'the fetish', ritual studies and Earth Traditions (Paganisms, Goddess movements). She has also co-edited volumes including *Indigenous Religions: Critical Concepts for Religious Studies* (2018), and is the managing series editor for Bloomsbury Studies in Material Religion.

Part I

RECIPROCITY AND KNOWING:
BEING IN TOUCH WITH THINGS

Chapter 1

Tattooing Ritual and the Management of Touch in Polynesia

SÉBASTIEN GALLIOT[1]

While tattooing primarily appears as a material practice involving technical skills, tactile experience, senses, aesthetical judgement, physical discomfort, pain and sometimes pleasure, most of the available literature on this topic has largely developed along the lines of 'tattooing as an expression of the self/identity', tattooing as a 'political discourse' or tattooing as a 'statement', as monitored and reported by Benson (2000: 244). As a result, the social sciences have considered tattooing as subordinated to language and mental representations, thus sharing the same subordination as the one to which the material culture was brought since the 1980s. Material culture studies showed that materiality was not a mere expression of cultural representations but could be producing culture. In other words, as Keane wrote, 'materiality is a precondition for the social circulation and temporal persistence of experiences and rules' (2008: 230). Thus, focusing one's reflections and investigations on touch within the field of religious materialities suspends the understanding of material culture as material expressions of culture, or merely as a sign ultimately referring to an immaterial/collective mental representation, to instead engage in a more pragmatic approach to religious practices.

I argued elsewhere (Galliot 2015a) that ritual efficacy not only rested on a postulated super-human agency but could also be achieved and assessed on very tangible, technical and sensible criteria, by elementary actions on matter, by the making of tools, by the importance attached to the work devoted to specific materials such as boar tusks and candlenuts. Eventually,

1 Aix-Marseille Univ., CNRS, EHESS, CREDO 7308, 13003, Marseille, France.

by applying a methodology initially intended for the comparative study of technical processes (Balfet 1991; Creswell 1996; Lemonnier 1993), I showed that ritual efficacy could also be achieved through the implementation of technical skills and efficacious actions which were usually confined to the domain of profane techniques.

This commitment to look at elementary actions, tools, hands and the social aspect of technological processes first developed in the margins of the French anthropological tradition concerned with making processes and with the description of *chaînes opératoires* (or 'operating sequences'), and occurring before the phase of circulation and the handling of artefacts. Here, understanding the role of touch within tattooing rituals leads us through different pathways, including the dialectical relation between what is touched and physically endured here and now, and has a postulated effect on the untouchable, intangible, invisible world, i.e. a domain of sociality that remains separate from material causality. In this chapter, I will try to bring a culturally oriented answer articulated with a practice-centred approach—or to borrow the term from Sillitoe (2017: 1-4) an *ethno-determinist* framework—to the following question: what can tactility tell us about religious experiences as they are lived and mediatised by the body?

Tackling the Maussian notion of 'techniques of the body' (Mauss 1973) that encompass embodied schemes of action and tacit knowledge had to wait several decades to become part of the anthropological agenda and to be re-injected in leading anthropological debates (Bourdieu 1998; Descola 2013: Ch. 4; Ingold 2013). Meanwhile, material culture, a contemporary popular field of research, was first studied from the angle of consumption, use and biography of finished goods (Appadurai 1986) without a real interest for the technical process and even less for the question of touch. It is no exaggeration to say that body techniques, artefact and touch have rarely been interpreted from anything but a symbolic angle.

For its part, Religious Studies as a discipline has also developed and been influenced by a Western logocentric and exegetical tradition proper to monotheist religions. In a nutshell, anthropological approaches to ritual have largely neglected to investigate how ritual activities can be shaped and transmitted through an engagement of the senses with various matters, precisely because artefacts (for example) have long been considered from a symbolic angle, in a language-like system of communication. The purpose of this chapter is to show how it is possible to complete the symbolic interpretation of the rituals with a fine ethnography of the sensory regime, that is, by taking into account technical actions and physical perceptions.

While the role of tactile experience has long been a central topic of investigation in developmental psychology, cognitive sciences, neurosciences and psychoanalysis, its consideration by social sciences and in particular by ethnology and anthropology remains marginal. In 2007, the French journal *Terrain* made a significant move by bringing this topic under ethnographical scrutiny with the publication of a special issue entitled 'Toucher'. In this issue, several contributions dealt with touch as a modality for the shaping the sense of corporate culture and for the acquisition and the transmission of practical knowledge (de Grave 2007; Pouchelle 2007; Sola 2007).

Moreover, the way perceptual modalities are prioritised during the process of skill acquisition and community shaping is context-dependent (Bromberger 2007: 8; de Witte 2011: 149). This is especially the case within the study of religions where, even within a single religious tradition such as Christianity, the attitude toward, for example, a religious icon can vary from one congregation to another depending on the historical period in which the icon is being touched, studied or engaged. As I will show below, this is also the case for tattooing practices in Polynesia where I exemplify how a relatively homogeneous technique can imply a great cultural variability regarding the role of touch.

To follow the main line of my argument, the observation that can be made about the study of touch as a modality of religious practice appears either as a sub-section of the anthropology of the senses within the study of material religion, or it is approached metaphorically through the symbolic meanings associated with it. While contributing to the study of the cultural and historical variability of the senses, and stressing that tactility among other senses can be a key modality of collective and religious experience, authors like Chidester (2018), Classen (2012), Harvey and Hughes (2018), Howes (2003), Laplantine (2005) and Montagu (1971) seem at the same time to have limited their scope to cultural values associated with touch, when explaining how the semantic field of touch and body perceptions serves to express religious belief and communication with divine and invisible entities.

A few decades before the corporeal turn in anthropology that led the discipline to follow Mauss' call and explore more systematically the culturally informed dimensions of body techniques, Michael Polanyi addressed the related question of tacit knowledge and human experience in a series of publications which remained at the margins of social science (1958, 1966). Yet, exploring touch within religious practice and belief also implies a dive into the embodied and tacit domain of experience which attracted anthropologists' attention a little bit later (Comaroff 1985; Csordas 1994; Jackson 1983; Turner 1994, 1995; Wacquant 2003). The physicality of collective experience has resisted anthropological investigations precisely because of this supposedly implicit and tacit nature which Polanyi attempted to analyse, but also because of the primacy given to language over gestures within the practice of ethnography. Thus, while most craftsmen or religious experts would certainly emphasise the crucial role haptics play in their everyday activities, tactility remains the less investigated mode of skill learning and religious behaviour.

To put the matter differently, if one follows Morgan's assumption that 'belief is what I know with my body' (2010: 9), then considerable ethnographic efforts need to be made in order to register the engagement of bodies in religious practices. Here I am far from pretending that we are facing a complete ethnographic void. In *The Pot King*, Jean-Pierre Warnier (2007) has rolled out a very rich ethnography to show how, in Cameroun, political subjection to a sacred king essentially relied on the interaction between the subject's bodies, artefacts and substances. Drawing on African data, Marie Nooter Roberts (2010) has also brilliantly shown the centrally of touch in mnemonic and divination practices, spirit possession and spiritual mediation. Amy Whitehead's (2018) research on the Virgin of Alcalá in Andalusia again demonstrates how fertile attention to touch can be for the understanding of devotional practices. Recent research in Melanesia and Polynesia have also brought new light on the constitutive blend of action, matters and invisible entities within religious experiences. This is exemplified by the ethnography of visual properties of the materials involved in the making process of Owa magical artefacts (Revolon 2012), and through the configuration of space in the *palo monte* rituals in Cuba (Kerestetzi 2018). In the same vein, the efficacy of magic can also rest on the very manipulation of stones in the Abelam 'yam cult' (Coupaye 2013). Ultimately, as Lemonnier (2012) stressed, after forty years of the study of cultural technology and material culture, there is no valid reason to rely on the 'opacity' of relationship between means and ends in ritual or to ignore the work of the hands and the role of touch in religion, nor any reason to oppose the significance of technique and materiality to the study of magic and religion. Thus, exploring the coupling of hands and matter in a religious context is even more relevant in the light of the acknowledgement of the constitutive blend between matter and belief in religious practices around the world.

TATTOO AND (NO) TOUCH

If one looks at the ethnographic literature devoted to tattooing, the question of touch is largely ignored. Most of the publications on tattooing look at it as a direct/primal scripture; a form of registration of the self (Caplan 2000; De Mello 2000) with the meanings of tattoo designs and the discourse of tattoo wearers of prime importance. Other studies tackle the history of the craft in Western and non-Western societies, as well as in relation with current indigenous tattoo revivals in various parts of the world.[2] However, recent research, including mine, shows a special interest in the ethnography of tattooing skill transmission: in Samoa (Galliot 2015b), in the Philippines (Salvador-Amores 2013) and in Switzerland (Rolle 2013).

That being said, there are unquestionably psychological, and psychoanalytical, approaches to tattooing that articulate more systematically the question of tactility, and the perception that the act of being tattooed, among other self-inflicted wounds and rituals involving inflicted pain on the body, is understood as a significant biographical episode for the construction of the psyche and the persona (Estellon 2004; Korff-Sausse 2004; Maertens 1978; Wiener 2004). But, with the exception of Maertens, these studies relate to the examination of Western individuals outside of a religious system; thus, they appear of little help for the present chapter's focus.

In other words, two main difficulties arise when one attempts to gather data on touch within tattooing rituals. The first difficulty relates to the scarcity of in-depth ethnographic accounts about tattooing rituals, which concentrate on tools and on the codification of designs rather than on elementary actions and perceptions of the bodies involved. The other difficulty relates to the fact that ethnographies of tattooing practices are, most of the time, disconnected from their socio-cultural and religious context to the point they are described as an autonomous domain. Thus, for instance, it is extremely difficult to reconstruct how tattooing rituals integrate with a system of belief and, by the same token, can be linked with the senses and tactility. First, because where tattooing rituals existed, they have often vanished with the establishment of Christianity (in the English and French colonies) and Islam (in the Maghreb) as state religions, and also with the centralisation of power during colonial times. Second, because

---

2 There is a rich literature on these topics. Here is a selection of the most noticeable recent works (Allen 2006; Deter-Wolf and Diaz-Granados 2013; Krutak 2014; Krutak and Deter-Wolf 2017; Kuwahara 2005; Mallon and Galliot 2018; Mangos and Utanga 2011; Te Awekotuku and Waimarie Nikora 2007).

where tattooing was studied by ethnographers, it was considered as an epiphenomenon classified in the 'arts', 'crafts' and 'ornaments' category. Yet, this does not need to be the case. Going beyond the more subdued notions of 'art' and ornamentation allows us to glean the powerful ritual efficacy at play through the medium of 'touch'.

TATTOO, TOUCH AND TRANSCENDENCE

One of the most researched contemporary tattooing rituals is found in mainland Southeast Asia where a long tradition of tattooing has been documented quite thoroughly (Cook 2007/2008; Lagirarde 1989; Rajadhon 1964; Scott 1896; Terwiel 1976; Tannenbaum 1987). Several categories of tattooing meant for different purposes are known in this area. Here, I will limit discussion to Thai protective tattoos (designated by the term *sak yant* or 'marking of sacred geometry') that are executed by experts such as revered laymen, monks and *sara* (traditional healers). By virtue of their religious status, these specialists can transfer power to their customer through the pigment and the tattooed image. To sum up very briefly Tannenbaum's detailed ethnography, these protective tattoos take *yantra* (magical figures derived from Buddha's teachings known as *katha*) in written form or encoded in a diagram, often combined with animal or divine representation, and render them efficacious with recitations of *katha* by the practitioner. They are meant for very down-to-earth purposes such as providing increased attractiveness, luck in business, protection against diseases, or invulnerability (which for example explains the propensity of tattooed Thai boxers). Beyond the pigment, an additional ingredient is crucial for the tattoo efficacy: medicine or exfoliated monk's skin.

Sak yant is relevant to help put into perspective our present concern regarding religion and touch, as it is associated with Theravada Buddhism which rests on principles of renunciation and asceticism. Tannenbaum (1987) and Cook (2007/2008), who studied tattooing in different parts of Thailand at different periods and with different theoretical agendas, both emphasise the very particular conception of the self this practice links with. Namely, a conception that is very far from the stereotypical Western one which draws on tattooing to produce a statement on the self, and to struggle against impermanence of worldly existence. The power transferred by *sak yant* and produced by monks and experts acts here and now on the bearer's body envelope (Tannenbaum 1987: 696) yet is dependent on the number of Buddhist precepts and the level of asceticism the practitioner conforms himself to. And, these precepts imply the strict regulation of his bodily and daily activities including his renunciation of materiality, even though its achievement actually needs a certain type of engagement with matter.

Paradoxically then our discussion on touch and religious tattooing starts with a case that denies any importance to tactility and self-consciousness through body perception. Rather, as Cook wrote, the conception of the self and corporeality 'are understood to be generative of power only when they are transcended' (2007/2008: 22). In addition, beyond reflecting a culturally grounded conception of the body, namely the one that predominates in Theravada Buddhism, *sak yant* follows the same rationale as the making and the carrying of amulets (Rajadhon 1964). This confers an interesting status to Thai protective tattoos as their efficacy is dependent on an interplay between religious asceticism and renunciation on one hand, and on material mediation on the other.

Interestingly, Rajadhon also reports that after the tattooing ritual, which takes place within the sanctuary of a Buddhist chapel, the tattooer would 'strike hard with his open hand on the tattooed *yantra* many times', until the designs emerged 'distinctly and prominently on the skin' (1964: 187). Without further development, the author underlines the fact that this step constitutes an even more painful ordeal than the tattooing itself. He goes on to report that the tattooed person or rather the efficacy of his protective tattoo was tested by being hit with a sharp instrument. This statement, as anecdotal as it may seem, shows quite clearly that even a theoretically disembodied ritual may manifest important tactile experience if one pays adequate attention to it. Unfortunately, none of the ethnographers of *sak yant* elaborates on that topic.

TATTOOING IN POLYNESIA

Next turning toward Polynesia, Alfred Gell made a significant move when he explored tattooing (1993) and then the agency of art (1998). By exploring these consecutively, he re-oriented research on art and artefacts to focus within a system of action, and not only within a system of meaning (Barthes 1964; Baudrillard 1996) or a system of value (Appadurai 1986; Kopytoff 1986). By combining Gell's attempts to explain, on one hand the cultural logic of tattooing and on the other the role of art in a system of social relations, I argue that he offered a radically new perspective on tattooing in general. His work makes it possible to see how the artefactual dimension of a tattoo articulates with its technical counterparts in a context of social relation. This is despite Gell himself not engaging in Polynesian fieldwork; he nonetheless drew on an extensive comparative reading on Polynesian tattooing, and on Sahlins' (1958) hypothesis of a homology between the islands' size and the degree of social stratification, in order to build an interpretative model which aimed at explaining the co-variance between islands' environments, cultural logics and tattooing techniques, meanings and positioning on the body. Gell also based his work on Anzieu's psychoanalytical approach of the skin and the self (1989). According to Anzieu, the skin and the tactile experiences this organ allows provide the constitutive representation of the self and its main functions. He goes on to define nine functions of the *Skin Ego* which were co-opted by Gell to explain what, in his analysis, can be understood as nine possible functions for the tattooing. However, in light of the available data, Gell had to restrict his analysis to only a few of the nine functions delimitated by Anzieu, and retained his broad statement that a tattoo, in general, has the symbolic status of a body envelope just like an additional layer of skin.

In our case, Gell's most convincing argument regards the technical schema of tattooing (blood-letting → scarring/healing → wearing/displaying). Posited in an evolutionary scheme, he proposed that marginal Polynesian societies (the Maori and the Marquesan) accorded more symbolic significance to the last step (the tattoo as an artefact) and thus manifested less standardisation and more individual idiosyncrasy in their tattooing. Gell links this with devolved political aspects characterised by an agonistic ethos which tends to express itself through displays of wealth and finery. This contrasts with central Polynesian societies among which blood-letting rituals and healing procedures (the Society Islands and Samoa) were more consistent with ancient hierarchical systems, and where rituals were designed to channel the flow of blood. Understood in this ritual context, blood is a fertilising substance and is the 'basic currency of social relations' (Gell 1993: 306).

Gell went on to make an analogy between tattooing and wrapping as a technical means to seal the person and the potential dispersal of his *tapu*. By *tapu*, he actually meant sacredness. I would rather use the term *mana*, i.e. the divine essence, the reproductive and political power. Roughly speaking, in many Pacific societies, the amount of *mana* a person is filled with can be lost, or contaminate others. For that reason, bodies have to be recharged, sealed, wrapped and protected. According to Gell, tattooing is linked with 'signalling the primary dispersal and subsequent containment of potentially dangerous *tapu*' (1993: 306). Although Gell over-interpreted his Polynesia data (Galliot 2019: Ch. 4), he nonetheless provides a refreshing theoretical framework which does not have any competitor so far. He obviously did not elaborate on the politics of touch in Polynesia, but his theoretical model acknowledges its relevance in considering the technical steps prior to the finished tattooed image. As a matter of fact, the marked steps in the making of a tattooed image produce very distinctive tactile perceptions through the skin. In this respect, I would add to Gell's analysis that it is not only relevant to look at the symbolic emphasis accorded to these steps (which do have importance in psychoanalytical terms), but it would also be fruitful to investigate the haptics of the process. For example, to what extent can the cultural importance of the scarring process during tattooing be based on the perceptions that are associated with it (itchiness, irritation, swollenness, inflammatory states, etc.)? Which body handlings are associated with the different technical steps? And to what extent do the tactile aspects of the ritual contribute to its efficacy?

As I suggested above, the problem with religious tactility is first a matter of ethnographic focus. Haptics, interoception and exteroception play a role in many religious rituals, sacred object manipulations, mediation practices and religious expertise. These aspects need to be looked at seriously. In order to begin to answer some of the questions I put above, I now turn to my own ethnography of the Samoan tattooing ritual.

TOUCH AND SAMOAN TATTOOING

Samoan tattooing is an emblematic ritual as most of its implementation involves bodies, and bodies only. In other words, this is a ritual in which transmission and efficacy do not rely on language, and where everything is mediated by the participants' bodies. Perceptions in question here vary from tactile-kinaesthetic (perceptions mediated by the touch of hands, or haptics strictly speaking) to somaesthetic and proprioception.

Contemporary Samoan tattooing ranges from a ritualised production of a standardised assemblage of designs (called *pe'a* for men and *malu* for women, see **Figures 1.1 and 1.2**) to more customised works based on the iconography of male and female above-mentioned categories. In order to produce these images, a hand tapping method relying on a mallet (*sausau*) and a set of small adze-shaped utensils (*autā*) tipped with boar-tusk needles or steel needles of various widths is used. All this is supervised and performed by a *tufuga tā tatau* (commissioned expert, literally a 'tattoo specialist') whose apprenticeship has been completed within one of the two traditional clans known as the 'aiga Sā Suʻa and 'aiga Sā Tulouena'. However, some *tufuga tā tatau* who own a title from another clan are nowadays also acknowledged by virtue of a connection between the origin myth of tattooing and one of their ancestors. As I argued elsewhere, Samoan tattoo practitioners rely as much on their filiation as on different versions of the tattooing myth of origin to legitimise their belonging to the category of *tufuga* (Galliot 2019: Ch. 5). This is the case for the name Liʻaifaiva which is currently used as a tattooing title by one *tufuga* who was bestowed it last year in Safotu, the village where it originates from.

Most of the *tufuga* as well as *pe'a* and *malu* wearers are of Samoan descent (living in Samoa or in diasporic communities in Australia, New Zealand and USA). However, as far back in history as we can go, Samoan tattoo specialists have always been open to performing the ritual on non-Samoans. And in the late 1990s they also started to take non-Samoan apprentices as a result of the intensification of their international travels, both into other Polynesian countries involved in ethnic tattoo revivalism, and in connection with the Western tattooing scene where they built professional relationships with Western tattooists and customers dating from the late 1980s when they started travelling abroad.

Figure 1.1 Samoan men displaying *pe'a*.

Tattooing Ritual and Touch in Polynesia 35

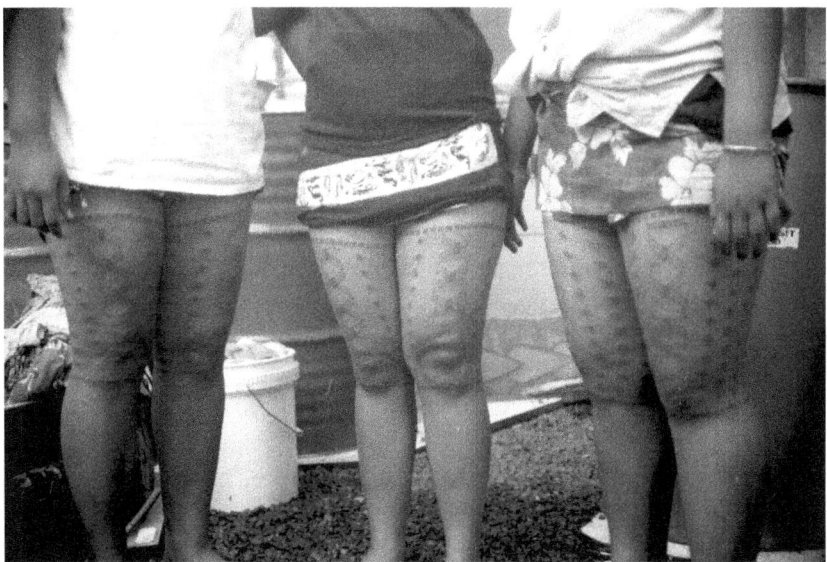

Figure 1.2 Samoan women displaying *malu*.

It is here important to recall the fact that tattooing is a once-in-a-lifetime ritual, and not only a commercial operation for performing a tattoo on a customer. Samoan tattooing is traditionally a three-stage collective male-focused initiation in the fashion of what has long been theorised by Van Gennep (1909), Turner (1969) or Bloch (1992). It involves the establishment of ritual relationships between participants, the settlement of a ritual space, its sacralisation by prayers, the separation of the recipients by prescriptions and proscriptions (*tulafono* and *fa'asā* in the Samoan language), and a closing ceremony during which initiates are released and allowed to carry on the normal course of their lives.[3] However, as noted, nowadays women are also tattooed, and the main difference in treatment between males and females has to do with the length of the tattooing operation. It requires five to ten days in a row to complete a *pe'a* (which extends from the waist down to the knees), whereas it takes only a few hours to cover women's thighs with a *malu*.

Having a ritual tattoo done by a *tufuga* is a costly procedure and there are a wide range of reasons, based on the social context of the wearer at the time of the operation, why someone might undertake this expense. For example, an individual can be tattooed prior to entering the village council of title holders (*fono o matai*) in order to perform various kinds of

3 For a detailed description, see Mallon and Galliot (2018).

duties (serving food, presenting valuables during inter-village ceremonial exchanges, serving kava[4] in the appropriate fashion, along with other things designated by the generic term *tautua*, i.e. service). Or it can be a celebration of an appreciated member of a kin group who is expected to serve his family and maybe in the future receive a chiefly title (*suafa matai*). It can also be an individual's celebration of their own accomplishments or success in a business or in an executive position in government. In fact, while it was quite rare in the 1990s and early 2000s to meet members of the Samoan intellectual or financial elite sporting ritual tattoos, it is fairly customary these days. Also, outside the context of inter-clan ceremonial relationships and village life and politics, wearers of *pe'a* and *malu* are broadly considered as flag-carriers, wearing a skin-deep national cultural heritage and displaying their cultural pride occasionally. In addition, most tattooing rituals involve several persons (male and/or female) being worked on during the same period of time by the commissioned expert and his group of helpers. This is explained not only by customary reasons (the fear of being tattooed alone without a tattoo partner) but also by practical reasons such as cost reduction and seizing the *tufuga*'s availability to undertake female tattoos beside male ones.

The above exploration is, by necessity, a somewhat superficial introduction to Samoan tattooing based on my own detailed fieldwork studying the apprenticeship and ritual transmission of tattooing. Samoan tattooing is literally a ritual work at every step: from the making of the tools to the final ointment that the initiate must use. It requires technical expertise and is locally called *galuega* (work, in the sense of men's physical work). Thus, the expression 'ritual work' is not to be understood metaphorically. In the same vein, the very act of tattooing is not just a symbolic death of the previously untattooed person before their re-emergence with their new status, but represents a real threat to life, as until recently undertaking this ritual could be a cause of extremely serious skin diseases, and sometimes death.

There are two special features to this Samoan tattooing ritual: (1) it is essentially speechless, i.e. it doesn't involve any secret revelation or designs exegesis that would be part of a communicable verbal content; (2) ritual performance and apprenticeship of ritual expertise are consubstantial, i.e. it is configured such that non-verbal and perceptual environment,

---

4 Kava (or 'ava in Samoan) is a drink made of water and pounded *Piper methysticum* roots. In Samoa, Tonga and Fiji, it is ceremonially distributed and drunk at the opening of important gatherings. It can also be consumed on a daily basis as a socialising beverage.

gestures and elementary actions are the privileged ways to access the knowledge that is being passed on. This modality of skill transmission is comparable to what Lave and Wenger have coined as 'situated learning' (1991).

Further, the **making of the tools** manifests a dichotomised use of the hands between the master and his apprentice. It is not necessary to detail every step of the manufacturing process here, but some operations are relevant. At the tool-making stage, the *tufuga* is in charge of most of the expert gestures, using both his hands and sometimes his feet, while the apprentice largely limits himself to holding things still (*taofi* = stopping/preventing from moving) for the *tufuga* (**Figure 1.3**). The *tufuga*'s tools are intended for his use alone; they must work with his hand size and how he holds things but must be technically useful as the boar-tusk handle must be the appropriate dimension to hold the needles which he also manufactures by hand. This needle-making operation depends on the alternative use of sight and touch to assess the right thinness of the piece of ivory from which the needles will be cut. He holds the ivory with two or three fingers of his right hand, and grinds it horizontally on a hone, regularly soaking it in water to remove the excess of ground enamel, and to cool the material (**Figure 1.4**).

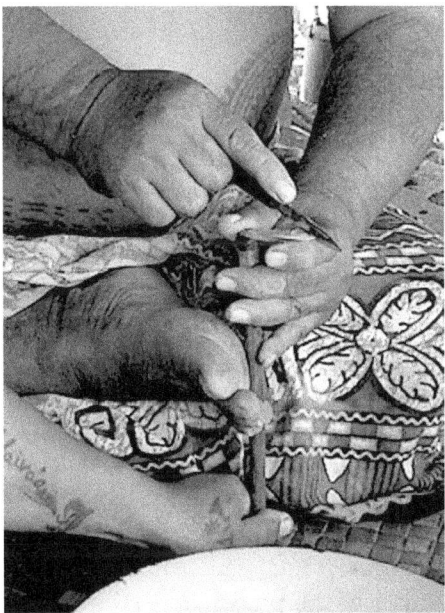

Figure 1.3 The apprentice's hand below holds in place the tool that is being made by the *tufuga* using his hands and feet.

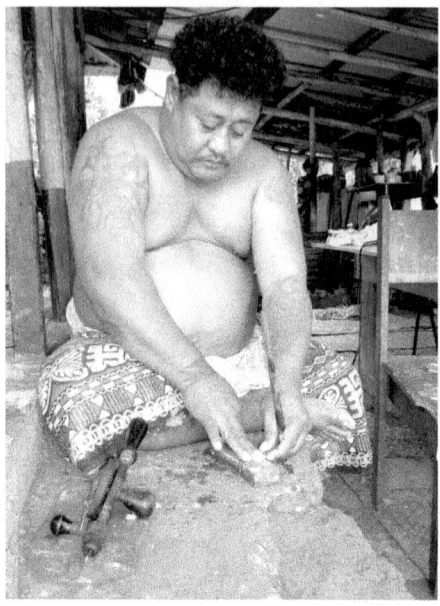

Figure 1.4 Making a tattooing needle.

After the selected tusk has been reduced to the intended dimensions, several tips are delimited with a knife and sharpened with a file made out of a sea urchin spine. This highly sensitive work necessitates frequent checking. The *tufuga* controls the making of the needles by applying the tips to his cheek. This allows him to assess the sharpness of the group of needles by using a soft part of his body. Notably, the efficiency of the completed tattooing tool (*autā*) is often tested on the specialist's own leg before being used in the ritual. Here then somaesthetic afferences channelled by a soft part of the expert's body are central for the making of efficient tools, which in return are necessary to ritual efficacy. I argue that this constitutes a striking example of the disruption of material causality into ritual actions.

At the stage of applying the tattoo, the work of the hands, the body movements and the positioning of the body in ritual space are also strictly controlled, according to the participants who do something with their hands and those who attend the ritual in a more passive way. This positioning according to agency contrasts with the customary management of space in other Samoan formal gatherings where bodies are regulated according to the status of the participants. The ritual space for the tattooing can be settled in any kind of sheltered area. It is configured in the fashion of two concentric circles of participants. In this space, the central circle of the action is occupied by the initiate ('*o le ta'oto* = the lying down), the tattoo master ('*o le tufuga*) and his two or three assistants (*o toso* = the stretchers), while at the peripheral circle are seated the relatives of the initiate and other voluntary participants. Here again, if one pays enough attention to it, the ritual management of touch is clearly at work.

The centre of the action is delineated between the expertise of the *tufuga* who makes fine lines and intricate designs with a very complex tapping technique and the role of the *toso* who stretches the skin of the *ta'oto*. The skin-stretchers must position their hands in order to harden and flatten the skin to the maximum of its elasticity, and at the same time they must hold the initiate's body still to prevent it from moving and compromising the expected visual result (**Figure 1.5**). Stretching is a task very onerous for the forearm muscles. Even though it does not require any specific apprenticeship, the task necessitates a specific positioning of the hands while stretching, as well as accurate hand-eye coordination between both assistants, and with the *tufuga*. This is made manifest by most inexperienced assistants who stretch the skin using their fingertips and thus cannot anticipate the movements of the surface of the body which is to be tapped by the *tufuga*; they need to learn to use the palms of their hands.

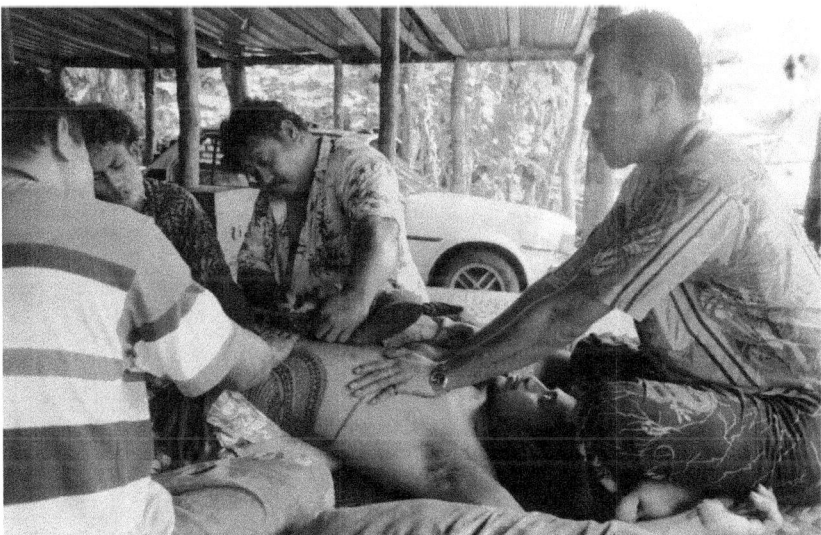

Figure 1.5 Stretching the skin for a tattoo.

After each sequence of tapping which rarely exceeds thirty seconds, the *toso* eases the pressure on the patient's skin and wipes away the blood and ink with a soft piece of fabric before repeating the same sequence of movements. The softness of the fabric used to wipe the blood can of course be evaluated through haptic perceptions. It is soaked in a bucket of water and squeezed so that it is just wet enough to clean the skin—the work surface. Thus, the cloth has to be spongy enough to absorb the excess of blood and ink, but dry enough to allow the skin to be stretched again without leaving too much humidity on it.

The peripheral circle occupied by other participants is characterised by inactivity and silent worshipping (*tāpua'i*) which, paradoxically, is an essential part of the ritual actions' success. The watchers sit cross-legged around the initiate being tattooed; they must wear no body ornaments such as necklaces, or flowers on the ears, and are expected to silently encourage the initiate and the *tufuga*'s group by their presence. Close relatives of the initiate can touch him or her, applying light pressure on the body (head, hands or feet; **Figures 1.6 and 1.7**). Occasionally, they also wave a fan to keep flies away and ventilate the members of the tattooing group. This is understood as a token of empathy and filial love (*alofa*), especially in the last steps of the operation when the initiate is exhausted; sometimes to the point of giving up. If this occurs, the *tāpua'i* group participate in the completion of the ritual through using their body positioning—a form of physical inaction.

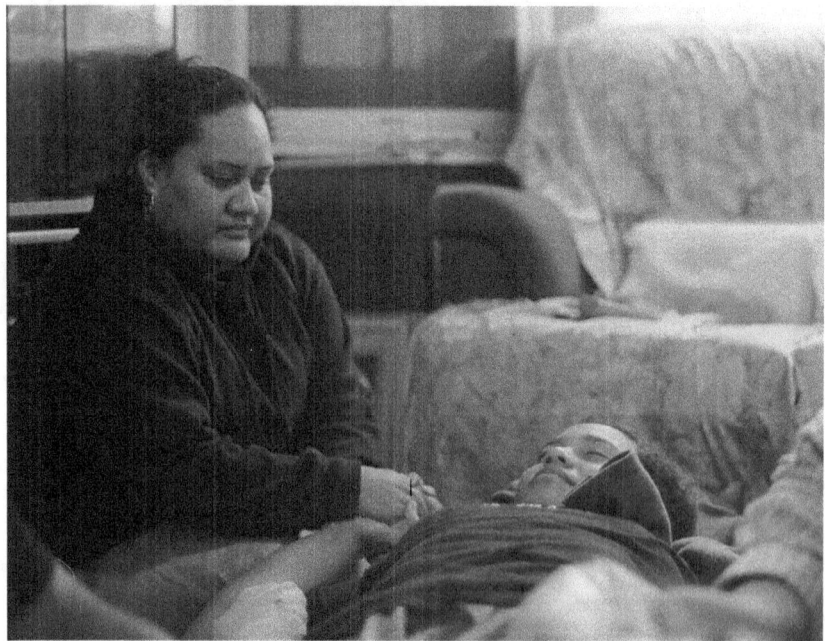

Figure 1.6 Applying pressure to the hand of the initiate.

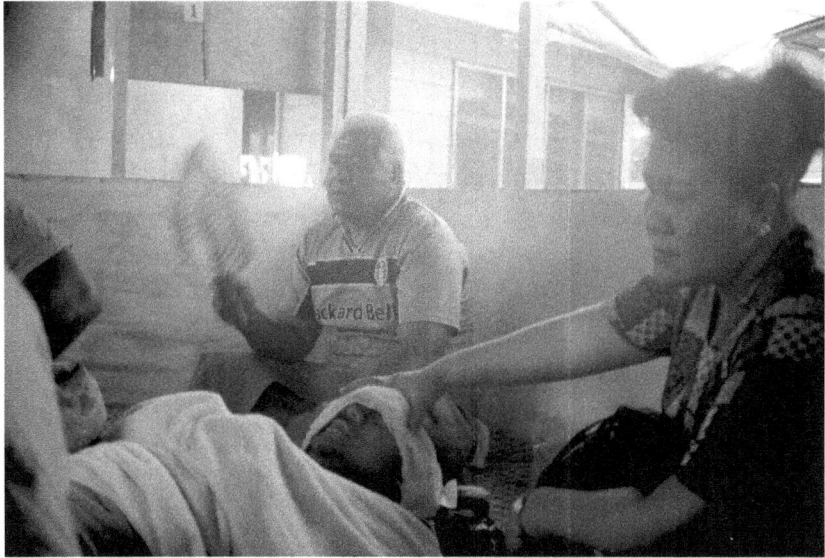

Figure 1.7 Applying pressure to the head, and fanning the initiate.

The initiate being tattooed is expected to do nothing other than cope with their situation passively, beyond repositioning their body according to the instructions given by the *tufuga* and *toso*. Somaesthetic inputs, i.e. the nature and severity of the perceived pain, depend on the portion of the skin being tattooed, and on the size of the tattooing tool in use. Tattooing the inside of the thighs, the torso or the knees is generally considered the most painful. Pain also varies throughout the session, usually starting with a localisable acute pain and moving to a duller and less localisable one. At this latter stage, of course, the brain has started to release endorphins and the patient feels numb and tired. After each tattoo session (usually five hours a day), the *ta'oto*'s wounded skin is washed with soap and massaged (*fō*) by an assistant or a relative (**Figure 1.8**).

During the duration of the ritual, the initiate must stay unshaved (if they are male), refrain from sexual intercourse and avoid going out at night alone as their sore, swollen and wounded skin is believed to attract malevolent beings. If the ritual rules are not followed, this usually affects the healing process and unusual scars and large skin infections can occur.

Figure 1.8 Washing the skin at the end of a tattooing session.

The final sequence of touches during the tattooing ritual is significant, and occurs during the *samaga*, or ointment ceremony. Initially, the focus of this gathering is to lift ritual prescriptions and proscriptions through a series of actions on the initiate's body. It is organised a few days after the last tattooing session. At this gathering are the initiate, the *tufuga*, his assistants and senior members (parents and title-holders) of the initiate's kin group. This meeting begins either with a moment of prayer said by a churchman or an elder from the initiate's family, or with a formal distribution of kava. This is a sanctification phase (*fa'apāia*) and is followed by two separate actions on the initiate's body. Often, the meeting is held for several initiates whose tattooing has been completed.

The first of these two actions occurs after the *tufuga* has briefly acknowledged the end of the work in front of the audience; he gets up, comes to the back of the group of initiates and gently applies some egg-white on the top of each head (**Figure 1.9**). He simultaneously whispers a short and often inaudible formula that is locally interpreted as a blessing (*fa'amanuia*) on the initiates. Then, assistants go on in front of the group with a receptacle filled with a mixture of coconut oil and turmeric powder with which they anoint the tattooed bodies (**Figure 1.10**). While the first movement recalls an ancient ritual action called *lulu'uga* that consisted in spreading green coconut water on someone's head in order to lift taboos on his person, the anointment is more complex to understand because of its multivalence. In

Polynesia and Micronesia, the combining of turmeric with coconut oil was (and still is on many islands) part of the major seasonal rituals (Lessa 1966; Sopher 1964), as well as crucial in birth and puberty rites, and funerals (Firth 1967; Galliot 2015b; Parmentier 1988; Turner 1884). In Samoa, it is also employed as a medicinal preparation and its use in the closing tattoo ceremony is linked to its antiseptic virtues and the relief it affords from the physical discomfort caused by tattooing. However, as this mixture is absent from the operation itself, its presence at the end of the ritual is also intended to neutralise the potentially harmful effect of the pigment and to give the *pe'a* or *malu* a lustre and unusual colour. In the contemporary Samoan context, this can also be interpreted as a ritual act ensuring a continuity with the ancient pre-Christian rites and ceremonies specific to the Polynesian region, while at the same time allowing an analogy between *sama* and *sanctum chrisma*, as sacred oils are believed to have the power to make the individuals visible to the gods and integrate the initiate into the community. Thus, whereas the inaugural prayer both Christianises the rite and enables the opening of a sacred space, the oil, through its shininess, authorises the presentation of the body in this space. The oil emphasises the visual impact of the work, celebrates the person's successful initiation and guarantees they are correctly introduced to the ancestors incarnated by the title-holders attending the event.

Figure 1.9 The *tufuga* applies egg-white on the head of an initiate.

Figure 1.10 An assistant anoints the tattooed body with a mixture of coconut oil and turmeric powder.

This anointing is followed by a distribution of fragrant necklaces, and by a short dance involving all participants but focused on the newly tattooed individuals who are expected to display their shiny tattooed body parts. During this dance, men acknowledge their physical fitness by slapping their tattoos, which will react by rising above the surface of the skin.

A second sequence of actions called *umusaga* involves a stereotyped series of speech exchanges and gift presentations. In contrast to the ritual work, this event is more wordy, since commissioned orators in charge of delivering speeches on behalf of both parties take centre stage. This phase is not specific to the tattooing ritual but to the generic status of the *tufuga* (expert craftsman and ritual specialist). In this respect, he is addressed with a special and formal lexical field reserved for his ritual office. Here, the purpose is recompense for the completed work. Although a stereotyped sequence of actions and speeches are delivered, we are now into a more political regime than a ritual one. Sensorimotor skills, physical contact and haptics are no longer relevant, and not prominent at all.

CONCLUDING REMARKS

The Samoan ritual of tattooing briefly described through the prism of physicality and touch leads us to consider the notion of ritual technology literally, as it involves a great deal of embodied skills. On one hand, this case contrasts with current developments in the professional Western tattoo industry that manifests a gradual withdrawal of touch of the hand to the body. The recent designing of a 3D tattoo printer monitored by software, requiring no human touch, is a striking example of this current state. Also, the popularity of rotary tattoo machines in the tattoo industry, together with the concern (from the tattoo milieu as well as from governments' health departments wishing to regulate the profession) to limit cross-contamination, tends to decrease the use of skilled hands and the importance of touch within tattooing practices.

Additionally, as shown here, Samoan tattooing contrasts with many approaches to ritual studies, as the required expertise for its proper implementation relies neither on divine intervention nor on a revelation from super-human entities, nor on the study of sacred scriptures sanctioned by a clergy. Rather it is a technical and relational skill that is acquired through the training of the senses, or as an 'education of attention' (Gibson 1979: 234; Ingold 2014). It combines habituation to strenuous postures (as sitting cross-legged for several hours is not usual), habituation to the right positioning of the hands, to the evaluation of the pressure and the force needed to adapt to various types of skin and differing skin elasticity, and to the production of sufficient strike force when using the mallet on the tattooing needles, with the tattooer's ability to memorise the numerous designs and complex assemblage of ornamental units which are stored nowhere else than on the initiates' bodies. However, the mnemonic capacities of the practitioner do not guarantee the efficacy of the ritual and quality of the image produced. Although the designs of *pe'a* and *malu* are standardised, the *tufuga* and his assistants always have to rely on the tactile perceptions available in the flow of activity in order to constantly re-adjust their intended design to the material constraints of the work environment. They first have to adjust the way they work to the recipient's body shape and skin type. They also have to adapt to the changing relational configuration of the rituals. Tattoo rituals feature variable categories of participants and recipients, i.e. people with variable status (untitled men and ladies, low titled men, high chiefs), variable level of expectations in terms of aesthetics and variable economic capacity. All these criteria do have an impact on the material implementation of the ritual, which is ultimately and subtly noticeable in the finished tattooed image.

In conclusion, as an alternative to Gell's symbolic emphasis on one of the tattooing universal technical steps to understand how it articulates within the kind of social systems in which it manifests, I proposed to rather look at the way the body perceives the tattooing process, in order to explore precisely if body perception could substantiate representations rather than the opposite. Taking a materialistic approach, I argue that emerging from the study of tattooing, when explored as a kind of excruciating body experience, are mental models and categories of social beings. The rare verbalisations that occur during the Samoan tattooing sessions are all oriented toward bodies, gestures and tools. Participants who *tāpua'i* the operation regularly utter short formulas acknowledging the movement of the hands (*malo le a'ao solo*) and the movement of the mallet (*malo le sausau*). Also, one of the best examples from the Samoan data is found in the term *soga'imiti* that applies to a young man who has completed the tattooing ritual. Local etymologies of this term agree on the idea that it is formed of *soga* + *mitimiti* which is basically understood as 'continuous itchiness', a sensation that universally occurs during the scarring of the skin after tattooing.

Samoan tattooing has the paradoxical effect of reinforcing the person by actually sensitising his skin. A *pe'a* covers half of the body and includes large solid black areas of ink on the back and on the thighs. While the ink injected into the skin does have a certain density that can be revealed by slaps (during the dance for example), the skin containing tattoo marks has the tendency to perceive tactile stimulations differently than the rest of the body. Thus, the effect this kind of ritual tattooing has more to do with a somaesthetic shift and a validation of strength than with an inscribed statement of status in a Polynesian hierarchy.

In this sense, this chapter could help in highlighting not only the importance of researching the material implication of tattooing, but more widely the heuristic value of undertaking fine ethnographies of senses and gestures as these allow a better understanding for non-verbal, non-symbolic, immediate and crucial aspects of religious practices.

BIBLIOGRAPHY

Allen, Tricia. 2006. *Tattoo Traditions of Hawai'i*. Honolulu: Mutual Publishing.
Anzieu, Didier. 1989. *The Skin-Ego*. New Haven: Yale University Press.

Appadurai, Arjun. 1986. 'Introduction: Commodities and the Politics of Value'. In Arjun Appadurai (ed.), *The Social Life of Things: Commodities in Cultural Perspective*, 3-63. Cambridge and New York: Cambridge University Press. https://doi.org/10.1017/CBO9780511819582.003

Balfet, Hélène (ed.). 1991. *Observer l'action technique. Des chaînes opératoires, pour quoi faire?* Paris: Ed. du CNRS.

Barthes, Roland. 1964. 'Réthorique de l'image'. *Communications* 4: 40-51. https://doi.org/10.3406/comm.1964.1027

Baudrillard, Jean. 1996. *The System of Objects*. London and New York: Verso.

Benson, Susan. 2000. 'Inscriptions of the Self: Reflections on Tattooing and Piercing in Contemporary Euro-America'. In Jane Caplan (ed.), *Written on the Body: The Tattoo in European and American History*, 234-254. Princeton, NJ: Princeton University Press.

Bloch, Maurice. 1992. *Prey into Hunter: The Politics of Religious Experience*. Cambridge: Cambridge University Press. https://doi.org/10.1017/CBO9780511621581

Bourdieu, Pierre. 1998. *Practical Reason*. Stanford: University of California Press.

Bromberger, Christian. 2007. 'Toucher'. *Terrain* 49: 5-10. https://doi.org/10.4000/terrain.5641

Caplan, Jane (ed.). 2000. *Written on the Body: The Tattoo in European and American History*. Princeton, NJ: Princeton University Press.

Chidester, David. 2018. *Religion, Material Dynamics*. Oakland: University of California Press. https://doi.org/10.1525/california/9780520297654.001.0001

Classen, Constance. 2012. *The Deepest Sense. A Cultural History of Touch*. Urbana, Chicago and Springfield: University Press of Illinois. https://doi.org/10.5406/illinois/9780252034930.001.0001

Comaroff, Jean. 1985. *Body of Power, Spirit of Resistance: The Culture and History of a South African People*. Chicago: University of Chicago Press. https://doi.org/10.7208/chicago/9780226160986.001.0001

Cook, Joanna C. 2007/2008. 'Tattoos, Corporeality and the Self: Dissolving Borders in a Thai Monastery'. *Cambridge Anthropology* 27 (2), Boundary Crossing: A Festschrift in Memory of Sue Benson: 20-35.

Creswell, Robert. 1996. *Prométhée ou Pandore. Propos de technologie Culturelle*. Paris: Editions Kimé.

Coupaye, Ludovic. 2013. *Growing Artefacts, Displaying Relationships: Yams, Art and Technology amongst the Nyamikum Abelam of Papua New Guinea*. New York and Oxford: Berghahn Books.

Csordas, Thomas J. (ed.). 1994. *Embodiment and Experience: The Existential Ground of Culture and Self*. Cambridge: Cambridge University Press.

de Grave, Jean-Marc. 2007. 'Quand ressentir c'est toucher. Techniques javanaises d'apprentissage sensoriel'. *Terrain* 49: 77-88. https://doi.org/10.4000/terrain.6061

De Mello, Margot. 2000. *Bodies of Inscription. A Cultural History of the Modern Tattoo Community*. Durham: Duke University Press. https://doi.org/10.1215/9780822396147

de Witte, Marleen. 2011. 'Touch'. *Material Religion* 7 (1): 148-155. https://doi.org/10.2752/175183411X12968355482466

Descola, Philippe. 2013. *Beyond Nature and Culture*. Chicago and London: University of Chicago Press. https://doi.org/10.7208/chicago/9780226145006.001.0001

Deter-Wolf, Aaron and Carol Diaz-Granados (eds.). 2013. *Drawing with Great Needles: Ancient Tattoo Traditions of North America*. Austin: University of Texas Press.

Estellon, Vincent. 2004. 'Tatouage sur corps ou l'envers de l'expression'. *Champ psy* 4 (36): 145–158. https://doi.org/10.3917/cpsy.036.0145

Firth, Raymond. 1967. *The Work of the Gods in Tikopia*. London: Athlone Press.

Galliot, Sébastien. 2015a. 'Ritual Efficacy in the Making'. *Journal of Material Culture* 20 (2): 101–125. https://doi.org/10.1177/1359183515578248

Galliot, Sébastien. 2015b. 'Le tatouage samoan et ses agents. Images, mémoire et actions rituelles'. *Gradhiva* 21 (1): 156–181. https://doi.org/10.4000/gradhiva.2969

Galliot, Sébastien. 2019. *Tatau Fa'asamoa. Un rite de tatouage polynésien dans l'histoire*. Paris: CNRS éditions.

Gell, Alfred. 1993. *Wrapping in Images*. Oxford: Clarendon Press.

Gell, Alfred. 1998. *Art and Agency: An Anthropological Theory*. Oxford: Clarendon Press.

Gibson, James. 1979. *The Ecological Approach to Visual Perception*. Boston: Houghton Mifflin.

Harvey, Graham and Jessica Hughes (eds.). 2018. *Sensual Religion. Religion and the Five Senses*. Sheffield and Bristol: Equinox.

Howes, David. 2003. *Sensual Relations: Engaging the Senses in Culture and Social Theory*. Ann Arbor: University of Michigan Press. https://doi.org/10.3998/mpub.11852

Ingold, Timothy. 2013. *Making: Anthropology, Archaeology, Art and Architecture*. London: Routledge. https://doi.org/10.4324/9780203559055

Ingold, Timothy. 2014. 'Religious Perception and the Education of Attention'. *Religion, Brain & Behavior* 4 (2): 156–158. https://doi.org/10.1080/2153599X.2013.816345

Jackson, Michael. 1983. 'Knowledge of the Body'. *Man*, New Series (June) 18 (2): 327–345. https://doi.org/10.2307/2801438

Keane, Web. 2008. 'On the Materiality of Religion'. *Journal of Material Religion* 4 (2): 230–231. https://doi.org/10.2752/175183408X328343

Kerestetzi, Katerina. 2018. 'The Spirit of a Place: Materiality, Spatiality and Feeling in Afro-American Religions'. *Journal de la société des américanistes* [online] 104–1: IX–XXV. https://doi.org/10.4000/jsa.15573

Kopytoff, Igor. 1986. 'The Cultural Biography of Things: Commoditization as a Process'. In Arjun Appadurai (ed.), *The Social Life of Things. Commodities in Cultural Perspective*, 64–91. Cambridge and New York: Cambridge University Press. https://doi.org/10.1017/CBO9780511819582.004

Korff-Sausse, Simone. 2004. 'Quelques réflexions psychanalytiques sur le Body Art'. *Champ psy* 4 (36): 171–183. https://doi.org/10.3917/cpsy.036.0171

Krutak, Lars. 2014. *Tattoo Traditions of North America. Ancient and Contemporary Expressions of Identity*. Arnhem: LM Publisher.

Krutak, Lars and Aaron Deter-Wolf (eds.). 2017. *Ancient Ink. The Archeaology of Tattooing*. Seattle and London: University of Washington Press.

Kuwahara, Makiko. 2005. *Tattoo: An Anthropology*. New York: Berg Publishers.

Lagirarde, François. 1989. 'Note on Thai Tattoo—Note sur le tatouage en pays Thai. Récits de voyage et regards d'ethnographes jusqu'à la fin du XVIIe siècle'. *Journal of the Siam Society* 77 (2): 29–39.

Laplantine, François. 2005. *Le Social et le Sensible: introduction à une anthropologie modale*. Paris: Téraèdre.

Lave, Jean and Etienne Wenger. 1991. *Situated Learning. Legitimate Peripheral Participation*, Cambridge: Cambridge University Press.
https://doi.org/10.1017/CBO9780511815355

Lemonnier, Pierre (ed.). 1993. *Technological Choices: Transformation in Material Cultures since the Neolithic*. London: Routledge.

Lemonnier, Pierre. 2012. *Mundane Objects: Materiality and Non-Verbal Communication*, Walnut Creek: Left Coast Press.

Lesser, William. 1966. *Ulithi: A Micronesian Design for Living*. New York: Holt, Rinehart & Winston.

Maertens, Jean-Thierry. 1978. *Le dessein sur la peau*. Paris: Aubier-Montaigne.

Mallon, Sean and Sébastien Galliot. 2018. *Tatau: A Cultural History of Samoan Tattooing*. Wellington: Te Papa Press.

Mangos, Therese and John Utanga. 2011. *Patterns of the Past: Tattoo Revival in the Cook Islands*. Auckland: Punarua Prod.

Mauss, Marcel. 1973. 'Techniques of the Body'. *Economy and Society*, 2 (1): 70–88.

Montagu, Ashley. 1971. *Touching: The Human Significance of the Skin*. New York: Columbia University Press.

Morgan, David (ed.). 2010. *Religion and Material Culture: The Matter of Belief*. London and New York: Routledge.

Nooter Roberts, Marie. 2010. 'Tactility and Transcendence: Epistemologies of Touch in African Arts and Spirituality'. In David Morgan (ed.), *Religion and Material Culture: The Matter of Belief*. London and New York: Routledge.

Parmentier, Richard J. 1988. 'Transactional Symbolism in Belauan Mortuary Rites: A Diachronic Study'. *Journal of the Polynesian Society* 97 (3): 281–312.

Polanyi, Michael. 1958. *Personal Knowledge: Towards a Post-critical Philosophy*. Chicago: University of Chicago Press.

Polanyi, Michael. 1966. *The Tacit Dimension*. London: Routledge and Kegan Paul.

Pouchelle, Marie-Christine. 2007. 'Quelques touches hospitalières'. *Terrain* 49: 11–26.
https://doi.org/10.4000/terrain.5651

Rajadhon, Phya A. 1964. 'Thai Charms and Amulets'. *Journal of the Siam Society* 52: 171–198.

Revolon, Sandra. 2012. 'L'éclat des ombres. Irisation, contraste et présence des morts aux îles Salomon'. *Techniques et culture* 58, Objets irremplaçables: 252–263.
https://doi.org/10.4000/tc.6299

Rolle, Valérie. 2013. *L'art de tatouer. La pratique d'un metier créatif.* Paris: Editions de la Maison des Sciences de l'Homme.
https://doi.org/10.4000/books.editionsmsh.3622

Sahlins, Marshall. 1958. *Social Stratification in Polynesia*. Seattle: University of Washington Press.

Salvador Amores, Analyn. 2013. *Tapping Ink, Tattooing Identities: Tradition and Modernity in Contemporary Kalinga Society, North Luzon Philippines*. Baguio: University of the Philippines Press.

Scott, Sir James. 1896. *The Burman: His Life and Notions*. London: Macmillan.

Sillitoe, Paul. 2017. *Built in Niugini: Constructions in the Highlands of Papua New Guinea*. Canon Pyon: Sean Kingston Publishing.

Sola, Christel. 2007. 'Y a pas de mots pour le dire, il faut sentir. Décrire et dénommer les happerceptions professionnelles'. *Terrain* 49: 37–50. https://doi.org/10.4000/terrain.5841

Sopher, David E. 1964. 'Indigenous Uses of Curcuma (*Turmeric domestica*) in Asia and Oceania'. *Anthropos* 59 (1/2): 93–127.

Ta Awekotuku, Ngauia and Waimarie Nikora. 2007. *Mau Moko: The World of Maori Tattoo*. Honolulu: University of Hawaii Press.

Tannenbaum, Nicola. 1987. 'Tattoos: Invulnerability and Power in Shan Cosmology'. *American Ethnologist* 14 (4): 693–711. https://doi.org/10.1525/ae.1987.14.4.02a00060

Terwiel, Baren J. 1976. 'Tattooing in Thailand's History'. *Journal of the Royal Asiatic Society* 2: 156–166. https://doi.org/10.1017/S0035869X00135580

Turner, George. 1884. *Samoa, A Hundred Years Ago and Long Before*. London: Macmillan.

Turner, Terence. 1994. 'Bodies and Anti-bodies: Flesh and Fetish in Contemporary Social Theory'. In Thomas Csordas and Alan Harwood (eds.), *Embodiment and Experience: The Existential Ground of Culture and Self*, 27–47. Cambridge: Cambridge University Press.

Turner, Terence. 1995. 'Social Body and Embodied Subject: Bodiliness, Subjectivity, and Sociality among the Kayapo'. *Cultural Anthropology* 10 (2): 143–170. https://doi.org/10.1525/can.1995.10.2.02a00010

Turner, Victor. 1969. *The Ritual Process: Structure and Anti Structure*. Ithaca, NY: Cornell University Press.

Van Gennep, Arnold. 1909. *Les rites de passage*. Paris: E. Nourry.

Wacquant, Loïc. 2003. *Body and Soul: Notebooks of an Apprentice Boxer*. Oxford: Oxford University Press.

Warnier, Jean-Pierre. 2007. *The Pot-King: The Body and Technologies of Power*. Leiden: Brill. https://doi.org/10.1163/ej.9789004152175.i-325

Whitehead, Amy. 2018. 'Touching, Crafting, Knowing: Religious Artefacts and the Fetish within Animism'. *Body and Religion* 2 (2): 224–244. https://doi.org/10.1558/bar.36491

Wiener, Suzanne. 2004. 'Le tatouage, de la parure à l'oeuvre de soi'. *Champ psy* 4 (36): 159–170. https://doi.org/10.3917/cpsy.036.0159

Sébastien Galliot is a cultural anthropologist at the Centre for Research and Documentation on Oceania in Marseilles. Between 2001 and 2013 he extensively studied the transmission and the transnational diffusion of Samoan tattooing ritual, and has recently published two books: *Tatau: A Cultural History of Samoan Tattooing*, written with Sean Mallon (Te Papa Press, 2018) and *Le tatouage samoan: Un rite polynésien dans l'histoire* (CNRS, 2019). Switching his fieldwork area from Samoa to Yap in Micronesia, he is currently researching areca-nut supply chains within a multi-site and global approach, from Yapese gardens and lagoons to corner shops in Guam and Saipan.

Chapter 2

Touching Deities: Offerings, Energies and the Notion of Touch in Guyanese Hinduism

SINAH THERES KLOß

'You can touch my shoulder', a middle-aged woman invited me when I first visited a *mandir* (temple) on a Sunday morning in Georgetown, the capital of Guyana, in 2011. We were lining up to revere the Shiva *lingam* (phallic symbol and manifestation of the Hindu god Shiva) and offer milk and ghee, which an individual or head of a small group would slowly pour over its top. The offering person, I would later find out, is called *jajman* in Guyanese Hinduism and is usually touched softly on his or her back or on the shoulder, either with the palm of a hand or its fingers, by accompanying spouse or children. Having briefly chatted with her during this regular service, the woman knew of my interest in learning about Hinduism in Guyana and was aware that I was visiting the *mandir* for the first time. She realised that I did not know what the usual procedures were, and thus kindly invited me to join her and her daughter in making the offering together, as a temporary ritual unit. I carefully touched her shoulder and watched the ritual, still unsure about its meaning and why it was necessary for me to touch her in this process.

In just a few months, this act of touching became usual for me during Hindu ritual services. As I found out, this was not the only relevant mode of touching: one could physically touch a person or deity but also visually touch him or her; one could directly or indirectly touch a *murti* (statue; representation and manifestation of a deity) by either creating tactile contact or by offering a material object that would transmit and facilitate touch. In this chapter I thus highlight the role of tactility in Guyanese Hindu ritual and conceptualise the notion of touch, which I propose to be distinct from contact. Drawing on the interrelationship of clothing and bodies and the exchange processes that occur during (acts of) mutual touching, I discuss that 'touched' clothing may be transformed into a person's material likeness and may be considered divine dwelling structures. The exchange of touched clothes is thus a means for religious communities and families to literally 'stay in touch' even in the context of migration. Therefore, this chapter raises questions such as: How is 'touch' facilitated and closeness created between giver and receiver through the exchange of clothing? How do Hindu notions of purity and pollution influence this understanding of touch? I elaborate that in the Guyanese Hindu context, gifts of (touched) clothing are not only relevant with regard to human beings, but they furthermore materialise and visualise relationships between people and deities. My findings are based on a multi-sited ethnography that consisted of participant observation and ethnographic interviews, conducted in Guyana and New York City between 2011 and 2017.

THE TRANSFER OF DIVINE ENERGIES

Approximately a year after my initial visit to the Hindu *mandir*, a long stretch of my fieldwork for my doctoral dissertation in Guyana came to an end. (I would continue my research with my Guyanese informants' friends and relatives in New York City.) For several months I had regularly visited the *mandir* in the neighbourhood for Sunday morning services, special religious ceremonies, readings, and even the cleaning of the mandir and the changing of the *murtis*' clothes. To show my appreciation to the community and as a thank you for the people's hospitality, I decided and was allowed to sponsor one of the Sunday services. This also gave me the opportunity to be the *jajman* on this Sunday and conduct the *puja* (ritual veneration of Hindu deities) at the *hawan kund* (ritual fire site) as well as the *arti* (the waving of fire in front of *murtis*). By this time my Guyanese Hindu friends, *pandits* (priests in the Hindu Sanatan tradition) and *pujaris* (ritual practitioners in the Hindu Madras tradition) had explained to me the significance of *puja*, its ritual elements and proceedings.[1] They had said that during *puja* auspicious energies emanate and spread into the atmosphere from the *hawan kund*, where the sacrificial fire burns. I had been advised to

---

1 For detailed descriptions and analyses of Guyanese Hinduism and the different Hindu traditions in Guyana, consult Smith and Jayawardena (1967); Williams (1990, 1991); Vertovec (1996); Bisnauth (2000); Younger (2004, 2009); Kloß (2016, 2017a).

sit close to the altar instead of at the back of the mandir, as the amount of energies and divine blessings I would receive would be higher the closer I sat to the ritual, and lower when sitting at the back of the temple.

According to Guyanese Hindus, during *puja* the circulating auspicious energies and blessings enter human and other physical bodies. People in the audience raise their right hands and arms during the offering of *sambrany* (benzoin resin) and *ghee* (clarified butter) into the sacrificial fire and fan the air with slow and wavy movements of the hand, thereby spreading and receiving the energies. During the fire offering, the offered substances are transformed into energy through the act of burning, enabling their transfer to the deity. This transfer is testified by and sensible through the particular smell of the visible smoke. While the *jajman*, *pandit* and other members of the offering unit, who usually sit on the left side of the *jajman*, receive the highest intensity, any person in the room benefits from their presence and sensory involvement in the ritual.

Touch remains an additional, effective and secure means of transferring auspicious energies and blessings besides atmospheric transfer. When touching the shoulder, arm or back of a *jajman* during the process of offering, energies are transferred through the body of the *jajman* to the touching parties. In some temple communities it is common that all people in the congregation move closer to the front of the building, where the ritual is conducted, and touch the body of a person seated or standing in front of them. The congregation thus forms a temporary unit, as it is physically connected to the ritual agent and receives blessings not only through energies spread in the atmosphere, but also through material exchange facilitated by touch (see **Figure 2.1**). In this context it has to be emphasised that my informants consider the realms of the physical and the spiritual to be in constant exchange with each other, as demonstrated by the transformation of material offering to spiritual energy during *puja*. As has been discussed for example by McKim Marriott, Hindus in general do not conceive of the strict, dualistic differentiations of immaterial and material substances, which are prominent in much of 'Western' thought (Marriott 1976b). This stresses the need of an inter-sensory approach to the notion of touch in the Guyanese context, as discussed later in this chapter.[2]

---

2   Marriott theorises that Hindus do not differentiate substances and codes for action but proposes the notion of merged 'substance-codes' (Marriott 1976a: 110). According to him Hindus perceive of a scale of substance-codes, of which some are relatively gross and others are relatively subtle. Substance-codes are thought to constantly circulate and infiltrate other entities or bodies (ibid.).

Figure 2.1. Hindus touching shoulders and performing a ritual unit during *puja*.

The relevance of tactility in Guyanese Hindu *puja* is further emphasised in the context of making offerings to deities. Usually Hindus strive to make an offering to every Hindu deity, present through visual representations and material manifestations such as *murtis*, posters and paintings. Although my informants usually describe these statues and images to be means that allow a devotee to 'focus the mind', they are also regarded as objects that provide dwelling structures for divine material substances and spiritual energies. Thus, when offerings are made, for example through the gift of a flower, they are placed on the *murti*'s body or draped in the proximity of the feet of the image. After placing the offering—which may also consist of fruits, sweets, clothing, jewellery, and with regard to a few non-Sanskritic deities even cigarettes and alcohol—the offering person first touches the feet or body, never the head, of the deity's statue or image, then quickly his or her own chest, ensuring the transfer of blessings to the devotee. This practice is called *charhaway* (Kloß 2016, 2019).

DRESSING DEITIES

Hindu murtis in Guyanese temples are usually adorned in Indian-style clothing and jewellery, defined as 'Indian Wear'. Indian Wear refers to a category of clothing in the Guyanese context, which is not worn on a daily basis but as 'dress up clothes' on special occasions celebrating for instance Guyanese Indian identity (e.g. on Indian Arrival Day celebrations) or during religious ceremonies (Kloß 2017b). During *puja* this Indian-style dress is given to the deities as gifts. When a person or household conducts *puja*, it is common that the *jajman* hands over pieces of cloth or clothing—a sari, dhoti, kurta, t-shirt or five yards of cloth—to the revered deity. When the financial circumstances of the *jajman* (and his or her household) allow it, sometimes all deities receive a sartorial gift. The *jajman* places the clothes near or on the *murti*, the *pandit* or *pujari* then opens the folded garment and places it on the *murti*, and the *murti* 'uses' it. After the *puja* is concluded the ritual practitioners take the clothes to either store them in the temple, where they are used as future *murti* clothing, or they may take them home as personal ritual clothes in their function as representatives of deities. At the time of my research in the early 2010s, *murti* clothing was changed twice a year in Guyana, and up to four times in Guyanese Hindu temples in New York (Kloß 2016).

Although cloth has always been part of Hindu ritual gift-giving practices, it has taken on a particular relevance in the Guyanese context. Emphasis is given to the exchange of clothing gifts, as these have a special capacity of storing for instance identities, substances of former wearers and spiritual energies, which can become absorbed and imbued in a garment. Clothes may thus 'take on' and store former wearers and consumers in a specific way. As Peter Stallybrass proposes, cloth has a particular aura due to the fact that 'it receives us: [it] receives our smells, our sweat, our shape even' (Stallybrass 2012: 69). Differentiating clothes, jewellery and food, he elaborates:

> Clothes receive the human imprint. Jewelry lasts longer, and can also move us. But even though it has a history, it resists the history of our bodies. [...] On the other hand, food, like jewelry, is a gift which joins us to each other, rapidly *becomes* us and disappears. Like food, cloth can be shaped by our touch; like jewelry it endures beyond immediate moment of consumption. (Stallybrass 2012: 69)

Cloth is shaped by touch and is thus transformed. From the perspective of my informants it also has to be emphasised that cloth mutually influences its consumers. Cloth and clothing impact human bodies by moulding them, as examples such as brassieres or corsets reveal, or it may cause wounds for example by rubbing on skin. Guyanese Hindus further believe that human bodies may also be impacted by receiving energies and substances stored in clothing, and interpret this as either positive or negative depending on context.

Humans and objects are thus in constant processes of exchange, hence transformation, and are not as distinct as they are often assumed to be. Bodies and clothing influence each other, as they 'exist in dialectic relationship to one another' (Entwistle 2011: 139). In the context of gift exchange, a gifted piece of cloth may consequently be understood to be a 'gift of a detached fragment of oneself; it links the giver and the receiver, bringing them into a more intimate relation yet creating a hierarchy in the process' (Norris 2010: 118).

While the aspect of hierarchy is discussed later in this chapter, it seems relevant to first exemplify how the transformation of bodies and clothes occurs and that used clothes are transformed into a person's material likeness. Material likeness is created for example through the transfer of substances such as body fluids. Body fluids maintain a link and (material) connection between garment and wearer, even when the piece of clothing is no longer worn. My informants consider for instance sweat to remain linked to a person, even when it has become a mere trace in cloth (Kloß 2016). Various scholars have documented the relevance of sweat in different cultural contexts with regard to the maintenance of connections and relations, most prominently in James Frazer's analysis of 'sympathetic magic' in *The Golden Bough* (1922). Here, Frazer discusses that according to the 'Law of Contact', 'things which have once been in contact with each other continue to act on each other at a distance after the physical contact has been severed' and that 'whatever he [a magician] does to a material object will affect equally the person with whom the object was once in contact, whether it formed part of his body or not' (1922: 11). Hence in numerous societies detached parts of bodies or body fluids such as sweat are considered to remain a link between object and body. Although Frazer's work has been influenced by early twentieth-century colonial mentality and evolutionist bias, which cannot sufficiently be discussed in this chapter, his elaboration on similarity, contact and imitation offers a foundation to the analysis of the idea that clothes are transformed into a person's likeness. For example, an effigy of a person can be created by adding the person's sweat to another material substance or object. In this way the object can be used to damage the 'owner' of the sweat, possibly an enemy (Taussig 1993: 52). Discussing Frazer's work, Michael Taussig highlights the fact that people from various socio-cultural backgrounds may consider likeness and similarity to be based on visual as well as material likeness (Taussig 1993). Visual similarity is thus not the only option to create likeness, as material similarities can be understood to be just as relevant. Likeness can be created by visual or material similarities, or a mixture of both. In the Guyanese Hindu context of exchanging pieces of garments, it is necessary to highlight that sweat and other essences of a former user imbued in a garment transform the garment into a (material) likeness of the person, or, as discussed later, of a deity.

TOUCH AND LIKENESS

Likeness is facilitated through touch. Touch is the mutual transmission of substances and essences between two or more entities, for example bodies and clothing. For heuristic purposes I differentiate contact from touch: I propose that contact refers to a temporary proximity and not a union of entities, and thus differs from the notion of touch, which refers to a process, transformation, an exchange or a transmission between entities. Thus, touch exceeds mere proximity or closeness and the act of touching implies more than the act of establishing contact (Kloß 2016: Ch. 6). As touch is necessarily reciprocal, Jo Turney rightfully emphasises that 'to touch' always implies 'to be touched' (Turney 2012: 305). A touch hence implies the transformation of the physical and spiritual levels of all objects in touch.

Touch is certainly not the only mode of sensing that is of relevance in Guyanese Hindu *pujas*. Touch has to be understood as an inter-sensory process and practice, and to define touch merely on the basis of tactility would reproduce an artificial distinction of the senses (Barnett 2012). As all senses are related and societies are based on 'interconnected sensory system[s]' (Classen 1997: 403), it is necessary to consider the 'interplay of the senses' (Howes 2012: 642) and apply an inter-sensory approach to conceptualise the notion of touch. For example, seeing can be understood as a mode of touching in Hindu traditions, in which the visual and the tactile cannot be considered to be unrelated. This is of relevance in the context of Guyanese Hinduism, in which the practice and concept of *darshan* further emphasises the need to conceptualise touch as an inter-sensory phenomenon. *Darshan* is the practice of religious seeing, the 'visual perception of the sacred' (Eck 1985: 3) and a 'physical relationship of visual intermingling' (Pinney 2001: 168), which takes place during *puja* when devotees gaze at images of deities, precisely the depicted eyes. It is not only the devotee who looks at the deity, but it is a mutual gazing at each other. According to Alfred Gell, darshan is

> ...very much of a two-way affair. The gaze directed by the god towards the worshipper confers his blessing; conversely, the worshipper reaches out and touches the god. The result is union with the god, a merging of consciousness according to the devotionalist interpretation. (Gell 1998: 117)

Darshan and practices of seeing facilitate touch through the mutual transmission of substances and essences, hence may also create likeness.

Touch is an intricate aspect of the practice of giving a sartorial gift, bearing the risk of pollution. Which modes of touch exist in relation to clothes and how are these affected by the notion of pollution? As indicated earlier, the interrelationship of clothing and bodies is created through acts of consumption; when substances and energies are transferred between bodies and dress and when mutual touch is created. According to my informants, the relevant modes of 'using' with regard to clothing are wearing and giving, both implying the act of touching.[3] Both modes of consumption—using through giving and using through wearing—indicate that bodies, skins or spirits are touched and relations between body and clothing are recreated. This is obvious when clothes are worn, but according to my informants also in the context of gift exchange. The giving of a gift necessarily leads to its transformation into a touched item. Even when a piece of clothing is only handed over to another person or to a *murti*, it has been consumed (as a gift), it has been used and touched.

Guyanese Hindus offer only 'new' garments to deities, as a means to lower the risk of offering a polluted garment. 'New' in this context can be translated to 'not having been worn', 'not having been given to a deity or a person before' or in general 'not having been (excessively) touched'. To minimise the risk of excessive touching, most garments remain folded and in the original transparent plastic cover in which they were purchased, even during the process of offering. Leaving the items neatly folded and thus partially hiding them from view is a practice that lowers the risk of exposing them to too many gazes and visual touching. Offering garments thus necessitates consideration and the negotiation of balancing conspicuous consumption—of recreating high(er) social status through demonstrations of capital spent—with ritual orthopraxy and efficacy.

3 Consumption and exchange, I argue, cannot be considered as distinct processes or concepts, since on the one hand consumption includes processes of exchange (between garment and body) and on the other hand exchange includes processes of consumption, for example in the process of incorporation, a process in the course of which the consumed item is transformed and partakes in the (re)constitution of the 'the personal and social identity of the consumer' (Gell 1986: 112) and the consuming body.

POLLUTION AND THE DEITY'S TOUCH

As clothes are among the most intimate objects for people and presumably deities, due to their proximity to bodies and their exchange with them, offering practices are necessarily influenced by the notion of pollution. 'Touched' clothes may be considered to be polluting or polluted as a consequence of their consumption. Offering polluted clothes renders the *puja* inefficient, meaning that no blessings and auspicious energies are received despite the amount of time, money and effort put into the preparation and implementation of the ritual.

The risk of pollution and measures for its prevention are pervasive in Guyanese Hindu temples. All groups and traditions implement specific dietary and teetotal rules, as well as dress codes that prohibit for instance the wearing of leather products and shoes in temples. In light of this, the invitation of the woman, described in the beginning of this chapter, to touch her shoulder while conducting the offering at the Shiva *lingam*, has to be understood as a risky practice for her. Even though auspicious energies could be transferred through her body to me, I could vice versa transfer any potential pollution from me to her, rendering her ritual ineffective. I recall that she had asked me, after having invited me to touch her shoulder, if I had eaten any 'rank' (polluting substances such as meat or eggs) earlier, a question which usually tacitly implies the question whether a person has observed all relevant rules and is 'clean'. She seemed reassured and felt at ease when I responded in the negative. Acts of touching someone's body and letting someone touch one's own body during the ritual process are thus expressions of trust, which are even more significant when questions of potential pollution are not addressed.

As touching is a mutual process and deities consume the objects given to them, questions concerning the deity's touch and its polluting potential have to be raised. According to Guyanese Hindus, when a deity touches an offering made by a devotee, this becomes imbued with divine substances and essences. After the deity has consumed an offering, it is shared with people in the congregation as *prasadam* (auspicious leftover, sometimes *prasad* or in the Guyanese context *parshad*) at the end of *puja*. Most commonly *prasadam* consists of food and fruits, which are distributed in equal shares to each person in the congregation to be consumed by the receivers, absorbing the deity's blessing and energies during this consumption. C.J. Fuller describes *prasadam* as

...the material symbol of the deities' power and grace. During *puja*, different substances—ash, water, flowers, food, or other items—have been transferred to the deity, so that they have been in contact with the images or, as with food, have been symbolically consumed by the deity in its image form. As a result, these substances have been ritually transmuted to become *prasada* imbued with divine power and grace, which are absorbed or internalized when the *prasada* is placed on the devotee's body or swallowed. (Fuller 2004: 74)

People often take *prasadam* home for family members who have not been present at a *puja*, but who are thus able to receive at least a small amount of distributed blessings. Aisha Khan affirms for the Trinidadian context that *prasadam* 'is imbued with divine attributes', that eating it is 'a blessing, and the act of distributing it is thus one important means of symbolically affirming bonds of camaraderie and reciprocity among kin, neighbors, and friends' (Khan 1994: 256). In Guyana, textiles and clothing function as another but significant kind of *prasadam*; a kind that is 'shared' as a whole with a limited number of people, usually only the *pandit*, who receives the blessing stored in this *prasadam*.

Prasadam is thus a concept that clearly marks and re-creates social hierarchy. When people agree 'to eat the leftovers of the gods [they] demonstrate their own inferiority to the gods' (Miller 1998: 80). The partial consumption of an object and its handing on reinstates the superiority of deities. This is similar to other practices in which people who accept partly consumed leftovers express their inferiority in relation to the prior consumers (Fuller 2004: 77). Such leftovers are usually referred to as *juthaa* or as having become '*juthaa*-ed', a term that usually only indicates human consumption and interaction, while *prasadam* refers to divine consumption and human-divine interactions. According to Khan, Caribbean Hindus make a 'conceptual distinction between divine contact (prasad) and mortal contact (juthaa)' (1994: 256), hence differentiate between divine and human touch.

My informants consider it impossible for divine essences to be dirty or polluting, as they are generated by superior beings. As I discuss elsewhere for the context of Guyanese Hindu gift exchange, pollution is a concept that emphasises relationality and social status (Kloß 2019).[4] The understanding

---

4   Here I consider that pollution has to be regarded as a process in which boundaries of the category dirt are performatively defined and recreated (Douglas 2005 [1966]). Notions of (im-)purity, dirt and pollution are intricately related to the maintenance of social order. Dirt, as the outcome of pollution, does not exist a priori, but is a socially constructed category of objects that social

whether specific energies and substances are polluted or not is thus relative and varies from the point of view of the different social actors. The evaluation of the substances and energies is related to the quality of the relationship between giver and receiver and depends on their relationality in social hierarchy and cosmic order. Energies are not considered 'dirty' or 'polluting' per se:

> Since purity and impurity are invariably relative qualities, leftovers that are polluted from the point of view of the superior party may still appear pure to the inferior. Hence, whether food prasada is actually described as the deities' jutha or not, it is not polluted, but pure, for the consumer, the worshiper. (Fuller 2004: 77)

In unequal relations, as is the case when humans give clothes to a deity, the energies and substances imbued in garments are potentially polluting. The gifts are considered *juthaa*, because they are imbued with substances from an inferior being from the perspective of the deity.

TOUCH AND MIGRATION

From the 1980s, influenced by Forbes Burnham's authoritarian rule and an economic crisis in Guyana, Guyanese Hindus—and other populational groups—have been migrating to North America in large numbers. They have particularly settled in the metropolitan centres of New York City and Toronto, where they have started to build temples and other social infrastructure necessary to maintain (and reinvent) their religious traditions (Younger 2004; Pillai 2020; Hangloo 2011; Ramey 2011; Plaza 2004). Even though numerous first-generation migrants have struggled to make a living in the new environment, the possibilities for them to afford sartorial offerings have increased due to the availability of, for example, cheap polyester saris, which are available from eight US dollars per piece. Most households in New York thus strive to offer each female deity a sari and each male deity a dhoti during their annual household rites. In some temples this leads to a large surplus of offered garments, which cannot be worn by the *murtis* and which cannot be disposed of, as they have become *prasadam*, are imbued with the deity's energies or may even be considered to still be in the possession of the deity (Kloß 2019). Some temple communities

---

actors use to define order and disorder (ibid.). When my informants consider a practice to be polluting, this indicates that the practice is transformative and potentially creates disorder.

have thus started to collect the surplus saris and dhotis, and send them to affiliated temples in Guyana, where they are used as *murti* clothing or for temple decoration, or are given to 'deserving' members of the community (Kloß 2016).[5]

Touched clothes thus become a means of visualising, materialising and manifesting group identity, for example of families and religious communities. They recreate the possibility of touch even among people who live in dispersed geographical locations, and in contexts in which visual, olfactory and auditive touch is impacted by physical distance and high costs of postal services, travel and initially also telecommunication. They become an intricate and material aspect in the creation of transnational communities (Halstead 2011). Their close relations to bodies and former consumers create intimacy and closeness that facilitate a means to literally stay in touch (Kloß 2016, 2018). The sending and receiving of touched clothing in transnational contexts, while also recreating distance and hierarchy evident in all gift exchange practices, becomes a way of (re-)constructing the senders' and receivers' presence and absence, both at home and in the diaspora.

CONCLUSION

Auspicious energies and blessings circulate during *puja* and enter human and other physical bodies. Tactile touch remains an effective means of receiving these energies. Touch may either be established by directly touching a *murti* or indirectly when creating touch through the giving of an offering to the revered deity. Cloth and clothing have a special capacity in facilitating touch and in storing wearers' identities, substances and spiritual energies, which become absorbed and imbued in a garment in the course of consumption. Humans and material objects such as clothing are in constant processes of exchange, hence transformation, which can be demonstrated for instance through the example of sweat. Sweat, similar to other body fluids, creates material likeness between a body and a piece of used clothing. Likeness—based on visual or material similarities, or a mixture of both—is facilitated through touch.

Touch is an inter-sensory process and practice and refers to the mutual transmission of substances and energies between two or more entities.

---

5 They are usually sent in barrels by specialised shipping companies. For an analysis of barrel-sending and barrel-receiving, consult Plaza (2014) and Kloß (2018).

Different modes of consumption, for example the consumption as gift or the consumption through wearing, imply the act of touching. 'Touched' clothes may be considered to be polluting or polluted as a consequence of their consumption, particularly through the former consumers' substances and energies. Deities, who engage in processes of touching as well, are not considered to pollute from the perspective of devotees. Their partial consumption is considered to create auspicious leftovers, referred to as *prasadam*. The transmission of substances and energies is hence evaluated as either good or bad, positive or negative, with regard to the relationship of the consuming entities and their relationality in social hierarchy.

As clothes and especially touched clothes are intimate objects, they become a means for families and religious communities to (re-)create, visualise and materialise relationships and identity, and facilitate a possibility of 'staying in touch' in the context of transnational migration.

BIBLIOGRAPHY

Barnett, Pennina. 2012. 'Folds, Fragments, Surfaces: Towards a Poetics of Cloth'. In Jessica Hemmings (ed.), *The Textile Reader*, 182–190. New York: Berg Publishers.

Bisnauth, Dale A. 2000. *The Settlement of Indians in Guyana, 1890–1930*. London: Peepal Tree Press.

Classen, Constance. 1997. 'Foundations for an Anthropology of the Senses'. *International Social Science Journal* 49 (153): 401–412.
https://doi.org/10.1111/j.1468-2451.1997.tb00032.x

Douglas, Mary. 2005 [1966]. *Purity and Danger: An Analysis of Concept of Pollution and Taboo*. Routledge classics. London and New York: Routledge.

Eck, Diana L. 1985. *Darśan: Seeing the Divine Image in India*. 2nd revised and enlarged edition. Chambersburg, PA: Anima Books.

Entwistle, Joanne. 2011. 'The Dressed Body'. In Linda Welters and Abby Lillethun (eds.), *The Fashion Reader*, 2nd edition, 138–149. Oxford and New York: Berg Publishers.

Frazer, James. 1922. *The Golden Bough: A Study in Magic and Religion*. New York: The Macmillan Company. https://doi.org/10.1007/978-1-349-00400-3

Fuller, C.J. 2004. *The Camphor Flame: Popular Hinduism and Society in India*. Revised and expanded edition. Princeton paperbacks. Princeton, NJ: Princeton University Press. https://doi.org/10.1515/9780691186412

Gell, Alfred. 1986. 'Newcomers to the World of Goods: Consumption Among the Muria Gonds'. In Arjun Appadurai (ed.), *The Social Life of Things: Commodities in Cultural Perspective*, 110–138. Cambridge and New York: Cambridge University Press.

Gell, Alfred. 1998. *Art and Agency: Towards a New Anthropological Theory*. Oxford: Clarendon Press.

Halstead, Narmala. 2011. 'Gift Practices in Guyanese East Indian Diaspora: Belonging, Loss, and Status'. *The Journal of Latin American and Caribbean Anthropology* 16 (2): 278–295. https://doi.org/10.1111/j.1935-4940.2011.01158.x

Hangloo, Rattan L. 2011. 'Sita Raam America: The Indo-Caribbean People in the United States'. *South Asian Diaspora* 3 (2): 241–242. https://doi.org/10.1080/19438192.2011.579466

Howes, David. 2012. 'Re-Visualizing Anthropology Through the Lens of "The Ethnographer's Eye"'. In Ian Heywood, Barry Sandywell, Michael Gardiner, Gunalan Nadarajan and Catherine M. Soussloff (eds.), *The Handbook of Visual Culture*, 628–647. London: Berg Publishers.

Khan, Aisha. 1994. 'Juthaa in Trinidad: Food, Pollution and Hierarchy in a Caribbean Diaspora Community'. *American Ethnologist* 21 (2): 245–269. https://doi.org/10.1525/ae.1994.21.2.02a00020

Kloß, Sinah T. 2016. *Fabrics of Indianness: The Exchange and Consumption of Clothing in Transnational Guyanese Hindu Communities*. New York: Palgrave Macmillan.

Kloß, Sinah T. 2017a. 'Manifesting Kali's Power: Guyanese Hinduism and the Revitalisation of the "Madras Tradition"'. *Journal of Eastern Caribbean Studies* 41 (1): 83–110.

Kloß, Sinah T. 2017b. 'Performing Authenticity through Fashion: Sartorial Contestations of Guyanese Indianness and the Creation of the Indian "Other"'. In Emanuela Mora and Marco Pedroni (eds.), *Fashion Tales: Feeding the Imaginary*, 327–44. Bern: Peter Lang.

Kloß, Sinah T. 2018. 'Staying in Touch: Used Clothes and the Role of Materiality in Transnational Guyanese Gift Exchange'. In Anja Bandau, Anne Brüske and Natascha Ueckmann (eds.), *Reshaping Glocal Dynamics of the Caribbean: Relaciones y Desconexiones, Relations et Déconnexions, Relations and Disconnections*, 351–365. Heidelberg: heiUP.

Kloß, Sinah T. 2019. 'Giving to Mother Ganga: Gift Exchange, Social Hierarchy and the Notion of Pollution in Transnational Guyanese Hindu Communities'. In Lawrence Aje, Thomas Lacroix and Judith Misrahi-Barak (eds.), *Re-Imagining the Guyanas*, 215–228. Montpellier: PoCoPages, Presses Universitaires de la Méditerranée. https://doi.org/10.4000/books.pulm.5537

Marriott, McKim. 1976a. 'Hindu Transactions: Diversity without Dualism'. In Bruce Kapferer (ed.), *Transaction and Meaning: Directions in the Anthropology of Exchange and Symbolic Behavior*, 109–142. ASA Essays in Social Anthropology. Philadelphia: Institute for the Study of Human Issues.

Marriott, McKim. 1976b. 'Interpreting Indian Society: A Monistic Alternative to Dumont's Dualism'. *The Journal of Asian Studies* 36 (1): 189–195. https://doi.org/10.2307/2053901

Miller, Daniel. 1998. *A Theory of Shopping*. Cambridge: Polity Press.

Norris, Lucy. 2010. *Recycling Indian Clothing: Global Contexts of Reuse and Value*. Tracking Globalization. Bloomington: Indiana University Press.

Pillai, Rupa. 2020. 'A Hinduism of Their Own: Emerging Guyanese Hindu Reading Practices in New York City'. *The Journal of Hindu Studies* 13 (2): 122–143. https://doi.org/10.1093/jhs/hiaa010

Pinney, Christopher. 2001. 'Piercing the Skin of the Idol'. In Christopher Pinney and Nicholas Thomas (eds.), *Beyond Aesthetics: Art and the Technologies of Enchantment*, 157–179. Oxford and New York: Berg Publishers.
https://doi.org/10.4324/9781003084808-9

Plaza, Dwaine. 2004. 'Disaggregating the Indo- and African-Caribbean Migration and Settlement Experience in Canada'. *Canadian Journal of Latin American and Caribbean Studies* 29 (57/58): 241–266. https://doi.org/10.1080/08263663.2004.10816858

Plaza, Dwaine. 2014. 'Barrels of Love. A Study of the Soft Goods Remittance Practices of Transnational Jamaican Households'. In Wiebke Beushausen, Anne Brüske, Ana-Sofia Commichau, Patrick Helber and Sinah Kloß (eds.), *Caribbean Food Cultures: Culinary Practices and Consumption in the Caribbean and Its Diasporas*, 227–255. Postcolonial Studies 18. Bielefeld: Transcript.
https://doi.org/10.14361/transcript.9783839426920.227

Ramey, Steven. 2011. 'Hindu Minorities and the Limits of Hindu Inclusiveness: Sindhi and Indo-Caribbean Hindu Communities in Atlanta'. *International Journal of Hindu Studies* 15 (2): 209–239. https://doi.org/10.1007/s11407-011-9104-9

Smith, Raymond T. and Chandra Jayawardena. 1967. 'Caste and Social Status among the Indians of Guyana'. In Barton M. Schwartz (ed.), *Caste in Overseas Indian Communities*, 43–92. Chandler Publications in Anthropology and Sociology. San Francisco: Chandler Pub. Co.; Chicago: Science Research Associates.

Stallybrass, Peter. 2012. 'Worn Worlds: Clothes, Mourning and the Life of Things'. In Jessica Hemmings (ed.), *The Textile Reader*, 68–77. New York: Berg Publishers.

Taussig, Michael T. 1993. *Mimesis and Alterity: A Particular History of the Senses*. New York: Routledge.

Turney, Jo. 2012. 'Making Love with Needles: Knitted Objects as Signs of Love?' *Textile: The Journal of Cloth and Culture* 10 (3): 302–311.
https://doi.org/10.2752/175183512X13505526963949

Vertovec, Steven. 1996. '"Official" and "Popular" Hinduism in the Caribbean: Historical and Contemporary Trends in Surinam, Trinidad and Guyana'. In David Dabydeen and Brinsley Samaroo (eds.), *Across the Dark Waters: Ethnicity and Indian Identity in the Caribbean*, 108–130. Warwick University Caribbean Studies. London: Macmillan Caribbean.

Williams, Brackette F. 1990. 'Dutchman Ghosts and the History Mystery: Ritual, Colonizer, and Colonized Interpretations of the 1763 Berbice Slave Rebellion'. *Journal of Historical Sociology* 3 (2): 133–165.
https://doi.org/10.1111/j.1467-6443.1990.tb00094.x

Williams, Brackette F. 1991. *Stains on My Name, War in My Veins: Guyana and the Politics of Cultural Struggle*. Durham: Duke University Press.

Younger, Paul. 2004. 'Guyana Hinduism'. *Religious Studies and Theology* 23 (1): 35–54.
https://doi.org/10.1558/rsth.v23i1.35

Younger, Paul. 2009. *New Homelands: Hindu Communities in Mauritius, Guyana, Trinidad, South Africa Fiji and East Africa*. New York and Oxford: Oxford University Press.

Sinah Theres Kloß is research group leader at the Bonn Center for Dependency and Slavery Studies (BCDSS) at the University of Bonn, Germany. She holds a PhD in Social and Cultural Anthropology from Heidelberg University. Her research interests include Caribbean Studies, Anthropology of the Senses, Postcolonial Theory, Religion and Material Culture Studies. Her recent books include the edited volume *Tattoo Histories: Transcultural Perspectives on the Narratives, Practices, and Representations of Tattooing* (Routledge, 2020) and the monograph *Fabrics of Indianness: The Exchange and Consumption of Clothing in Transnational Guyanese Hindu Communities* (Palgrave Macmillan, 2016). Her research group 'Marking Power: Embodied Dependencies, Haptic Regimes and Body Modification' focuses on the history of touch and different forms of body modification from a historical and anthropological perspective.

Chapter 3

Accommodating Crisis: Exploring the Dynamics of Touch and Material Devotion in Alcalá de los Gazules

GABRIEL BAYARRI AND AMY R. WHITEHEAD

This chapter contains two parts, each written by one of the authors, about the role of 'touch' and religion in the context of Alcalá de los Gazules in Andalusia, Spain. In the first section, Whitehead focuses on the local shrine of the Virgin of Alcalá, and three of the shrine's 'touch-oriented' everyday rituals. She argues that (a) the Virgin's personhood emerges through acts of devotional 'touch' and (b) that these ritual activities are not metaphorical, representational or symbolic of something else. They are, instead, 'real' and efficacious; and they inspire, inform and generate faith and devotion, not the other way around. This contributes to advances being made in the fields of material, sensual religion where 'belief' is not given priority in our analysis, but placed on a relational continuum where it is considered 'one' factor amongst many in the sensual entanglements of lived religious lives. In this case, the focus is on the rich, performative devotional activities that take place in the shrine of the Virgin of Alcalá.

In the second section, Bayarri moves emphasis away from shrine activities and onto the ways in which the Virgin has been accommodated in the homes of the townsfolk during, at the time of writing (2020), the Covid-19 pandemic. Having conducted a small-scale ethnographic study, he surveys the attitudes and views of the townspeople regarding the role of the Virgin in the personal management of the crisis in times when shrine access and acts of 'touch' are prohibited. Findings not only tested the people's varying degrees of devotion, they also revealed the significance of home devotionals where the Virgin's image is found on plaques, medals and home altars. Services such as virtual streaming, and the Virgin being processed through the town, also kept the Virgin 'in view' during this time. Arguably, because that which has been in physical touch with the shrine (including the image of the Virgin herself) is efficacious, the potency of the Virgin is able to be disseminated through the dynamics of Virgin-inspired materiality in the town.

I: SHRINE DEVOTION AND THE DYNAMICS OF TOUCH

Alcalá de los Gazules sits on a hilltop in La Sierra de Cádiz mountain range. It is one in a string of *pueblos blancos* (white villages) that stretch across the southern province of Cadiz in Andalusia. Each one of these 'white villages' (which are, in fact, small towns) houses a statue of the Virgin Mary; and each one has its own character that is inevitably entangled with the identities of the towns, their histories and their inhabitants. However, the Virgin of Alcalá enjoys a regional, national and even international popularity that other Virgins in the region do not. While the Virgin of Alcalá is particularly *milagrosa* (able to perform miracles), especially when it comes to curing illnesses and infertility, and offering protection, it can be argued that her popularity, indeed her personhood, at least for now, rests on the fact that she is physically accessible in her shrine and can be 'touched'.

Everyday Rituals and 'Touch'

I began research in Alcalá in 2007 after taking my Andalusian mother-in-law on a day trip from Cadiz to visit 'her Virgin'. Having recently started a PhD in the UK on the roles of religious objects in museums, this encounter not only changed my research topic, it changed what I thought I knew about religion. Accordingly, my 'fieldwork', which was more akin to enjoyable visits filled with meetings and conversations with different people, was carried out at different times over the course of eleven years. What follows are accounts of what I observed, experienced and learned from spending time at the shrine, and about how this unique, vernacular, lived religion 'works'. The word 'work' is not used lightly here. Devotees work with and for the Virgin, and consequently, the Virgin works for them. From the *ex voto* images that line the walls, to the actual Virgin herself, the shrine is filled with opportunities for ritual engagements, all of which readily invite the sense of touch. This, I argue, is generative. Acts of touch generate both tradition and belief.

I have here isolated three of the more popular rituals to support the argument that belief and religious text are not privileged, and that action both creates and generates faith, as well as the Virgin's personhood. These are: 'going under the mantle of the Virgin', the giving/taking of offerings and devotionals, and caretaking rituals. But first, some description of the Virgin and her shrine is required.

Figure 3.1 Image of the Virgin of Alcalá in her shrine.

The shrine of the Virgin of Alcalá is roughly six kilometres from the town itself, and it can be found at the end of a narrow, winding country lane. Upon arrival at the sanctuary, a large white complex can be seen, and within its walls lives Jose Luis, the *Santero* (the shrine caretaker) and his family, as well as the Virgin. The complex also houses a souvenir shop to accommodate the devotional requirements of shrine visitors. Things such as rosary beads, bracelets, necklaces, ceramic tiles and mini-temples akin to ancient Roman *lararium* can be purchased that depict the Virgin of the Saints (the local familiar name for the Virgin of Alcalá), and everything here has been blessed by the local priest. To get to the actual shrine where the Virgin resides, it is necessary to pass the shop, and then through a typically Andalusian Spanish *patio*, or courtyard, filled with plants, flowers and twittering birds. Two heavy wooden doors provide entry into the main shrine; and once inside, the point around which the sanctuary complex has been constructed becomes clear.

Central and elevated above the main altar, presiding over everything, is the Virgin of Alcalá (**Figure 3.1**). She, never 'it', is only three feet in stature, crafted from cedar wood, and sits on a pedestal that makes her appear to be quite tall. She has fine European features, pale 'skin' and lidless brown eyes. I was told that she never sleeps. She is always attentive to the needs of her people. The age of the Virgin varies depending on who one speaks with. Some people say she is about 600 years old, but others say she is older. Whatever her age, she has been a significant part of local life and identity for centuries.

The shrine itself is both a welcoming and working space, and it offers several different opportunities for devotional interactions to take place. For example, accessed through a set of stairs on the ground floor, the very chamber where the Virgin stands is designed to receive several visitors at once, and this access to the Virgin facilitates the ability to be in literal touch with her. It must be noted here that although Andalusia has a long and vibrant history of Marian devotion, it is rare for religious statues to be physically accessible on an everyday basis, a fact that further supports the claim that the shrine is unique and, for this reason, quite popular. Inside the chamber where the Virgin can be seen up close, one can see how every wooden finger is adorned with a gold ring: offerings given to her in thanks, adoration or on the premise of negotiation. As indicated in the following subsection, the Virgin is always donned with magnificent robe, or mantle, and this is the prime point for physical interaction with her (**Figure 3.2**). In fact, she has several ornate and different coloured mantles, which are also offerings, and these are changed by a group of elite women called the *camaristas* (literally 'chamber maids') in accordance with the liturgical year. These women (discussed in greater detail further along) are responsible for ritually bathing the Virgin, and for changing her mantle. Although the statue has ball joints, being made of wood means that she is rather fixed. Her mantle, on the other hand, is capable of movement. An extension of the Virgin, it is soft and tactile, and provides both a source of comfort and an appropriate medium for human and other than human interaction.

Figure 3.2 The Virgin's mantle.

Ritual Performance and the Mantle

The ritual protocol of going under the mantle is probably the most significant ritual that takes place in the shrine, and the chamber is a wide space where people can stand behind the Virgin and place her mantle over their heads. Having carried out this performance on several occasions during my time at the shrine (it is the first 'business' to be done upon arrival—in fact it would be rude to do otherwise), I can say that placing the Virgin's mantle over my head is an intimate practice, and from my experience, it is understandably revered. Although I am not Catholic (a fact that I made clear to the shrine caretaker before embarking on the research), I found being under her mantle to bring a sense of peace and even communion with her. I also felt a sense of being in communion with others who had carried out the ritual. In the darkness, it is still possible to see little notes that have been pushed under her small statue-feet. I could only guess the contents of these notes (I would not dare look); but certainly, their content would reveal petitions or requests, perhaps for the healing of a sick loved one, or perhaps some relief from unemployment. Depending on the time of year, there would often be a short queue of devotees waiting behind me when I would emerge from behind the mantle. People often emerge in tears and a box of tissues is positioned close-by. A sign that reads 'please don't kiss the mantle' sits on the Virgin's pedestal; this speaks to the ritual wear and tear that is a problem here. In 2018, I spoke to Arsenio (the lead figure in the *Hermandad*, or cult of the Virgin) and the local priest about the ritual and the potential for irreparable damage, but they both emphasised that what made the shrine unique was the opportunity of being able to be in contact with the mantle. However, as Bayarri highlights in Part II of this chapter, whilst no change to this ritual was ever expected, the Covid-19 virus meant changes had to occur in 2020.

While intimate, individual devotions are significant at the shrine, the Virgin's mantle also works to provide a literal medium through which collective local identities are reciprocally generated through the Virgin mother. William Christian writes in reference to Mary in the north of Spain,

> ...the symbolic role of Mary as village patron becomes a very important practical one. She is a significant factor in binding the villagers together as members of the same family. Just as the extended family stays together as long as the widowed matriarch is still alive and active, so the village stays together under the continued activity of a powerful image. This is how the

very essence of the village as home can come to be bound up in a revered image. (1989: 175)

In Andalusia, I witnessed the same—Mary acting as the 'widowed matriarch', providing a protective, warm, nurturing and loving presence; but in the town, because of the unique ritual, the Virgin of Alcalá provided a literal not metaphorical mantle under which her children could gather. In her shrine, devotees are not only able to touch her mantle, but to place it over their heads and literally feel enveloped and comforted by her, their divine mother and protector. Further, the significance of the mantle extends outward from the shrine and into the town. Daily rituals of being in touch with her, such as going under the mantle, or in the giving of offerings (discussed further along), are woven in the fabric of local knowledge, local belonging and local life. They form some of the ties that bind this maternal, totemic mother to her people, and accounts reveal that religious affiliation (believers or non-believers in the Catholic faith) makes little difference to this vernacular practice.

Despite the Catholic canonical relegation of religious images to the status of 'devotional' or 'symbolic' (things that refer to something else), the types of touch that the Virgin receives reveal both concepts to be rather impoverished. Touch is, in fact, as Marleen de Witte tells us '…a powerful medium of religious communication, not only between human beings, but also between humans and spirits' (2015: 262). It is not, however, only 'humans and spirits' that are mediated; performances of touch also mediate unspoken relational dialogues between so-called 'objects' and 'subjects'. These two categories are suspect, especially when dealing with questions about the relationships that take place between human persons and powerful artefacts such as the Virgin. In fact, the Virgin is both treated and understood by devotees in such a way as to encourage the notion of 'personhood'. She is, in fact, a 'statue-person' (Whitehead 2013a).

Understanding the Virgin of Alcalá as a 'statue-person' complements and builds on Graham Harvey's (2005) newer usage of animism which asserts that the world is full of persons, only some of whom are human. Harvey's animism is not so much concerned with how persons come into being, as it with how persons are treated or 'behaved towards' (2005: xi). This idea originates with A. Irving Hallowell's (1960) understanding of the Ojibwe ontological perspective that 'persons' exist all around us, and that this personhood can be inclusive of the objects, artefacts and the other beings who comprise the 'living world', depending on the quality of the relationship. Thus, building on Harvey (2005) and Hallowell (1960), the concept and practice of 'personhood' helps address the treatment of religious 'objects' such as the statue-person that is the Virgin of Alcalá, as well as how they can be better understood in the study of religions. In the context of the Virgin of Alcalá, ritually touching the Virgin's mantle (an extension of the Virgin) is a form of treatment that obscures and destabilises the categories of 'subject' and 'object', as well as the categories of 'representation' and 'symbolic'. This is because 'touch' goes both ways. If I am touching either the statue of the Virgin or her mantle, then she is also touching me in return. Michel Serres' notion of 'co-mingling bodies' is apt for supporting this position. He writes:

> The skin is a variety of contingency: in it, through it, with it, the world and my body touch each other, the feeling and the felt, it defines their common edge. Contingency means common tangency: in it the world and the body intersect and caress each other. I do not wish to call the place in which I live a medium, I prefer to say that things mingle with each other and that I am no exception to that, I mix with the world which mixes with me. Skin intervenes between several things in the world and makes them mingle. (Serres 2008: 80)

Not only does skin intervene; abstract notions of 'subjects' and 'objects' can be understood to 'co-mingle' (Serres 2008). The notion of 'co-mingling' is helpful because it re-frames understandings of religious 'touch' in terms of reciprocity, or being reciprocal. Co-mingling also presents opportunities for inter-subjectivity to be advanced in relation to material religious figures/objects. This framing has the advantage of placing physical touch interactions between the Virgin and her devotees on a relational continuum. It also supports the idea that personhood is a co-created 'happening'. When 'skins' (sensory surfaces, whether human or otherwise) come into contact/touch with one another, once estranged 'others' (subjects and objects) can be known through the senses, or the fingertips in the case of humans. Indeed, it is these apparently simple actions that generate faith, belief, knowledge and devotion (not the other way around). As S. Brent Plate points out: 'What seems trivial and easily overlooked, in the end, becomes foundational for religious environments and traditions' (Plate 2012: 162). In the case of the Virgin, touch has been the facilitating source of 'traditionalisation' at both individual and collective levels. Local heritage and group identity are maintained through the shrine site, and under the protective mantle of the Virgin.

Offerings and Devotionals

Like the centre of a spider's web, the shrine sits at the heart of the town's identity and religious life. Things are taken and left behind at the shrine (offerings), and things that have been blessed are bought and taken out (devotionals from the souvenir shop; see **Figure 3.3**). There's a flow, a currency and a kind of traffic, that runs through this sacred assemblage of a place that sits on the border of this world and the next. Negotiations made with the divine do not involve so-called normal currencies, or even normal circumstances. In fact, exchanges with the Virgin are often (but not always) made when some aspect of a person's life is felt to be out of his or her control, and divine assistance is being sought, and the intention with the giving of many of the objects found in the shrine is that they will stay in proximity to the Virgin. This keeps the devotee 'in touch' with the Virgin even when they are at a distance. I should note here that it is precisely because the Virgin is given gifts and treated in this way that she can be considered a powerful statue-person. This is evidenced on the walls of the shrine which are, for example, lined with hundreds of *ex voto* offerings. *Ex voto* images depict tragic scenes that happened in the region where the Virgin's miraculous intervention was seen or felt, some of which are over 250 years old. They also act as a local living record. Consequently, a family *ex voto* that remains in the shrine has the capability to inspire intergenerational faith, belonging and practice through its very presence which continually stands witness to the Virgin's miraculous power.

In this working shrine, worth mentioning, there is also a small statue of the infant Jesus, who sits in the main part of the shrine, housed in a glass box. This, too, requires a certain minimalist ritual, and involves the *Santero* removing the glass so that those who wish to have a child can 'touch' or 'tug' on the infant's genital area (covered in a cloth nappy). This is known to be one of the more potent actions one can take in the shrine. The ritual efficacy of touch, in the case of the fertility infant, is evidenced not only through numerous accounts but through the sheer amount of baby paraphernalia brought back to the shrine and left as visible evidence that the believers' prayers or requests had been fulfilled.

Figure 3.3 The shrine souvenir shop.

Existing on the strands of the web that issue forth from the shrine are devotionals that have been purchased at the shrine; as mentioned before, these things were either blessed at, or have once been in touch with, the shrine. Following James G. Frazer's (2005 [1922]: 11) notion of contagion, it can be argued that the townspeople are able to remain in touch with the shrine and the Virgin through plaques, images, medals and home altars. These things are extensions of the shrine that enable a continuation of shrine activities that, as Part II of this chapter discusses through ethnographic accounts, extend into the homes of the locals during this time of pandemic crisis. The fact that these domesticated devotional objects and images of the Virgin had 'co-mingled', been in touch with and/or moved through the shrine arguably confers a quality of efficacy through contagion.

Caretaking Rituals

There are two main forms of physically interactive caretaking at the Virgin of Alcalá's shrine. First, there is the *Santero*'s form of caretaking which involves day-to-day shrine maintenance and security, as well as changing of the rings and other jewellery placed on the Virgin's statue-body. Second, and more involved, are the caretaking rituals carried out by the *camaristas*. As mentioned prior, the *camaristas* are a group of women, each of whom has a kind of special status or standing, and who are responsible for more intimate aspects of the Virgin's caretaking. These women, accounts of whom are provided in Part II, are responsible for ritually changing the Virgin's mantles in accordance with the liturgical year, or for special occasions such as processions, or times of crisis. These rituals include changing her dress and mantle, including her petticoats, and ritually bathing her female artefactual body, which is often done while singing devotional songs. The type of touch involved in these intimate rituals is reserved for women only. When I asked the obvious question 'why', I was told that under no uncertain circumstances should the Virgin be looked upon by a man while undressed, and this is due to respect and to protect the Virgin's modesty. This treatment is one of the prime indicators of her personhood. She is not only a statue, but a 'woman'. The *Santero* added that the security cameras are even turned off while the Virgin's clothes are being changed. The only man allowed to see the Virgin disrobed is the local priest, and this is because of his vow of celibacy.

Modalities of caretaking, centred around who is permitted to touch the Virgin and who is not, denote gendered restraints aimed at protecting the Virgin's modesty and upholding an air of mystique through the creation of a taboo. Nevertheless, the ways in which the Virgin of Alcalá is 'touched' or 'not touched' are a prime indicator of her powerful position, her female gender and her personhood. 'After all, caretaking is also a form of crafting the invisible lines that create relations' (Whitehead 2018a) with things, persons (human and other than human), traditions and places, and these relations are quite real. In this case, touch facilitates (even underpins) belief, and mediates the sensually religious world.

The caretaking rituals discussed here, whereby the Virgin is bathed and dressed, are not 'pretend' gestures or what Alfred Gell calls 'make believe' (1998: 134). He writes: 'The essence of idolatry is that it permits real physical interactions to take place between persons and divinities. To treat such interactions as "symbolic" is to miss the point' (Gell 1998: 135). I agree with Gell. A real disconnect exists that has led scholars to treat these types of interactions as representational or symbolic when they should be taken seriously and understood on their own terms. Ritual interactions such as those outlined in this part of the chapter are powerful and within them exist transformative capabilities. As I have suggested before:

> This is why the ritual dynamics that take place in the ontologically 'unstable space' of the shrine of the Virgin are better understood as 'working relationships'. They are 'generated and generative', mutual, and co-created....
> (Whitehead 2018b: 217)

Applied to other forms of religious devotions and in other religious contexts, to think otherwise 'misses the point'. Moving away from a privileging of belief over tangible religious expressions means taking seriously the physical actions and activities carried out by religionists, and placing equal value (if not more in some cases) on sensual engagements.

The dynamic nature of the shrine, and the traditional performances that are sought, expected and performed by shrine visitors when in the presence of the Virgin, go beyond concepts of metaphor, representation and symbolism. This differs from the temporal dynamic that takes place when devotees are not in the Virgin's presence. And yet, although the language of 'symbolism', 'metaphor' and 'representation' is used by the people of Alcalá when describing the role of the Virgin in their domestic devotionals (as illustrated in Part II), it can be argued that the actual treatment of these devotionals defies any dualistic notion. Even when the Virgin is related with from afar, whether in the form of domestic devotions or through images of her bought in the shrine shop, the Virgin, with her geographical specification, is still 'the Virgin'; and she is the central, totemic, maternal and material religious figure around which town activities take place.

This section of the chapter is based on the author's fieldwork carried out at the shrine of the Virgin of Alcalá over an eleven-year period. It has discussed the vibrant and lively rituals and devotions that take place under 'normal', non-pandemic conditions at the shrine of the Virgin, and critically explored the different dynamics of and significances of touch that take place in the shrine, focusing primarily on day-to-day statue engagements, including those centred around the Virgin's mantle, offerings and devotionals, and caretaking rituals. Here, it has been argued that categories of subject and object mix, merge and 'co-mingle', giving way to the relational emergence of ontological possibilities such as personhood, aimed at helping us reimagine the nature of religion and the significant roles of religious artefacts, creativity and the senses, in ways that can shape our thinking beyond notions of symbolism and representation. In Part II, Bayarri explores how devotion to the Virgin is accommodated when the villagers of Alcalá are no longer able to visit the shrine or physically access the Virgin. Not only does this section reveal data regarding temporal relating, it also serves to measure levels of devotion beyond the shrine.

II: DOMESTIC DEVOTIONS IN TIMES OF PANDEMIC

Historically, various epidemics such as the plague or 'black death', flu and cholera were combated by the Alcaláine people through taking refuge in the sanctuary of the Virgin, where the lime on the walls sanitised the space, and where prayer and proximity to the Virgin shaped the way of administering the pandemics. Today, though, the villagers do not have that option (there are too many of them for the sanctuary to hold), and as such, in each house, the Virgin has an embodiment to which the villagers pray in times of need. And right now is a time of great need, such that a print drawn by a local artist has been distributed among the local houses so that the protection of the Virgin is provided against the current Covid-19 pandemic in each home.

In this part of the chapter, I try to understand how the current Covid-19 crisis is affecting the religious practices associated with the material figure of the Virgin of Alcalá de los Gazules (often referred to as the Virgin of the Saints). Through semi-structured telephone interviews, the conversations I had with the villagers covered their religiosity, their bond with the Virgin and the way in which the crisis may be contributing to the re-signification or re-interpretation of the practices associated with her.

My ethnographic study was made up of a total of eighteen testimonies taken from women and men aged between 25 and 70 years, all of them with knowledge about the religious practices associated with the Virgin of the Saints. My family link with the place made it easy for me to get in touch with the townsfolk, who were very willing to talk to 'Don Luis' grandson', and as such this part of the chapter adds an almost insider voice to the overall engagement with the statue-person that is the Virgin of Alcalá.

'The Virgin is Everywhere'

It was the beginning of the pandemic when in Alcalá de los Gazules, two local artists went around visiting the small shops. The artists were handing out little pictures (called 'stamps') representing the Virgin of the Saints covering the people of Alcalá with her mantle, protecting them from the Coronavirus (**Figure 3.4**). Quickly, the news spread through the town and, along with other representations, all the houses began to display a picture of the Virgin to protect them from the virus. The protection of the houses through the stamp recalled the biblical event in which the Hebrew people in Egypt had to paint the doors of their houses with lamb's blood, which would be a promise of protection. As many residents were claiming, the Virgin would act as a protector in the face of the pandemic, and one had to entrust oneself to her in order not to be affected. The villagers stated that in the stamp image 'the Virgin is showing her back, but she is not turning her back to the people; rather, the people are under her mantle'. This highlights the importance of the mantle in protecting the people of Alcalá. 'The mantle is a metaphor of protection', said Mari Santos (aged 58 years), a resident and small business owner.

Figure 3.4 Local artists' picture of the Virgin to protect every house from the Coronavirus.

Various testimonies explained the role that the Virgin was playing during the pandemic: Aurelio (58 years old) related that he had a nephew with Coronavirus who had been discharged from hospital, and that he had prayed every night for those affected. Elena, a 32-year-old woman, said:

'right now everyone is praying to the Virgin of the Saints'. Maria (aged 70 years), declared: 'faith is what will help the Virgin of the Saints heal [us]. She will do it. It will all end well.' Juan Carlos, the 54-year-old former Deputy Mayor of the United Left Party (Izquierda Unida) explained: 'the mantle creates intimacy. People are afraid of the present situation.' The reassurance that her protection would afford was expressed by a woman named Tere (55 years old) who stated: 'prayer will help end the Coronavirus. She will cover us with her mantle to protect us. The Virgin is helping us in our recovery.' Tere's intense faith in the Virgin came from a moment in her life when 'there was a miracle' and Tere was saved from being drowned. In an act of gratitude, she placed an *ex voto* (a painting of the miracle) to the Virgin in the shrine.

It was evident that because the characteristic touching of the Virgin in the shrine was no longer possible because of the pandemic, there were changes in the ritual approaches to the Virgin. Primarily, during the 'lock down' in March 2020, these changes included the Virgin being made present throughout town in temporary form, mainly through representations in homes. Below, I will discuss the dynamics of domestic devotion through the veneration of objects in the homes, with respect to the more ritualised moments of shrine devotion as discussed in Part I of this chapter.

The characteristic element of touch as the main construction of material religiosity and devotion with the Virgin is indisputable. However, from my research it was evident that her protective element was not simply represented in the figure in/of the shrine, and that the shrine's closing did not imply a sense of total loss, such that her devotees would feel almost orphaned. However, this appreciation varied according to the devotion of each of my interviewees, i.e. the people most linked to the shrine rituals of the Virgin, such as the *camaristas*, felt sad that they could not physically approach her and lamented: 'during the week, people always bring her flowers, and now we have not been able to dress her in the purple mantle of Lent'. Thankfully, as the pandemic situation began to improve in Spain, the *camaristas* were able to change the mantle of the Virgin. For the occasion, the *camaristas* chose the same embroidered mantle that was used during the Spanish Civil War (1936–1939), suggesting that the pandemic was interpreted by the townsfolk as a foe that had to be defeated with the divine assistance of the Virgin.

When asked about the imposed ban on touching the Virgin, though most of the Alcaláideans considered that touch is a fundamental part of the relationship with their Virgin, they found in their plaques, paintings or medallions sufficient material elements to develop a relationship of faith during the crisis. Many of the objects that they possessed in their homes had been acquired at the small shop of the shrine itself, and had previously been blessed in front of the Virgin. The Virgin, as noted by Whitehead in Part I, is understood by the people of Alcalá as a person—they speak of her as 'a happy person'—and the embodiment of the Virgin is understood to be in every figure, plaque or medal present in every house. 'We remember the Virgin in our joys and sorrows, and we feel the Virgin and her mantle even when she is not there', explained Mari Santos. Pictures, plaques, rosary—Antonia (aged 70 years), a *camarista*, and daughter of the *Santeros* ('Saint Keeper'), had everything in her house. When someone was in pain, she would give them a little plaque so that they could be cured with the support of the Virgin. She prayed for her children and for all those affected by the virus.

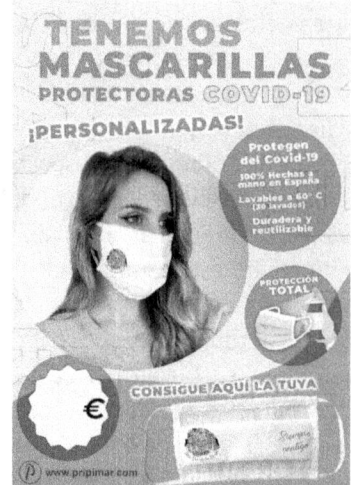

Figures 3.5 and 3.6 Advertisement for face masks created by the Brotherhood of the Virgin, published on Facebook, and detail showing the mask with the image of the Virgin.

A further example of the ways in which the Virgin has been embodied outside her shrine during this pandemic period is through the use of face masks (see **Figures 3.5 and 3.6**). The Brotherhood of the Virgin began to sell sanitary masks for two euros each that show the image of the Virgin. Soon, these masks began to be sold in various shops, as the villagers thought that the Virgin would act as a protector against the virus by not allowing the virus to enter their respiratory system.

There was, then, an evident need for the traditional tactile connection with the Virgin to continue in some form. The onset of the pandemic had broken the centuries-old practice, that even physical wear and tear of the figure and her clothes had not caused to stop. However, the need to mitigate the Coronavirus transmission risk meant the present *Hermandad* (religious brotherhood) were forced to propose to the Diocese a modification to the usual tactile relationship with the Virgin. The change during the pandemic has not altered the perception that physical approach to the Virgin is the most intimate way to establish a relationship with her, but it has shown that tactile engagement with the statue itself is not the only way to maintain a relationship with the Virgin.

However, for this new relationship with the Virgin to materialise, it has not been enough for the devout resident to believe in the power of the Virgin; he or she had to act, since it is through rituals that the effects of religious beliefs are renewed (Durkheim 1995 [1912]). The new active relational commitment between residents and the Virgin of the Saints seemed to be directed to the images, especially the stamp image, that the villagers possessed in their houses, and to the construction of small confined spaces for the veneration of the image (Molotch 2010). Francisca (aged 65 years), for example, missed going to the sanctuary. She would normally walk the Way of the Three Crosses near the sanctuary, but since she could not go out, she decided to reproduce the Three Crosses in her *cortijo* (traditional farmhouse from the south of Spain). She took six wooden slats and, tying them with rope, she made three crosses and placed one on the door of the *cortijo*, another by the side of the road and another inside her home; this way she could still walk. At Easter, she made herself a candle and painted a cross with markers. She was very confident that in this situation the Virgin would act to protect her. With the material expression of religiosity towards the Virgin during the pandemic concentrated in the symbols of the Virgin that are kept in the houses, a certain amount of creativity has been involved in designing spaces of domestic devotion.

The Virgin is everywhere; indeed, such is the prevalence of domestic devotion, as in the account of Francisca, that, to paraphrase the words of many villagers, a church has been opened in each house. This devotion is a demonstration of not just religious belief but the need for ritual action. Further, invoking the Virgin is not only aimed at ending the pandemic, but maintains the normal request-relationships by the townsfolk to her through prayers for family and friends, and in making various requests to her. The use of these visual representations of the Virgin, however, are not totemic symbols of her, but according to my ethnographic data, were considered by the people of Alcalá as 'the Virgin herself'; in effect they functioned much as a *murti* does for Hindus, in that the Virgin image is a physical manifestation of her and venerated as such.

Various Degrees of Devotion

The different testimonies from my interviewees revealed that in Alcalá, there are varying degrees of devotion to the Virgin. These range from residents who do not typically perform any kind of veneration, to those who go to the sanctuary whenever they can to visit her, including those who participate in the highly organised rituals of the *Hermandad*, such as the annual *Romería* (pilgrimage) of the Virgin, and the making of the *pregones* (proclamations). There were also residents who belonged to 'rival' *Hermandades*, that is, those who compete for a different religious identification regarding the moral practices of the Virgin, such as Vicenta (aged 53 years). Vicenta is devoted to the Virgin Mary of Nazareth, and she does not approve of the gold ornaments, clothes and grooming rituals of the Virgin of the Saints, nor of her joyful and festive character.

Younger people in the village seemed to be more reluctant to venerate the Virgin, although they had all participated in the *Romerías* and processions at some point; Elena (age 32), Juanmi (35) and Claudia (26) are cases in point here. However, regardless of the level of belief and veneration, appreciation and affection for the Virgin were expressed by all. Some people claimed that they did not believe in God, but they did believe in the Virgin of the Saints. Interestingly, even agnostics, polytheists or atheists in the village declared that no one should 'hurt the Virgin', and they noted they had various objects that represented her in their homes. This is not untypical of contemporary vernacular 'religious' practice as articulated by Linda Woodhead (2016) in her explorations of the 'no religion' category of individuals where doing often juxtaposes with assertions of non-belief.

All of the villagers in Alcalá appear to have gone through a process of socialisation linked, at different levels, to the figure of the Virgin. Many had been presented at birth to the Virgin in the shrine and introduced under her mantle. Others had even taken their new cars there, to be blessed by her. All my interviewees claimed to have representations of her in their homes; Mari Santos, for example, had a painting of the Virgin at the entrance of her house that belonged to her great-grandmother and was passed down from generation to generation—'In building our new house, I am the one with the painting now. And it is emotionally very important', she said to me.

The perspective with which the objects of domestic devotion are interpreted is a part of the material culture of the people of Alcalá. In this way, the Virgin represented and fulfilled the interests of the townsfolk themselves, with the Virgin having a powerful presence of intervention in Alcalá de los Gazules as well as in the adjacent villages of the Sierra de Cádiz. However, interviewees noted that her powers as represented in the domestic devotion objects suffered modifications once certain geographical limits were altered. Alcalá immigrants in other parts of the country recognised the loss of power that remoteness had, with some wondering, 'when we are praying to the Virgin, are we asking for the cure of all the people of Alcalá or beyond?' Notably, Gracia (53 years of age) claimed that she only had representations of the Virgin of Alcalá in her house in the village, but not in her house in Granada.

Domestic devotions to the Virgin also served, in varying degrees, as an approach to relatives who would otherwise be physically absent. People recognised that praying to the Virgin from their homes brought them close to their relatives, where online worship brought them closer to the community. This was represented in the notion of the Virgin as a 'mother': a relative who was asked for proximity and protection through the use of objects in their homes. Various testimonies showed that the Virgin of the Saints acted as a protector in a maternal metaphor in the face of the Covid-19 crisis: 'the Virgin of the Saints is like a mother', exclaimed Gracia. José Luis, the *Santero* of the shrine, felt the same: 'The Virgin is now in mourning, she is suffering for her children. Mothers are like that.... She is beautiful, but in mourning.' He continued: 'The Virgin is everything to me: my mother, my hope, my life.' 'She is our mother and reference, and we have learned to have a very special relationship. She is your refuge for the good and the bad, and the one you have to go to every little while if you don't feel that something is missing. And she is part of your family', concluded Arsenio (aged 54 years), the former mayor of the town and former '*Hermano* Mayor' of the *Hermandad* of the Virgin of the Saints.

From an analytical approach focused on the artefacts, the presence of domestic devotions illustrates the ways in which the people of Alcalá accommodated the Virgin in their homes during 'lock down' circumstances with the Coronavirus pandemic providing a space for the development of closeness at a distance; the Virgin was everywhere, not only in the shrine. The previously shrine-based tactile commitments, such as kissing the hand and then touching the image of the Virgin, as well as lighting candles, caretaking and praying, were expressed at homemade altars with plaques, rosaries, statuettes and other forms of material devotion. But the Virgin being everywhere meant she was online too, so next I wish to explore what is effectively e-devotion.

The Virgin on Social Networks

On 14 March 2020, on the Facebook page of 'Nuestra Señora de los Santos la Coronada', next to an image of the Virgin of the Saints, the text read: 'To the Virgin of the Saints, the one who on the walls of her sanctuary has the largest pictorial collection of *ex-votos* in Andalusia, let us ask for the miracle of a prompt solution necessary for the cessation of the Coronavirus.'

The message was one of many invocations that had been made to the Virgin of the Saints in the town of Alcalá de los Gazules after official data reported five cases of Coronavirus infection. The Holy Week processions were cancelled, and all prayers became virtual, being shared by Facebook in real-time, in a programme of daily events that included the greeting to the Virgin of the Saints at 9 pm. The pandemic forced the town to change the forms of religious expression to a new, technological model, which had a series of consequences on the perception of the figure of the Virgin of the Saints. The current pandemic has meant that devotees, with varying degrees of involvement, have experienced a virtual relationship with the Virgin. One crucial example is amending the historical physical request for miracles to virtual petitions made through social networks, thus transforming a part of the religious language based on *ex votos*, into, as the former *Hermano* Mayor indicated to me, invocations made on social networks.

At first, when designing the online programming, the idea was to record the Virgin in the sanctuary so that the villagers could approach her through daily visual contact. However, the poor network connection prevented this as regular occurrence, meaning the villagers had to give up both physical and visual online contact with the Virgin and develop an active relationship on social networks. However, the villagers were able to attend daily scheduled social-media masses and could use their social network space to express devotion and petitions to the Virgin against the pandemic, in lieu of the *ex votos* placed in the shrine.

Some testimonies from my interviewees reveal the way in which the townspeople related to the Virgin through social networks: they believed that Holy Week had still taken place, although without the street culture. Mari Santos explained that the '*Hermandades* have worked hard' and held various events online. She believed that salvation from the Coronavirus lay in believing in the Virgin and sharing the pain and joy with fellow residents, with Facebook having a strong relevance in the construction of online community ties. Interestingly, the online masses have re-signified the role of the younger members of families, as is the case with Juanmi (aged 35), who now had to connect to the Internet and prepare the worship for his mother—her ability to access domestic devotions to request healing for relatives and villagers was reliant on his technology skills. Various ethnographic testimonies I collect reinforced that villagers were praying to the Virgin through Facebook. These prayers were not through private messages, but by using the pages of devotion to the Virgin as virtual altars, where they shared their requests as part of the construction of a virtual public space. The case of Francisca is an example that represents this idea: she not only prayed for people who had Coronavirus but also wrote actively on Facebook asking people to build a collective prayer online, finding in the virtual support new forms of collective ties. As she stated to me: 'collective masses could have more strength among many people'.

The use of worship on the Internet was a part of the need to rebuild the worship spaces in times of shortage, because ultimately the devotees of Alcalá felt that they had to revitalise, at regular intervals, the collective feelings and collective ideas that gave unity and individualised the experience. In this way, worship and faith are elements that go beyond the pandemic, adapting to new spaces and forms. The *Hermano* Mayor Antonio (aged 60 years) said that the cult of the Virgin and the request for protection and refuge are maintained as they have been for hundreds of years: 'the *ex votos* before were created to fight cholera, with the plague, and now with the Coronavirus they have been reconstructed towards the social networks. We are in the age of Facebook instead of the age of the *ex votos*, but the Virgin remains the refuge.' His and the villagers' faith in the Virgin acting to help the village in times of trouble has strong historical precedent, and the next section explores how e-devotionals have not dampened this.

'The Virgin Is Coming to Visit Us'

It was 1929 when the Virgin emerged from her sanctuary to visit Alcalá de los Gazules. The reason for the multitudinous mobilisation was to pray to the Virgin to end the drought that was devastating the small economy of the peasant town. Throughout the twentieth century, the Virgin visited Alcalá for different reasons, such as the end of the Civil War, the evangelising missions, and other droughts that occurred (see **Figures 3.7 and 3.8**). In 1994 the Governing Board of the *Hermandad* of the Virgin established in the Statutes a frequency of every four years for the Virgin's visiting the town. The Virgin had received her canonical crowning, and local worship practices were institutionalised. Antonia, *camarista* to the Virgin, told of how on the day of the coronation there was no room in the street outside the sanctuary for all the people, so they held it in the esplanade near the Church of San Jorge. On that day, the Virgin was wearing a mantle that was more than 200 years old, restored for the occasion. 'That esplanade with 400 or 500 chairs, people standing. The bishop came…' Antonia recalled with a smile. She continued, 'This year, 2020, is the 25th year of the Virgin's coronation. There is a very strict protocol.'

Figures 3.7 and 3.8 Visit of the Virgin to Alcalá in 1929 and in 1949, praying for rain.
Source: historiadeAlcaládelosgazules.blogspot.com

The ritual of the Virgin's visit expressed her as a protective and maternal figure, strengthened the materiality of her figure and allowed the devotees to ask her favours. To announce her arrival, the villagers would hang their cloth pictures of the Virgin on balconies and windows, welcoming her. Nowadays, in view of the Coronavirus pandemic, the residents of Alcalá have already asked the Town Hall that when the confinement is over, a festive walk be made with the Virgin through 'her' olive groves, taking her from the Paseo de la Playa to the sanctuary, where she comes to Alcalá every four years for her visit. However, many residents have already begun to place their pictures with the image of the Virgin on their balconies (**Figure 3.9**), as if, in the current crisis, she was being processed outside in her normal cycle. In discussions with villagers it was clear that the general feeling was that: 'If we cannot go to see the Virgin, the Virgin comes to us.' Her image on the balconies is providing the residents of Alcalá with a significant framework within which they can orient themselves in their reciprocal relations, in their relationship with the world around them and in their relationship with themselves (Geertz 1973). The relationship with the Virgin of the Saints is a form of the collective group consciousness of the sacred. People, regardless of the level of their observance to her, claim to be devoted to the Virgin. She is a figure around whom community life and events happen, and this is expressed in the prints on the balconies, waiting for the 'visit of the Virgin'.

Figure 3.9 Photograph sent by a village resident in which one can see banners of the Virgin displayed on balconies.

Findings from this second part of the study into the ritual action around the Virgin of Alcalá suggest that the people in their daily continue remotely to generate a continuous bond with the sanctuary, with the community and with the Virgin herself as part of the same intimate structure. Even in the midst of the Covid-19 pandemic, the Virgin regulates social relations and the social and cultural cohesion of the community. Juxtaposing the touch-encouraging performances that take place at the shrine with the ways in which villagers are maintaining relationships with the Virgin in their lock-down homes allows for a deeper understanding of the significance of religious material cultures, the dynamics of temporal and physical relating, and how presence and touch are accommodated in a time of social, pandemic crisis. The continuance of the devotion to the Virgin, even if only in domestic surroundings, reinforces the notion that tactile commitments are crucial, so that even when prayers and requests can only be offered online, not placed at her feet under her mantle, altars, plaques, rosaries, statuettes and other forms of image-bearing material substances are crucial to the way that the people of Alcalá interact with her, and stay 'in touch' from afar.

ACKNOWLEDGEMENTS

Gabriel and Amy would like to thank the Toscano family for their generosity in providing us with so many contacts from Alcalá de los Gazules. We are especially grateful to the people of Alcalá, who with their sympathy, patience and affection have taken part in the interviews. We would also like to acknowledge and thank Jose Luis, the shrine *Santero*, for his hospitality over the years.

BIBLIOGRAPHY

Christian, William A., Jr. 1989. *Person and God in a Spanish Valley*, New Revised Edition. Princeton: Princeton University Press. https://doi.org/10.1515/9780691214757
de Witte, Marleen. 2015. 'Touch'. In S. Brent Plate (ed.), *Key Terms in Material Religion*, 261–266. London: Bloomsbury.
Durkheim, Emile. 1995 [1912]. *The Elementary Forms of Religious Life*. Translated and with an Introduction by Karen E. Fields. New York: Free Press.
Frazer, James G. 2005 [1922]. *The Golden Bough: A Study in Magic and Religion*. New York: Macmillan Company; Reprint New York: Cosimo Classics [citation refers to the Cosimo edition]. https://doi.org/10.1007/978-1-349-00400-3

Geertz, Clifford. 1973. *The Interpretation of Cultures: Selected Essays.* New York: Basic Books.
Gell, Alfred. 1998. *Art and Agency: An Anthropological Theory.* Oxford: Clarendon Press.
Hallowell, A. Irving. 1960. 'Ojibwa Ontology, Behavior, and World View'. In S. Diamond (ed.), *Culture in History: Essays in Honor of Paul Radin*, 19-52. New York: Columbia University Press. Reprinted in G. Harvey (ed.) 2002. *Reading in Indigenous Religions*, 18-49. London: Continuum.
Harvey, Graham. 2005. *Animism: Respecting the Living World.* London: Hurst & Company.
Johnson, Paul C. 2000. 'The Fetish and McGwire's Balls'. *Journal of the American Academy of Religion* 68 (2): 243-264. https://doi.org/10.1093/jaarel/68.2.243
MacWilliams, Mark. 2008. Review of *Animism: Respecting the Living World*, by Graham Harvey. *Religious Studies Review* 34 (4): 265.
https://doi.org/10.1111/j.1748-0922.2008.00315_1.x
Molotch, Harvey. 2010. Review of *Thinking Through Things: Theorizing Artefacts Ethnographically*, edited by Amiria Henare, Martin Holbraad and Sari Wastell. *Journal of the Royal Anthropological Institute* 16 (4): 907-908.
https://doi.org/10.1111/j.1467-9655.2010.01661_3.x
Plate, S. Brent. 2012. 'The Skin of Religion: Aesthetic Mediations of the Sacred'. *Crosscurrents* 62 (2): 162-180. https://doi.org/10.1111/j.1939-3881.2012.00228.x
Serres, Michel, 2008. *The Five Senses: A Philosophy of Mingled Bodies.* New York and London: Continuum.
Spyer, Patricia (ed.). 1998. *Border Fetishisms: Material Objects in Unstable Spaces.* New York and London: Routledge.
Turner, Victor. 1967. *The Forest of Symbols: Aspects of Ndembu Ritual.* Ithaca and London: Cornell University Press.
Turner, V. and A. Soucy. 2000. 'The Ritual Process: Structure and Anti-structure'. *Asia Pacific Journal of Anthropology* 1 (1): 152-153.
Tweed, Thomas. 2015. 'Space'. In S. Brent Plate (ed.), *Key Terms in Material Religion*, 223-230. London: Bloomsbury.
Tylor, Eduard. 1913 [1871]. *Primitive Culture*, 2 Vols. London: John Murray.
Whitehead, Amy. 2013a. *Religious Statues and Personhood: Testing the Role of Materiality.* London: Bloomsbury.
Whitehead, Amy. 2013b. 'The New Fetishism: Western Statue Devotion and a Matter of Power'. In Graham Harvey (ed.), *The Handbook of Contemporary Animism*, 260-270. London: Acumen.
Whitehead, Amy. 2018a. 'Touching, Crafting, Knowing: Religious Artefacts and the Fetish within Animism'. *Body and Religion* 2 (2): 224-244.
https://doi.org/10.1558/bar.36491
Whitehead, Amy. 2018b. 'Devotional Bodies, Working Shrines: The Dynamics of Devotion in a Marian Shrine'. *Magic, Ritual and Witchcraft* 13 (2): 212-230.
https://doi.org/10.1353/mrw.2018.0018
Woodhead, Linda. 2016. 'The Rise of "No Religion" in Britain: The Emergence of a New Cultural Majority'. *Journal of the British Academy* 4: 245-261.

Gabriel Bayarri is a PhD candidate in the Departments of Anthropology and Sociology at two universities (Cotutelle agreement): the Macquarie University of Sydney, where he works as casual staff, and the Complutense University of Madrid, where he is an honorific collaborator. As a political anthropologist, his research focuses on the sociology of violence and the construction of rhetoric and identities of far-right political movements. During the last nine years, Gabriel has worked in the Latin American context, specifically in Brazil, where he has analysed postcolonial power structures. He currently collaborates as a research fellow in the following research groups: Centre for Research on Extremism (C-REX, Oslo University), Centre for Right-Wing Studies (CRWS, University of California, Berkeley) and Centre for Research into Global Power, Inequality and Conflict (RGPIC, Macquarie University). Gabriel is currently developing approaches that investigate the correlation between material religion and broader socio-political processes.

Amy R. Whitehead is a Senior Lecturer in Social Anthropology at Massey University in Aotearoa New Zealand. An Anthropologist of Religion/Religious Studies scholar, she is the author of *Religious Statues and Personhood: Testing the Role of Materiality* (2013), as well as several journal articles and chapters for edited volumes. Amy's primary areas of research concern the material and performance cultures of religions, the 'turn to things' in the Study of Religions, the development of new approaches to animism and 'the fetish', ritual studies and Earth Traditions (Paganisms, Goddess movements). She has also co-edited volumes including *Indigenous Religions: Critical Concepts for Religious Studies* (2018), and is the managing series editor for Bloomsbury Studies in Material Religion.

Chapter 4

The Heathen Lyre: On Religion, Music and Touch

ANDY LETCHER

> Then Scilling and I with our clear voices,
> before our glorious lord, struck up our song;
> sung to the hearpe, it rang out loudly.
> (From *Widsith*, translated by Bella Millett, reprinted with permission)

Music has a strong claim to being a human universal. There is no known extant human culture without it (Trehub, Becker and Morley 2015). The earliest musical instruments, flutes made from animal bones, date to around 40,000 BCE, though it is likely we have been playing and singing for far longer (ibid.). Seen from such a perspective, modern Western culture's tendency to divide musicians (the few) from non-musicians (the many) is unusual, but even so it presupposes a ubiquitous *musicality* that allows the latter to appreciate the former (Blacking 1973; Hoeschele et al. 2015; Honing et al. 2015; Trehub, Becker and Morley 2015). Western culture may be alone in having industrialised music production and consumption, but humans everywhere have invested large amounts of time and resources into making, mastering, playing and listening to musical instruments (Bates 2012). The proverbial anthropologist from Mars would have to conclude that music forms an intrinsic part of our behavioural ecology. We are inescapably *Homo musicus*.[1]

While no universal structural characteristics of music have been found, music's profound ability to occasion affect has been noted and utilised everywhere (Trehub, Becker and Morley 2015). This is perhaps why it is so often found in intimate relationship with that other, probably, human

---

1 With thanks to Alison Heatherington for the Latin. Thanks are also due to Roger Landes for supplying some of the harder-to-source papers cited herein.

universal: religion. In religious or ritual contexts music can help arouse us to ecstatic frenzy, carry us on shamanistic journeys or calm us to reflective quietude (Becker 2004; Huron 2015; Partridge 2013; Power, Collins and Burnin 1984; Rouget 1985). Where language struggles, music can express the complex and contradictory multiplicity of emotions or feelings of transcendence that arise in religious practice (Ralls-Macleod and Harvey 2017). And music provides a ready suite of metaphors with which to grasp ultimate metaphysical meaning: rhythm, harmony, consonance, dissonance, frequency, vibration, reverberation, higher octaves, the blues, the funk.

While the purported evolutionary origins of music and its cognitive effects upon the brain have stimulated a huge research effort (Hoeschele et al. 2015; Honing et al. 2015; Snowdon, Zimmermann and Altenmüller 2015; Morrison and Demorest 2009; Koelsch 2014), this intersection of music and religion remains somewhat under-theorised and under-explored (see Laack 2015 for a thorough review). There have been some notable studies of music within contemporary Paganism (Chase 2006; Weston and Bennett 2013), of indigenous music-making and religion (Ralls-Macleod and Harvey 2017) and of the relationship between music and trance (Rouget 1985; Aldridge and Fachner 2006; Becker 2004). In popular music studies, Christopher Partridge, adopting a Durkheimian approach, argues that rock and pop can have a religious function by offering a 'profane' challenge to the 'sacred' mores of mainstream culture (Partridge 2013). Nonetheless, Christopher Lehrich (2014) laments the lack of theorisation about music and religion within the study of religion, despite the fact that some of the founding fathers made significant overtures in this direction: for example, Rudolf Otto, Gerardus Van Der Leeuw, Johan Huizinga, Max Weber and Alfred Schutz (Lehrich 2014; Neitz and Spickard 1990; Laack 2015). Doubtless the breadth of the domain opened up by religion and music presents theoretical and methodological challenges (Laack 2015), but one way in which to limit the field is to add in a third category, as I do here with *touch*.

Touch is not typically the first sense we think of in relationship to music, or if it is then we use it as a metaphor: music *moves* us, *strikes* a chord. For most of us in the modern West, touch is incidental to our musical consumption (or, in the erotic domain, music is supplemental to touch). We feel the curve of the earphones as we slide them in place, or the texture of the smartphone screen beneath our fingertips. Few of us handle CDs anymore though increasing numbers are returning to vinyl and the old-school pleasure of lowering a needle into a treasured LP's grooves. But thereafter touch is forgotten as our attention shifts away from the skin to whatever inner realm of memory and affect we've conjured as we soundtrack our lives. No longer do we have to physically place ourselves within earshot of someone meaningfully disturbing the air for our aesthetic pleasure. Only when we do, at those intermittent occasions of live music, can we feel the pressure waves on our skin, the low frequencies in our guts. Then perhaps we remember the bodily sense of music and touch.

And yet all music originates with touch, even that produced entirely on a laptop. To consider music through touch immediately shifts focus away from the listener to the makers of 'humanly organized sound' (Blacking 1973); away from music abstracted into MP3s or notes pinned down on staves, to the tactile process of musicking (the very act of making music at a particular moment in a particular context, Becker 2004), of hands, fingers and feet (sometimes other body parts too) coaxing sound from things that vibrate. It draws us to what ethnomusicologist Marko Aho calls 'the tangible in music' (Aho 2016), for as Nietzsche reminds us in *Twilight of the Idols* (§10), 'all rhythm still speaks to our muscles' (Nietzsche 2004 [1889]: 45).

In this chapter, then, I want to examine the intersection of music and touch by looking at our relationship with musical instruments, those myriad artefacts wrought with human ingenuity that, as St Augustine put it in his definition of music, allow us 'to make controlled variations of sound in the right way' (cited in Crossley 1951: 127). What are doing when we touch an instrument? What exactly is it that we are touching, and what has that to do with religion?

On one level instruments are purely denotative: things that, through the time and long repetition required to make those controlled variations, become as it were extensions of the body. Thus, at the denotative level, a harp and a Fender Stratocaster are simply devices that allow for the production of sound in related ways via the vibration of plucked strings, while imposing limitations upon the player that restrict the available timbres and possible styles.

But instruments are also *connotative,* and powerfully so, signs that exist within complex webs of meaning before even a note is sounded and the music begins. So at the connotative level the harp and the Fender Stratocaster are quite different, and come already embedded in a range of meanings that shape, if not determine, the likely gender, race, class and personality of the player, the context of performance, the acceptable 'habitus of listening' (as Judith Becker puts it, 2004) that goes with their being played, and so on. In other words, Jimi Hendrix playing *the Star-Spangled*

Banner might not have had the same cultural impact had he played harp. This abundance of meaning readily extends into religiosity.

Consider the lyre, an instrument that I'm going to use as the hook for this chapter. Though for the most part obsolete in Western Europe, it nonetheless shimmers with religious or close-to-religious significance. Whether in the cherubs of Baroque art or the cartoons of *The New Yorker*, it's an instrument that is replete with heavenly associations. These probably stem from its ancient connection with the Greek god of light and learning, Apollo. Apollo, it is said, mastered the instrument and, in one version, placed it permanently in the night sky as the constellation *Lyra* to memorialise Arion, the tragic bard who rode on the back of a dolphin. The lyre too has sailed beyond the stars, albeit in the hands of *Star Trek*'s Mr Spock.

Though chiefly associated with Apollo, the Greek myths tell us the lyre was invented or discovered by the more ambivalent figure of Hermes. And the pictorial evidence from vases reveals that, in the form of the deep-voiced *barbitos*, it was also played by followers of Dionysus who, if Nietzsche is to be believed, is the divine antithesis of Apollo. Arion too is supposed to have invented the dithyramb, a hymn sung and danced in honour of Dionysus. Meanwhile singers of Homeric epic invoked all the gods to the hypnotic accompaniment of a four-string lyre, the *phorminx*.

But of all the Greek myths, none is more resonant than that of Orpheus, the lyre's most famous champion. Orpheus charmed both animals and gods with his virtuosity, persuaded Hades to release the shade of his beloved Eurydice, but failed at the last by breaking the injunction against looking back. Orpheus still very much haunts the Western imagination, such that his instrument 'represents all poets, all trees and the world itself' (Wroe 2011: 11). Even Bertrand Russell conceded that 'Orpheus is a dim but interesting figure' (Russell 2004 [1946]: 26).

The Western preoccupation with ancient Greece has left us, therefore, if not with the living instrument then a set of deeply engrained cultural meanings and associations. The lyre still signifies the highest art, inspired perhaps by the muses: hence our *Lyric* theatres, *lyric* poets, and even our *lyricists*. But as we shall see, the lyre is associated with another epoch, the so-called Dark Ages in northwestern Europe, through which it has accrued other, more earthy, heathen associations.

Meanings vary and change, hence the ethnomusicologist Eliot Bates writes that 'the same instrument in different sociohistorical contexts, may be implicated in categorically different kinds of relations' (Bates 2012: 364). Two musicians ostensibly playing the same *denotative* instrument may not be playing the same *connotative* instrument at all. An analysis of music and touch therefore requires a careful examination of the context of the musicking, but as I shall argue, to do so goes against another deeply engrained Western tendency, that of abstracting music and musical instruments from their context. What I want to suggest here is another alternative reading based on recent understandings of animism.

In this chapter, then, I share my own experiences of acquiring and learning to play a replica Dark Age lyre, within a context of modern Paganism, and in doing so I freely dance between my scholarly and participatory voices. The arguments against the idea of supposed etic, scholarly objectivity and for situated, reflexive, dialogical positionality are legion, persuasive and need not be rehearsed here. But the principal reason for using my insider voice is that, as Andrew Blake noted, words about music are somewhat superfluous (Blake 1997). To understand music, religion and touch one really needs to *experience* it, not read about it at one remove. So to read about what religion, music and touch mean *for others* is simply to add yet a further, unnecessary distanciation.

THE TROSSINGEN LYRE

A little over two years ago I took delivery of a new, specially commissioned instrument, a replica Dark Age lyre. The lyre was made for me by a skilled Breton luthier, Benjamin Simao, who specialises in re-creating ancient instruments, and it is a facsimile of a six-string instrument found in a grave in Trossingen, Germany. The remains of twenty-six 'Germanic' lyres have been unearthed by archaeologists in England (most famously at Sutton Hoo), Germany, the Netherlands, Denmark, Norway and Sweden. These date from the fifth to the mid-thirteenth centuries (Hillberg 2015). Of these, the lyre at Trossingen is one of the most complete and best preserved. Made with exquisite craftsmanship, it has been dated to around 580 CE (ibid.), a time when much of Europe was not yet Christian.

The Trossingen lyre accompanied a man in his thirties who was laid out with various other grave goods, including a sword (ibid.). His coffin was bed-shaped, its ridge carved into the form of a serpent. The lyre was exquisitely made, a high-status object, striking to behold. It was hollowed out from a solid block of maple and fitted with a thin, resonant soundboard, also of maple. The bridge was of willow, and its six tuning pegs of hazel and ash. Most striking of all, it was richly decorated using a technique known to us as *kolrosing*. Images were cut into the surface of the wood with a sharp knife, and then the grooves rubbed with a mixture of powdered charcoal, oil and wax to leave the wood tattooed. The soundboard shows two phalanxes of warriors marching towards one another on either side of the bridge, separated by a massive spear; the arms and back are covered with serpents, entwined in great knotted masses known unceremoniously to archaeologists as 'Germanic animal style II' patterns (Hillberg 2015: 11). Clearly this was an instrument that mattered, but then that seems always to have been the case with the lyre.

Though ancient Greece casts a long shadow, the lyre probably originated much earlier in ancient Mesopotamia, perhaps as early as the third millennium BCE (Wachsman et al. 2001). From there it spread to North, East and West Africa (where it is still played today, Racy 2006), across the Mediterranean to ancient Greece and Rome, and then upwards through Europe to Germany, the Baltic countries, Scandinavia and Britain. In Anglo-Saxon England it was probably called a *hearpe* (though by the height of the Middle Ages it had fallen from favour to be replaced by the more familiar, multi-stringed instrument we know as a harp). Of limited compass, sometimes consisting of as few as five, six or seven strings, the lyre is nonetheless capable of complex music. In places where it is still extant it is used to elicit moments of both Apollonian calm (as in Ethiopia, where the *begena* typically accompanies devotional song) and Dionysian ecstasy (as in Kenya where the *nyatiti* is used to lay down pentatonic riffs that wouldn't seem out of place in EDM). My first challenge, however, was to work out how to play it at all.

Learning any instrument is, as ethnomusicologist Marko Aho notes, a tangible thing. 'Musical instruments', he says, 'are played with human bodies and that deserves some thought' Aho (2016: 1). Aho studied the Finnish *kantele,* and made the tactile and at times painful process of his learning to play this traditional psaltery, which is organologically related to the lyre, the focus of considerable thought (ibid.). '[T]here exists', he says, 'a fundamental connection between music and body *movement*: people gesture to music everywhere, swaying their bodies to the beat, tapping their feet, or mimicking the movements they witness in musical performance. Musicians control their instruments by movements that are intended to carry essential musical meaning' (ibid.: 2, emphasis original). By movements, of course, but also by touch.

For Aho, touch refers to perception, of, say, the strings under the fingers, but also of proprioception, 'the sense of body movement and position involved...when playing musical instruments' (2016: 4). Acquiring the necessary muscle memory, of knowing which string to play when, but also the proprioceptive memory of how and where to place the hand and fingers, required hours of repetitive practice. Though candid about his limitations, Aho reached a point, citing John Baily, where the *kantele* became 'a type of transducer, converting patterns of human movement into patterns of sound' (ibid.: 3).

Aho had the advantage of having a living tradition of *kantele* playing on which to draw. By contrast I had next to nothing, just the instrument, my own ideas and musical imagination, and the online suggestions of a handful of similarly-minded enthusiasts. Yet almost everything about the Dark Age lyre is disputed.

The Anglo-Saxon *hearpe*, mentioned in poems such as *Beowulf* and *Widsith*, may not have been a lyre at all but a harp (Boenig 1996). The lyre may have been used to accompany song or played solo, though the image of the *scop* strumming his lyre in the mead hall—of which we find hints in the fragments of surviving Anglo-Saxon poetry—may itself have be a romantic and nostalgic harking back to a practice that was long gone and remembered only vaguely (Niles 2003). The strings of the lyre may have been sounded with a plectrum or the fingers, and if the latter the fingertips or the nails. Players may have damped strings with the left hand to leave chords that could be strummed with the right (the so-called block and strum method), or sounded strings using both hands. The strings may have been tuned to a pentatonic scale; or following the suggestion of one Hucbald, who flourished in the 8th century, to the first six notes of a major scale; or some other unrecorded variant. The intonation might have been set using Pythagoras' strict derivation of perfect fifths and fourths (which produces sullen, dissonant thirds), or to the harmonics of the lowest string using the much sweeter-sounding just intonation; or to some unknown piquant arrangement that would sound very out of tune to modern ears conditioned to the artifice of equal temperament.

Even after a hefty evaluation of the available evidence, Christopher Page could only conclude in the broadest terms that the 'execution was probably vigorous and designed to elicit a strong, bright sound from the strings.... The music—at least among the advanced players—was probably textured, involving various configurations designed to build up a self-sufficient sound picture. Yet the materials played may have been extremely simple, the essence of the art consisting of constant variation upon an iterated foundation' (Page 1981: 210). Fascinating but hardly prescriptive.

Page is right to imply that there is great creative freedom within restricted forms. The luthier who built the original Trossingen lyre was highly skilled and could easily have added extra strings if the music of the day required them. That they didn't, and that other Dark Age lyres had six strings, suggest that such an austere limitation was deliberate and existed perhaps as a challenge to would-be players. What can you do with such a limited palette? Contemporary African lyre players dazzle with their virtuosity and doubtless Dark Age minstrels did too. The desire to find 'constant variation upon an iterated foundation' proved, for me at least, an irresistible challenge.

In the end, mostly through trial and error but also by studying a little medieval harp technique and plentiful YouTube videos of the diverse playing styles of a number of extant lyre traditions in Africa, I arrived at my own idiosyncratic technique.[2] With no pressure to be historically authentic (whatever that might mean) I settled on just intonation and Hucbald's tuning: it's remarkably versatile and invites music that toggles between two chords (i and iim). My style is shaped by my modern musical enculturation and tastes (such as a fascination with traditional music, unusual time signatures, polyrhythms, loops, and scales marginalised in Western music), by the cognitive and physical limitations of my fifty-year-old body, and by constraints imposed by the instrument itself. Certain patterns seem to 'fall out' of the instrument, its ergonomics and set-up, such that I find it steers my hands and leads me to new discoveries. Like Aho's *kantele*, the lyre has become for me a kind of transducer.

But as I've argued above, an instrument is not just a physical device used to make sound but a potent sign, a conduit of meaning. I could have learnt, say, the guitar but instead I chose a long-dead instrument with very limited musical appeal, albeit one redolent with cultural associations. The question remains, why? What is it that I think I'm touching?

I'd like to say I've always wanted to play the lyre and that it was a long-cherished dream come true. In fact, when fellow scholar Jenny Blain introduced me to hers back in 1997 at the Contemporary Paganism conference at King Alfred's College Winchester, I dismissed it as limited beyond musical use. It was rather a gradual falling in love where the *idea* of the lyre caught me long before the instrument itself.

While miserable and bullied at boarding school I took solace in astronomy and spent many happy evenings observing the Ring Nebula, an object that sits in Arion's constellation, *Lyra*. Many years later, remembering this, I wrote a tune called *Lyra* that became one of those significant pieces of music in the very early days of my relationship with my wife. We both

---

2 I have compiled a YouTube playlist that shows examples of many of the lyre traditions and players mentioned here, including a video of myself. The playlist is complete and fully operational at time of writing. It is available at: https://bit.ly/2IwW4mq

liked the name and were to have given it to our first daughter who, tragically, was stillborn. Playing my lyre therefore has profound autobiographical significance, and I do so in part out of a kind of Orphic grief, as a way of remembering and honouring my lost daughter, but in part also as a comforting hand offered back to my younger self, to tell myself that all will eventually be well.

Then there are the more obviously spiritual resonances. I am a Pagan, an eclectic Druid with Heathen leanings and as such have carried the nickname 'Andy the Bard' for some twenty years. Contemporary Druidry attempts to revive, recreate or reimagine the religious practices and worldviews of the Iron Age, when it is believed the original Druids flourished (Letcher 2001). A form of nature spirituality, it is profoundly concerned with *awen*—a Welsh word usually translated as 'inspiration' but which I prefer to render as 'that which flows'—and with reinvigorating something akin to ancient bardic performance.[3]

Heathenism similarly attempts to revive, recreate or reimagine the religious practices and worldviews of so-called Germanic or Northern peoples of the Dark Ages and Viking period (Wallis 2003; Blain 2001), times which also had genres of oral, epic recitation by *scops* in Anglo-Saxon England and *skalds* in Scandinavia. In recent years I have found myself increasingly drawn to Anglo-Saxon heathenism, but whether from the Iron or Dark Ages, this passion for recreating an indigenous bardism has led me to the lyre (as well as other ancient instruments) that might offer some kind of conduit to worldviews that are for the most part lost. That an anagram of my name happens to be 'Chanted Lyre' also proved an irresistible coincidence.

Psychedelics, too, have formed an essential part of my spirituality, specifically my relationship with our most famous British hallucinogenic mushroom, the Liberty Cap, or *Psilocybe semilanceata* (Letcher 2006, 2007, 2013). Increasing numbers of psychedelic-seekers, especially those who have returned from medicine-ceremonies in the Americas, are now asking what would be an appropriate ritual context in which to consume mushrooms here. Different formats are being tried but most agree that music powerfully determines the mood, ambiance and elicited affect of

---

3 In traditional oral cultures bards recite epic poetry, hold the memories of important events and of significant lineages, and are able to compose or improvise panegyrics (see Bloomfield and Dunn 1992). By contrast, contemporary bardism, which has emerged in literate cultures, is concerned with the performance of music, poetry, story and song, and is characterised by nostalgia for, and the evocation of, an imagined pagan past. See Letcher (2001).

psychedelics (Kaelen et al. 2017): hence music, especially song, always forms part of traditional medicine ceremony (Shanon 2011). Psychedelics remain illegal in the UK, but I'm optimistic that situation might change in the medium term. By mastering the lyre my hope is to be able to provide live, extemporised music that can express and contour the affectual terrain of a ceremony with an instrument that powerfully connotes the ancient, pagan past. We can easily imagine this past as being more connected to one another, to the ancestors and to place.

Here, various scholars have noted that instruments distant to us in space or time are amenable to a process of 'othering' that is extremely attractive to practitioners of alternative spiritualities, like myself (Granholm 2011). Thus Koji Matsunobu found that the appeal of the Japanese *shakuhachi* for North American students of the instrument 'was not so much cultural aspects of Japanese music as [the] spiritual aspects of human experience they identified in Japanese music' (Matsunobu 2011: 275). Matsunobu's informants read the instrument through a Western Orientalist discourse of 'universal spirituality' in which meaning came to reside wholly in its sound and not the very particular Japanese cultural context from which it originated.

That an othering of the past forms an important dimension of contemporary northern European Paganism and Native Spiritualities, my own included, is well attested (Rountree 2018). Kennet Granholm writes that the 'pre-Christian religions of Europe are perceived as exotic, as they represent that which is beyond the mainstream in contemporary society, and as such they are an appealing "tradition" to turn to in the esoteric search for perennial wisdom' (Granholm 2011: 539). This othering extends to music, and Granholm describes a growing scene of Heathen Metal and Neofolk bands in northern Europe who identify with the culture and religioning of the Dark Ages and the Viking periods. As part of this, the lyre is undergoing a small, but noteworthy revival as a *heathen* instrument.

That this is happening outside of historical re-enactment, Early Music circles or traditional Scandinavian folk music—where European iterations of the lyre have made limited impact beyond a few enthusiasts—is largely down to one Norwegian musician, Einar Selvik. Originally the drummer of Gorgoroth, a Heathen Metal band, Selvik formed Wardruna, a Neofolk offshoot, in 2003 (Granholm 2011). Mixing ancient instruments (drums, horns, the lyre and the bowed lyre or *tagelharpa*) with electronic textures, samples and found sounds, and with a trilogy of albums based on the ancient writing and magical system of the runes, Wardruna create atmospheric soundtracks that conjure an imagined heathen past. When their music was used in the History Channel's show *Vikings* (2013–) they gained an international following that includes Metal fans, practising heathens and what might be termed cultural heathens, that is, those who reflexively identify with the heathen past through lifestyle choices such as hairstyles and tattoos, but in a secular sense (though the boundary between all three is often blurred). Selvik, it should be noted, is an outspoken Heathen practitioner.

Selvik has hitherto played and recorded with a replica of seventeenth-century heptachord lyre found at the Norwegian town of Kravik, but has recently taken possession of a Trossingen lyre also made by Benjamin Simao (Simao personal communication). His status as an international heathen musician has elevated the status of the lyre, provided contemporary musicians with a genre and something of a repertoire, brought renewed attention to the instrument's spiritual connotations and, by virtue of his impeccable Metal pedigree, conferred the lyre with a sense of alterity. In short, he has played a large part in manufacturing the 'heathen lyre'.[4]

To conclude this section, then, my musical and autobiographical motivation to learn the lyre, to train my body to coax aesthetically ordered sounds from its six strings, has coincided with a revival, albeit small-scale, of the instrument in northern Europe. This revival is happening within the broader context of a resurgence in Paganism and native spiritualities, as part of which ancient musical instruments are being employed to signify otherness and alterity, as well as connection to place (Granholm 2011; Rountree 2018). The high profile of musicians such as the openly heathen Einar Selvik has generated sufficient interest in the lyre to support a handful of full-time professional luthiers, and reframed the lyre as a northern European, heathen instrument.

---

4   Here, mention must also be made of traditional Norwegian singer, Øyonn Groven Myhren—who has developed a unique modern lyre technique to accompany her haunting medieval ballads—and Dutch NeoFolk artist, Kati Ran, who like Selvik evokes the pagan past through her songs and videos. Likewise, in Britain, 'Kate and Corwen' are druids, luthiers and folk musicians who have done much to popularise lyres through their appearances on TV and at festivals, as well as with their online presence. There would, of course, be no lyre, heathen or otherwise, without the handful of luthiers across northern Europe who have worked out how to make these instruments for modern musicians.

ANIMISM, MUSIC AND TOUCH

In this section I want to return to the question of how we might begin to study the intersection of religion, music and touch. In particular I want to argue for an animistic reading of musical instruments, one justified by phenomenological study, that stresses not just the personhood of certain instruments, but their rootedness in complex webs of often religious meaning. To begin I examine the antithesis of an animistic reading, namely organology, that severs instruments from their cultural contexts.

An example is instructive. While writing this chapter I went to see the collection of musical instruments at the Pitt Rivers Museum, Oxford. Like most collections, the instruments are arranged and classified according to the Hornbostel-Sachs system. Developed in 1914, this discriminates instruments according to their means of sound production. It helped systematise the formal study of musical instruments known as organology. Under this system a lyre, technically a chordophone, may be defined as a 'string instrument whose strings are attached to a yoke which lies in the same plane as the soundtable...and consists of two arms and a crossbar' (Wachsman et al. 2001).

Lurking in a rather forgotten cabinet in the Pitt Rivers are two African lyres from Kenya and Uganda respectively, both looking rather the worse for wear. Their hide soundtables are rumpled and flaccid, their gut strings frayed. Strum one of these and they'd likely snap in two. I always feel sad seeing instruments in museums but especially so with these lyres now that I know of what music they're capable. It seems a travesty of the luthier's art that things meant to be touched and brought to life, that may have been someone's treasured companion for many years, are imprisoned in soundless cabinets, there to gather dust in perpetuity. I am not alone. Eliot Bates writes that '[i]nstrument museums are mausoleums, places for the display of the musically dead, with organologists acting as morticians, preparing dead instrument bodies for preservation and display' (Bates 2012: 365). He laments the cursory labelling of a *saz* in the Musical Instrument Museum in Phoenix, Arizona for being 'bereft of stories about the particular instrument, how it came to be in the museum or its pre-death life in the hands of living players'.

Organology is a modern, Western practice. From the whole, complex, messy, lived reality of musicking, with all its rich and complicated meanings, organology dissects out just the instrument for its object of study, which now falls somewhere between utilitarian artefact and objet-d'art. The instrument becomes something to be looked at, to be prodded, poked, measured and compared by experts, but rarely if ever played. That it ever was, or that it had a pre-death life, becomes a secondary issue.

Anthropologist Tim Ingold critiques this kind of thinking in regard to material things, which he attributes to Aristotle's lasting distinction between form (*morphe*) and matter (*hyle*). This pervasive *hylomorphism*, he argues, privileges some agent acting to impose form upon inert or passive matter (Ingold 2013). Rather than invert the terms of the opposition to attribute some kind of agency to matter (an attempt he finds problematic), Ingold seeks to transcend it altogether in what he calls an 'ontology of animism'. He does this by contrasting objects and things. *Objects* for Ingold are fixed, have definite boundaries but only truly exist in the mind. The world about us consists rather of *things* that have permeable boundaries and exist in a state of continual process. Thus a lyre as an abstracted *object*, defined according to the precise terms of Hornbostel-Sachs, may well exist in the pages of an organological journal. But in the real world, actual lyres, being *things*, get worn and warped through use, gain a patina from sweat and smoke, have parts that are repaired or replaced, are affected by the weather and how often they're played. Lyres, even those imprisoned in cabinets, are always in process through their life-cycle. In a world of *things* there is no separating an instrument from the fingers that touch it, the air it moves, the ears and bodies that respond, the meanings, religious or otherwise, it conveys.

This cutting out of *objects* from a world of *things* is a familiar habit in the West. Consider the matter of 'religion'. Scholars of religion are not only aware that religion 'can be defined, with greater or lesser success, more than fifty ways' (J.Z. Smith, cited in Braun 2000: 4), but that the category itself is a Western discourse with its roots in Judaeo-Christian worldviews that acts to 'manufacture' its object of study (Braun 2000; McCutcheon 1997). For Russell McCutcheon, 'it is the act of scholarship itself that..."invents" such categories as religion, myth, ritual, sacrifice, pilgrimage, etc., uses them to construct theoretical models...and then "maps" these models onto what might otherwise simply be termed observable human behaviors' (cited in Arnal 2000: 22). Thus 'religion' often has no cognate term in other cultures, for whom the idea does not translate. Moreover, it comes replete with Protestant connotations that equate religion with 'belief', connotations that obscure the fact that religion is first and foremost something *done*. We might better talk of religioning (see Harvey 2013b) (as some already do with *musicking*).

Music is not included in McCutcheon's list but ethnomusicologists have long been aware that the same principle obtains. Owing to the fact that

Western culture learned in the Middle Ages to transcribe music in such a way that it could be faithfully reproduced at a later date (other attempts at transcription have been less successful), we have become adept at abstracting 'music' from musicking. We can transcribe and record humanly organised sound that would otherwise be lost, and subject it to analysis as if it had some independent, ideal existence.

But as with religion, 'there are many societies that have no word for "music" and do not isolate it conceptually from dance, drama, ritual or costume' (Blacking 1987: 3). For example, amongst Bantu-speaking cultures of East Africa, 'the word for drum, *ngoma*, has been extended to include singing, dancing, hand-clapping, and ululating on social occasions' (Rice 2014: 6). Similarly, our routine assumption that music can be 'beautiful' has no obvious parallel in many indigenous cultures, for whom music's value rests instead on its 'usefulness for a specific purpose: a song may be good for curing, [or] good for dancing, etc.' (Nettl, cited in Ralls-Macleod and Harvey 2017: 11). Indeed, so closely are music and its functionality related in indigenous contexts that ethnomusicologist John Blacking grew to know what was happening in the Venda agricultural year simply by the songs that were being sung (Blacking 1973).

Furthermore, the idea of a 'musical instrument' in an organological sense is a Western notion, a cutting out of the denotative from the connotative that is so habitual we forget such a move would be nonsensical in many cultures. Thus, for example the *ngombi* harp, once consecrated within the Bwiti religion in Gabon, becomes the mouthpiece of the Sister of God, *Nyingwang Mebege* (DeVale 1988). As *Nyingwang Mebege* rules the night, the consecrated *ngombi* can only be played during the hours of darkness, and is otherwise kept in a dedicated light-proof enclosure. The *ngombi* becomes her body such that the 'tuning pegs are her ribs, and the strings are her sinews and tendons' (DeVale 1988: 151), while the resonator is her womb, and the sound holes are her breasts and birth canal. Moreover, the 'four higher-pitched strings of the *ngombi* are female, the lower four, male' (ibid.: 150), hence 'the polyrhythmic play of the two hands represent gender relations' (Maas and Strübelt 2006: 113). There is no way to separate the denotative 'harp' from the connotative webs of meaning that arise from its personhood and the context in which it is played. To do so would be to impose Western categories of thought that misread what the *ngombi* means to Bwiti initiates.

To return to Tim Ingold's point, we might say therefore that the *ngombi* is a porous, processual *thing* that exists within an ontology of animism. Ingold deploys various metaphors—things, lines, threads, processes, improvisation, gathering together, meshwork—to challenge the hegemony, as he sees it, of hylomorphism, but he does not go so far as to attribute things with personhood (Ingold 2013). Here, I do. I want to suggest that doing so not only allows for a richer understanding of the overlap of music, religion and touch, but is also warranted phenomenologically: to continue the example, Bwiti musicians don't see the *ngombi* as a thing, but very much as a person.

Personhood is the key to understanding animistic worldviews. For animists the world is full of persons, only some of whom are human (Harvey 2005, 2013a, 2013b). In animistic cultures personhood may be attributed to things that seem bizarre to modern, materialist Westerners: plants, trees, animals, rocks, buildings and indeed musical instruments. The point is not that personhood and humanity are equivalent—a rock-person behaves as a rock-person, not as an attenuated human in rock form—but rather that an animistic worldview is one of immersive and radical relationality, where correct relations must be maintained with the other-than-human-persons with whom we share the world. Thus it would be improper for the *ngombi* to see the light of day, or to be played in anything other than an all-night Bwiti ceremony. To do so would be inconsiderate.

Two ethnomusicologists who lay a path towards an animistic reading of musical instruments are Eliot Bates and Sue Carole DeVale. Bates asks the question of why some instruments (like the lyre) become so imbued with meaning, whereas others (like the tuba) do not. His answer might be surprising to an organologist: instruments are *subjects*. 'Guitars seem to have a propensity to teach their owners how to play them, gods live in or are channeled through certain instruments, and other instruments such as the Anatolian saz...mediate interpersonal disputes in communities' (Bates 2012: 364). He calls therefore for the 'study of the *social life of musical instruments*' (ibid., emphasis in original).

DeVale meanwhile draws attention to the importance of musical instruments in ritual (1988). Instruments, she argues, can participate in ritual in either a *receptive* or a *transitive* mode. 'In the receptive mode, the instrument is the focus of the ritual; that is, a ceremony or ritual procedure is performed on or for the instrument itself' (DeVale 1988: 127). An example might be an offering made to the tree which will ultimately be transformed into, say, a drum, or a prayer offered each time an instrument is played. In the transitive mode, however, the instrument 'is an active agent in ensuring the efficacy of a ritual performed' (ibid.: 127), such as the guitars and drums used to occasion trancing during American Pentecostal services (as described in Becker 2004).

If DeVale and Bates go some way to escaping the gravitational pull of hylomorphism that Ingold decries, they do not go quite as far as the attribution of personhood to instruments. Yet, this may be extremely common in other-than-modern cultures, if not the norm. Such a reading certainly offers a fruitful interpretation of the original Trossingen lyre, for while the worldview of the Dark Ages is lost beyond dim glimpses, those beautifully carved *kolrosing* images clearly situated the lyre within a complex worldview. Their meaning would have been understood by performers and audiences alike, who would have known, for instance, the implication of all those snakes. Cross-cultural comparison is suggestive: each of the strings might have represented a god or a planet or an ancestor. The instrument may have had a myth of origin or rituals to accompany its making and playing. To play it might have been to achieve balance or harmony with the fundamental forces of the cosmos; to channel inspiration from a deity; or at the very least to have exchanged praise-songs for gold. Unlike the lyre today, it probably engendered solidarity not alterity. But above all, I would suggest, it may have been regarded as alive in some sense or possessing personhood: in the Anglo-Saxon poem *Widsith*, *Scilling* might actually refer to the *hearpe*, not another scop.

So much for the past, but how might an animistic reading be helpful today? Don't we regard musical instruments in, well, a purely instrumental way? When we name the parts of a fiddle as the head, neck, belly and body, aren't we being knowingly anthropomorphic?

Though I haven't researched this formally, I can at least offer the suggestion that animistic readings of instruments remain surprisingly common, following a straw poll of my Facebook friends. Of the hundred or so comments I received, a clear majority of musicians (around 80%) affirmed that they regard their instruments as alive in some sense or as possessing personhood. While the figure is noteworthy, a high proportion of my friends are practitioners of animistically-minded alternative spiritualities—Pagans and Neo-shamans—so this probably shouldn't be taken as indicative of musicians as a whole. Likewise, some of my friends are vocal atheists and it would have been surprising if they'd replied in the affirmative. What was more interesting to me were the people who denied their instruments personhood, but nonetheless expressed emotional attachment that went beyond aesthetics or sentimentality. Some even attributed emotions to their instruments, such as saying they sulked if not played frequently enough. Nonetheless all agreed that instruments, by virtue of being extensions of the body, came alive or allowed the music to come alive. A Facebook poll is not an academic research methodology. It is rather a crude, self-selecting sounding board. However, it certainly opens up suggestive avenues of research.

As for myself, I am a card-carrying animist. Much of the thought within the new understanding of animism (see Harvey 2005, 2013a, 2013b) stems from the work of Irving Hallowell among the Ojibwe, for whom all things are forced by the necessities of grammar to be animate or inanimate. Recalling what has become an iconic encounter, Hallowell writes that '[s]ince stones are grammatically animate, I once asked an old man: Are all the stones we see about us alive? He reflected a long while then replied, "No, but *some* are."' (cited in Harvey 2005: 33). When I consider my own musical instruments I realise that the same obtains: not all of them are alive but *some* are. My Border bagpipes in G are alive, while my lower-pitched set in D are not. My mandolin is sprightly with a tricksy personality, but my twelve-string cittern is just an instrument. My lyre is certainly alive and I chose Benjamin to be my maker because his instruments quiver with vitality. I have no way of telling you what the difference is. That's just how things appear to me. I gravitate towards my instruments with personhood and neglect the others. They invite me to play.

An animistic reading, therefore, not only rejects the tendency to hylomorphism identified by Ingold but is, I suggest, very much warranted phenomenologically. If we truly want to understand religion, music and touch, then a good starting point is the realisation that for many musicians, their instruments possess personhood. I suspect, though I cannot prove, that this tendency is ancient.

A CADENCE, OF SORTS

I'm finishing writing this chapter in a café, on a sunny morning in September, and I can see through the window that outside on the tables a woman and a man are jamming on guitars. I'm itching to know what they're playing, but they're drowned out by the martial sounds of Beethoven on the café's PA. I'm hard against my deadline so I'm staying put, but now, as I'm typing this, I see that they're leaving. Like most of the music that humans have ever made, theirs too has disappeared. I shall never know what it was. I'm feeling frustrated, unresolved.

This chapter has been, if not an improvisation, then certainly an extemporisation. I've approached writing it exactly as I would playing the lyre, following the chains of thought, letting the ideas guide me. Traditionally, you'd expect me to end this with a sensible, well-rounded conclusion, a final resolving chord, but at the risk of leaving you frustrated too, I want to finish with something more open-ended and ambiguous.

For, as you've probably already noticed, in making the distinction between the denotative and connotative meanings of the lyre, I've been guilty of making exactly the kind of unhelpful analytical incisions that I decry in my animist *apologia*. Indeed, to come at the subject through the categories of 'religion', 'music' and 'touch' is to try and stitch back the parts with yet further analysis, an act that's ultimately as fruitless as dissecting an animal to find where the life is. To write about music at all is to be stuck on the wrong side of the glass, looking mournfully at the jam happening outside. I've felt that tension with every paragraph.

Musicking was ancient when the Trossingen lyricist was buried. It's so old it probably even pre-dates our obtaining language. It remains with us, in religioning and secular contexts, because it continues to do what it has always done, namely, to express the complexities of human feeling in ways that words simply cannot do. If we really want to understand religion, music and touch, in the end we have to get up from the table, step outside and join in the jam.

BIBLIOGRAPHY

Aho, Marko. 2016. *The Tangible in Music: The Tactile Learning of a Musical Instrument*. Abingdon: Ashgate. https://doi.org/10.4324/9781315527017

Aldridge, David and Jörg Fachner (eds.). 2006. *Music and Altered States: Consciousness, Transcendence, Therapy and Addictions*. London and Philadelphia: Jessica Kingsley Publishers.

Arnal, William E. 2000. 'Definition'. In Willi Braun and Russell T. McCutcheon (eds.), *Guide to the Study of Religion*, 21–35. London: Cassell.

Bates, Eliot. 2012. 'The Social Life of Musical Instruments'. *Ethnomusicology* 56 (3): 363–395. https://doi.org/10.5406/ethnomusicology.56.3.0363

Becker, Judith. 2004. *Deep Listeners: Music, Emotion and Trancing*. Bloomington and Indianapolis: Indiana University Press.

Blacking, John. 1973. *How Musical Is Man?* Seattle and London: University of Washington Press.

Blacking, John. 1987. *'A Commonsense View of all Music': Reflections on Percy Grainger's Contribution to Ethnomusicology and Music Education*. Cambridge: Cambridge University Press.

Blain, Jenny. 2001. *Nine Worlds of Seid-Magic*. London: Routledge.

Blake, Andrew. 1997. *The Land Without Music: Music, Culture and Society in Twentieth Century Britain*. Manchester: Manchester University Press.

Bloomfield, Morton W. and Charles W. Dunn. 1992. *The Role of the Poet in Early Societies*. Cambridge: D.S. Brewer.

Boenig, Robert. 1996. 'The Anglo-Saxon Harp'. *Speculum* 71 (2): 290–320. https://doi.org/10.2307/2865415

Braun, Willi. 2000. 'Religion'. In Willi Braun and Russell T. McCutcheon (eds.), *Guide to the Study of Religion*. London: Cassell.

Chase, Christopher. 2006. '"Be Pagan Once Again": Folk Music, Heritage, and Socio-sacred Networks in Contemporary American Paganism'. *The Pomegranate* 8 (2): 146–160. https://doi.org/10.1558/pome.8.2.146

Crossley, Goulbern W. 1951. 'St. Augustine's "De Musica": A Recent Synopsis'. *The Musical Times* 92 (1297): 127–129. https://doi.org/10.2307/933234

DeVale, Sue Carole. 1988. 'Musical Instruments and Ritual: A Systematic Approach'. *Journal of the American Musical Instrument Society* 14: 126–160.

Granholm, Kennet. 2011. '"Sons of Northern Darkness": Heathen Influences in Black Metal and Neofolk Music'. *Numen* 58 (4): 514–544. https://doi.org/10.1163/156852711X577069

Harvey, Graham. 2005. *Animism: Respecting the Living World*. London: Hurst & Company.

Harvey, Graham (ed.). 2013a. *The Handbook of Contemporary Animism*. Durham: Acumen. https://doi.org/10.4324/9781315728964

Harvey, Graham. 2013b. *Food, Sex and Strangers: Understanding Religion as Everyday Life*. Durham: Acumen. https://doi.org/10.4324/9781315729572

Hillberg, Julia. 2015. 'Early Lyres in Context: A Comparative Contextual Study on Early Lyres and the Identity of Their Owner/User'. Master's thesis in Archaeology, Lund University. Accessed 3 October 2018 from http://lup.lub.lu.se/luur/download?func=downloadFile&recordOId=7855733&fileOId=8893341.

Hoeschele, Marisa, Hugo Merchant, Yukiko Kikuchi, Yuko Hattori and Carel ten Cate. 2015. 'Searching for the Origins of Musicality across Species'. *Philosophical Transactions of the Royal Society* B 370: 20140094. https://doi.org/10.1098/rstb.2014.0094

Honing, Henkjan, Carel ten Cate, Isabelle Peretz and Sandra E. Trehub. 2015. 'Without It No Music: Cognition, Biology and the Evolution of Musicality'. *Philosophical Transactions of the Royal Society* B 370: 20140088. https://doi.org/10.1098/rstb.2014.0088

Huron, David. 2015. 'Affect Induction through Musical Sounds: An Ethological Perspective'. *Philosophical Transactions of the Royal Society* B 370: 20140098. https://doi.org/10.1098/rstb.2014.0098

Ingold, Tim. 2013. 'Being Alive to a World without Objects'. In Graham Harvey (ed.), *The Handbook of Contemporary Animism*, 213–225. Durham: Acumen.

Kaelen, Mendel, Bruna Giribaldi, Jordan Raine, Lisa Evans, Christopher Timmerman, Natalie Rodriguez, Leor Roseman, Amanda Feilding, David Nutt and Robin Carhart-Harris. 2017. 'The Hidden Therapist: Evidence for a Central Role of Music in Psychedelic Therapy'. *Psychopharmacology* 235 (2): 505–519. https://doi.org/10.1007/s00213-017-4820-5

Koelsch, Stefan. 2014. 'Brain Correlates of Music: Evoked Emotions'. *Nature Reviews Neuroscience* 15: 170–180. https://doi.org/10.1038/nrn3666

Laack, Isabel. 2015. 'Sound, Music and Religion: A Preliminary Cartography of a Transdisciplinary Field'. *Method and Theory in the Study of Religion* 27: 220–246. https://doi.org/10.1163/15700682-12341339

Lehrich, Christopher I. 2014. ,The Unanswered Question: Music and Theory of Religion'. *Method and Theory in the Study of Religion* 26: 22–43.
https://doi.org/10.1163/15700682-12341266

Letcher, Andy. 2001. 'The Role of the Bard in Contemporary Pagan Movements'. PhD thesis, King Alfred's College, Winchester.

Letcher, Andy. 2006. *Shroom: A Cultural History of the Magic Mushroom*. London: Faber and Faber.

Letcher, Andy. 2007. 'Mad Thoughts on Mushrooms: Discourse and Power in the Study of Psychedelic Consciousness'. *Anthropology of Consciousness* 18 (2): 74–97.
https://doi.org/10.1525/ac.2007.18.2.74

Letcher, Andy. 2013. 'Deceptive Cadences: A Hermeneutic Approach to the Problem of Meaning and Psychedelic Experience'. In Anna Waldstein (ed.), *Breaking Convention: Proceedings of the Interdisciplinary Conference at the University of Kent, Canterbury 2011*. London: Strange Attractor.

Maas, Uwe, and Suster Strübelt. 2006. 'Polyrhythms Supporting a Pharmacotherapy: Music in the Iboga Initiation Ceremony in Gabon'. In David Aldridge and Jörg Fachner (eds.), *Music and Altered States: Consciousness, Transcendence, Therapy and Addictions*, 101–124. London and Philadelphia: Jessica Kingsley Publishers.

Matsunobu, Koji. 2011. 'Spirituality as a Universal Experience of Music: A Case Study of North Americans' Approaches to Japanese Music'. *Journal of Research in Music Education* 59 (3): 273–289. https://doi.org/10.1177/0022429411414911

McCutcheon, Russell T. 1997. *Manufacturing Religion: The Discourse on Sui Generis Religion and the Politics of Nostalgia*. Oxford: Oxford University Press.

Morrison, Steven J. and Steven M. Demorest. 2009. 'Cultural Constraints on Music Perception and Cognition'. *Progress in Brain Research* 178: 67–77.
https://doi.org/10.1016/S0079-6123(09)17805-6

Neitz, Mary Jo and James V. Spickard. 1990. 'Steps towards a Sociology of Religious Experience: The Theories of Mihaly Csikzentmihaly and Alfred Schutz'. *Sociological Analysis* 51 (1): 15–33. https://doi.org/10.2307/3711338

Nietzsche, Friedrich. 2004 [1889]. *Twilight of the Idols and The Antichrist*. London: Dover Publications Inc.

Niles, John D. 2003. 'The Myth of the Anglo-Saxon Oral Poet'. *Western Folklore* 62 (1/2): 7–61.

Page, Christopher. 1981. 'Anglo-Saxon Hearpan: Their Terminology, Technique, Tuning and Repertory of Verse 850–1066'. PhD thesis, University of York. Accessed 3 October 2018 from http://etheses.whiterose.ac.uk/13998/1/258618.pdf

Partridge, Christopher. 2013. *The Lyre of Orpheus: Popular Music, the Sacred and the Profane*. Oxford: Oxford University Press.
https://doi.org/10.1093/acprof:oso/9780199751396.001.0001

Power, David, Mary Collins and Mellonee Burnim. 1984. *Music and the Experience of God*. Edinburgh: Concilium.

Racy, Ali Jihad. 2006. 'In the Path of the Lyre: The Tanburah of the Gulf Region'. *Musiké* 2: 97–122.

Ralls-Macleod, Karen and Graham Harvey. 2017. *Indigenous Religious Musics*. Ashgate: Routledge.

Rice, Timothy. 2014. *Ethnomusicology: A Very Short Introduction*. Oxford: Oxford University Press. https://doi.org/10.1093/actrade/9780199794379.001.0001

Rouget, Gilbert. 1985. *Music and Trance. A Theory of the Relations Between Music and Possession*. Translated by Brunhilde Biebuyck. Chicago: University of Chicago Press.

Rountree, Kathryn, ed. 2018. *Contemporary Pagan and Native Faith Movements in Europe: Colonialist and Nationalist Impulses*. New York and Oxford: Berghahn.

Russell, Bertrand. 2004 [1946]. *History of Western Philosophy*. London: Routledge. https://doi.org/10.4324/9780203487976

Shanon, Benny. 2011. 'Music and Ayahuasca'. In David Clarke and Eric Clarke (eds.), *Music and Consciousness: Philosophical, Psychological, and Cultural Perspectives*, 281–294. Oxford: Oxford University Press.
https://doi.org/10.1093/acprof:oso/9780199553792.003.0077

Snowdon, Charles T., Elke Zimmermann and Eckart Altenmüller. 2015. 'Music, Evolution and Neuroscience'. *Progress in Brain Research* 217: 17–34.
https://doi.org/10.1016/bs.pbr.2014.11.019

Trehub, Sandra, Judith Becker and Iain Morley. 2015. 'Cross-cultural Perspectives on Music and Musicality'. *Philosophical Transactions of the Royal Society* B 370: 20140096. https://doi.org/10.1098/rstb.2014.0096

Wachsmann, Klaus, Bo Lawergren, Ulrich Wegner and John Clark. 2001. 'Lyre'. *Grove Music Online*. Accessed from https://doi.org/10.1093/gmo/9781561592630.article.50534

Wallis, Robert 2003. *Shamans/Neo-shamans: Ecstasies, Alternative Archaeologies and Contemporary Pagans*. London: Routledge. https://doi.org/10.4324/9780203417577

Weston, Donna, and Andy Bennett, eds. 2013. *Pop Pagans: Paganism and Popular Music*. Durham: Acumen. https://doi.org/10.4324/9781315729688

Wroe, Anne. 2011. *Orpheus. The Song of Life*. London: Jonathan Cape.

Andy Letcher, PhD, is a Senior Lecturer at Schumacher College (UK) where he leads the MA Engaged Ecology. He is the author of *Shroom: A Cultural History of the Magic Mushroom* (Faber and Faber, 2006) and has written papers on subjects as diverse as psychedelic experience, fairies, the spirituality of environmental protest movements and kinship in a world of animism. He is a folk musician who plays English bagpipes, low whistle and Dark Age lyre.

Chapter 5

Being There: Anglo-Indian Roots Tourism Experiences

ROBYN ANDREWS

In earlier research with Anglo-Indians in New Zealand I learnt of a number of second- and third-generation Anglo-Indians who have travelled to India, or are planning to, in order to investigate their family roots in situ. With the increased popularity of genealogical tracing through DNA analysis and the availability of technologically-enhanced archival searches of recently archived material, family history information is more accessible than ever before. Television series such as *Who Do You Think You Are?* reach vast audiences and possibly add to the popularity of this type of tourism. It is this phenomenon that my research, and this chapter, seeks to explore, drawing on the experiences of Anglo-Indians or their descendants[1] returning to India specifically to investigate their family roots. A significant theme explored here is the intense emotional reaction of those involved, when encountering significant objects and places linked to their ancestors. What began, from necessity, with technologically mediated virtual searches from afar, culminated with encounters with the material reality of their ancestors, including being able to touch—both with their hands, and their corporality—objects previously touched by those ancestors. This was the highlight for many. A number of aspects of their experiences resembled pilgrimage journeys—in that there was a preparatory build-up to the trip, there were visits to specific locations such as churches (as sites of significant historical moments, and keepers of heritage objects) and the descriptions of journeys included notions about their 'sacredness'. A result

---

1 I refer to both Anglo-Indians (as defined further in this chapter) and their descendants as Anglo-Indians from now on.

of this experience was that returnees seek to distinguish themselves from tourists by drawing on a personal claim based on physical and emotional connectivity with the places they visited, thereby distancing themselves from tourists who visit the sites without such connection or claims. This was demonstrated in the way they described their journeys with terminology other than 'roots tourism', calling on terms such as 'family pilgrimage' or 'ancestral quest' instead.

In this chapter, in order to explore the significance of Anglo-Indian returnees' physical proximity (including touch) to sites significant to their ancestors, I employ Walter Benjamin's (1968) work which has been used to understand objects and their aura, as well as the idea of authenticity, from the perspective of disciplines from critical museum and heritage studies (for example, Schwabsky 2017; Naumova 2015) to anthropology (for example, Das 2014). The empirical materials I draw on are descriptions of experiences that either I was directly privy to, or were recounted to me or made available through another medium such as social media. I begin, though, by looking briefly at literature on the phenomenon of roots tourism, before turning to scholarship relating to the aura of objects, the significance of touch and of sharing spaces through epochs.

ROOTS TOURISM

There are a number of researchers writing about the phenomenon of roots tourism, collecting accounts, for example, of second-generation Nigerians from the US and Canada returning to Nigeria (Clarke 2006). A significant scholar in this area is Paul Basu who writes of descendants of Scottish immigrants returning from Commonwealth countries to Scotland (2001, 2004a, 2005) and also, in alignment with findings of this chapter, about this phenomenon being a form of pilgrimage (Basu 2004b). He has this to say about the phenomenon of genealogical tourism:

> Since the publication of Alex Haley's seminal family saga, Roots (1976), genealogical research has become an almost global pastime and, aided by the internet and relatively cheap air travel, genealogy-related tourism has become an important revenue-earner for numerous 'old countries' throughout the world. (Basu 2005: 153–154)

He adds that he concurs with David Lowenthal in observing that diasporas (or members of diasporas) 'are notably heritage hungry...' (Basu 2005: 154) and that there is quite a lot of work being carried out exploring the experience of descendants revisiting their 'old countries', by which Basu means the old colonising European countries. There is little substantial scholarship, however, on areas such as India, except on the practice of regular visits to family still residing in India.

Basu also argues that the term 'roots tourism' is often rejected by those on ancestral quests returning to the country of a forebear's origin. Based on my participants' responses I would concur: while it may be a useful phrase to encapsulate the general idea of travelling to places in pursuit of connecting spatially with one's roots, it does not do justice to the experience. As Basu says:

> ...many participants in these journeys [...] are keen to distance themselves from what they perceive as the superficial consumerism of tourism [...]. 'I am not, and never will be a tourist in Scotland', asserts an informant from Canada. 'To me it was a pilgrimage, a searching for roots', recalls a New Zealander of her journey. (2004: 154)

Also picking up this theme of naming the quest for roots are Blunt, Bonnerjee and Hysler-Rubin (2012) who include a discussion of ancestral quests by first- and second-generation Anglo-Indians, the community I define shortly, in their article 'Diasporic Returns to the City: Anglo-Indian and Jewish visits to Calcutta'. Their focus is Anglo-Indians' connection to the city as 'home', 'both in terms of genealogical "roots" and the material spaces of urban dwelling, which span the domestic home and urban neighbourhood as well as the wider city' (Blunt, Bonnerjee and Hysler-Rubin 2012: 31). They comment that while some Anglo-Indians go back to the city for a holiday, other first-generation Anglo-Indians are reticent about seeing what India is like now. They would rather keep their memories intact. Yet others go *because* of their memories, with one interviewee commenting: 'when we go back to Calcutta it's not like we go back as tourists...we go back for the memories' (ibid.). Blunt and Bonnerjee also write about the calendrical timing of returns; for example, one-time returns to re-experience a Calcutta Christmas (Blunt and Bonnerjee 2013: 231). Some who have brought their children back note that the children are interested to see homes their parents had lived in, and schools they had attended. This resonates with my findings too, as the children of first-generation returnees indicated that they would particularly like to go back to India with their parents—both in order that their parents could show them around and because they felt it would be a good opportunity for their parents to revisit.

THE SENSORY: TOUCHING THE PAST

The empirical data I collected pointed to the significance of touch and touching as a way of reconnecting with or claiming an object that one is already related to through personal history. I argue that there is a sense of specific objects being imbued with essence or significance, or aura in Walter Benjamin's (1968) sense, which is only accessible through proximity to the objects. While Benjamin wrote primarily of objects of art, the same sense that objects are more than just the atoms they comprise is at the heart of the idea I explore here.

In writing of art pieces and their reproductions, Benjamin discusses what is worth more, the original or its reproductions (Schwabsky 2017: 93). I propose that this idea, and the different arguments made for each viewpoint, may be applied to the relationship between the original historical record, or place, or artefact (for example, a tombstone) and its archived digital reproduction, whether photographed or reproduced in some other way.

Rickly-Boyd gives one of the clearest discussions of Benjamin's sense of objects of art, including his position on aura and authenticity, in her article, 'Authenticity and Aura: A Benjamin Approach to Tourism' (2012). It is based on Benjamin's essay 'The Work of Art in the Age of Mechanical Reproduction' (1968). I quote her at length:

> Benjamin states that 'the presence of the original is the prerequisite to the concept of authenticity' [...]. However, he also suggests a more complex understanding of authenticity as tied to tradition and ritual—'The authenticity of a thing is the quintessence of all that is transmissible in it from its origins on, ranging from its physical duration to the historical testimony relating to it' [...]. Furthermore, aura, 'the unique value of the "authentic" work of art always has its basis in ritual', argues Benjamin, [...]. 'Aura' is an experience, an engagement, defined as a 'strange tissue of space and time: the unique apparition of a distance, however near it may be' [...]. The desire to get in touch with this uniqueness, to engage more closely with aura, is the catalyst for reproduction; ironically however, it is the aura, and therefore authenticity, which deteriorates with mechanical reproduction, as it, 'detaches the reproduced object from the sphere of tradition' [...]. (Rickly-Boyd 2012: 270)

Benjamin does not argue that the reproductions do not have value, but that it is the value of the *original* which makes reproductions so desirable. He does argue, unsurprisingly, that reproductions do not have the aura or authenticity of the original. This would explain why people still go in pursuit of observing particular original objects: for example, going to the Louvre to see the original painting of the Mona Lisa, visiting museums, and travelling generally to see the sights and places firsthand (notwithstanding the attempt in Las Vegas to reproduce iconic buildings from around the world). In the same way, I argue that 'roots tourism' journeys are embarked upon because those journeying desire to see and be in the presence of objects and places of ancestral significance to them, though there may be records and reproductions they could view digitally from afar.

Taking Benjamin's idea of an object's aura further is anthropologist Veena Das who writes about the relationship between aura and storytelling, whereby the stories people tell of an object belong to, and add to, its aura. She writes about 'the interpenetration' she observed in 'people's discussion of persons and things specific to the lifeworld from which they emanate' (Das 2014: 292–293), and that the stories she heard told about particular 'things', such as 'a tile with the picture of a god placed on a rock at the corner of two roads' (2014: 293) or even objects such as a transformer or a tube-well, added to the aura of the object. Commodities, therefore, that are valued and used, or retained, rather than becoming quickly obsolete, build up aura. In a similar manner, anthropologist Brian Spooner, contributing to Arjun Appadurai's *The Social Life of Things*,[2] draws on Benjamin's work to say that age, and especially antiquity, bestows aura on objects such as the 'oriental' carpets his work focused on (Spooner 1986: 220).

To tease out the significance of embodying certain shared spaces, or places, I draw on Alevtina Naumova's (2015) work on the 'lived experiences of heritage in living history museums' (as she subtitles her article). She discusses visitors to Toronto's Mackenzie House Museum's living history spaces, which are set up for visitors to 'feel' through their bodies the 'object-person transactions', what it would have been like to be in such rooms or homes, historically. She drew the following conclusion from watching visitors engaging with the materiality of the space they visited:

...touching moves the past into the domain of immediacy, translating stories of the seemingly remote and inaccessible past into a lived and, at times, highly intimate experience of the present. Touching, then, becomes a form

---

2 Appadurai (1986: 6) seemed to be getting at this same idea when he wrote of the Trobriand Islanders' Kula ring system of exchange, and the significance of certain objects to (and because of) those who had possessed them earlier. That is, commodities have social lives.

of interaction with people who used these objects before, a form of time travel. (Naumova 2015: 3)

Of course, in such museums, as Naumova writes, the 'spaces' and situations have been deliberately set up in order for visitors to engage with them, so 'the interaction between the imagination and the material world' (2015: 2) can take place. Though, in contrast, Anglo-Indian returnees visit the actual spaces of significance to their ancestors, these places provide a similar opportunity for this type of phenomenological engagement. When they are inside a building, or in other spaces of significance to their ancestors, they have the opportunity for a realistic, fully embodied, sense of what it would have been like for their ancestors to have been there.

ANGLO-INDIANS

Turning now to the returnees I write of: Anglo-Indians are a minority community of mixed Indian and European descent. The community originated as a result of various European groups making their home in India from the very late fifteenth century onwards. From the liaisons that ensued, a culturally distinct minority community was established in India. They are defined in Section 366(2) of the Indian Constitution which states that:

> An Anglo-Indian means a person whose father or any of whose other male progenitors in the male line is or was of European descent but who is domiciled within the territory of India and is or was born within such territory of parents habitually resident therein and not established there for temporary purposes only.

Socially and culturally Anglo-Indians are habitually more 'Western' than 'Indian' in their practices and worldviews. For example, they are Christians, mostly have English as their mother tongue and European names. Another characteristic attributed to Anglo-Indians in India is a 'culture of emigration', as British anthropologist Lionel Caplan termed it (Caplan 1995, 2001). This is based in large part on the fact that more than half of the population left India after the country gained its independence from Britain in 1947.[3] Those who left, and are still leaving, mostly do so because they felt or feel insecure about what a future in India offers themselves and their

---

3 It is not possible to know population numbers with any certainty as Anglo-Indians have not been enumerated separately in the national ten-yearly census since 1951.

children, for example, in terms of maintaining their lifestyles and cultural practices, obtaining meaningful employment, and finding socio-culturally suitable marriage partners. Many of the early migrants were afraid of negative repercussions after centuries of aligning themselves with the British during the time of the Raj. Mostly, then, their migration was driven by a complex combination of economic, political and cultural insecurity. They typically migrated to English-speaking Commonwealth countries, with Britain, Canada, Australia and even New Zealand being the most popular. Given that they have been leaving en masse from the 1940s, and some well before then, there are now second- and third-generation Anglo-Indians in those countries. And a number of them are very interested in the land and history of their parents, grandparents or great-grandparents.

INVESTIGATING ANGLO-INDIAN RETURNS

In earlier research with the community in New Zealand, as part of a qualitative survey interview to ascertain their experiences of identity, I asked participants if they had ever visited India (or returned, for those who were first-generation migrants). I came to understand that there were a number of Anglo-Indians of the second and subsequent generations who had been to India, or who were planning to visit. A number also made it clear that they are keen to experience this country that they have an intriguing, and often proud, familial connection to.

I learned from the earlier research that the focus for return visits from second- and third-generation descendants was to locate church records of births (or more commonly baptisms, being more likely to be recorded), marriages and deaths, and to visit cemeteries to locate graves and 'pay their respects' to their deceased relatives. They also said they were interested in searching for the homes relatives had lived in, and other geographical sites significant to their family's past, for example, schools and parish churches. For the current research I was especially interested in what returnees seek or sought (to do, and to find), how they found their experience of going back and what it means or meant to them.

The research comprised three main methods of empirical data collection: participant-observation, interviews and social media posts. The first, participant-observation, involved accompanying people on their genealogical journey, taking part in day-to-day events with them. As I accompanied Anglo-Indians on their journeys, I collected accounts of their experiences besides interviewing them before, during and after their travels. I write in detail about one of these return journey experiences later in this chapter. The second source of material was informal focused interviews with returnees whom I did not accompany on their journey. I interviewed them about their plans and expectations as they prepared to go, and again after they returned, about their experiences and reflections. The third data source, one I had not initially anticipated using, were various social media sites. Returnees used these for their own record, and to keep friends and family informed of their progress, often on a day-to-day basis. I sought and received permission to draw from these sites, changing identifying details when I did so. The immediacy of the postings, both on blog sites and Facebook platforms added significantly to the sense of following their journey. In many cases the emotions of the day are recorded in rich and affecting detail.

QUEST MOTIVATIONS

Looking now at some of the findings, I begin with the way participants who had very recently returned to New Zealand from India described what it is they were doing, or proposing to do, in returning to India. My question, which elicited the responses below, was 'How do you describe the journey to others?'

> An exploration of family history, mainly through the church where my family used to worship in Delhi. (second-generation man, early thirties, NZ-born)

> It's all about family really: reconnecting with my cousin who I haven't seen since we were both children, and finding out more about family from the past through records in churches over here. I want to add to my family tree that I've been constructing since the 1980s. (second-generation woman, mid-fifties, UK-born)

This woman continued, explaining that she had managed to get 'so far' with her genealogical research but some details were alluding her, and she hoped to be able to fill some gaps by looking at records in churches in Kolkata, where her family was from. The details she talked about wanting to find included the names of godparents at baptisms, and the residential address of the parents. Another person I spoke to said:

When people ask me why I am going to Kolkata I say 'Ancestral Pilgrimage' because I am very clear about my purpose. Roots Tourism[4] is the same thing and I have had many friends at this stage of life who mention wanting to do the same. (fourth-generation woman, early sixties, NZ-born)

One of the families whose journey I followed set up a blog titled 'Discovering our ancestors: A journey to India'. They described it to me as their 'family roots tour' of India. They travelled extensively from the south to west to north, following a long and varied family history in India. As they said, 'We have two hundred years from Shimla to South India to cover.'

ONE RETURN JOURNEY

In this section I present a case study, or detailed example, which I have selected as it exemplifies so many aspects of what others talked to me about. It follows the journey of two sisters from New Zealand whose great-grandparents (Frederica and Robert Hay) met and married in Calcutta (now Kolkata), in St Paul's Anglican Cathedral in 1869. Later that same year the newly married couple migrated to New Zealand where they began their family.[5] The two sisters, one in her late fifties and the other in her early sixties, who have cousins of similar ages, had carried out a lot of research before I met them. Until then they had used digital archives such as geni.com and ancestry.com, as well as physical archives: the early settler's museum in Otago and the British India Office in London. They had been able to reconstruct considerable portions of the story of the lives of their great-grandparent couple, but learnt almost nothing about the bride's mother, or her family. I knew that what they really hoped would emerge from the trip was information about this great-great-grandmother—Frederica's mother, whose name on Frederica's wedding record is written as 'Emuan'.

Some months before we met in Kolkata I had put them in touch with an archivist to try to find more material before they arrived.[6] When they were preparing for the trip I had stressed that we might not uncover any further information. They understood this but said it would be enough to walk

---

4 While this research participant did use the words roots tourism, it was almost certainly because she had just read my information sheet, and my project description used this term.
5 For more details see Andrews (2018).
6 The archivist had not been successful when we met her in Calcutta.

where their great-grandmother had walked, and see some of what she had seen. Which is what they did.

Some months before we left for India they had invited me to be a Facebook 'friend'. I noted that one of the sisters changed her profile photo and the background photo as she prepared to journey back to India. The background was an iconic image of the Taj Mahal, and the profile photo was of her great-grandmother, Frederica.

On the first day in Kolkata, a Monday in December 2018, we met up and planned the details of our week together, guided by what they wanted to see and do, and augmented by what I thought I might be able to assist them with through my contacts.[7] We began that day with the most obvious starting point, the cathedral where their great-grandparents were married, and its archives where the marriage records were held. Below is the Facebook post made by one sister the evening after our visit.

> *Quite an emotional morning as we arrived at St Paul's Cathedral in Kolkata. We walked down the aisle of the Church our Indian Great Grandmother got married in before travelling to NZ in 1869. After all these decades and generations the past and the present aligned as we walked her footsteps. I read a prayer for the departed sitting quietly in a pew. We, my cousins as well, felt some urgency to do the research now before the knowledge is lost. It was our mothers who knew her and told us about her. Interestingly the second purposeful task today was seeing if we could get access to some highly secured non-public archives which has proved most difficult even with a local archivist on the ground here in Kolkata. We met with [the Bishop], told our story and we now have full access thanks to Dr Robyn Andrews, the Social Anthropologist who set it up and is here with us. I certainly felt we had some divine assistance in this.*

I made two observations that day which are not recorded above. One of the sisters wore Frederica's silver ankle bracelets, which had been joined together, repurposed as a necklace. It was important for her to bring back, and to be wearing, and so to be physically in touch with, these links to her past. She also wore an 'Indian' ethnic top she had purchased in the local market the day beforehand.

The other observation was of our shared response to the prohibition of taking photographs within the interior of the cathedral. Rather than accept this rule we sought 'special permission' for photographs of the sisters near the front of the church, close to where their great grandparents married. The argument we deployed in seeking permission was that they had travelled from so far away and they had family connections with the

---

7 Since 2000 I have been a regular visitor to Calcutta and have built up a network of contacts, both through academic interests and friendships.

space.⁸ It was granted, as long as we took only a couple of photos and were discreet about it (**Figure 5.1**). The sisters expressed gratitude that others also recognised the significant moment of connection with their past.

Figure 5.1 Two sisters in Saint Paul's Anglican Cathedral in Calcutta, standing on the same spot their great-grandparents had stood when they married.

8 In *At Home in the World*, Michael Jackson (1995) also writes of this when he describes Australian aboriginals' sense of belonging and connection with a particular piece of land, and their sense of entitlement and rights to be there, due to their relationship to the space and place.

We had planned that day to also visit the cathedral's archives to view the marriage registry, but the office was closed on Mondays. Instead, we made our way through the busy midday traffic to Bishop House, where the Bishop's office was located, across the road from the cathedral. From earlier research, the sisters had learned that their Anglo-Indian great-grandmother was the daughter of Frederik Hay, a Lieutenant Colonel in the British Army, based in West Bengal's Fort William when his daughter was born. As I have indicated, the sisters had not managed to find out anything more about her family, so were hoping there would be records of her parents' marriage, and of the birth of Frederica. I had learned earlier that the records from Fort William's now deconsecrated church were stored by the Church of North India (CNI), at Bishop House. We requested an interview with the Bishop for access to these records, if not for us then for the archivist. The Bishop generously saw us that very afternoon, and gave permission for the archivist to access the documents which were in storage right above the room in which we met. As the Facebook post indicates, the sisters were delighted to be granted permission for the archivist to look through the record books for them. In India, as in other places no doubt, making a request in person carries import that mail, electronic or otherwise, or even a phone call, fails to convey.

The next day we visited West Bengal's State Archives, as this was where the young archivist who was looking for more family information was based. While there we were told, just as a matter of interest, that the old Fort William Church, or Chapel, is now used as the Fort's Library. It is likely that the sisters have family connections to that church, in that significant events probably took place while Frederica's father was stationed there. This information about the church now being the library became useful a few days later.[9]

The third day saw us back at the cathedral, and this time we were able to view the marriage registers. Again, the sisters wore carefully selected clothing and jewellery, with the other sister wearing a gold locket that had belonged to Frederica. They had knowledge of the details held in these records, but until then had not seen the record book. Their excitement at seeing the names written so long ago was tangible and I offered to take as many photos as they wanted, and that the officers on duty permitted (**Figure 5.2**).

> 9 Since this visit in December the archivist has begun looking through the archival records, and so far, in an index book, has found evidence that Frederica was baptised in the 'Old Church Calcutta'. So not in the Fort, and not in Agra, as ancestry.com has it recorded. She is currently continuing her search.

Figure 5.2 The sisters trace their fingers along the lines in the register recording the marriage of their great-grandparents.

On the fourth day we visited local attractions, all of which had existed when the sisters' forebears lived in the city. Also on that day they attended a wedding of Indian friends of theirs who now reside in New Zealand.

Our final day together was a Friday. One of the sisters documented what occurred in her Facebook post that evening:

On our last day in Kolkata the unbelievable happened that I am going to try my best to explain. We had been told by many that we would most likely not gain access to Fort William where our Great Grandmother was born and where our Gt Gt Grandfather was a Lt Colonel in the British Army in the 1840s so we didn't try to set this up prior to arriving other than having a letter of introduction from the NZ Indian Consulate. So in true kiwi fashion we rocked up to one gate where they offered us tea while they asked higher ranking permission on our behalf. Then we got redirected to another gate and as luck would have it within 2 minutes the very personable 3 Star General arrived. We were escorted into headquarters reception, waited 20 mins till sign-off was given. We were then escorted into the secure compound. Unbelievable experience, totally awe inspiring. We were unable to take photos other than these few. The Indian Army were so kind and helpful I felt like hugging the officers that made this possible.

To gain access we had needed to request access to a specific part of the Fort. It is a national security area and we could not wander around, even with an escort. Grateful for the information from the State archivists, we requested access to the Fort's library, the old chapel at the time Frederica and her parents were there. That is where we were taken by an armed guard, only after handing in our phones and cameras, and still encountering strict security at a number of checkpoints. Once in the library we were free to move around, look at the beautiful preserved ceiling and windows, and at a plaque that may well have been commemorating the activities of Frederick Hay's regiment.

On the way back in a taxi from the Fort, one sister asked me if I believed in divine intervention. She made it clear that she did, and that she felt they had been 'looked after' while on their journey to Kolkata. This was their last day and both sisters said the week-long trip had exceeded all expectations. They added that it had been an emotional journey too. One posted this after arriving back in New Zealand:

It has certainly been a sacred journey. It feels a bit like we have reclaimed and honoured her [Frederica] and our mothers. When I was told about her as a seven-year-old, in the same breath I was told 'do not tell anyone'. It has taken a few generations to heal this!

One of the sisters emphasised again in the follow-up interview that 'It was the most important overseas trip I've done, because it had such a deep sense of purpose to it.' The other sister affirmed that this applied to her also. These are very well-travelled people who have taken several travel adventures, from Nepal to Italy to days of isolated kayaking in American rivers.

Even though their original purpose was to retrieve more genealogical information, and this did not eventuate, they still felt the journey was enormously significant. They seemed surprised by the source of the journey's most significant impact, that of just being there, as described in the interview excerpted here.

> '...there's one level of knowing the information, but there's a whole new level in being there, and retracing those steps, and being in the presence of places where your ancestors have been. And that was the real feeling of the pilgrimage part, that your ancestors stood in that place. And so it made that information real. And it felt real, really. There was a head-heart connection, a cellular connection to that place, and I had had no expectations around that. Even though we were going to the church that she married in. Until we walked down the aisle and things just....'

RA: *Then that struck you.*

> 'Yeah, that was the meeting of the past and the present and that was a big impact.'

This is just one story but others I have collected are also very positive, as long as a number of factors have been thought through, as suggested by research participants and written about elsewhere.[10]

DISCUSSION

Past and Present Aligning

The sense of the 'past and present aligning' as expressed above and earlier in a Facebook post, is the same notion Naumova (2015) describes after watching visitors engaging with the materiality of the space they visited in the living museums. In the section titled 'Touching the past with one's body', as I have quoted earlier, she notes that: '...touching moves the past into the domain of immediacy, translating stories of the seemingly remote and inaccessible past into a lived and, at times, highly intimate experience of the present. Touching, then, becomes a form of interaction with people who used these objects before, a form of time travel' (Naumova 2015: 3). In the case of the sisters this sense was generated through being in the places and spaces that had been so significant to their forebears. The 'objects'

---

10 I discuss these more pragmatic issues in an article currently under review.

were the spaces and places themselves, as well as the registers, as I discuss further along.

Other reflections about returnee experience of the past and present aligning, felt through their bodies being in particular spaces, included those from the adult daughter of a New Zealand family. In early 2019 she travelled extensively in India with her mother and brother to verify and add information to their already comprehensive set of records, and to just 'be' in some significant places. She reports in their family blog:

When we stepped into the graveyard the atmosphere shifted and the stillness suddenly felt permeated with history. Due to a completely by chance but exciting find back in Mumbai, in a death records book at St. Thomas' Cathedral, we had verified for certain that [her great-great-great-grandfather] had been buried in [named town]. He could only be somewhere in the very graveyard we were standing in!

Unfortunately, the graves were badly dilapidated and the various engravings that still existed were barely legible. [His] grave would now be 164 years old and the likelihood of finding an intact headstone was very low.

Knowing [he] was there in that graveyard and actually to be standing on that random patch of earth [...] (that we had studied so closely on Google Earth) was a surreal feeling! I am glad we made the trip into the unknown.

Touch is a two-way relationship, which in the case of visiting graves, can be initiated by the living just by being there, and by certain actions, as described here:

We placed a small ring of marigolds on the remains of the headstone (that looked to be a simple cross) and said the Lord's Prayer together.

The mother's comment near the end of the family blog was redolent with imagery conveying a sense of physical proximity, of whole of body touch:

After 5 days of walking in the footsteps of our great Indian ancestor, [...], we had experienced many glimpses of the man and his life and felt that we had got a little closer to the father of [her grandfather], the common ancestor of all of us in NZ, and the ancestor we share with his only other living descendants, the [named] family, in France.

Another young man in his early thirties, whose grandmother had migrated to New Zealand, was on his second journey to India to try to find out more about his ancestors. He was very aware that at times he had been sharing physical space with his ancestors, telling me, in an interview:

> 'What was on my mind really, was when we were going through the old parts of Delhi, I was thinking, "my ancestors would have been on these roads going to church on Sundays". But they would be going on a rickshaw, or horse and cart, [that is] a *tonga*. And there would have been less buildings, there would have been no paved road, but this is the route that they would have taken. So, I was thinking that this was exactly the same route my ancestors, seeing the Red Fort, everyday when they went to church. That was going through my mind.'

> RA: *How did that feel?*

> 'That was very surreal. Very surreal. 'Cause again, it was a hot dusty Delhi day, and I was just imagining nineteenth-century Delhi, 1870s. Only twenty years after the mutiny.'

Touching the Past

Another participant, in India at a similar time, described the moment and impact of seeing and being able to handle church record books in this way: 'The highlight for me was to see the writing, the signatures, of these people who are related to you. To hold the books, and the very paper that they held.' Benjamin's idea of an object possessing an aura explains the response such an original authentic object generates in someone for whom it is historically and genealogically significant.

While handling such old and significant material objects can feel like touching a sacred object, the very materiality of it can also offer challenges. The photo in **Figure 5.3**, provided by another returning participant, is of record books from a church in Northeast India. The participant was given access to this pile of record books in various states of repair, and disrepair, by the minister at the church she visited. They had worn gloves to handle the books' fragile paper and spines, and masks to lessen their reaction to allergens they were stirring up. This person told me that she had managed to get some work done with the record books before being denied access by a church caretaker. She did not manage to re-contact the minister who had granted her access and so was unable to continue her search for extra information about her family in her remaining time in the city. She was sure she had been tantalisingly close to retrieving more information from the records, so this was recalled as a frustrating experience.

Anglo-Indian Roots Tourism Experiences 131

Figure 5.3 Record books of a church in Northeast India.

CONCLUSIONS

What transpired to be most significant to the returnees about these journeys is to see the things their ancestors had seen, to walk where they had walked and to hold what they had held: to be able to be physically in touch with, and feel that connection to, their ancestors through objects and spaces. While they were interested in finding more information about their forebears, to add to what they had gathered through virtual searches, it was 'being there' in the presence of an object or space that was incomparable. The idea of significant objects possessing an aura recognised (perhaps subconsciously) by those who are related to it through their forebears makes sense of this. Being able to touch those aura-endowed objects with one's hands in the case of, for example, record books, or the whole of the body in spaces such as churches, became the unanticipated highlight for those I spoke with. It aligns too with Benjamin's (1968) idea of the value of reproductions in comparison to the originals. But in the case of objects and spaces of genealogical significance it was even more than just recognition of the value and aura. The mingling of the present and past, of people who are genetically, corporally, linked to others who once had a connection with the same objects, was also achieved through touching and being touched, through tactile connection between their forebears from the past and themselves in the present. Drawing on Naumova's (2015) idea, which highlights the temporal dimension, adds a further layer of understanding the significance to those who are able to experience touching such objects and spaces.

It is not surprising, then, that just as Paul Basu (2004b) says his informants on similar genealogical quests did not take kindly to being referred to as tourists, neither did those I spoke to. One of the sisters I travelled to Kolkata with wrote the following in a Facebook discussion about this very issue:

> *If a tourist is someone who is travelling or visiting a place for pleasure then it does not quite fit, it goes much much deeper and is much more purposeful. Well that is how it played out for [us]. On the surface 'Roots Tourism' fits in the beginning as motivation for travel but the experience is much more profound in my personal experience. The closer it got to traveling the greater the purpose and reality of it emerged. So, in a way Roots Tourism morphs into Ancestral Pilgrimage. A longing to reconnect and honour ancestors. The trip became a place where the past and present reconnected...*

They reconnected in a tactile and material way, in a way that 'information' about links between ancestors and themselves did no justice to. Being in the presence of objects and in the spaces, and bringing particular objects, such as jewellery, to those spaces was what gave the visit its heightened significance. That many of these experiences occur in churches and spaces associated with churches, such as archives and graveyards, brings the material I discuss in this chapter in alignment with the focus of this book. Churches and their officers act as enablers, and gatekeepers, in their roles of storing and safeguarding heritage objects.

For those returnees I write of here the key factor that seemed to be at play was 'being there' versus seeing things digitally. This gives access to the aura of certain spaces and objects that is not otherwise possible. That this occurs and is felt so keenly makes a visit more than just about seeing things, that a tourist may do, as the things seen and touched have such personal significance. As the experiences of people whose journeys I have documented indicates, being in the presence of objects and places of genealogical significance is very much more than a way to corroborate information, and very much more affecting than these returnees anticipated it would be.

BIBLIOGRAPHY

Andrews, Robyn. 2018. '"Did You Know Your Great-Grandmother Was an Indian Princess?" Early Anglo-Indian Arrivals in New Zealand'. In S. Bandyopadhyay and J. Buckingham (eds.), *Indians and the Antipodes: Networks, Boundaries, and Circulation*, 210–232. New Delhi: Oxford University Press.
https://doi.org/10.1093/oso/9780199483624.003.0008

Appadurai, Arjun (ed.). 1986. *The Social Life of Things: Commodities in Cultural Perspective*. Cambridge: Cambridge University Press.

Basu, Paul. 2001. 'Hunting Down Home: Reflections on Homeland and the Search for Identity in the Scottish Diapora'. In Barbara Bender and Margot Winder (eds.), *Contested Landscapes: Movement, Exile and Place*, 333–348. Oxford: Berg.
https://doi.org/10.4324/9781003085089-25

Basu, Paul. 2004a. 'My Own Island Home: The Orkney Homecoming'. *Journal of Material Culture* 9 (1): 27–42. https://doi.org/10.1177/1359183504041088

Basu, Paul. 2004b. 'Route Metaphors of "Roots-Tourism" in the Scottish Highland Diaspora'. In Simon Coleman and John Eade (eds.), *Reframing Pilgrimage: Cultures in Motion*, 153–178. London: Routledge.

Basu, Paul. 2005. 'Roots Tourism as Return Movement: Semantics and the Scottish Diaspora.' In Marjory Harper (ed.), *Emigrant Homecomings: The Return Movement of Emigrants, 1600-2000*, 131–150. Manchester: Manchester University Press.

Benjamin, Walter. 1968. 'The Work of Art in the Age of Mechanical Reproduction'. In *Illuminations: Essays and Reflections*, edited by Hannah Arendt. New York: Schocken Books.

Blunt, Alison and Jayani Bonnerjee. 2013. 'Home, City and Diaspora: Anglo–Indian and Chinese Attachments to Calcutta'. *Global Networks* 13 (2): 220–240.
https://doi.org/10.1111/glob.12006

Blunt, Alison, Jayani Bonnerjee and Noah Hysler-Rubin. 2012. 'Diasporic Returns to the City: Anglo-Indian and Jewish Visits to Calcutta'. *South Asian Diaspora* 4 (1): 25–43.
https://doi.org/10.1080/19438192.2012.634560

Caplan, Lionel. 1995. '"Life is Only Abroad, Not Here": The Culture of Emigration among Anglo-Indians in Madras'. *Immigrants and Minorities* 14 (1): 26–46.
https://doi.org/10.1080/02619288.1995.9974850

Caplan, Lionel. 2001. *Children of Colonialism: Anglo-Indians in a Post-Colonial World*. Oxford: Berg.

Clarke, Kamari Maxine. 2006. 'Mapping Transnationality: Roots Tourism and the Institutionalization of Ethnic Heritage'. In K. Clarke and D. Thomas (eds.), *Globalization and Race*, 133–154. Durham, NC: Duke University Press.
https://doi.org/10.1215/9780822387596-007

Das, Veena. 2014. 'Actions, Expressions and Everyday Life: Recounting Household Events'. In Veena Das, Michael Jackson, Arthur Kleinman and Bhrigupati Singh (eds.), *The Ground Between: Anthropologists Engage Philosophy*, 279–306. Durham, NC and London: Duke University Press. https://doi.org/10.1215/9780822376439-013

Jackson, Michael. 1995. *At Home in the World*. Durham, NC: Duke University Press.

Naumova, Alevtina. 2015. '"Touching" the Past: Investigating Lived Experiences of Heritage in Living History Museums'. *International Journal of the Inclusive Museum* 7: 1–8. https://doi.org/10.18848/1835-2014/CGP/v07i3-4/44486

Rickly-Boyd, Jillian M. 2012. 'Authenticity & Aura: A Benjaminian Approach to Tourism'. *Annals of Tourism Research* 39 (1): 269–289.
http://www.sciencedirect.com/science/article/pii/S016073831100082X.
https://doi.org/10.1016/j.annals.2011.05.003

Schwabsky, Barry. 2017. 'Aura as Medium: Walter Benjamin Reconsidered'. *Raritan: A Quarterly Review*: 92–100.

Spooner, Brian. 1986. 'Weavers and Dealers: The Authenticity of an Oriental Carpet'. In Arjun Appadurai (ed.), *The Social Life of Things: Commodities in Cultural Perspective*, 195–235. Cambridge: Cambridge University Press.
https://doi.org/10.1017/CBO9780511819582.009

Robyn Andrews is a Social Anthropologist at Massey University, New Zealand. She completed her PhD in 2005 based on ethnographic research with Kolkata's Anglo-Indian community. She continues her research involvement with Anglo-Indians in India and the diaspora employing mainly ethnographic, narrative and life story research methods. Her research focus has been on migration and diaspora (particularly in New Zealand), and their practice of Christianity, and of pilgrimage. In addition to her book, *Christmas in Calcutta: Anglo-Indian Stories and Essays* (Sage, 2014) she has published academic articles and book chapters, as well as articles in community publications. She is the co-editor of the *International Journal of Anglo-Indian Studies* and regularly co-organises Anglo-Indian Studies workshops for scholars working in the area.

Part II

CRAFTING DEVOTION:
RITUAL LABOUR

Chapter 6
The Senses and Their Absences in Balinese and Tamil Hinduisms

GRAEME MACRAE

Clifford Geertz famously described Balinese religion as an 'orthopraxy' rather than an 'orthodoxy' (1973a: 176–177). What he meant was that it consisted primarily of doing things, rather than thinking things—a system of ritual practice more than a system of belief—with knowledge embedded more in hands and bodies than in minds. This was obviously a simplification and a generalisation, but there was, and still is, truth in it and since then we have been reminded from many quarters (e.g. Harvey 2018: vii) that this is substantially true of most of the old religions prior to the rise of the 'great world religions'. In Bali there has long been debate among an intellectual elite about matters ostensibly theological but in fact closely linked to the politics of ethnicity and caste (Picard 2011) and nowadays carefully selected and curated fundamentals of Hindu theology are taught in schools. But for most ordinary Balinese, their religion[1] means the making of offerings (*sesajen* [Indonesian], *banten* [Balinese]) to a pantheon of invisible beings who preside in various ways over human affairs. While this pantheon includes the high gods of universal Sanskritic Hinduism and even a highly abstract supreme deity, it also includes closer-to-home deities of earth and the forces of nature, and spirit beings that inhabit mountains, rivers and forests as well as specific trees, rocks and sacred or powerful

---

1 There is no indigenous Balinese term that corresponds to the English 'religion', but the Sanskrit *agama*, conventionally translated as religion, has been known for a long time and has come into widespread use in Bali over the past few decades. Prior to that the (Arabic) term *adat* was more commonly used, with a meaning closer to 'custom'.

places. But closest and most meaningful of all are the ancestors who reside in deified form in the family temple that occupies the uphill-eastern corner of every houseyard. All have power to influence human affairs and all require constant attention by way of offerings.

Offerings range from *saiban/banten jotan*, the tiny mounds of rice on tiny squares of banana leaf that are placed around every houseyard every morning, to huge elaborate assemblages of fruit, flowers and flesh arranged on bamboo frames constructed for major temple ceremonies. The performing arts (music, dance, drama) are likewise understood essentially as offerings, as to a lesser extent are the visual and plastic arts. The ideology of this system of offerings is that they are sincere and disinterested expressions of respect and gratitude to the invisible beings, but the underlying logic is essentially a quasi-economic one—of an implicit (but rarely explicit) expectation of reciprocal exchange across the boundary between the visible (*sekala*) and invisible (*niskala*) worlds. The currency of this exchange lies in the purity of motivation involved in preparation of the offerings, but also in their aesthetic qualities, because the gods are understood to have much the same tastes as humans, for beauty and harmony of colour, smell, sound and taste.[2] The music is melodious, the incense fragrant, the colours bright and lively, the fruit always colourful even if not fresh, the compositions variously dramatic and harmonious. Entering a Balinese temple at night when a major ceremony is in progress is a veritable feast for the senses, with the complex rhythms of multiple *gamelan* orchestras playing simultaneously, the bells of the high priests ringing and their voices chanting,[3] the floor ankle-deep in the flowers of used offerings, the overpowering fragrance of flowers and incense in the tropical air, the white, yellow and checkerboard cloth, the red and gold ornamentation of the temple itself and the mass of people, also mostly clad in white and gold, pressing in on all sides.

But, as Geertz also noted (1973b: 379, 401), the ceremony itself is an almost anticlimactic culmination of hours, days or weeks of preparation (*ayahan*). For women this consists of an endless daily round of making smaller offerings—weaving the trays from banana leaves and young coconut fronds (*busung*) and assembling the more or less complex combinations

---

2 This interpretation of the logic of offerings is essentially my own, but Ramseyer (2002: 137) makes a similar analysis.

3 The five sounds that must be heard at a temple ceremony are *kulkul* (slit gong), *kidung* (singing of sacred texts), *gamelan* (the traditional orchestra of drums and gongs), *genta* (the *pedanda* or priest's bell) and chanting of *mantra* (Rucina Ballinger, pers. comm.).

of flowers and foods inside them. Men's contribution to ritual labour is less regular but more intense and collective. For major ceremonies, which typically occur both in village temples and in households several times a year, groups of men (community or family) work together cleaning, repairing and decorating the temple or houseyard, erecting flags, banners and bamboo shelters, then preparing the ritual offerings of food. This involves slaughter of a range of livestock, always chickens, usually ducks, often pigs and occasionally dogs and other more exotic fauna. Blood is drained and mixed into *lawar*—finely chopped mixtures of vegetables, coconut and spices. Carcasses are butchered, and meat is processed in various ways— minced for *sate* which is laboriously pressed onto bamboo skewers and grilled over charcoal; entrails spread over bamboo frames in decorative forms; whole chickens spread-eagled onto tall offerings; with parts put aside for beings of the underworld, *bhutakala*, whose tastes and ideas of beauty are more ambiguous than those of humans and gods.[4] This work takes place over hours, days or weeks in crowded courtyards, either hot and dusty or wet and muddy, fuelled by endless glasses of sweet black coffee, sweet snacks and, at the end, a shared meal of rice and ritual food. After the ceremony most of the food makes its way home as *lungsuran*—the leftovers of the gods which are more nutritious, spiritually as well as physically, than ordinary food. *Ayahan* is also a feast for the senses, but a more challenging one: of heat, dust, the smell of fresh and roasting meat, coffee, smoke from cooking fires and cigarettes, the screams of dying animals, the raucous two-stroke engines of mills for mincing coconut and meat, and the bawdy banter[5] of village men working together. Every sense is involved— except apparently touch—or is it?

Running through this apparent chaos is a certain unhurried calm, among groups of men who have known each other all their lives, many of them close relatives, sitting together in small groups, preparing and assembling offerings, splitting bamboo and whittling it into sticks and skewers, pressing minced meat onto the skewers, grilling it over charcoal fires, tearing, cutting and folding banana leaves to wrap it in, tidying and sweeping. And at this level, touch begins to enter the picture, albeit through the back door. Participation in local *ayahan* of this kind was my

---

4 The standard view of offerings to *bhutakala* is that they prefer offerings of stale, rotten and otherwise unwholesome materials, but a recent article by Acri and Stephen (2018) argues convincingly that this is not so, and that these offerings are also assembled with aesthetic care and that *bhutakala* are in fact merely a different kind of deity, rather than anti-deities.
5 I have it on good authority that women's banter is even bawdier.

mode of apprenticeship in community and culture, and provided my passport into the networks through which my research has been facilitated ever since.[6] But the lessons of those hours, days, weeks, months are embedded in memories of bodily discomfort—of the heat, dust, noise, but also the hard gritty surfaces on which we sat, cross-legged, the smooth dry feel of bamboo, the razor-sharp carbon steel blades of Balinese knives and cleavers, bevelled and honed on one side only, the greasy texture of fat-rich meat up to my vegetarian elbows, the sticking of shirt and sarong to sweaty body, the comfortable comradely press of my neighbours' knees and shoulders.

Had I been female, I would probably have worked with women on their *ayahan*—the less spectacular, slower, steadier production of offerings for daily use, rising regularly to peaks for frequent ceremonies—a relentless round that forms the calendrical backdrop to their domestic lives. The primary materials of these offerings are young coconut fronds (*busung*), leaves of the jaka tree (*ron*) and banana leaf, woven into small containers and simple decorative shapes, but they also form the foundation of a dazzling array of more elaborate offerings. Images of Bali by both foreign and local artists are replete with images of women engaged in this task which in many respects defines their lives. I have spent many hours with this work as the background to my conversations with both men and women but I have never paid it the attention I perhaps should have.[7] What I do know is that *busung* and other leaves are pleasant materials to work with—relatively soft, pliable, non-toxic and non-abrasive—easy on the hands,[8] although the slivers of bamboo used to stitch them together are hard and sharp and learning to use them accurately takes time and effort (Martin 2018: 35). The work is also easy on the mind and for many women there is a

---

6 This chapter is based primarily on sensorially embedded memories of my PhD research in a neighbourhood of Ubud, Bali from 1993 to 1996. Since then I have returned to Bali almost annually to research other matters, but occasionally I find myself in the situations described here and little has changed. My observations of Tamil ritual were made during a three-month visit in 2001–2002. My research over the years has been partially funded by Auckland and Massey Universities. I am grateful also to the friends, Balinese and otherwise, who have taught me all I know about Bali. Most recently some of them, notably Diana Darling, Michel Picard, Rucina Ballinger and Carol Warren, have contributed welcome suggestions and corrections to this text.

7 The definitive text on women's offerings is Brinkgreve and Stuart-Fox (2002).

8 In recent years, as coconut trees become scarce in the more urbanised parts of Bali, *busung* has been imported from East Java and Sulawesi and these varieties are said to be inferior and harder on the hands.

soothing, meditative rhythm to it. In larger households or temple settings, women work in groups, so it is also a context for sisterly conversation and good-humoured (and equally bawdy) banter. But behind these comfortable images of traditional culture, is the reality of the constant need to produce, exacerbated by the relentless round of ceremonial deadlines,[9] the ever-increasing scale of ritual, especially in more prosperous parts of the island, and the competing demands of paid work outside the household. This tension between the benign ideology of ritual and the demands of its performance is one of the defining features of Balinese lives today, especially for women (Hobart, Ramseyer and Leemann 1996: 132; Nakatani 2003).

While most Balinese recognise that the process of making one's own offerings is spiritually desirable, households of higher status and wealth have always had servants who often do a lot of the more menial parts of ritual labour, but in the increasingly monetised and commodified economy driven largely by tourism, increasing amounts of the production of offerings are outsourced to commercial providers. At the bottom end of this market are the women who sell small quantities of readymade offerings for daily use in local markets, to be bought by women, or more likely the servants of women, who head busy households or who work outside their homes. At the top end are the households of (mostly) Brahmin women who specialise in the production of more elaborate offerings for bigger ceremonies.[10] These may be beyond the knowledge and experience of many women and are prescribed by the high priests (*pedanda*) of these Brahmin households. In between are backyard industries of varying scale, established by entrepreneurial women to supply this growing market and employing the labour of women with few other skills of value in the new economy—only these embodied skills they have known since they were children.

---

9 Most Balinese are members of the congregations of at least three temples, each of which has a major ceremony (*odalan*) every 210 days. There are also intensified peaks of ordinary household offerings at full and new moon and (approximately) fortnightly peaks in the complex calendar in which 'weeks' of different length intersect in complex and irregular ways. At the family/household level there are life-cycle ceremonies (*manusa yadnya*) beginning with birth and at regular intervals thereafter, and finally the enormous ritual cycle surrounding death (*pitra yadnya*). Taken together, it is rare for a household to go more than a week or two without some kind of ritual beyond the ordinary.
10 This system has been long established for major ceremonies (e.g. Connor 1995: 542), but has increased in recent years.

But, behind this emerging socio-economic analysis, and more relevant to our purposes here, is the question of what happens to these embodied skills when they are redeployed to commercial ends. What happens to the purity of motivation and the meditative pleasure which form at least part of ordinary domestic production of offerings for home use? I don't know and the research hasn't really been done, but what we do know is that production and use of commercially produced offerings are seen by at least some Balinese as compromised and inherently inferior.

During the 1990s, cheap staplers began to become available in Bali and some women started using them to assemble their offerings, as well as in packages of cooked food sold in markets and on streetsides. Stapling is quicker and easier than pinning with the traditional bamboo slivers and does not require collection and preparation of raw materials beforehand. At the time, however, this created quite a furore of public debate as to whether this method violated the unwritten rules for (natural) materials and even more so the spirit embodied in the process of preparing offerings. Eventually high-ranking *pedanda* in Parisada Hindu Dharma, the official organisation of Balinese Hinduism, ruled that staples were allowable in the interests of efficiency in an era of time-scarcity. Since then, staples have become widely used and are no longer a matter of concern. While there is a general consensus that the best offerings are the ones you make yourself, similar minor debates have occurred over the use of other artificial ingredients, especially plastics and food colouring, which are creeping into everyday use.

The justification routinely used for pragmatic innovations in materials or technology is that while outward things change, what really counts and must remain constant is the inner meaning of the offering, of which the key ingredient is the intent (cf. MacRae 2002 on renovations of Tamil temples). Offerings believed to be made in (rumoured) offering-factories staffed by non-Hindu migrants from Java are used by some people, and regarded as inferior by others, but the line which few people would cross is using ingredients recycled from previous offerings (Martin 2018: 90).

To what extent my Balinese friends understand the practice of their religion in similarly sensory terms I don't know, but aside from the embodied experience of unintended discomforts, the senses privileged in Balinese ritual practice are those favoured by the gods—sight, sound and smell—and the preferred flavour is harmonious sweetness. Taste and especially touch by contrast seem to be either ignored, devalued or perhaps even deliberately avoided. Is this perhaps a reflection of Hindu values of purity and fear of the pollution which can be transmitted by touch and taste?[11]

TAMIL NADU

In another corner of the Hindu world, in the deep south of India, the main sites of religious practice are also temples, ranging in size and style from simple stones in the ground to 'vast complexes, with multiple sanctuaries, subshrines, mandapas, corridors, courtyards, tanks and gopuras' (Michell 1995: 73). But at the centre of them all is a 'womb chamber' (*garbha griha*) in which dwells the deity, sometimes in an iconic form such a *lingam*,[12] but more commonly in the form of a stone or bronze image (*murti*). *Murti* are neither images of the deity nor receptacles for him/her—they *are* the deity—the deity is physically embodied in them, even if (s)he is also embodied in other *murti* in other places. The *murti* '...is not a mere image... [but]...a person...fully corporeal, sentient and intelligent' (Appadurai 1981: 1). The literal meaning of the Sanskrit term *murti* is 'form' and the semantic implication is that it is the physical form in which the deity manifests his/her self or 'takes form' (Eck 1986: 48).

Consequently the deity/*murti* is treated as a person, legally, but also morally, practically and domestically. (S)he is woken in the morning, bathed, fed, clothed and performs his/her public duties throughout the day until the process is reversed and (s)he is put to bed at night. All this attention is conducted by hereditary priesthoods and takes the form of embodied functions such as bathing with water, oil and milk, feeding with suitably sanctified food, and wrapping and unwrapping with cloth (Fuller 1984; Mohan 2015: 139). Deities and priests are linked by daily practices of touch. Essentially similar practices, understandings and relationships with deities pertain also in other religious contexts, including parts of the Roman Catholic world (Whitehead 2018: 226). In Marian shrines of southern Spain, not only priests, but also ordinary worshippers engage tactually with the deity, whereas in most Tamil temples such intimacies are not

---

11 The work of waste management and recycling in Bali is done largely by non-Hindu immigrants from Java, partly because of Balinese disinclination for contact with dirty or polluting materials.

12 Aniconic forms include natural forms such as stones, rivers and trees, but also sculpted ones such as *lingam*—an upright cylindrical post commonly interpreted as a phallic image, but essentially an abstract representation of Shiva (Eck 1986: 44–46).

available to ordinary worshippers. But, as Alfred Gell says of 'idolatry' in general, 'it permits real physical interaction...between persons and divinities' (Gell 1998: 135; see also Whitehead 2018: 221).

In Tamil Nadu, this interaction begins as soon as soon as worshippers enter the temple gates. In the outer courtyards of major temples there are always people enacting their own embodied forms of communication with the deity, including prostrations, hopping/jumping, gymnastic-type exercises and vigorous slappings of their own bodies. The central act of worship is physical approach to the deity, which in major temples can mean queuing for hours, or at major festivals even for days. The climax, which may only be for a matter of seconds, is the face-to-face encounter with the deity, and especially the making of eye-contact with him/her. This is called *darshan*. While most etic understandings of *darshan* emphasise the obvious visuality of its workings, more emically informed ones recognise that *darshan* transcends the visual: 'Merely to observe the image does not amount to real darsana.... The observer must feel..."in the deity's immediate presence"...[it is] a subjective experience implying a heightened sense of awareness. For devotees blessed with the faculty of subtle sight the image is a sentient being, but for those with the limited faculty of gross sight it remains a lifeless statue' (Bennet 1990: 192–193). In other words, *darshan* implies that the visual is not only visual, but 'a mutually complicit merging of subject-object positions' (Coorlawala 1996: 24)—'an exchange of perspectives between devotee and deity that involves an intersensory visual, tactile and olfactory empathy' (Mohan 2015: 139), an intimate emotional/spiritual experience more akin to being 'touched' by the deity than simply seeing him/her from a distance.

Much of this formal worship in major temples is now packaged in discourses of pan-Hindu ideology of Sanskritic theology originating from north India. But historically and culturally, these southern temples are the upper end of a pyramid grounded on thousands of local village shrines devoted to local village deities. Susan Bayly (1989: ix) refers to these as 'deities of blood and power' whose tastes are unashamedly carnal— primarily for blood and flesh. On a dusty roadside in the very deep south I once stumbled unprepared into one such shrine where, amid blaring music and a sense of powerful energies in the semi-darkness, I came face to face with a goddess (whose name I decline to repeat here[13]) with effigies of mangled human bodies hanging from her mouth but also cradling a baby. Her story is of thwarted romance turned into vindictive anger and

---

13 Invoking the names of powerful deities is not generally considered respectful, let alone prudent.

revenge against men, who can avert her wrath only by acts of dangerous bodily sacrifice such as fire-walking. In more typical village temples, most of which are dedicated to local mother-goddesses (*amman*) with similar appetites, the demand for sacrifice can usually be satisfied with the bodies of non-human animals, documented in disconcerting detail by the Rev. H. Whitehead (1921), but throughout Tamil Nadu, the more dedicated devotees celebrate major temple festivals with self-inflicted pain by piercing cheeks and tongues with steel skewers, self-flagellation with studded whips and hanging from hooks impaled through the flesh of the back.

While *darshan* is arguably a form of 'touch' mediated by the visual, these other forms of self-violence also involve touch of a kind, but the currency of them appears to be sacrifice in the form of pain or even death. The point of this detour into deepest Tamil Nadu is that while the core Hindu interaction between deity and worshipper(s) is common with Bali, the forms of the deities are different and, more importantly for our purposes, so are the sensory means by which humans communicate with them. As Howes and Classen (citing Geurts), put it, different cultures have different 'sensory orders', which need to be understood in their own terms (2014: 12).

BALI

Meanwhile, back in Bali, the ritual goes on—endlessly—but not all of it is directed to deities of temple, locality and community. Parallel to and intertwined with this is an equally endless round of life-cycle ceremonies (*manusa-yadnya*), to do with the path of living beings through this life and beyond, where they eventually become purified, depersonalised and deified ancestors in the family temple. Here, however, dealing with corporeal humans, touch is less conspicuous by its absence.

Babies are believed to be reincarnated ancestors and when newly born are believed to still be partly in that other (*niskala*) realm. They spend their early weeks somewhat insulated against the everyday (*sekala*) world by being held, mostly in the arms of a succession of female relatives. When a baby is three months old, a ceremony called *telubulanin* is performed, in which the central act is the touching of the baby's feet, for the first time, onto the earth, deified as Ibu Pretiwi (mother earth).

While the human life-cycle involves periodic transitions between *sekala* and *niskala* realms, the ritual status of humans is also defined in contradistinction to the domain of lesser animals and the wildness of the natural world in general.[14] The key ritual of transition from animality to proper human status is *masanggih/mapandes/matatah*, popularly known as 'tooth filing'.

Finally, at the end of human life, comes the most important ceremonial cycle of all, of which cremation of the body is but the most spectacular and best-known moment. The purpose of this ritual cycle (*pitra-yadnya*) is to progressively re-transition the person from their embodied life in the *sekala* world, back to the deified ancestral realm from whence they came and which is their true home.[15] The key metaphors for this process are of progressive 'purification' and breaking of attachment to the *sekala* world. But the practices involved are much more embodied and sensory than these metaphors might suggest. One of the first steps is washing the body, which is done primarily by the women of the family, with flowers and holy water (*tirta*). But wider family, neighbours and friends often push and jostle to, if nothing else, at least lay a hand on the body as it is bathed.[16] The body is then wrapped in white cloth by the women of the family and carried by the men of the neighbourhood (*banjar*) to the local cemetery where it is sometimes cremated immediately, but more often buried temporarily until an appropriate time for cremation.[17]

Later in the cycle, fragments of bone are salvaged from the ashes, and ground, again collectively, with all close kin being sure to at least place a hand on the mortar. The resulting powder is mixed with water to form a paste which is fashioned into an effigy of the deceased person.[18] This then becomes the subject of one or more further stages of release of the soul from its earthly embodiment.

Dead bodies are, like blood, especially menstrual blood, highly polluting and this pollution is transmitted primarily by touch, so a lot of everyday Balinese body language and spatial orientation is designed to physically avoid pollutions of this kind. But in the case of cremation, such cautions are abandoned and in the bathing of the body, touching the most polluting of entities is actively sought. Death ritual is however followed by periods

14 The clearing of forest, the pacification of local nature-spirits and the establishment of properly defined boundaries between humanised and natural domains is a key process of historical settlement of new land and of principles of spatial planning and management in general (MacRae 1997: 123).
15 The terms *pulang* (Indonesian) and *budal* (Balinese) meaning to 'return home' are often used as euphemisms for death.
16 For an extended description and discussion of this washing, see Connor (1995).
17 This description of funerary ritual is fairly generalised as details vary considerably between villages, lineages and castes (Connor 1995: 540).
18 The details of this ritual vary considerably, but the general pattern is common.

during which the family and community remain polluted until subsequent rituals of purification.

These (and other) life-cycle rituals involve relationships with humans, living, dead or deified, and even the deified/depersonalised ancestors in the family temple are arguably more tangible and immediate than the more abstract deities of community temples.[19] And this concreteness and closeness is reflected in the much more tactile practices of these ritual. Is touch somehow more intimate, more 'human' than the other senses? Does it come into play when the relationships are with persons, deities and beings with whom we have more human-like relationships—as worshippers at Marian shrines and other places of Catholic pilgrimage often do? And is it mere coincidence that Tiffany Field refers to touch as 'the mother of all senses' (2001: 76)?

Finally, there is the 'much wider notion of senses' alluded to by Graham Harvey in 'his Foreword to this series, including 'senses of place, decorum, decency…and others' including the sense of 'the uncanny' (2018: ix) which obviously extends into senses of the numinous, being in the presence of god or supernatural powers of some kind, which many of us experience at times. This meta-sense is (in a sense) at the heart of much religious experience, but it is not experienced uniformly. The profound sens-ations and revelations that the pioneers of the Abrahamic religions experienced in the deserts of the Levant seem both the same (in phenomenological terms) and different (in cultural terms) from the ways in which Mbuti Pygmies experience the Congo rainforest (Turnbull 1968) and/or aboriginal peoples of Central Australia experience the landscapes of their ancestral 'dreamings' (Hogan and Randall 2006). What is common is our inherent capacity for this kind of experience, but what varies are the ecological and cultural contexts in which it is experienced.

In Bali, local oral histories are replete with accounts of the founding of temples, villages and kingdoms following an experience (usually by a wandering king or holy man) of supernatural light, sound, water, movement or simply a 'sense' at a particular location (usually in a forest). Similarly, in the neighbourhood I know best, the community's relationship with a local royal house is based on the story of a *kris* (a wavy-edged ceremonial dagger) which appeared mysteriously at the workshop of a smith, but caused such sensory disruptions of nocturnal heat and vibration, which he recognised as signs from the *niskala*, that he attempted to deliver it to the

---

19 A partial exception to this generalised contrast is that the sacred objects (*pretima*) which belong to most temples, and are sometimes anthropomorphic in form, are handled and cared for in a way more reminiscent of Tamil deities.

palace of the royal house to which the community was ritually attached. The story need not be related in detail here (see MacRae 1997: 251), but their attempts to deliver it were thwarted in various ways and the *kris* eventually led them to a newer and even more local palace, for which it is to this day a sacred heirloom on which the success and prosperity of the palace has depended for over a century. The point, however, is the manner, at once grossly sensory, but also subtly uncanny, in which the *kris* (itself a kind of deity) communicated its wishes to its human hosts. Stories of this kind, involving *kris*, are common across Indonesia.

The logic here is that underlying the ordinary (*sekala*) world apparent to our normal senses is an invisible (*niskala*) world usually obscure to ordinary sensory perception, but breaking through occasionally in the form of sensible heat, light, sound, water or movement. The *niskala* is also apprehensible through a more subtle meta-sense granted only to a few gifted individuals. I once waited, with the people of my neighbourhood, at midnight in a mountain graveyard, for the spirit of the surrounding forest to re-enter a new *barong*[20] whose mask was made of wood from this place. Many of us witnessed nothing beyond a generalised sense of the *niskala*, but those with eyes to see saw the lightning flash of blue fire when the spirit entered.

But it is also said that this meta-sense is there in us all, awaiting only the opportunity. Old people in Bali remember the time before electric lighting, motorised transport and electronic sound obscured darkness, silence and distance. They speak of the sense[21] of the *niskala* they had in those days—of how close it was, all around, and how easily they could sense it, in unusual sights and sounds, but also in the meta-sense of 'something there'. Such stories are easy to dismiss as peasant superstition, but what they refer to is also the very stuff of old religion, and perhaps not altogether lost from newer religions.

What then can we conclude from this recitation of religio-sensory exotica from two extreme corners of the global Hindu-scape? Obviously, and not very originally, that both the everyday practice and the defining experience of (at least some) religion are utterly entwined with and mediated by sensory experience. Second, that while touch seems at first glance virtually absent from the sensory extravaganza of Balinese religion, it is

20 A *barong* is a deity embodied in a large puppet in forms vaguely mammalian, but also reminiscent of the Chinese dragons from which they are likely descended.
21 The term often used for this kind of feeling or 'sense' is *rasa*—an Indonesian and Balinese word from Sanskrit, meaning taste or flavour, but also sensation more broadly—roughly equivalent to the English 'feeling'.

in fact there between the lines, and becomes more evident the closer we look at the entire repertoire of Balinese religion. Third, as Amy Whitehead (pers. comm.) has reminded me, all the senses are to a degree reciprocal, at least when they involve contact between living beings. *Darshan* is a powerful image of this reciprocity, in the cultural language of Hinduism, but *darshan* is also conceptualised as a kind of touch, mediated through the eyes. And of all the senses, touch is inherently the most reciprocal. Fourth, however, as Sarah Pink reminds us, the five senses defined in Western classification do not actually operate in isolation—'Everyday experience is multi-sensual, though one or more senses may be dominant in a given situation' (Pink 2009: 14, citing Rodaway 1994). The same is true of religious experience, and while the senses are nominally separated in the common understandings embodied in language, at the level of primary experience they are less so. As much of religious experience lies at this primal level, we should perhaps question the utility, if not the validity, of their separation at the level of analysis, as Graham Harvey implied at the very beginning of this series (2018: ix). Fifth, this is made clearer as soon as different traditions are placed in comparative perspective. As Howes and Classen (citing Geurts), put it, different cultures have different 'sensory orders', which need to be understood in their own terms (2014: 12). While the religions of Tamil Nadu and Bali are both nominally Hindu and indeed have significant areas of overlap at both ideological and practical levels, the sensory regimes by which they operate are quite different—the one emphasising a kind of 'touch' disguised as sight at an individual level, the other multi-sensory overload at a collective level in which touch is downplayed in relation to the other senses.

And finally, between the lines of all this description we should not forget the sub-text of labour—manual, tactile and endless, but also unequally distributed. Behind the romantic image of the beautiful Balinese woman devotedly making or placing offerings, is a sometimes harsh reality of too much work, not enough time, pressure to perform and fear of *niskala* consequences if she gets something wrong. The woman who speaks of the meditative satisfaction she gets from her ritual labour also speaks sometimes of how hard it is to keep it up. And nowadays the reality is that most offerings are made by the poorest class of women—those without a foothold in the tourist industry. She makes her own offerings, but also ones for her employer, or to sell in the market, or perhaps she sells her ritual labour, the skill embodied in her hands, in the local offering-factory of her more entrepreneurial high-caste neighbour. The ritual economy is probably the second largest sector of the Balinese economy (after tourism), but ritual is also economic in a deeper sense. All this labour is notionally for the gods—in the form of disinterested gift, but, as we have seen above, it may also be understood as a disguised quasi-economic transaction across the boundary between gods and humans. However this, too, obscures the fact that some of the temple ritual that men devote so much time to is in fact sponsored by people of high status—often palaces, but sometimes businessmen or politicians—and it serves to build their symbolic capital through the most powerful means in Balinese culture. The unpaid labour of thousands of people, working ostensibly for their temples and gods, forms an invisible, or at least obscured, stratum of contribution to this class-like form of inequality. An extended analysis of the political economy of ritual production and labour in Bali has yet to be made, but this is not the place for any more than this brief reference to it.[22] What is being commodified and exploited here is not really touch itself but, as Marx taught us long ago, human labour—in all its embodied sensuality. While the better-known parts of Marx's theory have little to say about the senses, in his earlier work, influenced by both Fournier and Feuerbach, sensory experience was an important theme (Howes 2003). If, however, economic privilege and Bourdieusian manipulations of capital(s) entail control over labour—the kinds and amounts that people do—this necessarily entails a regime of sensory privilege. It is not the senses themselves that are commodified, but the commodification/exploitation nexus is accompanied by inequalities of sensory experience.

CODA

Writing in April 2020 at the height of the Covid-19 pandemic, it is impossible to ignore the contradictory meanings of touch which it has brought into focus—that human touch is on one hand the danger to be most avoided, but simultaneously there is loss, in conditions of isolation, of the reassurance of touch that people most need in times of fear and uncertainty. These two faces of touch are perhaps what makes it the most enigmatic of senses and especially potent as a vehicle of ritual processes. Tamil Nadu is neither a hotspot nor free of the virus, but Bali appears to be mysteriously relatively free of it despite the kind of touch most explicitly to be avoided being precisely the kind that occurs in collective ritual—the pressing together of hundreds or thousands of bodies and the consequent

---

22 My PhD thesis (MacRae 1997) and subsequent writings (1999) are probably the closest to date, but the real work remains to be done.

mutual contact with substances and surfaces. Under-testing and under-reporting are suspected, while theories abound, including the predictably Balinese one that 'Bali was spared because of the good karma and prayers of the Balinese people' (Neubauer and Samsura 2020).

BIBLIOGRAPHY

Acri, Andrea and Michele Stephen. 2018. 'Mantras to Make Demons into Gods: Old Javanese Texts and the Balinese *Bhūtayajñas*'. *Bulletin de l'École française d'Extrême-Orient* 104: 141–203. https://doi.org/10.3406/befeo.2018.6271

Appadurai, Arjun. 1981. *Worship and Conflict under Colonial Rule: A South Indian Case*. Cambridge, London and New York: Cambridge University Press. https://doi.org/10.1017/CBO9780511557934

Bayly, Susan. 1989. *Saints, Goddesses and Kings: Muslims and Christians in South Indian Society 1700-1900*. Cambridge: Cambridge University Press. https://doi.org/10.1017/CBO9780511583513

Bennett, P. 1990. 'In Nanda Baba's House. The Devotional Experience in Pushti Marg Temples'. In Owen M. Lynch (ed.), *Divine Passions. The Social Construction of Emotion in India*, 189–296. Berkeley, CA: University of California Press.

Brinkgreve, Francine and David Stuart-Fox. 1992. *Offerings: The Ritual Art of Bali*. Singapore. Select Books.

Codron, Sandie. 1999. 'The Art of Offering in Bali'. *Indonesia and the Malay World* 27 (79): 157–176. https://doi.org/10.1080/13639819908729940

Connor, Linda H. 1995. 'The Action of the Body on Society: Washing a Corpse in Bali'. *The Journal of the Royal Anthropological Institute* 13 (3): 537–559.

Coorlawala, Uttara Asha. 1996. 'Darshan and Abhinaya: An Alternative to the Male Gaze'. *Dance Research Journal* 28 (1) (Spring): 19–27. https://doi.org/10.2307/1478103

Eck, Diana. 1986. 'Darshan of the Image'. *India International Centre Quarterly* 13 (1), IMAGES (March): 43–53.

Field, Tiffany. 2001. *Touch*. Cambridge, MA: MIT Press. https://doi.org/10.7551/mitpress/6845.001.0001

Fuller, Christopher. 1984. *Servants of the Goddess: The Priests of a South Indian Temple*. Cambridge. Cambridge University Press.

Geertz, Clifford. 1973a. '"Internal conversion" in contemporary Bali'. In *The Interpretation of Cultures: Selected Essays by Clifford Geertz*, 170–89. New York: Basic Books.

Geertz, Clifford. 1973b. 'Person, Time and Conduct in Bali'. In *The Interpretation of Cultures: Selected Essays by Clifford Geertz*, 360–411. New York: Basic Books.

Gell, Alfred. 1998. *Art and Agency: An Anthropological Theory*. Oxford: Clarendon Press.

Harvey, Graham. 2018. 'Series Foreword'. In Graham Harvey and Jessica Hughes (eds.), *Sensual Religion: Religion and the Five Senses*, vii–ix. Sheffield and Bristol: Equinox. [Or see pages xi–xiii in this volume.]

Hobart, Angela, Urs Ramseyer and Albert Leemann. 1996. *The Peoples of Bali*. Oxford: Blackwell.

Hogan, Melanie and Bob Randall 2006. *Kanyini* (videorecording). Sydney: Hopscotch Entertainment.

Howes, David. 2003. 'Marx's Skin'. In *Sensual Relations: Engaging the Senses in Culture and Social Theory*. Ann Arbor, MI: University of Michigan Press. https://doi.org/10.3998/mpub.11852

Howes, David and Constance Classen. 2014. *Ways of Sensing: Understanding the Senses in Society*. London: Taylor & Francis.

MacRae, Graeme. 1997. 'Economy Ritual and History in a Balinese Tourist Town'. Unpublished PhD thesis, University of Auckland.

MacRae, Graeme. 1999. 'Global Village or Neo-Negara? Acting Global, Thinking Local in a Balinese Tourist Town'. In Linda Connor and Raechelle Rubinstein (eds.), *Staying Local in the Global Village: Bali in the Twentieth Century*. Honolulu: University of Hawaii Press.

MacRae, Graeme. 2004. 'Who Knows How to Build a Temple? Religious and Secular, Tradition and Innovation, in Contemporary South Indian Sacred Architecture'. *South Asia: Journal of South Asian Studies* (n.s.) XXVII (2).

Martin, Emily. 2018. 'The Art of Dealing with the Gods: Balinese Women and Ritual Labor'. Unpublished BA Hons thesis, University of Colorado.

Michell, George. 1995. 'Architecture and Art of Southern India: Vijayanagara and the Successor States'. *The New Cambridge History of India* I:6. Cambridge: Cambridge University Press.

Mohan, Urmila. 2015. 'Dressing God: Clothing as Material of Religious Subjectivity in a Hindu Group'. In Adam Drazin and Suzanne Kuchler (eds.), *The Social Life of Materials: Studies in Materials and Society*, 137–152. London and New York: Bloomsbury. https://doi.org/10.4324/9781003087175-11

Nakatani, Ayami. 2003. 'Ritual as "Work": The Invisibility of Women's Socio-Economic and Religious Roles in a Changing Balinese Society". In Thomas Reuter (ed.), *Inequality, Crisis and Social Change in Indonesia: The Muted Worlds of Bali*. London and New York. RoutledgeCurzon.

Neubauer, I.L. and L. Samsura. 2020. '"No Miracle": What Explains Bali's Low Coronavirus Cases?' *Al Jazeera* (3 May). https://www.aljazeera.com/news/2020/05/miracle-explains-bali-coronavirus-ases-200502035557649.html

Picard, Michel. 2011. 'From Agama Hindu Bali to Agama Hindu and Back: Toward a Relocalization of the Balinese Religion?' In Michel Picard and Remy Madinier (eds.), *The Politics of Religion in Indonesia: Syncretism, Orthodoxy, and Religious Contention in Java and Bali*. Abingon: Routledge. https://doi.org/10.4324/9780203817049

Pink, Sarah. 2009. 'Situating Sensory Ethnography: From Academia to Intervention'. In Sarah Pink (ed.), *Doing Sensory Ethnography*. London: Sage Publications. https://doi.org/10.4135/9781446249383

Ramseyer, Urs. 2002. *The Art and Culture of Bali*. Basel: Museum der Kulturen Basel and Schwabe & Co.

Turnbull, Colin. 1968. *The Forest People*. New York. Simon and Schuster.

Whitehead, Amy. 2018. 'Touching, Crafting, Knowing: Religious Artifacts and the Fetish within Animism'. In Graham Harvey and Jessica Hughes (eds.), *Sensual Religion: Religion and the Five Senses*. Sheffield and Bristol: Equinox.

Whitehead, Henry. 1921. *The Village Gods of South India*. Second edition. London: Oxford University Press.

Graeme MacRae did his PhD research in Bali in 1993–1996 and he has returned there most years since. Ritual was central to his early research but his more recent focus has been on various intersections of development, environmental and food security issues. He has also conducted secondary research in (far north and far south) India. In his spare time he teaches anthropology at Massey University.

Chapter 7

Death Doulas and Coffin Clubs: Exploring Touch and the End of Life

SUZI GARROD AND BRONWYN RUSSELL

This chapter explores touch in relation to dying and preparations for death from the position of real-life accounts involving touch. Garrod is an end-of-life doula, otherwise known as a death doula. Her work in England entails supporting the dying as they reach their end of life. In the first part of this chapter, she explores through anonymised case studies how non-religious holistic approaches offering therapeutic touch at end-of-life helps provide spiritual, emotional and practical support to both the dying and their caregivers. In the second part, Russell explores the phenomenon of coffin clubs in New Zealand. Here, coffin club group members face death practically and creatively through the physical crafting of the box that they, or a loved one, will be buried or cremated in. Death doulas and coffin clubs, each offer unique insights into death-related phenomena, or 'death work', that advances understandings about the relationships between death, religion and the sense of touch.

I: DEATH DOULAS

'Touch is the first sense we develop in the human embryo and the last to diminish in old age' (Hess 2014: 23–25). It is arguably our most fundamental means of contact with the world (Hertenstein et al. 2009: 566) and a powerful sensory way through which to communicate presence, emotion, comfort and support, particularly at end of life. Touch is also 'a powerful medium of religious communication, not only between human beings, but also between humans and spirits' (de Witte 2011: 150). Dying can be an extremely lonely, isolating and frightening experience and 'religion often serves as a defense mechanism that keeps anxiety at bay' (Soenke, Landau and Greenberg 2013: 106). Some religious faiths and spiritual traditions have sought to eliminate the fear of death and dying through rhetoric and ritual frameworks which offer hope or the promise of rebirth or an afterlife. In Britain, however, the increased medicalisation of death (Walter 1994) and growing trend towards 'no religion' (Woodhead 2017: 245) have led to many people becoming unfamiliar and uncomfortable with the process of dying. As a result, the dying often feel abandoned or ostracised by society, as family and friends avoid touching or even being around them because they are frightened by the reality of death, their own mortality, or simply do not know what to do or say (Mendoza 2017). This is where death doulas can step in to help the dying and their families approach death differently. Death doulas are also known as end-of-life doulas, soul midwives or death midwives, although there are some differences between their practices.

Over the last fifteen years of working with the dying and their families, I have found that the therapeutic effects of touch extend far beyond the physical. Notwithstanding the body's measurable physiological response to touch, in which the stimulation of sensory receptors on the skin activate the release of the hormone oxytocin, known for its positive effects on well-being and relaxation (Cronfalk et al. 2009: 1204), meaningful and compassionate touch has been shown to address the 'physical, psychological, social and spiritual aspects of suffering experienced by persons with advanced illness' (Mitchinson et al. 2014: 11). In my death doula practice, I have consistently observed how the simple act of physical contact at the end of life, ranging from holding hands to gentle massage, reflexology, acupressure or reiki, can positively impact my clients' perceptions of their physical, emotional and spiritual well-being. The following reflections and anecdotal observations are based on both my personal and clinical experiences with the dying.

Case 1: My First Time

The first dying person I touched was my aunt, who died of metastatic stomach cancer at the age of 53. Moni and I were very close. She was only sixteen years older than me and, in many ways, felt more like my older sister than my aunt. A few months before her death, having undergone extensive surgery and two years of aggressive chemotherapy, she chose to stop all conventional treatment after receiving the news that any future medical intervention would be purely palliative, not curative.

Prior to Moni's death in July 2005 I had never even been near a dying person, let alone sat by their bedside as they took their last breath. I had no training, no experience of what the dying process entailed, and absolutely no understanding of what was happening to her or what she needed from me. In the final weeks and days of her life, whenever her rasping breath became panicky or her wide-open eyes wildly searched mine in pain, fear or confusion, I felt scared, utterly impotent and useless. Not knowing how else to help her, I would intuitively reach out to hold her hand, gently touch her face, kiss her forehead and repeatedly reassure her that she was safe, loved and not alone. It was a heart-breaking experience. With hindsight I believe both Moni and I, indeed all the friends and relatives who sat in vigil during those final days, may have been comforted by a religious ritual or prayer. However, none of us held any spiritual beliefs that offered hope or eased our collective existential fear of death. We simply floundered our way through the dying process without consciously knowing how to help her. At the time my ministrations felt inadequate, yet I now realise that my instinct to simply reach out and physically touch my aunt as she was dying was a meaningful and helpful way to communicate my presence and love when she was anxious or in pain. A study on the existential experiences of palliative care patients receiving touch in the form of soft tissue massage, observed that compassion and 'physical nearness created a bond of trust' that was found to 'compensate for the pain of existential isolation' (Cronfalk et al. 2009: 1209). Anxiety and patient demoralisation 'characterised by feelings of hopelessness, isolation and being trapped and without future' (ibid.) were reduced when the patients felt acknowledged and connected to the therapist. Looking back, I can see how those final liminal moments of connectedness with Moni as she dipped in and out of consciousness, transitioning between acceptance, fear, hope or despair, had an equally existential impact on me. Touching her not only touched my own sense of helplessness and fluctuating states of acceptance, it also dispelled my death denial, made me confront my own mortality and facilitated the necessary process of grief. On a spiritual level, being fully present at the end of Moni's life led to my exploring the possibility of belief in an afterlife for the first time ever. In the final few days she would reach out her hand as if to touch someone at the end of the bed and call out the names of her deceased mother and two sisters. A few seconds later she would turn her head away and close her eyes, as if to say 'no, I'm not ready'. On the evening of her death, her breathing changed, her face softened, she appeared more peaceful and when she called her mother's name, she smiled. I was holding Moni's hand as she took her last breath and felt a palpable shift of energy in both her body and the room. There was a deep sense of peace, an air of sacredness and an indescribable stillness which, to this day, leads me to describe her death as simply beautiful. Despite the absence of religious ritual or prayer, touching my aunt as she was dying was a profoundly spiritual experience. Though challenging and painful on so many levels, being present at Moni's death had a hugely positive impact on me and ultimately changed the direction of my life and my career entirely. I was no longer afraid of death, no longer wary of touching the dying or sitting in vigil with the dead, and I felt compelled to share this acceptance of death and my perception of the sacrality of dying with others. Moni's death led directly to my becoming a death doula and I have since supported the dying in hospices, nursing homes, hospitals and at home. I also run death cafes, facilitate end-of-life planning workshops and teach others how to offer holistic support to the dying.

Before moving on to present my subsequent clinical experiences with palliative clients, it is important to briefly consider the ethical and safety implications of touching the dying. People who are dying are, by definition, vulnerable in both a physical and emotional sense, and their wishes must be respected when it comes to being touched. Therefore, seeking permission from the client/patient themselves is paramount. If they drift in and out of consciousness, are too weak or not lucid enough to give explicit consent, or if tacit approval through non-verbal communication is unclear, family members or healthcare professionals should be consulted. It is vital to remember that whilst touch can be soothing for palliative care patients it can also be intrusive or threatening, even physically painful in some cases. Renz asserts that in this liminal sphere of dying, 'every impression means pressure and may reactivate a traumatic experience' (2016: 161). Whilst this highlights the absolute need for sensitivity and respect when touching the dying, Renz's statement may equally be applied to caregivers. Not everyone is comfortable around death and many like me, when I first sat with Moni, will have had little or no exposure to the dying. The increased medicalisation of death, heavily criticised by Ivan Illich in the 1970s (Clark 2002: 905), has resulted in less general exposure to sickness and the dying. Despite contemporary hospice and compassionate community initiatives which are actively seeking to increase community engagement in end-of-life care (Kellehear 2013: 1071), 'the wider medical system continues to regard death as something to be resisted, postponed or avoided' which has led to 'the loss of the capacity to accept death and suffering as meaningful aspects of life' (Clark 2002: 905). As such, the lack of prior exposure to death may cause distress to some people who might perhaps be experiencing the fragility and coldness of a dying person's hand for the very first time. Touching the dying requires having to face the stark reality of impending loss and the truth of one's own mortality, which might be too overwhelming and traumatic for some people. Notwithstanding these subjective emotional considerations, there are also some physical safety issues that need to be addressed in relation to touching the dying. Open wounds posing a risk of infection, thin, fragile skin due to dryness or lymphoedema, osteoporosis and tumours are all examples of contraindicators that must be carefully considered when touching a dying person (James 2016).

In the following case studies, all ethical, physical and emotional considerations were sensitively addressed either through a clinical consultation with the client or joint discussions between client, family members and multi-disciplinary medical teams. My reflections and client observations are entirely anecdotal and were not part of a randomised controlled trial. Where possible, however, reference is made to clinical studies that support the observed results.

Case 2: Jenny – Touching My Scar

Jenny was a 58-year-old woman, married for 35 years with two children in their late twenties. When she first came to my clinic, Jenny was in remission from breast cancer and seeking massage therapy to help release scar tissue that had developed as a result of her mastectomy. A few months later she received the news that her cancer had returned with metastases detected in her liver and lungs. Her condition was now terminal. As the disease progressed, our therapy sessions took place at Jenny's home and focused on providing relief from the increasing lymphoedema in her feet, legs, arms and abdomen.

In the beginning, much of the touch associated with Jenny's complementary therapy sessions with me revolved around the physical symptoms of her condition. Her post-operative scars responded well to massage, the tightness and redness around her ribcage and the elasticity of her skin improved as the physical scars healed. Eventually she was able to move her left arm without feeling the pain that had previously extended into her armpit and mid-back. Over time, this scar tissue massage proved to be more than just physically helpful, it also had a positive emotional effect on

Jenny. She told me she had felt 'ugly, deformed and no longer a whole, sensual woman' since her mastectomy and that having someone other than herself touching her scars made her feel nurtured and accepted.

As Jenny's condition deteriorated, the physical benefit of touch was further noticeable in the reduced swelling around her lower limbs following our lymph drainage sessions, which provided temporary relief from the pressure caused by the build-up of fluid in her tissues. Towards the end of her life Jenny had to be admitted to hospital several times for the fluid to be manually drained from her abdomen and chest cavity. Each time she returned home, she called to ask if I could visit. The touch she experienced in hospital was 'purely functional not personal', she told me, 'the medical staff are too busy and nowhere near as present as you are'.

Jenny clearly valued the conversations, time and human intimacy that our sessions of gentle hand, leg and foot massage provided. She would often alternate between talking about her death or her funeral wishes and drifting into sleep whilst I worked on her legs. As her physical symptoms became less treatable, it became clear that touch therapy provided far more emotional than physical comfort. The massages helped her feel more relaxed, less anxious and more able to talk about difficult topics, such as where she wanted to die and what the final second of her life might feel like. As Bronwyn mentions later in this chapter, these conversations that Jenny and I shared about death occurred organically. If she wanted to talk about it, we did; if she didn't, we would either talk about something else or Jenny would close her eyes. Over time, I was able to empathically sense whether Jenny was sleeping or simply closing her mind to the subject.

One day she mentioned that she felt isolated and alone, as her husband did not hug or even really touch her anymore. Cognitively she rationalised that he was nervous her delicate skin might tear or bruise, 'or that all the fluid would burst out' if he held her. Emotionally, though, she perceived his lack of touch as a rejection and it rekindled her belief that she was ugly and no longer loveable. I asked permission to invite her husband into the room to teach him how to apply gentle acupressure on Jenny's toes, to help calm her nervous system and encourage relaxation. The soothing benefit of this gentle touch, as well as the easy eye contact it established between them as he sat at her feet, not only helped Jenny relax, it also helped re-establish a level of intimacy with her husband. He no longer felt frightened of touching her, felt more included in her care and much less helpless. Eventually he also felt confident enough to perform gentle massage on her legs and arms, mimicking my strokes and gentle acupressure massage until he felt confident to do it on his own.

Case 3: Colin – Easing My Anxiety

Colin was 65 and suffering from a terminal respiratory disease that leads to fibrosis (scarring) and an irreversible decline in lung function. He had experienced sudden breathing difficulties whilst on holiday and had collapsed whilst walking up a flight of stairs. His subsequent diagnosis and progressive breathing difficulties led to him rapidly becoming physically weaker and unable to walk very far. Moreover, he now subconsciously associated climbing stairs with becoming ill and had developed chronic anxiety and panic attacks. For the last few months, Colin and his wife had resorted to sleeping on a sofa-bed in the living room, as he was physically and psychologically unable to walk upstairs to their bedroom.

When I first met Colin, in late June, I began by teaching him some mindfulness breathing practices to ease his anxiety. He found it difficult to remain focused on counting the breaths due to his diminished breathing capacity and began to panic. I sat in front of him and asked him to place both hands palm up on his knees. I placed my hands on top of his, held his gaze and slowed my own breathing down, gently pressing my hands into his on the out-breath, and lifting them slightly on the in-breath. The touch and guided breathing calmed him down within a few minutes. He began to slow his own breathing rate to match mine and we practised the mindful counting exercise for 10 minutes together. His wife told me he slept in his chair for an hour after I left.

Over the next few sessions, I introduced EFT or Tapping (EFT International 2020) as a strategy to help Colin relax and address his irrational association between ascending stairs and falling ill. I also taught his wife Diane how to apply the tapping routine on Colin, how to give him a gentle reflexology foot treatment and gentle hand massage to help him relax and sleep; also how to apply these techniques on herself to reduce her own anxiety levels. This touch therapy was helpful for them both and meant that I was able to step back to allow them to navigate their last few weeks together feeling more in control of their emotions and less helpless.

Colin died with his family by his bedside just two months after my first visit. I heard later that Diane had shown their children how to massage Colin's feet and hands, they had all practised the breathing techniques together to help with his (and their own) anxiety during the last few hours, and Diane had continued to gently touch the EFT tapping points around his face until he died. Colin's case demonstrated how touch can not only help the dying but also those caring for them. Knowing that they could do something for him meant the family felt less helpless and touch therapy had eased their own anxiety just as it had done his. After the funeral, Diane told me that she and Colin had spent two nights together in their own bed before he was taken to hospital. They had installed a stair lift and he had successfully overcome his panic attacks to ascend the stairs one last time before he died.

Case 4: Uschi – Let Me Go

Uschi was a 77-year-old woman with end-stage heart and kidney failure. She was first diagnosed in 2000 and over the next seventeen years had astounded medics with her resilience, positivity and determination to stay alive. On numerous occasions the family were told she was at the brink of death, yet every single time she would declare 'I don't want to die' and somehow make a miraculous recovery. She was a medical enigma. In December 2016 she was once more rushed to hospital after the onset of intense unexplained pain. Doctors diagnosed acute septicaemia and pneumonia, and she remained in hospital until her death on 15 January 2017.

Uschi was my mother. Throughout those last weeks of her life my father and I visited her daily, spending hours by her bedside. In the final few days, we took turns to sit in vigil overnight so that she was never alone.

Uschi was determined to maintain her independence and dignity to the end and always took great pride in her personal appearance. Despite her increasing frailty, she would somehow get out of her hospital bed, shuffle to the bathroom and be washed and dressed, with perfectly styled hair by 8 AM, shortly before dad and I arrived. Towards the end as she became weaker and unable to even sit up, she would ask me to brush her teeth, comb her hair and moisturise her face before letting dad see her, insisted on fresh pyjamas every day and always asked 'Do I look OK?' before he came in. The healthcare staff, aware of the great importance Uschi laid on personal hygiene, would offer to give her a bed bath to make her feel fresh and clean. This physical touch, though practical in nature and slightly uncomfortable for mum as her body became weaker, vastly improved her sense of well-being. Her face literally lit up after her basic needs were met by these practical yet compassionate acts of touch.

Jewish law relating to those who are actively dying (within three days of death) is pertinent here, as the Talmud states that 'whosoever touches him [a goses, someone who is close to death] or stirs him sheds blood' (Baeke, Wils and Broeckaert 2011: 783). Rabbi Moshe Feinstein's interpretation of the twentieth-century understanding of the goses is that 'touching does not refer to basic care needs such as cleansing and providing liquids by mouth to overcome dryness...[whereas] routine hospital procedures, such as drawing blood or even taking temperature, have no place in the final hours of a patient's life' (Kinzbrunner 2004: 564). What stood out most for me when my mother was actively dying was how she reached out to touch us, in order to clearly communicate her love and her wish to be let go. In the final three days of her life, she took advantage of every fleeting conscious moment to look each of us in the eyes, squeeze our hands, say 'I love you' and then state very clearly 'Let me go.' She knew what she wanted and successfully communicated her feelings not only through her words but also through touch.

In their clinical study into the communication of touch, Hertenstein et al. were able to demonstrate that 'touch does, in fact, possess the possibility of communicating distinct emotions' (2009: 572). Study participants were able to decode emotions such as anger, fear, love and gratitude simply through touch alone. My mother's successful non-verbal communication of her wishes through the touch of her hand on ours confirmed their findings. Bronwyn's experiences at coffin clubs also reaffirm the significance of tactile communication towards the end of life, both to comfort and to teach. Goldschmidt and Van Meines posit that as a dying person approaches the final stages of life, caregivers 'will attach more significance to the flicker of light in the eyes, the rhythm of breath, or the squeeze of one's hand to indicate awareness' (Goldschmidt and Van Meines 2012:15). As verbal communication steadily becomes more difficult, both the dying person and caregivers naturally begin to place greater emphasis on non-verbal means to express their feelings or wishes, particularly focused touch.

Specifically drawing on my experience of Moni's death and my feeling that a ritual or prayer may have helped ease her anxiety towards the end, I used focused touch to anoint my mother's hands, feet and forehead with oil during the final hours of her life. She had been raised a Catholic but no longer practised; however, my hope was that she might subconsciously recognise the ritual touch and its subtle connection to the Roman Catholic Sacrament of Anointing the Sick (Catholic Answers 2004), and that this would comfort her in some way. Rather than reciting a prayer or the Sacrament of Confession as I anointed her, I sang a German lullaby that she used to sing to me as a child and expressed my gratitude, love and goodbyes. I like to believe that this final ritual consoled my mother in some way. Certainly, touching her in those final days and hours as she was actively dying comforted me and helped me come to terms with having to let her go.

In his documentary on touch as the forgotten sense, Chang states: 'We touch, and we know we exist, it's how we connect to the outside world.' He describes the skin as being 'our border on the world, the edge where we begin and end' (Chang 2013). Touch presents the dying with an opportunity to connect not only to the outside world but also to their inner and spiritual worlds.

In the same way that being gently held or touched helps to soothe a crying baby, being touched in the form of religious ritual or basic human compassion at the end of life can soothe both the dying and those they leave behind. Davies asserts that words spoken in ritual, whether religious or profane, become powerful and that these 'words against death', even if they are drawn from 'secular' sources, are performing a 'religious' function (2017: 243). Perhaps the same is true for touch. Touch against death, whether drawn from religious or secular sources, holds a deeply spiritual purpose. It brings comfort, peace, connectedness and a sense of the sacred, at a time when we might otherwise feel frightened, anxious, isolated and alone.

II: COFFIN CLUBS

I began going to Katikati Coffin Club as fieldwork towards achieving my Master's degree in Social Anthropology. Every week for the better part of a year, I attended the club and helped build personalised coffins (including my own). There, I found, was craftwork: the crafting of coffins, of relationships, of an environment in which to discuss death, the crafting of stories. A coffin club is an incredibly tactile place, in part because of craftwork. Touch is used to craft coffins, but also as a form of communication and as a medium for storytelling.

The first coffin club was formed ten years ago in Rotorua, New Zealand. Katie Williams, the founder, describes the idea for a coffin club as striking her 'like a bolt out of the blue'. She got in touch with some 'old blokes' she knew who liked woodwork, and from there, the first coffin club was born. Over the past decade, the idea has grown. There are clubs popping up all over New Zealand. There has also been significant interest globally. More than fifty countries have asked how to start clubs in their own communities. Katie has given a TEDex talk and been interviewed by a number of different groups (TEDex Talks 2019). Documentary makers (both film and radio) have come to explore coffin clubs and talk to those who attend. The movement is gathering momentum. As Katie states: 'In our own little way, we are making quite a difference to the concept of death and dying' (Freethink 2018).

The values that were core to the formation of a coffin club were a need to create a space in which people could talk freely about death, and to provide a way for people to put their personal stamp on their coffins. Katie states that when 'oldies' talk about death and dying, often they are met with resistance from their families, with statements like 'But you aren't allowed to die!' and 'We won't be able to manage without you.' Katie says 'that's a load of crap, and it doesn't help' (Death Hangout 2019). She talks about how, throughout life, people represent their individual personalities through style, interests and hobbies. Katie asked herself, 'Why should it be any different in death?'

Katie advocates for what she calls 'the loving touch'. She states that as people get older, they are more likely to be deprived of interaction, particularly touch (Death Hangout 2019). The coffin club is designed to provide an environment in which people can feel safe expressing themselves creatively and emotionally, particularly with regard to death. Part of this communication is through touch.

A typical day at a coffin club starts with greetings and catch-ups with everyone. Then it is down to business. Some people break off to join the starter group. This is the group who build the bones (excuse the pun) of each coffin. They cut out a base, sides, ends and lid, and screw them altogether. When the coffin is constructed, it is passed on to others for finishing. This group sand the coffins, affix the handles, prime and paint it, and line it. This way, every coffin has many hands working on it. At any one time, there are about five or six coffins being worked on. This means that everyone takes part, and that if someone is unable to help build their own coffin, there are many people who are willing and able to do it for them.

It is more than simply building a coffin, though. As mentioned, one of the aims of the founder was to create an environment in which people feel comfortable expressing their thoughts and feelings about death, dying, grief and loss. The coffin club succeeds in this. Woven throughout the building of coffins are conversations about emotions, pain, grief and death. There are members who continue attending long after they have finished their coffin. Some have been attending for years. They do so for different reasons. Often it is for the friendship and fellowship that they find at the club. Camaraderie is strong and jokes flow freely. Some people come for the sake of the crafting; for a creative outlet and to learn new skills. Some people come for the tools. Gary, a man for whom woodworking seems almost a religious experience, said: 'They have better workbenches here than I have at home.'

When I began attending Katikati Coffin Club, I thought that there would be dedicated 'talking about death and grief' time. I assumed that at some point during the gathering, everyone would sit in a circle and talk about how they were feeling about their situation or loss, and that ideas would be shared and sympathy expressed. I could not have been more wrong. Yes, thoughts and ideas are shared, and yes, sympathy is expressed, but it is done organically. If someone needs to talk, they do. If they do not want to talk, they keep quiet. There is no pressure, and most often these conversations occur while performing a task, such as sanding, lining or painting a coffin. I think the real power of the group comes from this: the freedom to let conversation flow where it needs to, and the acceptance of expressions of grief. It allows room for empathy.

Touch: My Background

I have worked as a physiotherapist for more than nine years. Physiotherapy requires a huge reliance on touch: as a tool for diagnosis, in treatment techniques, as reassurance, support and sometimes even as a deterrent. My hands are the tools of my trade and I would be lost without them. They see better than my eyes, have a longer and more accurate memory than my mind and are more eloquent than my words. I truly respect the power of touch. To me, touch is a form of communication, one which carries more weight than simply speaking.

As Suzi highlights, however, it is more than simply communication. I believe that touch, when administered with care, can be healing and empowering, and that as humans, we need positive touch as much as we need food and water. I see this often in my work as a physiotherapist; the comfort people receive from touch, and the depression of someone starved of it. Perhaps it is because of the value I place in touch that I quickly recognised how important it is at the coffin club. It is an incredibly tactile place. Every aspect of building, decorating and lining a coffin involves the hands: construction, sanding, painting, lining. It extends beyond that, though. Touch is also used to communicate, to teach and to comfort.

Touch as Communication and Communion

In the coffin club, touch is integral to communication. The firm handshakes in greeting, the hugs offered in times of support. The slaps on the back in acknowledgement of a job well done, the gentle cuffs on the shoulder to emphasise a joke. The fleeting, tangible acknowledgements of connection. It was through touch that I felt the acceptance of the group. I felt their acceptance through their shoulders, leaning in to work together on the same coffin. When I started woodworking, I received tactile signals of approval: a slap on the back, a squeeze on the shoulder. These were sometimes accompanied by a 'She's alright, this one', but more often, were simply silent signs of encouragement and approval.

As a novice woodworker, I need a lot of instruction, and in the workshop, there are times when it is too loud for conversation. Power tools generate a considerable amount of noise. Combine that with the use of earmuffs, and you have an almost impenetrable communication barrier. This is when tactile communication becomes invaluable. The blokes use touch to guide and instruct me. A gentle touch to the shoulder, a repositioning of my elbow, a tap on the forearm as a stop signal. Even if talking is possible, sometimes learning through touch is simply faster and easier. Thus, touch became an informant for my research.

As Suzi has shown, there is much scholarship concerning touch. Perhaps this is in part because there are so many ways in which to administer touch. Loving, gentle, comforting, erotic, guiding, parenting, as punishment and to torment. In the coffin club, the majority of touch I observed was in empathy, friendship, acceptance or guidance. Touch has long been recognised as a way to establish and build relationships (Classen 2012; Field 2001; Howes 2018; Ibañez-Tirado 2018; Montagu 1986). Cross-cultural studies show that despite differences in practice and belief surrounding touch, one thing holds true: touch is social, not simply individual (Howes 2018).

Touch is particularly relevant in the coffin club for three reasons. First, it has been shown to alleviate stress, depression and anxiety (Field 2001). These are an acknowledged part of bereavement (Kübler-Ross 1969). Second, it is widely recognised that many older adults are deprived of touch. As people age, their tactile needs increase (Montagu 1986). Ironically, this increase in need corresponds with a stage in life when people are touched less often (Field 2001). Field (2001) posits that the reason for this is that there are taboos surrounding adults and touch. Montagu (1986) supports this, claiming that fear of aging causes a failure to understand and meet the needs of the aging population. And to me, touch is relevant in the coffin club because it is a medium through which my research has taken place. It has many functions within my research, as I will continue to explore in this chapter.

The touch deprivation discussed above is what Katie Williams was referring to when she spoke of aging adults missing out on 'loving touch' (Death Hangout 2019). It is one of the reasons she began the first coffin club, and touch continues to be part of the non-verbal communication that happens within the group. It is never talked about within the group, to my knowledge. From my observations, however, I feel it is an important part of why people come to coffin club, tying into friendship, fellowship and comfort.

Touch, Movement and Tools

One of my favourite tasks is sanding. We do it outside in the concreted courtyard area. Working outside means I can hear the rustling of the nearby trees, smell the woodsmoke and feel the breeze playing across my face. A coffin is balanced on two sawhorses and we sand it down ready for painting. I like it for its tactility. It is much like physiotherapy—I use my hands to feel for imbalances. I find myself treating the coffin if it were a patient; I close my eyes and run my fingertips over the lid, following the grain of the wood. Finding a rough patch is like finding a knotted muscle in a person's back. There is the double satisfaction of finding it, and of knowing that you will soon be rid of it. The wood initially feels gritty. After sanding, it feels as smooth as the skin on the inside of a person's wrist. It is incredibly gratifying.

Another incredibly tactile task is lining a coffin. Many hands must work together. It is like watching a dance. Hands smooth out plastic into the corners of the coffin, so it does not create an unwanted hammock. It needs to lie flat against the wood; if it is too tight, it will create a sling which will hold the corpse up off the base of the coffin. This is unacceptable, as the plastic could tear and drop the body abruptly. After the coffin has been lined with the obligatory layer of plastic, it is lined with fabric of the owner's choosing. Ruched white satin, a treasured handmade quilt, an old sleeping bag; anything can be used. Hands tuck fabric into corners and pleat it carefully so it does not bunch.

Invariably, I am charged with stapling the plastic and fabric to the wood. The staple gun is heavy and prone to jamming, and my hands are the strongest. I have to get close to the inside of the coffin to get the angle right. This means ducking under arms, reaching around shoulders, leaning into a many-armed hug. I look at the hands around me. They are wrinkled, liver-spotted, gnarled, bearing the marks of decades of hard work and the tell-tale signs of arthritis. They have painted and unpainted nails, many rings, no rings, bracelets, no bracelets. They all work together to make this final of the coffin as perfect as they can.

At the coffin club, hands and tools are almost synonymous. A tool is 'a device that is activated by human agency' (Ingold 2000: 300); one that lends itself to manipulation (rather than automated use) and becomes an extension of their users. The hand itself is also a tool. It can grip, flex, pinch, squeeze, dig, knead. Every movement is subject to minute variations, and therefore has infinite possibilities, making each individual's movements unique (Ingold 2013). Over time and with repetitive movement, hands become more skilled and protected from injury (through callouses). They collect scars and other signs of use. This results in a tool which is perfectly adapted for the task it is undertaking. It also means that hands can reveal the story of an individual's life (ibid.: 116–117). This expands on the idea of 'touch as communication', making hands not only the medium for communication, but the story themselves.

While observing and participating in the coffin club I noticed movement. More specifically, I noticed repetitive movement, and what effect it had on club members. Tasks such as sanding and painting are repetitive. The arms and body move in unison, drawing the paintbrush or sandpaper to and fro over the surface of the coffin. Concentration is required to ensure the strokes are even, smooth, parallel and that no areas are missed. I noticed that the longer people were engaged in such a task, the more they relaxed. Tension drained from their bodies; their shoulders dropped, their grip loosened and their posture softened.

It was more than just a physical response, however. These repetitive tasks also fostered conversation. I noticed that people were far more likely to talk about difficult subjects while performing these tasks. There is something meditative in the repetitive movement, concentration and muted sounds of the tasks that calm the mind and encourage discussion. This observation was validated by Gloria. I asked her how she found the coffin club as a space in which to express her thoughts, grief, concerns and ideas. She replied that the tasks, particularly sanding, were soothing, and stimulated conversation. She also commented on how having something to do with her hands and somewhere to look made talking about difficult topics easier.

When thinking about the convergence of movement and thought, I turned once again to the work of Ingold. He writes of the biographical elements of walking. Ingold writes that in undertaking a task as repetitive and familiar as walking, the walker is transformed, not simply geographically, but biographically. In the planning stages of taking a walk, it is a task which the walker intends on undertaking. But once the walker is walking, they *become* their walking. They are their steps, their breath, the blisters on their feet. They are perpetually modified by it, vivified by its movement and with completely new experiences gained by the time the walk is completed. The walker, in the act of walking, becomes a different person (Ingold 2018: 23).

Ingold's work on walking informed my ideas about movement at the coffin club. Sanding is similar to walking, in that there is a progression. There is an origin (a rough coffin), a destination (a smooth coffin), rhythmic movement and the space for thoughts to flow. Perhaps, as Ingold posits, the sander becomes their sanding. They are their wide-legged stance, their swaying torso, their sensitive fingertips and the metrical motion of their arms. The sander watches without seeing, mostly using their hands to guide them. The space for thought is immense.

Crafting and Creativity

Touch, movement and the use of tools brings us to crafting. This is a crucial part of the coffin club. The term 'crafting', in this context, refers to the making of something, but also to the crafting of a narrative. Hedtke and Winslade state that crafting an aesthetic, tangible object is a 'creative process that is shaped by stories, meaning, actions, and rituals' (2017: 18). The 'doing' of crafting allows for room for the rituals and storytelling needed to find meaning in grief, loss, death and dying.

When a new member arrives at the club, they are measured for their coffin, taking into account height, depth and width. After measurements have been taken and recorded, the member then chooses what shape coffin they prefer (rectangular, cone-shaped or traditional) and what kind of handles they would like (wooden, plastic or rope). These preferences are followed to make a basic coffin. After that, it is up to the member to decide how they want it decorated. Some people leave it plain so friends and family can write messages on it at their funeral. Others choose to paint pictures on their coffin. I have seen coffins painted in a wide range of colours, with flowers, birds and beloved pets depicted on the lid. People have designed their coffins to look like pool tables, packing crates and kayaks. Every facet of the coffin is chosen carefully, and each coffin is a representation of the person it belongs to. The sky is the limit, as long as it can be made from plywood.

The reflective nature of crafting is highlighted in the scholarly works of Hedtke and Winslade (2017), Letherby and Davidson (2015) and Rogers (2007). By producing a work of art, the craftsman is simultaneously presenting an expression of themselves to others, and to themselves. This seems particularly relevant in light of the personal nature of the craftwork in the coffin club. Creating a personalised coffin is a form of self-expression. It allows others to see into who the artist is and allows the artist to explore their identity. It is a form of storytelling.

Marg is a kind, quirky and somewhat abrupt woman. She does not instigate conversation often. When she does participate in the conversation, it is always insightful and often hilarious. Over the course of a couple of months, I asked her a few times how she planned on decorating her coffin. Each time I asked, she had a different idea. Pink, then purple. Flowers one week, birds the next. Maybe dragonflies, or bumblebees. She seemed overwhelmed by options.

I was surprised, then, when I arrived one week to find Marg painting her coffin an incredible neon green. I asked her about it. She told me the story simply. Her granddaughter had died when she was 13, after battling leukaemia for two years. Frances described her granddaughter's funeral. The coffin was a brilliant lime green, and all of Marg's granddaughter's family and school friends covered it with their messages, drawings and handprints. It became very clear why Frances had chosen to paint her own coffin green. 'They say they're going to heal them. It's a load of crap.' Her granddaughter would have been 21 this year.

My research project has emphasised the importance of crafting, touch and creativity for performing death work in a coffin club, but it is more than that. It is an incredibly human thing to do. Whether we carve religious statues, fashion home altars, cook sacred food or build a coffin the size of a jewellery box to hold a stillborn baby, we are crafting. We are using our hands to express our ideas, beliefs, thoughts and intentions. We are crafting our stories, and feeling to the edge of our understanding of those stories. We are making things, while making sense of things.

Conclusion

It has been more than a year since I first attended Katikati Coffin Club. I remember being incredibly nervous. I felt out of my depth and had an acute case of imposter syndrome. I was sure I would be viewed as an interloper. I need not have worried. I was welcomed with open arms. I have learnt a lot. Hands-on skills, such as how to use a router and a table saw. I have learnt about the practicalities of death work; the legalities and basic practical needs that are required when someone dies. I have learnt about the ways people find meaning in death and grief by attending the coffin club.

Woven throughout every facet of the coffin club is the importance of touch, movement and crafting. Touch is intrinsic to every aspect of the club. It is used to guide and instruct, and to demonstrate empathy and love. Movement is a by-product of the work of building a coffin, and has its own effects. It can soothe, relax and allow for meditative thought and conversation. The creativity of designing, building and decorating a coffin contributes to this. As people tell their story through their crafting, their hands and their touch, they are also able to narrate and find meaning in their loss and grief. And as they craft their coffin, they also craft the relationships and social environment around them and it is these characteristics of the coffin club—touch, movement, creativity, crafting and socialisation—which make it such an effective space for sharing experiences of grief and loss. It is a haven, a safe space in which to share emotions and experiences, free from judgement. In performing a practical aspect of death work, coffin club members are also working on grief and loss. Woodwork, death work and the work of grief, all occur simultaneously. And therein lies the beauty.

BIBLIOGRAPHY

Baeke, Goedele, Jean-Pierre Wils and Bert Broeckaert. 2011. '"There is a Time to Be Born and a Time to Die" (Ecclesiastes 3:2a): Jewish Perspectives on Euthanasia'. *Journal of Religion and Health* (Springer Science and Business Media LLC) 50 (4): 778–795. Accessed 5 February 2020. https://doi.org/10.1007/s10943-011-9465-9

Catholic Answers. 2004. 'Anointing of the Sick'. Accessed 5 February 2020. https://www.catholic.com/tract/anointing-of-the-sick.

Chang, Kun. 2013. 'Touch: The Forgotten Sense'. *Vimeo*. Video File. Accessed 5 February 2020. https://vimeo.com/71964645.

Clark, David. 2002. 'Between Hope and Acceptance: The Medicalisation of Dying." *BMJ* (Clinical research ed.) 324 (7342): 905–907. https://doi.org/10.1136/bmj.324.7342.905

Classen, Constance. 2012. *The Deepest Sense: A Cultural History of Touch.* Chicago, IL: University of Illinois Press. https://doi.org/10.5406/illinois/9780252034930.001.0001

Cronfalk, Berit Seiger, Peter Strang, Britt-Marie Ternestedt and Maria Friedrichsen. 2009. 'The Existential Experiences of Receiving Soft Tissue Massage in Palliative Home Care: An Intervention'. *Supportive Care in Cancer* (Springer Science and Business Media LLC) 17 (9): 1203–1211. Accessed 26 January 2020. https://doi.org/10.1007/s00520-008-0575-1

Davies, Douglas. 2017. *Death, Ritual and Belief: The Rhetoric of Funerary Rites*. 3rd edition. London: Bloomsbury Academic.

de Witte, Marleen. 2011. 'Touch'. *Material Religion: The Journal of Objects, Art and Belief* (Informa UK Limited) 7 (1): 148–155. https://doi.org/10.2752/175183411X12968355482466

Death Hangout. 2019. 'Let's All Join the Coffin Club with Katie Williams'. YouTube video file. https://www.youtube.com/watch?v=tgAL89oODgQ&t=189s.

EFT International. 2020. 'What is EFT Tapping'. Accessed 5 February 2020. https://eftinternational.org/discover-eft-tapping/what-is-eft-tapping/.

Field, Tiffany. 2001. *Touch*. Cambridge, MA: MIT Press. https://doi.org/10.7551/mitpress/6845.001.0001

Freethink. 2018. 'New Zealand's Coffin-Building Club Helps Seniors Approach Death Positively'. YouTube video file. www.youtube.com/watch?v=18uwoX2k37A.

Goldschmidt, Barbara and Niahm Van Meines. 2012. *Comforting Touch in Dementia and End of Life Care*. London: Singing Dragon.

Hedtke, Lorraine and John Winslade. 2017. *The Crafting of Grief: Constructing Aesthetic Responses to Loss*. New York: Routledge. https://doi.org/10.4324/9781315686806

Hertenstein, Matthew J., Rachel Holmes, Margaret McCullough and Dacher Keltner. 2009. 'The Communication of Emotion via Touch'. *Emotion* (American Psychological Association [APA]) 9 (4): 566–573. https://doi.org/10.1037/a0016108

Hess, Samantha. 2014. *Touch: The Power of Human Communication*. Portland: Fulcrum Solutions LLC.

Howes, David. 2018. 'The Skinscape: Reflections on the Dermalogical Turn'. *Body and Society* 24 (1–2): 225–239. https://doi.org/10.1177/1357034X18766285

Ibañez-Tirado, Diana. 2018. 'Intimacy and Touch: Closeness, Separation and Family Life in Kulob, Southern Tajikistan'. *Ethnography* (SAGE Publications) 19 (1): 105–123. https://doi.org/10.1177/1466138117723650

Ingold, Tim. 2000. *The Perception of the Environment: Essays on Livelihood, Dwelling and Skill*. New York: Routledge.

Ingold, Tim. 2013. *Making: Anthropology, Archaeology, Art and Architecture*. New York: Routledge.

Ingold, Tim. 2018. *Anthropology and/as Education*. New York: Routledge.

James, Jo. 2016. 'Imperial College Hand Massage'. YouTube video file. Accessed 6 February 2020. https://www.youtube.com/watch?v=vfp4VULUQG8&t=966s.

Kellehear, Allan. 2013. 'Compassionate Communities: End-of-Life Care as Everyone's Responsibility'. *QJM* 106 (12): 1071–1075. Accessed 26 January 2020. https://doi.org/10.1093/qjmed/hct200

Kinzbrunner, Barry M. 2004. 'Jewish Medical Ethics and End-of-Life Care'. *Journal of Palliative Medicine* (Mary Ann Liebert Inc) 7 (4): 558–573. Accessed 2 May 2020. https://doi.org/10.1089/jpm.2004.7.558

Kübler-Ross, Elisabeth. 1969. *On Death and Dying: What the Dying Have to Teach Doctors, Nurses, the Clergy and Their Own Families*. New York: Scribner.
Letherby, Gayle and Deborah Davidson. 2015. 'Embodied Storytelling: Loss and Bereavement, Creative Practices and Support'. *Illness, Crisis & Loss* (SAGE Publications) 23 (4): 343–360. https://doi.org/10.1177/1054137315590745
Mendoza, Marilyn A. 2017. 'Touch the Dying'. *Psychology Today UK*. Accessed 30 January, 2020. https://www.psychologytoday.com/gb/blog/understanding-grief/201703/touching-the-dying.
Mitchinson, Allison E., Carol Fletcher, Hyungjin Myra Kim, Marcos Montagnini and Daniel B Hinshaw. 2014. 'Integrating Massage Therapy Within the Palliative Care of Veterans with Advanced Illnesses: An Outcome Study'. *American Journal of Hospice and Palliative Medicine* 31 (1): 6–12. https://doi.org/10.1177/1049909113476568
Montagu, Ashley. 1986. *Touching: The Human Significance of the Skin*. 3rd edition. New York: Harper & Row.
Renz, Monika. 2016. 'Spiritual Care Interventions'. In Monika Renz, *Hope and Grace: Spiritual Experiences in Severe Distress, Illness and Dying*. London: Jessica Kingsley.
Rogers, J. Earl. 2007. 'Introduction'. In J. Earl Rogers (ed.), *The Art of Grief: The Use of Expressive Arts in a Grief Support Group*, 3–8. New York: Routledge.
Soenke, Melissa, Mark J. Landau and Jeff Greenberg. 2013. 'Sacred Armor: Religion's Role as a Buffer against the Anxieties of Life and the Fear of Death'. In Melissa Soenke, Mark J. Landau and Jeff Greenberg, *APA Handbook of Psychology, Religion, and Spirituality* Vol. 1: *Context, Theory, and Research*, 105–122. American Psychological Association. https://doi.org/10.1037/14045-005
TEDex Talks. 2019. 'The Coffin Club: Makers of Fine and Affordable Underground Furniture with Katie Williams', TEDxAuckland. YouTube video file. https://www.youtube.com/watch?v=HKn6ibHJ-Zg.
Walter, Tony. 1994. *The Revival of Death*. Oxford: Routledge.
Woodhead, Linda. 2017. 'The Rise of "No Religion" in Britain: The Emergence of a New Cultural Majority'. In Linda Woodhead, *British Academy Lectures, 2015-16*. British Academy. https://doi.org/10.5871/bacad/9780197266045.003.0011

Suzi Garrod is a death doula and bereavement counsellor, and the founder of Next Steps for Living, Dying, Grieving. She has worked in the death and dying field for over fifteen years, integrating her psychotherapeutic, end-of-life and complementary therapy skills to offer deep listening and gentle touch therapies within the community, in hospices, care homes and hospitals. Working in close partnership with St Luke's Hospice (Plymouth, UK) and Kingsbridge Age Concern, Suzi trains and coordinates local networks of compassionate community volunteers, offering practical and emotional support to friends, relatives and neighbours who wish to spend their last days at home. Three years ago, Suzi decided to return to part-time study, to broaden her understanding of death within religion and culture, and to develop a more scholarly approach to her practical end-of-life work. She is currently completing her Master's thesis which explores barriers to integrating death doula approaches within UK healthcare settings.

Bronwyn Russell has worked as a physiotherapist for nine years, in New Zealand, Australia, England, Scotland, India and Nepal (and a few other places in between). Her jobs have included working with children with disabilities and people recovering from amputations, burns and reconstructive surgery, in chronic pain management and musculoskeletal physiotherapy. She is now back in her home country of New Zealand. A few years ago, Bronwyn decided to return to study. A friend suggested social anthropology, and Bronwyn has never looked back. She is currently finishing a thesis towards her Master's degree, which explores coffin clubs in New Zealand.

Chapter 8

Touch and Other Senses: Feeling the Truth in Basket Divination

SÓNIA SILVA

In basket divination, the source of truth is not the diviner, but Kayongo, an ancestral spirit. In order to access spiritual knowledge, which is deemed free of human bias, the diviner as well as his clients open themselves to Kayongo, attuning their senses. What, then, are the human senses at work in basket divination, a centuries-old technique well known in the vast region of Africa where Zambia, Angola and the Democratic Republic of the Congo share borders? How do those senses relate to one another, and what are the aesthetics of such sensorial relations?

Two human senses come immediately to mind: sight and hearing. The significance of these sensorial modalities in basket divination reflects the important fact that the diviners and consulters both focus their gaze on the symbolic material pieces contained in the basket and engage in dialogue at key junctures. Yet, an account of basket divination exclusively focused on the sensory work of the eyes and ears would remain incomplete. I argue that in basket divination the distant senses of sight and hearing are in close collaboration with the near, affective senses of touch, kinaesthesia and pain. No sense is superior to another; all senses matter.

A brief note on terminology and sensory differentiation is in order. By 'touch' I mean not only active touch, a sensorial modality sometimes known as haptic touch, but also its kinaesthetic extension to other parts of the moving body. I also place touch under the same umbrella as pain, suggesting that these three senses—touch, kinaesthesis and pain—share an affective quality that is distinct from the more analytical tenor of vision and audition. Kayongo's knowledge is not only seen and heard; it is also felt with the hands, the moving body and the aching heart. By distinguishing between distant, ratiocinative senses and the more affective, near senses, and focusing attention on their conjoining rather than their separation and opposition, I hope to deepen our understanding of the role of the senses, the body and material religion in divination and other practices deemed religious.[1] Moreover, to conceptualise this collaboration between the senses in the same activity, I employ Birgid Meyer's concept of sensational forms. Meyer explains: 'Sensational forms are authorized modes for invoking and organizing access to the transcendental.... Sensational forms are part of a specific religious aesthetics which governs a sensory engagement of humans and the divine and each other' (2010: 751).[2] The religious aesthetics of basket divination is, for the most part, one of synergy and sensory attuning and cooperation. In the language of sense studies, we may speak of these moments as instances of cosensing, intersensoriality and synaesthesia.

SEEING

Let us start with sight. In the Luvale language spoken in Chavuma, a district of northwestern Zambia where I have conducted two years of ethnographic research between 1995 and 2011, to divine (*kutaha*) is to see.[3] Diviners are seers, or *vakakutaha*. Although Luvale speakers will often designate particular material oracles by their name—the divination basket is known as *lipele*, and the pounding pole, for example, is known, more prosaically, as pestle (*mwishi*)—they are as likely to refer to these and other oracles by the generic term *chitaho*, or 'the thing used for divining (or seeing)'. Tellingly, *chitaho* refers as well to a particular oracle that consists of a of wooden mortar, or some other container, filled with medicated water. Here, diviners peer into the water to see the truth revealed in images. In basket divination, diviners shake the contents of their baskets in an upward direction

---

[1] Other authors who have studied the senses in the context of divination include Andermann (1991), Devisch (1991), Igreja (2015), Palmeirim (2010) and Stroeken (2008).

[2] See also Csordas' idea of 'somatic modes of attention' (1993). On the relation between religion and aesthetics understood as sense perception, see Plate (2005).

[3] My publications on the topic of basket divination include Silva 2011, 2013, 2014 and 2016. For other authors who have written on the same topic, see, for example, Andermann (1991), De Boeck and Devisch (1994) and Turner (1975).

and then observe the resulting symbolic configurations. Consulters highly value the fact that they can see Kayongo's messages.

In basket divination, the importance of the sense of sight is also revealed in other ways. At the start of every séance, diviners enhance their eyesight by rubbing their eyelids with red clay. The diviners' eyes are said to be sharp like the eyes of the spotted eagle-owl (*Bubo africanus*), a nocturnal bird. Diviners receive their gift of clairvoyance during their formal initiation into the divining profession, when the officiant in charge applies a medicine known as *misozo* onto their eyelids. Reportedly, this potent medicine clears their vision and removes the blur that is characteristic of ordinary eyesight.

I should mention that the sense of sight is paramount in countless divination methods throughout Sub-Saharan Africa. Similar to the basket diviners who practice in northwest Zambia, the Zulu diviners in South Africa have their eyes treated with potent medicines in order to enhance their clairvoyance (Ngubane 1977: 86–87). In Tanzania, the ancestral spirit that dwells in oracles is called the 'eye' (Stroeken 2008: 477). Among the Kuranko of Sierra Leone, it is said that diviners with extraordinary insight have four eyes, and that their second sight transcends ordinary vision. Michael Jackson reports that, during divination, the Kuranko seers often close their eyes to 'see' the truth (2013: 36–37). Elsewhere in Africa, this idea of the blind seer is more elaborated. In Chad, the Mundang compare the blind man's cane to divination since both are able to guide and orient the sightless (Adler and Zempléni 1977: 40). In southern Sudan, the Dinka aver that blind people possess special powers of insight. It is also worth noting that the Dinka word *coor* (meaning blind) is cognate with the word *car* (to divine) (Lienhardt 1961: 68).

Interestingly, this common association of vision with spiritual insight and truthfulness has led a number of Africanist anthropologists to draw a provocative parallel between divination and Positivist science—two systems of knowledge—and diviners and Positivist social scientists—two types of social analysts. According to Igor Kopytoff, the Suku of the Democratic Republic of the Congo know (they do not simply believe) that their ancestors exist, their system of thought being comparable to the nineteenth-century ideal of Positivism (Kopytoff 1981: 718). For Jackson, the Kuranko pebble method that he studied in Sierra Leone is akin to social science; like the Positivist scientist, the Kuranko diviner is 'allegedly passive and receptive, the technique allegedly objective, the procedure allegedly impersonal' (2013: 37). This thought-provoking parallel serves as an important reminder that Western scientists and philosophers do not have a monopoly over the production of knowledge, or even the idea of detachment and objectivity (Silva 2016).

In order to produce true knowledge, the Cartesian seer reduces vision to an objectifying gaze that is directed toward the object. Erwin Straus captures this stance well when he describes it as a 'standing over-against' rather than a being 'side by side' (Straus 1963, 370). The Cartesian seer grasps the skeleton of things, identifying and stabilising them.[4] Yet vision should not be reduced to the philosophical and epistemological definition it has acquired in Western thought, a tendency that Paul Stoller describes as a foundational 'sensual bias' (1989: 7), and Stroeken identifies as a form of cultural sensotyping (2008: 472).[5] Although concepts such as 'visualism' (Ihde 1979) and 'oracular centrism' (Jay 1993) have been instrumental in the work of critiquing the Cartesian definition of sight, we must be wary of the resulting tendency to downplay or even deny the role of vision in in religious and cultural life. Ihde addresses this problem in his essay on 'Vision and Objectification' (1979), and Tim Ingold (2000) returns to the same issue in his critique of Edmund Carpenter's seminal study of Inuit sensory experience (Carpenter 1973). Why did Carpenter diminish the role of eyesight in the Inuit perception of their environment? Ingold asks. 'Could it be because [Carpenter] took with him into his study a preconceived notion of vision, as analytic and reflective rather than active and generative?' (Ingold 2000: 253). According to Ingold, it is possible to combine the perception of the Inuit lifeworld with 'a thorough-going ocular-centrism, albeit of a kind radically different from that with which we are familiar in the West' (ibid.). I agree.

Positivists are not the only analysts whose epistemological vocabulary conveys a close kinship between knowing and seeing. Basket diviners value truth, objectivity and detachment as much as Positivists do, and yet they do not imagine themselves as Cartesian observers of static and mute objects. It is also perfectly possible to celebrate the distant sense of sight without disparaging the near senses as unreliable and untrustworthy. The human senses rely on each other. In basket divination, sight partners

---

4 On the Cartesian seer, see among others, Ihde (1979: 82–92), Straus (1963: 370) and Fabian (1983: 105–142).

5 It is of interest that the Luvale verbs 'to see' and 'to hear' may carry affective qualities. Sometimes the verb to see (*kumona*) means to experience, as in *kumona malwa*, meaning to see (that is, to experience) hardship. While *kwivwa* means 'to hear', this verb is also used in the sense of tasting, smelling and feeling. The first meaning of *kwivwa* listed in Horton's Luvale dictionary is 'to sense' (Horton 1953).

with hearing and touch in the important task of gaining access to truthful knowledge.[6]

HEARING

Let us now consider the distant sense of hearing. Basket divination is never a silent activity. While the sense of sight enables both diviners and consulters to visualise Kayongo's messages, diviners are expected to verbally explain these messages to their clients, most of whom are incapable of interpreting the rapid succession of configurations. Many consulters quickly identify a number of pieces, such as the carved wooden figurines known as Lunga (Man), Pwevo (Woman) and Katwambimbi (Mourner). Beyond this basic level, however, the number of clients who are able to read the fast series of configurations, one at a time and in succession, drops considerably. For this reason, diviners speak throughout the séance, alternating between formulaic passages and more colloquial communication.

What about the consulters, do they remain silent? Although the consulters depend on the translation work of basket diviners to access Kayongo's knowledge, they do not remain in silence. The formal structure of the séances facilitates their verbal participation. When the diviner is rapidly translating Kayongo's material communication into the medium of words, describing what he sees in his oracle, he expects his clients to repeat his statements verbatim at the same pace and intonation. When he has grasped an important piece of knowledge, he lowers his basket and says, *ngungwehhh*, which prompts his clients to retort, *ehhh*. Now, the diviner snaps his fingers, signalling his clients to clap once. At this point, his clients are expected to confirm or deny his claims. They pose new questions to the diviner, a procedure known as *kusukula*, and the session continues. While the diviner's formulaic speech enables the consulters to repeat his statements—passively receiving Kayongo's knowledge and gradually developing an understanding of the reasons behind their suffering—the diviner's act of lowering his basket signals to the consulters that they are expected to ask questions and confirm or refute specific statements. I have never heard anyone in Chavuma claim that the act of hearing (*kwivwa*) is the quintessence of basket divination, even though to hear and to listen

---

6 On the differentiation between distal and proximal senses with the aim of showing their collaboration rather than separation, see Fischer (1997), Harvey (2018) and Howes (1991a and 1991b).

are an indispensable part of every consultation. Rather than defining their role simply as hearers, the consulters see themselves as both listeners and talkers. Hence the indirect answer they may give their interlocutors during their journey to a diviner. If asked where they are going, they may reply, *natuya nakushimutwila*, we're going to converse.

Since the 1990s, a prolific decade in divination studies, a number of scholars have focused on the verbal negotiation between clients and diviners. In a passage dealing with gourd rattle divination (spirit possession) and book divination (examination of Arabic books) in Bunyole, Uganda, Susan Whyte states, 'all clients retain a degree of autonomy in relation to the diviner, who solicits and respects their opinions' (1997: 73). On the topic of television divination in post-civil war Gorongosa, a district of Mozambique, Victor Igreja asserts, 'the client emerges as an unequivocal agent in the production and consumption of divinatory knowledge' (2015: 708). These and other authors share the idea that the study of speaking, hearing and replying deepens our understanding of the multiple ways in which the consulters shape the outcomes of divination, asking us to shift our focus from the diviners alone to the relationship between diviners and their clients.[7] On its own, vision is likely to empower the diviners who are equipped with enhanced sight, authenticating their statements and legitimising their work. The activity of divination is inseparable from issues of power, being well described as an 'aesthetics of persuasion' (Meyer 2010: 749). By carefully listening to the diviners' statements, the consulters are able to access spiritual knowledge in comprehensible terms, and ask back. Verbalisation allows the consulters not only to quietly and passively listen and observe but also to actively participate by confirming or rejecting specific statements. In basket divination, sight separates, hearing connects; sight enunciates, hearing engages.

And yet, it is not always warranted to categorically oppose sight to hearing. Let us momentarily return to Ingold's work on the human senses. In addition to critiquing the tendency to ignore or minimise the importance of vision outside so-called Western societies, he also notes the tendency in anthropology to contrast and oppose sight to hearing. Among the criteria of distinction, as he puts it, 'are that sound penetrates whereas sight isolates', 'that the auditory world is dynamic and the visual world static' and 'that to hear is to participate whereas to see is to observe from a distance' (Ingold 2000: 251). As Ingold goes on to remark (ibid.: 252), these sets of

---

7 In addition to Igreja (2015) and Whyte (1997), see Graw (2009), Parkin (1991) and Wilce (2001).

oppositions speak louder to the preconceptions of researchers than to the sensory experiences of their subjects of study.

In the study of divination, this tendency to categorically distinguish between vision and audition finds its parallel in the change of focus from the figure of the diviner to that of the consulter. We will be better served by an approach that acknowledges the value of both sides, and questions both the tendency to oppose sight to hearing and the erroneous assumption that these sensorial modalities always occupy the same position in the power dynamics of particular séances.

A case in point is television divination in Mozambique. Here the seers are not the diviners but their clients, and the diviners' role is to urge their clients to see the image of those individuals who made them suffer on a 'television screen' consisting of a wooden board. Diviners ask their clients to see those images 'for themselves' (Igreja 2015: 705–717). In addition to this focus on vision, here largely under the consulters' control, Igreja reports that the clients are also expected to describe the images they see on the 'screen' and discuss them with one another (ibid.: 708). In television divination, vision and audition are not mutually exclusive. These two modalities depend on one another, and the activity of divining is perfectly well described as both to see and to dialogue.

TOUCHING

Thus far I have shown that the distant senses of sight and hearing play a key role in basket divination. These senses, however, are not alone. In fact, without the near senses of touch, kinaesthesia and pain, the eyes of both diviners and consulters would lack a focal point, and their words turn to silence.

Let us revisit the typical séance. In order to access Kayongo's truth, the basket diviner employs a material mediator: a coiled basket about eight centimetres deep and thirty centimetres wide, filled with thirty or so symbolic pieces of different shapes, sizes and materials. Seated on a goat skin, one leg outstretched and the other bent sideways, the diviner grabs his oracle by the sides, feels the round shape of his basket and the tight coils woven with the strong roots of the *mukenge* tree (*Combretum zeyheri*). He also senses the weight of the divining pieces through the basket. Philosophers refer to this awareness of distal objects through a tool as extended touch (Fulkerson 2016: 7).

My attention so far has been focused on so-called active or haptic touch, that is, on the work of the hands as instruments of knowledge (Chidester 2000: 62). In the Luvale language, the act of touching with one's hands is known as *kusalika*. The diviner, however, does not simply and quietly hold his basket, inviting his clients to look inside; he also shakes his basket in an upward motion, *seku, seku, seku*, as the Luvale speakers onomatopoeically evoke the sound of upward shaking. For this reason, the Luvale may sometimes apply the term *lwalo*, typically reserved for a winnowing basket, to the *lipele*, suggesting a kinaesthetic resemblance between the act of shaking the *lipele* and the women's work of winnowing food stuffs, such as pestle-pounded rice grains and dried *tukeya* fish. The active sense of touch engages the somatic sense of kinaesthesia. From Greek *kinein* (to move) plus *aisthēsis* (sensation), kinaesthesia is defined as the sensation of movement.[8]

This relation between touch and kinaesthesia should not come as a surprise. In the act of touching, we do not only use our hands and fingers. We also move the elbows and shoulders, the trunk and legs, and the feet and toes. We actively move and feel with nearly every surface of our body because our body receptors are located not only on the skin but also in the muscles, joints and tendons (Fulkerson 2016: 3). As Fulkerson puts it, 'there is some truth to the claim that we touch with our whole body' (2016: 7). We also learn with our whole body. In Chidester's words, 'in the kinaesthetic movements of the body, tactile information is acquired. For the study of religion, kinaesthesia calls attention to embodied movements—kneeling, standing, prostrating, walking, climbing, dancing, and so on—not only as types of ritual performance but also as instruments of knowledge' (2000: 71).[9]

Note that the act of holding the *lipele* and shaking it in a vertical motion is not in the least secondary to the acts of seeing and hearing. This important point is clearly reflected in the Luvale descriptive terms used to designate the technique of basket divination. I mentioned earlier that the diviner is a seer, and that to divine is both to see and to talk. In addition, basket divination differs from other methods available in northwest Zambia on the basis of the modus operandi of its divining instrument. While the rubbing board, for instance, operates by rubbing one piece against another, as its name suggests, the divining basket works by shaking

---

8 For the relation between tactile perception and kinaesthesis, see for example Fulkerson (2016: 2), Loomis and Lederman (1986) and Paterson (2007: 21).

9 On touch and tactility in Religious Studies, see Brown (2009), Chidester (2000, 2005), Hughes (2018), Promey (2014) and Whitehead (2018).

it upward; hence its descriptive name, *ngombo yakusukula*, 'the oracle that is operated by shaking it'. This designation is widespread in the vast region where Zambia, Angola and the Democratic Republic of the Congo share borders. Consider the following terms: *ngombo yakusekula* in the Luvale-speaking areas, *ng'ombo yakusekula* in Ndembu territory (Turner 1975: 213), *ngombo ya cisuka* in Chokwe country (Bastin 1988: 20) and *ngoomb ya chisuk* in Luunda land (De Boeck and Devisch 1994: 104). This occurrence of the same descriptive name over thousands of kilometres and across ethnic and linguistic differences is not fortuitous. While, to my knowledge, only the Luvale people refer to their divination basket as *lipele*, they share the designation *ngombo yakusukula* with the Ndembu, Luunda and Chokwe, among others. Without the diviner's embodied knowledge of how to operate the divination basket—and, consequently, without the basket itself—the diviner's eyes would lack a focal point. The bodily act of shaking the basket gives all the séance participants a physical anchor where they may focus their gaze and base their dialogues.

To better grasp the importance of basket shaking, we need to briefly consider the diviner's apprenticeship. To access Kayongo's knowledge, diviners must undergo a long and challenging apprenticeship during which they will not only memorise the names and symbolism of the the thirty or so divining pieces, a key component of their training, but also learn how to toss the basket's contents in mid-air while ensuring their landing inside the basket. Learning the symbolism of divining pieces goes hand in hand with learning how to operate the divining instrument.

The basket divination student apprentices himself to a senior diviner. He joins his master on divining trips in the region of northwestern Zambia or to locations further afield, such as the Western province of Zambia and the Zambeze province of neighbouring Angola. As an apprentice, or *pumba*, the soon-to-be diviner learns by assisting his master as needed. He may carry his master's large carrying basket, which contains the *lipele* and other paraphernalia, including the distinctive bell-shaped *musambo* rattle, the *somo* horn and the bundle of broken arrows. He may help his master set up the liminal space of his séances by laying a dried goat skin on the sandy ground, and positioning the *lipele*'s paraphernalia within arm's length. During his master's séances, the apprentice may swiftly grab any divining pieces that might land on the ground. He may also help the consulters play their part in the séance by repeating the diviner's statements along with them. In due time, the senior diviner will on occasion hand out his basket to his student, encouraging him to divine. Diviners learn their new skill through practice, repetition and perseverance, eventually incorporating (literally, bringing into the body) their new working tool and religious mediator.[10]

Thanks to these long apprenticeships and the subsequent opportunities to practice as professional diviners, these men are able to perfectly coordinate the act of shaking their baskets with their visual reading and verbal translation of material configurations—a case of intersensoriality, as Howes terms the coming together of the senses (2005: 7–12). I would also suggest that basket divination in an example of learned synaesthesia, a case in which one sensorial stimulus arouses impressions in another sensorial register. In the literature on this fascinating topic, the classic example of sensory blending is coloured hearing. Here, an auditory stimulus produces both auditory perceptions and coloured visual images (Marks 1978: 83–93; Straus 1963: 214–230). In the case of basket divination, the accomplished diviner apprehends his own act of physically operating the oracle as both kinaesthetic perceptions and material images,[11] engaging in a form of kinaesthetic seeing.

We have come a long way since Aristotle judged the sense of touch as metaphysically and morally inferior to the other senses, and Kant demeaned the sense of touch, as well as smell and taste, as brutish and servile.[12] Thanks to the interdisciplinary work of contemporary researchers, we know that touch holds an indispensable place in the human sensorium (Paterson 2007: 9) as well as the messier fields of religious, cultural and social life.[13] The activity of basket divination asks us to acknowledge the importance of seeing and hearing while at the same time taking into account that the séance participants would see nothing and hear nothing without the presence of two mediators: the divination basket that contains true statements in objectified form, and the diviner's skilled body that holds the oracle and shakes it. The divinatory truth is visible, audible and tangible.

> 10 On skill and incorporation, see Leder (1990: 30–31). On practical knowledge or *praktognosia*, see Merleau-Ponty (1962 [1948]: 140). See also Meyer's idea of 'religious didactics', during which 'the senses are called upon and tuned in a way that yields a habitus' (Meyer 2006a: 23).
> 11 The idea of learned synaesthesia has been recently developed in interesting ways by Casini (2017), Watson (2014) and Whitelaw (2008).
> 12 See Aristotle (1968) and Kant (1966 [1790]). On the history of the human senses in Western thought, see Paterson (2007), Serematakis (2018) and Synnott (1991).
> 13 Many authors have dealt with the topic of the senses in its relation to religious, cultural and social processes, among them Classen (1998, 2005a, 2010), Csordas (1993), Geurts (2002), Howes (1991a, 1991b, 2005, 2015) and Hsu (2008).

FEELING PAIN

Any study of the sensory form of basket divination would remain incomplete without briefly considering one last somatic sensation that can neither be seen nor shared: pain. Diviners describe their feeling of pain (*kwivwa kukola*) as a sensation of pressure, and they ascribe that painful feeling to Kayongo. As they put it, Kayongo causes their heart and head to 'change' (*kwalumuka*). Diviner Sangombe described the experience of being possessed by Kayongo as an upward movement (*kukatuka*) from the heart toward the head, a growing pressure in the chest and an increasingly faster and heavier heartbeat that he described by means of ideophones: *luku luku luku luku* (a pounding sound) and *palakanyi* (pressure). In his effort to describe the experience of being released from Kayongo's grasp, Sangombe spoke of a downward movement, *hehhhh* (sighing) and *nyeka nyeka nyeka nyeka nyeka* (lowering or sagging). Often reported by basket diviners, these opposing sensations of pressure also appear in a famous *lipele* song:

> This feeling of pressure, my *lipele*
> This feeling of lightness, *lipelehhh*

It is no coincidence that in northwestern Zambia the heart is described as a site of understanding. People say that the process of thinking (*kushinganyeka*) takes place in both the head and heart. Diviners wish that their hearts may have, as they express it, openings of understanding. In the words of diviner Sangombe,

> Let the throat have openings, let the heart have openings. When the diviner lays his hands on the *lipele*, may he have openings of understanding like the openings of a banana stalk. This is no trivial matter. When the heart in the chest hurts, kwi!, you start moving like the cowry shell moves in the river sand. This is how it is.

Another famous *lipele* song evokes this conjoining of different organs and abilities:

> Lyaya lyaya
> The sun has set
> The eagle owl does not miss its prey
> And thinking is in the heart

To explain their heartaches, diviners link their recurrent physical symptoms to their own trajectories as basket diviners. Diviner Sakutemba told me how he became a basket diviner. He had been living an ordinary life in Chavuma, cultivating cassava in the fields, catching fish in the flooded plains located on the west bank of the Zambezi River and selling his catches for good money in the local market. Then, he fell seriously ill with pains in his chest, headaches and moments of lunacy. When Sakutemba's relatives took him to a basket diviner, they confirmed their suspicion. Sakutemba had been caught by his maternal ancestor in the form of Kayongo, the cruel ancestral spirit who forces some of his male descendants to become basket diviners. According to Sakutemba, although his physical condition improved as a result of that consultation, his initial symptoms of chest pains, headaches and mental disturbances returned periodically, becoming the sensorial markers of his professional identity as a basket diviner.

It is also instructive that diviners explain their heartaches by linking each séance to the initiation ritual that all diviners undergo prior to joining the divining profession. At some point in this night-long ritual—in itself a rich sensorial form in which the senses of the ritual participants become attuned to Kayongo—the senior diviner in charge reportedly presses a tiny needle tip into a small portion of the sacrificed cockerel's heart, which he tells the initiate to swallow. In divinatory symbolism, the crowing cockerel, which announces the sunrise, stands for clairvoyance. The needle tip symbolises the diviner's sharpness. In addition to this symbolism, however, the needle is said to cause a piercing pain in the diviner's own heart when he is in the midst of divining. This sharp pain signals to the diviner that a new divination point has been revealed.

Pain is therefore experienced as a sensory intensification of stimuli received through the senses of vision and kinaesthesia working in synergistic concert. When, by shaking his basket, the diviner reveals, or makes visible, a new divination point, he feels pain.[14] As soon as he turns the new piece of knowledge into words, his heart stops aching. Note that pain is a particularly powerful communicator due to its sensory intensification and

14 As such, the experience of pain in basket divination appears to corroborate the so-called intensive theory of pain, a theory that refutes the more prevalent idea that pain is a distinct sensorial mode typically known as nociception. According to the intensive theory of pain, 'the primary function of pain experience is to indicate when the stimuli that are sensed whenever anything is perceived by means of a sensory modality exceed a significant level of intensity' (Gray 2014: 89). On synaesthesia and pain, see Marks (1978: 93–98).

episodic structure. Being the only sense that hurts, pain places upon the sufferer an affective call.[15]

Moreover, when the diviners report a feeling of pain, they are not speaking symbolically or metaphorically. They assured me that the pain they feel in their chest is a physical pain. Thanks to their accounts, it also become clear that their experience of synaesthesia involves not only two senses, as previously stated, but three modalities: sight, kinaesthesia and pain. That which they experience as movement, they see as images; and that which they see as images and sense as movement, they feel as pain. In this regard, the exemplary work of basket diviners in northwest Zambia offers a valuable contribution to the study of synaesthesia, an area of research in which little attention has been given to culturally shaped forms of learned synaesthesia as well as synaesthetic experiences involving the sensation of pain.[16]

SENSING THE TRUTH

Echoing Plato's distinction between the senses and reason, Aristotle associated sight with knowledge, and touch with affect, a notoriously persistent dualism in the history of Western thought. In *Phenomenology of Perception*, Merleau-Ponty offers a powerful critique of the tendency to sever the intellect from the body, and relegate the body to the servile status of the 'handmaid of consciousness' (Merleau-Ponty 1962 [1948]: 139). More recently, numerous authors have espoused this critique, arguing that corporality is a generative principle, and that the body perceives and acts of its own accord.[17] The 'sensory turn' in the humanities and social sciences builds on this ground-breaking scholarship by showing that the body perceives and acts through the senses. As Ingold puts it, 'the whole body perceives, [and] meaning is generated within the contexts of its activities of looking, listening and so on' (2000: 284).[18] In our quest for knowledge, we rely as much

15 On the concept of pain and the correlated notions of sensory intensification, episodic structure and affective call, see Gray (2014) and Leder (1990: 73).
16 Exceptions to this research trend are, for example, Casini (2017), Watson (2014) and Whitelaw (2008).
17 Important contributions to this large body of literature on the body and embodiment include Csordas (1993, 1994: 37), Jackson (1989: 119–136 and 199) and Leder (1990: 5–7).
18 For an historiographic account of the transition from 'text' to 'embodiment' to the 'sensory turn' in the human sciences, see Cox (2018) and Howes (1991a: 3–4, 1991b).

on the intellect as we do on our senses, and depend as much on our distant and ratiocinative senses as we do on our near and affective modalities. The idea that sight and hearing are superior senses is biased and myopic. All senses are similarly incomplete. Hence their readiness, as Straus words it, to 'complement each other and become a genuine being-together' (Straus 1963: 230).

In this chapter, I have shown that the senses of sight, hearing, touch, kinaesthesia and pain work together to good effect in the sensorial form of basket divination, making the transcendental 'sense-able' (Meyer 2006b: 9). The diviner's motor skills and his sense of kinaesthesia enable him to shake the basket, offering his gaze a material anchor. Adding to his sense of kinaesthesia, as well as his vision, the experience of pain lets the diviner know when he has laid his eyes on the right configuration in response to his queries. While the eyes interpret the successive configurations, the feeling of pain lets the diviner know when truthful patterns have surfaced. In basket divination, the senses cooperate with one another. Sight and touch do not work separately, the eyes seeing, the hands holding and shaking the oracle, and the heart aching. These modalities work in synergy and synaesthesia. At the centre of this complex religious practice stands the diviner's body, shaking his *lipele* and producing a different configuration with each upward shake. The oracle's name, *ngombo yakuseluka*, or the 'oracle that operates by shaking it', speaks to the centrality of the body, the sense of touch and material religion in basket divination.

While I have, for the purpose of this study, separated the senses at work in basket divination, beginning with the distance senses of sight and hearing and gradually transitioning to the near senses of touch, kinaesthesia and pain, my intention was never to create a rift between these two sensorial categories, and much less resurrect the old mind-body dualism in a new guise. In basket divination, all these senses work in tandem and for the same purpose: the revelation of ancestral truths. While sight as well as hearing play a key role in séances, opening up a channel of communication between the diviner and his clients, it is not possible to access truthful knowledge based on these two senses alone. In lieu of the idea of a hierarchy of the senses, let us welcome their creative collaboration, and celebrate the indispensable role that the human senses, the moving body and material objects play in lived and sense-able religion.

BIBLIOGRAPHY

Adler, Alfred and Andras Zempléni. 1972. *Le bâton de l'aveugle: Divination, maladie et pouvoir chez les Moundang du Tchad*. Paris: Hermann.

Andermann, Lisa. 1991. '"To Render Visible": Making Sense among the Ndembu'. In D. Howes (ed.), *The Varieties of Sensory Experience: A Source Book in the Anthropology of the Senses*, 203-209. Toronto: University of Toronto Press.

Aristotle. 1968. *Aristotle's De anima, Books II and III (with certain passages from Book I)*, translated from Greek, with introduction and notes by D.W. Hamlyn. Oxford: Clarendon Press.

Bastin, Marie-Louise. 1988. 'A propos du panier divinatoire Tshokwe'. *Arts d'Afrique Noire* 68: 19-27.

Brown, Candy Gunther. 2009. 'Touch and American Religions'. *Religion Compass* 3/4: 770-783. https://doi.org/10.1111/j.1749-8171.2009.00154.x

Carpenter, Edmund. 1973. *Eskimo Realities*. New York: Holt, Rinehart and Winston.

Casini, Silvia. 2017. 'Synesthesia, Transformation and Synthesis: Toward a Multi-Sensory Pedagogy of the Image'. *The Senses and Society* 12 (1): 1-17. https://doi.org/10.1080/17458927.2017.1268811

Chidester, David. 2000. 'Haptics of the Heart: The Sense of Touch in American Religion and Culture'. *Religion and Culture* 1 (1): 61-84. https://doi.org/10.1080/01438300008567140

Chidester, David. 2005. 'Tactile Imagery in American Religion and Politics'. In Constance Classen (ed.), *The Book of Touch*, 49 68. Oxford: Berg.

Classen, Constance. 1998. *The Color of Angels: Cosmology, Gender, and the Aesthetic Imagination*. London: Routledge.

Classen, Constance. 2005a. 'McLuhan in the Rainforest: The Sensory Worlds of Oral Cultures'. In David Howes (ed.), *Empire of the Senses*, 147-163. Oxford: Berg.

Classen, Constance (ed.). 2005b. *The Book of Touch*. Oxford: Berg.

Classen, Constance. 2010. 'Foundations for an Anthropology of the Senses'. *International Social Science Journal* 49 (153): 401-412. https://doi.org/10.1111/j.1468-2451.1997.tb00032.x

Cox, Rupert. 2018. 'Senses, Anthropology of'. In Hillary Callan (ed.), *The International Encyclopedia of Anthropology*, Vol. 10, 5411-5422. Hoboken, NJ: Wiley Blackwell.

Csordas, Thomas J. 1993. 'Somatic Modes of Attention'. *Cultural Anthropology* 8 (2): 135-156. https://doi.org/10.1525/can.1993.8.2.02a00010

Csordas, Thomas J. (ed.). 1994. 'The Body as Representation and Being in the World'. In Thomas Csordas (ed.), *Embodiment and Experience: The Existential Ground of Culture and Self*, 1-24. Cambridge: Cambridge University Press.

De Boeck, Filip and René Devisch. 1994. 'Ndembu, Luunda and Yaka Divination Compared: From Social Engineering to Embodiment and Worldmaking'. *Journal of Religion in Africa* 24 (2): 98-133. https://doi.org/10.2307/1581328

Devisch, René. 1991. 'Mediumistic Divination among the Northern Yaka of Zaire'. In Philip M. Peek (ed.), *African Divination Systems: Ways of Knowing*, 112-132. Bloomington, IN: Indiana University Press.

Fabian, Johannes. 1983. *Time and the Other: How Anthropology Makes its Object*. New York: Columbia University Press.

Fisher, Jennifer. 1997. 'Relational Sense: Towards a Haptic Aesthetics'. *Parachute* 87: 4–11.
Fulkerson, Matthew. 2016. 'Touch'. In Edward N. Zalta (ed.), *The Stanford Encyclopedia of Philosophy*. https://plato.stanford.edu/archives/spr2016/entries/touch/
Geurts, K.L. 2002. *Culture and the Senses: Bodily Ways of Knowing in an African Community*. Berkeley: University of California Press. https://doi.org/10.1525/9780520936546
Graw, Knut. 2009. 'Divination as Hermeneutic Encounter: Reflections on Understanding, Dialogue, and the Intersubjective Foundation of Divinatory Consultation'. In William A. Christian Jr. and Gábor Klaniczay (eds.), *The Vision Thing: Studying Divine Intervention*, 459–477. Budapest: Collegium Budapest.
Gray, Richard. 2014. 'Pain, Perception, and the Sensory Modalities: Revisiting the Intensive Theory'. *The Review of Philosophy and Psychology* 5 (1): 87–101. https://doi.org/10.1007/s13164-014-0177-4
Harvey, Graham. 2018. 'Introduction'. In Graham Harvey and Jessica Hughes (eds.), *Sensual Religion: Religion and the Five Senses*, 1–18. Sheffield and Bristol: Equinox.
Horton, A.E. 1953. *A Dictionary of Luvale*. El Monte, CA: Rahn Brothers.
Howes, David. 1991a. 'Introduction: "To Summon All the Senses"'. In David Howes (ed.), *The Varieties of Sensory Experience: A Sourcebook in the Anthropology of the Senses*, 3–21. Toronto: University of Toronto Press.
Howes, David. 1991b. 'Sensorial Anthropology'. In David Howes (ed.), *The Varieties of Sensory Experience: A Sourcebook in the Anthropology of the Senses*, 167–191. Toronto: University of Toronto Press.
Howes, David. 2005. 'Introduction'. In David Howes (ed.), *Empire of the Senses*, 1–21. Oxford: Berg.
Howes, David. 2015. 'Sensation'. In S. Brent Plate (ed.), *Key Terms in Material Religion*, 193–199. London: Bloomsbury.
Hsu, Elisabeth. 2008. 'The Senses and the Social: An Introduction'. *Ethnos* 73 (4): 433–443. https://doi.org/10.1080/00141840802563907
Hughes, Jessica. 2018. 'The Texture of the Gift: Religious Touching in the Greco-Roman World'. In Graham Harvey and Jessica Hughes (eds.), *Sensual Religion: Religion and the Five Senses*, 191–214. Sheffield and Bristol: Equinox.
Igreja, Victor. 2015. 'Intersections of Sensorial Perception and Imagination in Divination Practices in Post-war Mozambique'. *Anthropological Quarterly* 88 (3): 693–723. https://doi.org/10.1353/anq.2015.0042
Ihde, Don. 1979. 'Vision and Objectification'. In *Technics and Praxis*, 82–92. Dordrecht, Holland: D. Reidel. https://doi.org/10.1007/978-94-009-9900-8_7
Ingold, Tim. 2000. 'Stop, Look and Listen! Vision, Hearing and Human Movement'. In *The Perception of the Environment: Essays on Livelihood, Dwelling and Skill*, 243–287. London: Routledge.
Jackson, Michael. 1989. 'Knowledge of the Body'. In *Paths Toward a Clearing: Radical Empiricism and Ethnographic Inquiry*, 119–136. Bloomington, IN: Indiana University Press.
Jackson, Michael. 1996. 'Introduction'. In Michael Jackson (ed.), *Things as They Are: Phenomenology, Radical Empiricism and Anthropological Critique*, 1–50. Bloomington, IN: Indiana University Press.
Jackson, Michael. 2013. 'How to Do Things with Stones'. In *Lifeworlds: Essays in Existential Anthropology*, 31–50. Chicago: University of Chicago Press.

Jay, Martin. 1993. *Downcast Eyes: The Denigration of Vision in Twentieth-Century French Thought*. Berkeley: University of California Press.
https://doi.org/10.1525/9780520915381
Kant, Immanuel. 1966 [1790]. *The Critique of Judgement*. Translated by J.H. Bernard. New York: Hafner.
Kopytoff, Igor. 1981. 'Knowledge and Belief in Suku Thought'. *Africa* 51 (3): 96–110.
https://doi.org/10.2307/1159605
Leder, Drew. 1990. *The Absent Body*. Chicago: University of Chicago Press.
Lienhardt, G. 1961. *Divinity and Experience: The Religion of the Dinka*. Oxford: Clarendon Press.
Loomis, Jack and Susan Lederman. 1986. 'Tactual Perception'. In K. Boff, L. Kaufman and J. Thomas (eds.), *Handbook of Perception and Human Performance*, 1–41. New York: Wiley.
Marks, Lawrence E. 1978. *The Unity of the Senses: Interrelations among the Modalities*. New York: Academic Press.
Meek, C.K. 1931. *Tribal Studies in Northern Nigeria*. London: Kegan Paul.
Merleau-Ponty, Maurice. 1962 [1948]. *Phenomenology of Perception*. Translated by C. Smith. London: Routledge and Kegan Paul.
Meyer, Birgid. 2006a. 'Religious Sensations: Why Media, Aesthetics and Power Matter in the Study of Contemporary Religion'. Inaugural Lecture, VU University, Amsterdam, 6 October 2006.
Meyer, Birgid. 2006b. 'Media and the Senses in the Making of Religious Experience: An Introduction'. *Material Religion* 4 (2): 124–134.
https://doi.org/10.2752/175183408X328262
Meyer, Birgid. 2010. 'Aesthetics of Persuasion: Global Christianity and Pentecostalism's Sensational Forms'. *South Atlantic Quarterly* 109 (4): 742–763.
https://doi.org/10.1215/00382876-2010-015
Ngubane, Harriet. 1977. *Body and Mind in Zulu Medicine: An Ethnography of Health and Disease in Nyuswa-Zulu Thought and Practice*. London: Academic Press.
Palmeirim, Manuela. 2010. 'Discourse on the Invisible: Senses as Metaphor among the Aruwund (Lunda)'. *Journal of the Royal Anthropological Institute* 16 (3): 515–531.
https://doi.org/10.1111/j.1467-9655.2010.01637.x
Parkin, David. 1991. 'Simultaneity and Sequencing in the Oracular Speech of Kenyan Diviners'. In In Philip M. Peek (ed.), *African Divination Systems: Ways of Knowing*, 173–191. Bloomington, IN: Indiana University Press.
Paterson, Mark. 2007. *The Senses of Touch: Haptics, Affects and Technologies*. Oxford: Berg.
Plate, S. Brent. 2005. *Water Benjamin, Religion, and Aesthetics: Rethinking Religion through the Arts*. New York: Routledge. https://doi.org/10.4324/9780203997734
Plate, S. Brent (ed.). 2015. *Key Concepts in Material Religion*. London: Bloomsbury.
Promey, Sally M., ed. 2014. *Sensational Religion: Sensory Cultures in Material Practice*. New Haven, CT: Yale University Press.
Ryle, Gilbert. 1949. *The Concept of Mind*. New York: Barnes & Noble.
Seremetakis, C. Nadia. 2018. 'Tactility'. In Hilary Callan (ed.), *International Encyclopedia of Anthropology*, Vol. 11, 5987–5995. Hoboken, NJ: Wiley Blackwell.
Silva, Sónia. 2011. *Along an African Border: Angolan Refugees and Their Divination Baskets*. Philadelphia: University of Pennsylvania Press.
https://doi.org/10.9783/9780812203738

Silva, Sónia. 2013. 'Remarks on Similarity in Ritual Classification: Affliction, Divination, and Object Animation'. *History of Religions* 53 (2): 151–169. https://doi.org/10.1086/673184

Silva, Sónia. 2014. 'Mind, Body and Spirit in Basket Divination: An Integrative Way of Knowing'. *Religions* 5 (4): 1175–1187. https://doi.org/10.3390/rel5041175

Silva, Sónia. 2016. 'Object and Objectivity in Divination'. *Material Religion* 12 (4): 507–509. https://doi.org/10.1080/17432200.2016.1227638

Stoller, Paul. 1989. *The Taste of Ethnographic Things: The Senses in Anthropology*. Philadelphia: University of Pennsylvania Press. https://doi.org/10.9783/9780812203141

Straus, Erwin. 1963. *The Primary World of Senses, A Vindication of Sensory Experience*. Translated from the German by Jacob Needleman. London: Collier-MacMillan.

Stroeken, Koen. 2008. 'Sensory Shifts and "Synaesthetics" in Sukuma Healing'. *Ethnos* 73 (4): 466–484. https://doi.org/10.1080/00141840802563923

Synnott, Anthony. 1991. 'Puzzling over the Senses: From Plato to Marx'. In David Howes (ed.), *The Varieties of Sensory Experience: A Sourcebook in the Anthropology of the Senses*, 61–78. Toronto: University of Toronto Press.

Turner, Victor. 1975. *Revelation and Divination in Ndembu Ritual: Symbol, Myth, and Ritual*. Ithaca, NY: Cornell University Press. https://doi.org/10.7591/9781501717192

Watson, Marcus R. 2014. 'Synesthesia and Learning: A Critical Review and Novel Theory'. *Frontiers in Human Neuroscience* 8: 98. https://doi.org/10.3389/fnhum.2014.00098

Whitehead, Amy. 2018. 'Touching, Crafting, Knowing: Religious Artefacts and the Fetish Within Animism'. In Graham Harvey amd Jessica Hughes (eds.), *Sensual Religion: Religion and the Five Senses*, 215–236. Sheffield and Bristol: Equinox.

Whitelaw, M. 2008. 'Synesthesia and Cross-Modality in Contemporary Audiovisuals'. *The Senses & Society* 3 (3): 259–276. https://doi.org/10.2752/174589308X331314

Whyte, Susan Reynolds. 1997. *Questioning Misfortune: The Pragmatics of Uncertainty in Eastern Uganda*. Cambridge: Cambridge University Press.

Wilce, James. 2001. 'Divining Troubles, or Divining Troubles? Emergent and Conflictual Dimensions of Bangladeshi Divination'. *Anthropological Quarterly* 74 (4): 190–200. https://doi.org/10.1353/anq.2001.0040

Sónia Silva is an Associate Professor of Anthropology at Skidmore College. She is the author of *Along an African Border: Angolan Refugees and Their Divination Baskets* (University of Pennsylvania Press, 2011), a study of divination and divining baskets (*lipele*) among Angolan refugees in Northwest Zambia. This and other publications on the topic of divination draw on two years of ethnographic fieldwork in Northwest Zambia, and are inspired by the concepts of lived religion, material religion and existential anthropology. Presently, Silva is researching the role of the colonial idea of the fetish in the early representation of Africa in European and North American museums as well as the demise of the 'fetish' beginning in the 1960s, when curators reframed the African religious objects in their displays as modernist art imbued with spirituality.

Part III

TOUCH, RITUAL EFFICACY AND COMMUNICATION

Chapter 9

'I am broken, I am remade. And I am held tightly through all that comes between.'—BDSM and Religioning on the Edge

ALISON ROBERTSON

> I have only two arms to hold you. Let my ropes be an extension of my form, let me wrap my love around you and keep you held in my arms longer and stronger than my own limbs ever could. As I hold this length of hemp line in my hand let me lock eyes with you as it passes from my will to yours, and brings us into a shared space, a sacred space, outside of our other worries. Let us dwell in each other's presence.... In these times of pain and desperation I offer up this as a safe space to be the true you that you cannot show to the outside world.
> —B. Harrington, 'The Many Paths of Earthly Bondage'

The inclusion of BDSM (put simply, Bondage, Domination, Sadism and Masochism) in a collection of work about religion may not be an immediately obvious choice, but it is one I could justify in several ways. I am not going to focus on BDSM practised as a part of named religious tradition, although such practitioners exist. Neither am I going to take the currently best travelled path in the academic study of BDSM and examine its potential to produce experiences of transcendence. Instead I wish to set aside views of religion which require the idea of distinct binaries such as sacred/profane or matter/spirit. I see no such neat separation between the things people do in their everyday lives and the things they do in designated 'religious' spaces. Religion cannot be separated from the material situation in which it arises, and/or to which it responds, and this means that religion can be found everywhere and anywhere: in all 'the places where humans make something of the worlds they have found themselves thrown into' (Orsi 1997: 7). The play-space of BDSM is one such place of 'adult ritual play' (Taves 2009: 159) within which challenging forms of touch are employed to shape powerful and transformative experiences. This kind of idiosyncratic ritualising enables a person to remake themselves, and to share the results of that remaking. Whether it occurs inside or outside the aegis of a named religious tradition or institution is irrelevant to its power, place and value within the lives of the individuals concerned. Understanding this requires moving away from an essentialist view of 'religion-as-a-thing' (Nye 2000: 466) and towards religion as an element of human existence shaped to and by individual lives involving constant and fluid processes of exploration and creation; a shift best signalled with a corresponding shift from noun to verb—religion to religioning. By framing the practice of BDSM as religioning I do not say 'BDSM is a religion', since the determiner 'a' feeds the very binaries I have discarded to reach this point. Nor do I impose or presume an acceptance of 'religious' as a part of the self-understood identity of my research participants. What I do say is that BDSM, and other such practices, can and do function within individual lives as religioning activities, and so the religioning offers an analytical lens through which the meaning and significance attached to their kink by (some) kinky people can be understood. As I unpack the use and nature of touch in the context of BDSM, its potential as a source of world-, meaning- and/or story-making will also be revealed.

SETTING THE (BDSM) SCENE

The sense of touch incorporates both pleasant and unpleasant sensation, can take both violent and gentle forms and be used to express the full range of human emotions. But, when the term is used in general conversation it seems to infer the gentler end of these possibilities: it may be literally true to say that Boxer A touched Boxer B's face in order to bring an end to their bout, but that feels like a strange way to put it. Something that is described as 'touching' is usually something that has created gratitude, empathy, perhaps melancholia, while something that creates rage, jealousy or discomfort is described with other words. Words the English language offers for violent or intrusive forms of touch generally carry a more negative weight of associations and an implication of (non-consensual or undesired) harm being done. Striking, beating, pinching, biting, slapping, punching, cutting, smacking and similar terms are all examples of touch less likely to be considered warmly. However, the consensual activities of BDSM commonly involve such touches and more of the same kind. The term is typically considered an 'overlapping abbreviation' (Tanos 2003) that stands for some combination of Bondage and Discipline, Domination and submission, Sadism and Masochism, or Sadomasochism and (possibly) Slave and Master, an understanding which places pain- and power-exchange at the heart of what BDSM is.

The research from which the material that follows is drawn took the form of forty-six qualitative semi-structured interviews conducted with forty-four self-identified practitioners of BDSM. My requirements for participation in the research were only that they had some real-world experience of doing what it is that they do (playing), and that this was important to them. Various aspects of this, including their understanding of contested terms and accounts of personal experience, were unpacked and explored through reciprocal and dialogic conversations.

Drawing on the material thus collected, I am able to offer this summary of the nature of BDSM as practised by my participants: a collection of activities (usually called play) that involve the conscious and consensual use of pain, perceptions about pain, sensation, emotion, restraint, power, perceptions about power or any combination of these, for psychological, emotional and sensory pleasure. This builds on a foundation offered by Staci Newmahr (2011b), but is extended to better reflect the forms of play in which participants to my research engaged; to further enhance that reflection it should be noted that while all individuals who responded to my call for participants recognised themselves and their activities in the term BDSM, it was generally considered too narrow a term to denote the complexities of their practice and the link of that practice with identity. The generally preferred label for their identity was 'kinky' and the term 'kink' was used in two ways: as an umbrella term for the entire array of behaviours and relationships (including ones they did not perform themselves) associated with fetish, BDSM, D/s (Dominance and submission), DD (Domestic Discipline), SM (Sadomasochism) and other activities such as body modification; and as an indicator of individual placement within that larger milieu, with individuals referring to their 'kink(s)'—an individual portfolio of interests and associations drawn from the larger pool of all kinks that can be woven into self-understanding and identity. An exhaustive list of specific kinks is not really possible, but my research included both practitioners of more common practices (bondage, spanking, flogging) and of more unusual, extreme or edgy ones (electro-play, cutting, enemas). Among my research participants BDSM was primarily used as a general descriptor for performative elements of kink or, more specifically, the practising into existence of one's personal kinks, whether or not the practice fitted into the areas covered by translating the acronym.

CHALLENGING TOUCHES

BDSM is troublesome and potentially distressing for an observer because it does involve violence, pain, discomfort, restraint, the physical and emotional exercising of power by one person over another. It involves the deliberate creation of sensations (and emotions) presumed to be unpleasant and, although always done consensually and for mutual satisfaction, it can look otherwise. Common understandings of the kinds of activity associated with BDSM carry with them assumptions that the qualitative experience of such sensations is universally the same for all and that what is unpleasant in the moment must always remain so. It thus remains a common view that someone consenting to be hurt must be psychologically damaged in one way and someone wishing to inflict consensual pain must be psychologically damaged in another. BDSM represents a spectrum that extends from light bondage as part of foreplay to detailed torture scenes that are 'hands-on, up close, teeth and snarling and bruises that don't show off well after the fact' (Kaldera 2010: 106). It is perceptions of the latter that feed the kind of judgements which might encourage people at the other end to distinguish themselves from the category. Engaging in BDSM, whether or not you choose to call it that, carries social risks that include psychiatric diagnosis, social discrimination (e.g. job loss) and criminal prosecution (Khan 2014). The infamous 'Spanner' case (R v Brown 1993), which forms much of the basis for the current legal status of consensual BDSM in the UK, judged BDSM practices to be 'the indulgence of cruelty by sadists and the degradation of victims' (Templeman LJ, 83) which is not only 'dangerous and injurious to individuals' but 'if allowed...harmful to society generally' (82). Even the (minority) opinions in favour of accepting that free consent removed criminality declared BDSM to be 'repulsively wrong' (Lowry LJ, 115) and found it 'astonishing' that the existence of such consent was not in doubt (Slynn LJ, 121).

The Spanner judgements also reveal a simplified view of consensual BDSM as based in the ability of participants to experience pain directly as pleasure and/or to take pleasure directly from creating pain. Not all BDSM involves pain, but even its explicitly sadomasochistic forms are far from that simple. My research participants' descriptions of receiving consensually inflicted pain reveal multiple ways of experiencing it: pain can be surrendered to, so as to be felt as it is, without judgement; it can be grappled with in a struggle to hold it and survive it, or to feel the triumph of not being destroyed by it; it can be welcomed for its power to break, cleanse or transform; it can be endured or weathered as the state in which one exists for those moments; it can be submitted to and accepted as something being given with their acceptance, an expression of service, commitment or love; and it can be embraced or delighted in because the sensations themselves are, or can become, pleasurable. Any of these might be combined with others or passed through as distinct stages of the same experience and all involve and require the input, connection and corresponding experiences of the inflictor, so that the scene as a whole is co-constructed. It cannot be assumed that all recipients of pain are masochists or givers of it sadists, as those terms are commonly understood, neither can the power distribution within a scene be automatically inferred from who feels what.

BDSM practices are violent—although practitioners would probably reject this word as carrying too great a burden of moral judgement—they are often painful and/or humiliating and they trespass on bodily integrity, but they are not experienced as either the indulgence of cruelty by one at the expense of another or as a simple physiological quirk that makes what 'should' be painful directly into pleasure. Madeleine, who plays on both sides of the experience, described processing the feeling of pain as 'transubstantiation' because she transforms sensations devoid of physical pleasure into 'an offering', while the process of inflicting it is a twofold experience of 'enabling or bringing about this transition but…[also] you're sacrificing your humanity to do it'. Making such transformation is, at least in part, dependent on many factors rather than an inbuilt ability—Marie speaks for many so-called masochists when she observes, 'I stubbed my toe the other day, and it was horrible…. And I was thinking "how is this that just one knock gets me swearing and yet I can bend over and have someone beat me repeatedly and love it?"'. The answer lies partly in the crucible formed by the context of the experience as a whole (Robertson and Wildcroft 2016) and partly in the type of pain being delivered. Molly described forms of play which involve 'pain which I will ride and endure' because although that form of pain is a sensation in which 'I can't find the pleasure place' it will give her physical marks, in which she finds a different kind of pleasure. She also spoke of the enjoyable physicality of 'my real pleasure-pain…. I don't even think of it as painful.' This distinction between a combined pleasure-pain and experiences where the pleasure derives from 'having done them rather than out of doing them at the time' (Ivy) is a common one. Molly's play-partner Michael described some of the complex layers that contribute to his pleasure in creating these different pains for Molly. These layers include 'a sense of release—isn't exactly the right word', physical satisfaction 'in the ache of your muscles from having used them' and pleasure in 'having taken you [Molly] to a place that you've enjoyed and liked'. Mistress Marina spoke of the pleasure in 'taking control of myself…I could do something really damaging that could then wreck everybody's lives or I could, just one second before it becomes that, say "OK you can breathe now"' and of the consensual submission of her partners as enabling her to be comfortable with 'the feeling of power'. For pussikin (who chooses not to capitalise her name as an expression of her identity as a submissive) someone giving her pain is something that 'kind of [pause] solidifies me. It says…that I'm here. I'm real. And [pause] I guess that I matter enough…that someone would take the time to hurt me, put the energy into it.' For Rocks the enjoyment is not precisely in the infliction of pain but in 'the reactions that come back' and 'the fact that here is somebody who has not merely given you explicit permission to hit them; they're getting off on it! … It's that slight twisting of everything…that I enjoy.' BDSM play seems to blend experiences of dysphoria and euphoria in ways that render 'twisting of everything' one of the clearer descriptors of its qualities.

BDSM is clearly mutually pleasurable but that pleasure is complex and the shared, reciprocal nature of the experience may not be obvious to a bystander, even if they are kink-friendly. Aey shared with me an account she had written after a fellow attendee of a kink club shared their understanding of a play encounter that she experienced as an intimate dance 'like a symphony—melodically moving through an area, intensity increasing, reaching crescendo, then fading into gentleness again':

> He said 'we were watching you play…you were so relentless…like a treadmill at the gym.… We could see you were hitting him harder and harder, as if to say "You will respond! You will respond!" [You were] determined to get a reaction from him, and he wasn't giving it'…[and I thought] is that what it looked like? Well, I suppose it did. His face was turned to me and they were at a distance. They wouldn't have seen his occasional faint smile—the peaceful, almost glowing aura.… They saw the impacts, not the dance. They saw him under the impacts, not his body humming. They see S&M—not the music.

The difference between the impacts and what Aey calls the 'body-hum' is qualitative and not directly observable and so understanding the use and experience of touch in BDSM challenges common perceptions about pleasurable, loving and reciprocal touch. For kinksters, though, their play constitutes a shared 'exploratory journey to joy' (Ben). That journey is primarily built through the sensation of touch and responses to touch. Such a playing with sensation must, however mild the activity, always find a point between trust and violation. A spanking or a flogging does literally and, in the UK at least, legally constitute actual bodily harm; *R v Donovan* [1934] defines actual bodily harm as including any hurt or injury that is more than transient or trifling and that interferes with health or comfort. However, this not necessarily experienced by a consenting recipient as a violation unless it goes beyond previously agreed limits or either party fails to recognise the desire of the other to stop. It need not be pleasant in the moment but, to be play rather than abuse, it must not cause harm of the kind created by an undesired violation of intimacy.

Understanding intimacy as the experience of one person accessing what would usually be inaccessible in another person makes it clear that intimacy which is forced is also terrible, as in the case of rape. BDSM requires consent to take place which, in turn, requires trust. It is always open to the risk of that trust being betrayed, meaning that BDSM activity is not inherently a violation 'but it is potentially so, always and deliberately' (Newmahr 2011b: 178). It plays with the distinction between violation of the body and violation of trust. Some people and some scenes play further from the point of violated trust than others but sometimes finding the point of balance between the two, the precise edge between intimacy and violation, is the aim of the play. In walking along that edge, it is possible to create liminal spaces of both uncertainty and potential and so to explore such things as power, intimacy, vulnerability, trust, responsibility, identity, place, belonging and connections between self and other.

EDGES AND LIMITS

Deliberately creating and experiencing high-risk edges is edgework. This concept initially focused on the boundaries between physical absolutes like life and death or consciousness and unconsciousness and the exploration of these through extreme sports like skydiving (Lyng 1990). Later work has recognised that non-corporeal, emotional or psychological edges such as control/abandon or safety/danger can take as much skill to navigate and return from safely as physical edges (Newmahr 2011a). The intimacy/violation edge described above is one such edge and analysing a single kink scene might incorporate multiple conceptual edges; the experience however is always described as being on 'the edge', without identification of any specific boundary.

The term edge-play is in common use in the kink scene, although its exact meaning is contested. For some it signals forms of play that would make 'somebody look twice' even if there is no one present to actually witness it, because 'you know certain things are just going to do that' (Stoney-face)—play with needles, blades and electricity are likely to fit this category; for others it is play 'where you can kill them by accident if you're not careful' (Aey) with play on the edge being simply 'how far I can push things, before I have to stop...the edge of life and death' (Mistress Marina); and for still others the edge is found in precisely the same balance of intimacy/violation that makes all play possible, the point at which 'it is acceptable on this side of what you're doing and unacceptable on the other, whether it's psychological or physical', and to play there is simply to ask yourself 'can you balance on that razor-edge?' without falling over it (Barry).

Discourse about edges in kink is further complicated by the idea of limits. Negotiations of personal limit are an important part of the preparation for play with a new partner, and consent is given in the context of those negotiations. However, the intensity and power of play is determined by how close it comes to those limits so that while they are, broadly speaking, the things that an individual does not wish to do or to have done to them, they might also be 'hard' or 'soft'. They can also change, not just as experience increases but because of different situations, relational dynamics and so on. Personal limits are 'not about how much you can take. It's when it stops being fun' (Griff), so things which are not enjoyable (in even the ambivalent, complex ways that pain, shame and discomfort are enjoyed within kink settings) indicate places upon which play should not trespass. Establishing these hard limits is thus the beginning of creating the edge between integrity and violation where play can take place, but it is only the beginning. Pushing limits can be a tool for creating more intense, powerful experiences of constructive discomfort for both parties—a process Douglas Ezzy identifies within pagan rituals as making 'space and time for transformations of soul' (Ezzy 2014: 16). Through such embodied performances people can directly address matters of deep concern or perceived threat, and the opportunity to reflect on those matters, as they pertain to themselves, is opened up. This iterative process is neither wholly conscious nor fully articulated; both limits themselves and processes of their exploration are at least as much somatic and emotional as they are cognitive, which is why pushing them is not (necessarily) a violation of consent. It is also why safe-words are a potentially important part of play. An agreed safe-word is a word which, if spoken by either party, stops the play immediately, demonstrating the centrality of trust to the play relationship. For limit-pushing play, as with Ezzy's discomfiting rituals, 'people do it because it feels right' (2014: 5), and the enriching nature of the experience is thus primarily somatic and emotional.

Experiences of the edge as described by Lyng (1990, 2012)—including altered perceptions of self, situation, space and time, dissolution of the self-object boundary and/or a sense of 'hyper-reality'—could result from most kinks (Easton and Hardy 2004). This means that an activity could be classed as edgework even if the actor would not call it edge-play, and care must therefore be taken not to assume edge-play and edgework are interchangeable terms. Newmahr, aware of the distinction, describes all kink play as edgework. Seen against its broader social context it clearly pushes normative, social, emotional and psychological boundaries; it explores 'the edges of morality...the liminal spaces between liberty and constraint, kindness and cruelty, and goodness and badness' (Newmahr 2011a: 698). It is in fact rooted in a foundational edge between intimacy/violation and the risk of betrayed trust inherent in that. All kink flirts with these edges, and in doing so it first creates and feeds the tension between potential danger and potential transformation and then, ultimately, resolves it. The 'potential for human actualisation' (Ferrell 2005: 78) is inherent in experiencing the edge; players who have successfully negotiated it can later understand and use 'their own potential to break through what they have come to regard as unalterable...limits' (Bromley 2007: 290). In this understanding kink is thus not only edgework, but spiritual edgework in that it uses deliberate constructions of risk to create experiences through which it is possible to discover and rediscover new ways of being, knowing and relating.

SHARING TOUCH

The centrality of touch to BDSM activities for the recipient of the sensation is clear—a person is hit and feels the sensations created by the blow; a person is bound and feels the bonds against their flesh and the resistance as they shift their muscles against those bonds. But, as I have emphasised already,

BDSM is intimate. It is also usually a relational, shared and co-constructed experience. It is worth noting that activities like self-bondage and self-spanking are practised within the Kink Scene, but they are much less common than relational kink. Since touching always also entails being touched and, as I shall show, the forms and processes of play rely upon responses to touch, it follows that the experiences created through such a process cannot be properly understood as isolated and internal to a single individual. As experiences are co-constructed by both/all players, they are also shared, reciprocal and so intimate. That these things can be created in positively valued forms through violence, discomfort, pain and distress renders BDSM a counter-pleasure (MacKendrick 1999), transgressing popular understanding of what is and is not desirable.

Touch is the deep and formative sense that it is at least partly because of its inherent reciprocity. It is a relatively common joke in the Kink Scene that many Dominants prefer not to hand-spank because of the nasty stinging sensation it creates for their poor delicate palms, but this joke illustrates the truth that to be willing to hit someone, to cut into or clamp their flesh, requires a corresponding willingness to feel the sensations that delivering such sensation will create. Even if a Dominant saves their palm by using a strap or a cane, such an implement 'transcends tool into extension of self really easily' (Stoney-face) during the process of play, and so the presence of a tool is not experienced as an interruption to the experience of touching and being touched. Touch is, of all our senses, perhaps the hardest to muffle or deny—absent a physiological problem, the surface of the skin is always sensitive and an awareness of what is touching us at any given moment is always available if we choose to access it (Sheets-Johnstone 2009). Touch not only expresses emotions that already exist, but it can create new ones or instantly recall prior experiences, and this might render otherwise desirable touches unpleasant; in Newmahr's (2011b) account of becoming involved in kink as part of her research she recounts how emotional associations with spanking ruled it out as an activity for her, although she was willing to engage in forms of play most kinksters would categorise as far more extreme, while some spanking aficionados would not class their kink as falling into the category of BDSM at all (Plante 2006). Touch is also productive of intimacy, a concept often casually assumed to be inherently positive, but which can be forced and terrible; it can create closeness and communicate compassion, but also pain, rage, fear and damage.

Touch is thus the foundation of BDSM activity—even sensory deprivation equipment involves touching and being touched—and the different, complementary experiences of the top and bottom players are intertwined. Although BDSM is sometimes described in terms of role-play, this is misleading when touch is considered; the touches shared during BDSM play are real and produce real sensations: when my research participants spoke of flogging they meant the actual, physical, real-world striking of flesh with an implement designed for that purpose, when they spoke of cutting they meant the deliberate slicing open of skin. A beating is a real thing. Even if it is stopped after the first blow, that blow was actually felt by both giver and recipient, and it is not really possible to know what that sensation will be like or how you will respond to it until, as Madeleine succinctly put it, 'the minute that the belt hits the arse'. The challenging nature of these kinds of touch means that some people choose to restrict their involvement wholly to fantasy but if real-world experience is desired then the risk that it won't prove enjoyable must be taken. That step is the first one in finding that edge between intimacy and violation where it is possible to 'discover things about myself that I didn't know' (Molly).

CO-CONSTRUCTING PLAY-SPACES

When the right balance can be found, play creates an other-where, an '"as if" or "could be" universe' (Seligman et al. 2008: 7) experienced as fully real and authentic, within which different potentialities can be shaped and explored. This does not happen inside the isolated mind of a single subject but in and through performed relationship. The presence of other people in a given space, even without any deliberate or direct communication between them, changes the experience each has of that place. When connections and communications are overt, explicit, intended and/or directed, as they are in the context of kink, and especially when those communications include something as intimate and foundational as touch, a collaborative and co-constructed experience is the result.

A typical BDSM scene involves a person (or several) giving or creating sensation, wielding whatever tools are being used and generally directing the scene overall, and a person (or people) on the receiving end of this. Common descriptors for these roles are 'top/topping' and 'bottom/bottoming'; put simply, a top is the person using the flogger while the bottom is the person being flogged. These terms describe the mechanics of a scene only and players often prefer other terms that also reflect their relational dynamic such as Dom/Domme and sub(missive). Not all kink relationships involve play or power-exchange and, for those that do, play does not always involve the Dominant partner taking the top role, but my focus here is on the processes of play and in such a context top/bottom as descriptors of role are sufficiently clear.

All BDSM play occupies a physical space, whether it is a dedicated playroom, the space around a piece of play-designed furniture (such as a St Andrews Cross or a spanking bench) at a club or a party, or simply an ordinary room in an ordinary house with everyday furniture. But successful play also happens within a different space, distinct from everyday reality. This play-space is 'practiced into existence' (Lindquist 2005: 158) through a continuing loop of actions performed by the top upon the bottom, and reactions to those by the bottom which then feed the responses and next actions of the top. This is likely to start gently and become more intense as all parties become more immersed in the play: 'You build it up. It's almost like a vortex. You're building it up as you're going along' (Mistress Marina). Aey says that this 'doesn't consciously happen...because you're so deeply focused it tends to happen naturally', while Cee suggests that it begins as a conscious and intentional process but changes as the feedback loop is formed so that 'to start off, yes, I'm very conscious of what I am, what I'm doing. But as it goes on, if you're getting really good feedback with that person and you're connecting you are actually completely oblivious to what you're wearing, what you're doing. Everything just seems to naturally flow...what we started off last night doing, and what we ended up doing were two completely different things, because I feed on that person.' But, whether conscious or not, this is not a mechanical process; it is not simply the act of flogging, or spanking or bondage which creates it. While mechanical, technical play is possible and would create many of the same physical sensations (although experienced differently), the kind of play-space being described here is relational, both created by and creating connection between the players. Ben compared this relational kind of play with kink that is solely for the gratification of a sexual urge, saying: 'It's not like going to a prostitute where you get your thing done and then you get out. It's not about that...the whole concept is, for me the whole approach is different. It's about giving joy and receiving joy. The whole phrase here is giving and receiving.'

This giving and receiving is multi-directional, and all players involved both give and receive sensation, emotion and connection. The specific qualities of these are different—the sensation of hitting is distinct from the sensation of being hit—but there is a shared knowledge of the mutually constructed nature of the experience. Ultimately it is felt that 'he's doing this to give me pleasure as much as it gives him pleasure' (cate, who, like pussikin, chooses not have her name capitalised), with all the many-layered complexities of pleasure in this context taken as read in that claim. This idea of play as mutually pleasurable is crucial to relational kink. Without it, in a situation where one partner simply goes through the motions to please the other, the connection necessary to create a fully realised play-space would not be present. Colin described the discovery, towards the end of his marriage, that his wife had explored kink as much as she ever wished to do: 'There was a night that I will never, ever forget, when she sat on the side of the bed pulling on some stockings and she said "God, I hate doing this".' This discovery meant that 'That was it. It was finished, gone', and he no longer found play with her pleasurable. Michael does play with people who are not Molly, but he experiences this very differently to play with her, saying he is just 'a stunt-arm' on these occasions; the play is still enjoyable and he does have to like someone he's going to play with because 'if you're not able to empathise and be in touch...you're going to make a mistake' but 'I am removed. I am not in that moment of that situation in the same way that...I am when we [him and Molly] do our thing.' It would still be possible to transgress the intimacy/violation boundary in this kind of play, but it is much less likely that either player would want to get close to that edge without a more intense mutual connection.

This kind of relational play requires both 'give and take', not only in the sense that 'I enjoy giving somebody something else, I enjoy what they give in return' (Damien) but in the sense of reactions and communication. If the reactions are not there for the top to read, with the bottom 'literally laid there like a plank' (Damien), the top may well then be confused as to whether the bottom has got anything from the play thus far and, consequently, unsure about what to do next. This communication is not purely verbal but takes place 'in the body' (Demon); 'it's the eye contact, it's body reaction, it's breathing' (Cee). It is not just about the 'wriggling around and squeaking' (cate), but about empathy, 'the energy that's around' (Nomad), 'interchange' (Barry) and the 'glorious dance...that you do together' (Aey). Ben explains it this way: 'BDSM is a relationship. Full stop. You are in a relationship with another person. And in order to enjoy, it's a bit like paella—the prawn, the chicken, the saffron, the cloves...each have to lose a little bit of themselves and absorb a little bit of the others and so it makes it a fantastic dish. So, if you think of a relationship as a paella or a pilaf or whatever...not only mixing ingredients together, each ingredient willingly loses a bit of themselves and gains the other.'

All participants need to understand all this at some level to make the connection that the play-space draws on. It is made 'absolutely together, unequivocally. Regardless of the roles being taken' (Griff). Mistress Marina agrees that 'the two of you need to make it together. I think if you've got someone with you that's not reading off the same page you can't go there.' Most of the people with whom I spoke had had experiences where things just did not work. The description cate gave is typical: 'I just got funny vibes from it. I couldn't fully relax and so I just had to stop...[the bubble] just wasn't there for me. I was doing it because I could...I could do it if I wanted too and I was doing it because I could, and I thought I would try it because I'd never actually played without the relationship before, so I thought I would try it to see what it was like and it did absolutely nothing for me, basically.' The connection is more than trust; for play to create this other world seems to require something 'more than just trust, it's also about bonding that occurs. When you can bond that deeply with someone.... And the bonding occurs as a process. It doesn't just happen at any one point; it's something that takes place over time' (Javelin). For pussikin, the top and bottom form two parts of a whole 'like a hook and eye, I've got one part, and it either fits with a partner or it doesn't.' She suggests that without both parts 'you can have kinky sex, but you can't have BDSM'. The implication here is that kinky sex does not dance along that line between intimacy and violation, although it might appear to. It does not actively embrace the risk of trust betrayed. The distinction pussikin draws is that between doing and being, as suggested by Newmahr—'people who do SM engage in it as a means to a (sexual) end. People who "love SM", by comparison, view SM as an end in and of itself' (Newmahr 2010: 329). For the kind of transformative ritualising play that has been discussed here to be deliberately sought it seems likely the players will be in the latter group, although this love might be discovered after an unexpectedly powerful play-experience.

The existence of the play-space relies not just on the practice, but on the relationship being enacted in that space. Play both creates and requires a bond between the players, so that as people play together more often they can also play more intensely and enter into their shared world more completely. The process of forming the play-space is initiated by the actions of the top performed upon the bottom; the bottom is the heart of the space; the connection and interactions of the players form and maintain the space, and the edges of it are held/defined by the top. And so, the world is changed, and a new space is created within which powerful experiences can occur.

BALANCING ON THE EDGE

I have observed above that the things which happen in a play-space are really felt, both somatically and emotionally, in the space of an as-if world. In describing 'rites of terror', Whitehouse and Lanman express surprise that such rituals are really painful, and truly terrifying. As they see it 'the costs of participation seem to be out of all proportion to the imputed symbolic value' (2014: 679). It might similarly be said that the levels of pain, fear, humiliation, etc. experienced within a play-space are disproportionate to the role being played. The confusion in both cases is the same: these ritual events are not symbolic or conceptual, they are real; players are not acting, but living an alternative reality. The reality of the experience gives it immediate, visceral power, whether or not a symbolic meaning is ascribed later.

This account by pussikin illustrates how different forms challenging touch create edges for her during play:

> This is something I've only done with my Master; I think I would only do it with my Master. This thing...it's like a bag you get in, and there's pockets inside for your arms and when it's zipped up it fits pretty much skin-tight all over. There's straps on the outside to tighten it up anywhere it's loose. I couldn't even [pause] I couldn't even move my fingers...I've never been so still [pause]. So still. And with a blindfold as well, stuff always freaks me out more if I can't see. Some people like it, it makes them feel safe. Held...I mean you can feel it gripping every part of you, so you are literally being held [pause] but I didn't find that comforting. For me it's scary. Not being held per se I mean [pause] but being held like that. Being held so still and left alone. Thinking you're left alone [pause]. For me it's scary. It was the closest to being totally immobile I've ever been, and it was [pause] a serious head-fuck. Serious. Total. I don't know how long I was in it for...I mean I was whimpering within minutes. Maybe seconds. I ended up screaming. There's just something about not being able to move...something like [long pause] melting, maybe. Fading away. I can take a lot of pain. I mean I've been beaten until my skin starts to lift and been happy to carry on but this [pause] I think, maybe, pain kind of [pause] solidifies me. It says...that I'm here. I'm real. And [pause] I guess that I matter enough...that someone would take the time to hurt me, put the energy into it. But that immobility was the opposite to that.... Am I really real? [laughs] And that tells you all my hang-ups, right there!

Although this experience was genuinely distressing it was also affirming; pussikin feels she learnt something from it, 'something about how I...

touch the world'. The vulnerability needed for that learning requires a level of trust pussikin could not simply give to anyone, because it is real vulnerability, arising in a place of real fear. Thus, the experience is not simply one of facing fear but also of trust given and justified. An edge is also necessarily created for the other player in this scenario because he must recognise himself as someone who is not only capable of deliberately creating this extreme of distress but of gaining fulfilment from that process. Rocks described this as a process through which 'you have pushed into dark places and you have come back again and, yes, you can be this nasty person but you're not. You don't have to be. You can unleash the beast and you can put it back in the bottle again.' This kind of exploration, recognising/accepting that 'forbidden side' (Rocks) in oneself, is fraught with emotional risk. Confrontation of it is made possible through the trust of the other player. Both pussikin and her Master are present on the edge, and they can only return safely from it together—he must help her to realise and accept her own reality and she must help him to accept the beast and return it to the bottle where it lives.

Griff described a scene of a similar kind at some length, emphasising how real the experience became for his partner—'she was convinced I was going to cut her up. She wouldn't safe-word, because she thought "if I'm going to safe-word he's going to kill me"'—and the reciprocal impact that such a successful creation of fear had on him:

> I had absolutely convinced her that there was no way out. That she wasn't going to get up. That she wasn't going to grab things. Because it just doesn't happen. And you know I just slowly took away all the options, leaving her with the only logical conclusion which is 'I'm going to die'. There is no way to [pause] describe that. And not in a good way, not only in a good way. Because that was the most intense scene I've ever done. Since and before. You know how some people say, 'I don't think I could ever kill anyone', or 'I think I could'. Right, you don't actually know until you're in the situation. And because I played it well I was in that situation. She was on the floor with various cuts of meat written out on her in marker, with a saw and a chisel and a knife. All there—the bathtub was lined with plastic—it was all there. I could have done it.... [But] here's the thing, here's the thing. At that [long pause] because I've never been in that frame of mind before [pause]...you have to be convincing, you have to be convincing. And I could have done it, as in physically. I mean everything was there. But I couldn't. I discovered that there is [pause] an absolutely huge brick wall at that point in my brain that stops me from taking that further. There is absolutely no way I would ever kill anyone...but you know what, I realised that I didn't know that wall was there before. Now I do.

Griff's account reveals how the two of them mutually constructed power, fear, control and vulnerability through the process of play; if the bottom he was playing with had not responded in the right way, Griff could not have taken either of them as far as he did, neither could he reach or confront that edge alone. Her experience of the edge was fear for her life, his was the fear of his own capacity for violence. Underlying both of these complementary edges is that edge between fidelity/betrayal that is always present when one person surrenders control to another. Both parties were therefore necessary to make an edge they could walk together and return from safely and, since such a powerful experience takes time to assimilate, that return may require a relationship of longer duration than the play itself. The process of play is thus not the exploration of an isolated self but what Cee describes as 'the interaction of two like-minded souls...wanting to experience something on mutual ground'. When pussikin told me 'I am broken. I am remade' by play she was not describing something that is isolated within her, inflicted by an uninvolved outsider which she then constructs post-fact into a positive experience, because she also said, 'I am held tightly through all that comes between.' In relational kink no one is alone on the edge; it could not exist if they were because, as Cee observes, 'At that moment in time with edge-play, I am theirs and they are mine.'

CONCLUSION: SPIRITUAL EDGEWORK, PERSONAL RELIGIONING

I have called the touch involved in BDSM challenging, and so it is. It is challenging to understand the pull to experience discomforting and dysphoric forms of touch, whether you feel that pull yourself or not; it is challenging to touch in ways that create pain and distress and challenging to surrender oneself to such touches; challenging to develop the skills needed to create intense sensations and challenging to accept that the doing is enjoyable or satisfying. But none of these challenges are grappled with in isolation. When we touch we are touched in return, and, in its touching of 'boundaries of the self that one does not allow to be crossed mundanely' (Bauer 2014: 111), BDSM pushes that reciprocity to the edge of violation: to engage in BDSM is to at least begin an active exploration of the point at which the experience of touch might become violation for you and to discover what can be discovered in the places you make and find along the way. BDSM requires being both the giver and the recipient of trust, with the inevitable risk that such trust can be betrayed. In such a space of performed vulnerability it is possible to achieve access to aspects of oneself and of other that could not occur 'outside these spaces of potential violation' (Newmahr 2011b: 179). Balancing at the edge between violation and trust inherent in BDSM allows for 'the discovery of things about myself that I didn't know' (Molly). This is spiritual edgework that 'gives me sensations and it gives me thoughts...to re-examine life through this experience' (Simon/Effie); that fills 'the hole in my life [that] needs to be filled by me. By knowing who I am...that knowledge of knowing who you are' (Griff) ; that 'creates a closeness that other things don't...you have that moment, or however long it takes when you feel so close to another human being' (Oliver); that helps 'me push past that next, impossibly, inflexible barrier, that part of me...that thinks I'll never do that, I can't' (Rita); 'that makes me feel that I am whole' (Kaz). This is religioning at its most fundamental, an active engagement with discovering what it means to be human within the worlds in which we find ourselves.

BIBLIOGRAPHY

Bauer, Robin. 2014. *Queer BDSM Intimacies.* Basingstoke: Palgrave Macmillan. https://doi.org/10.1057/9781137435026

Bromley, David. 2007. 'On Spiritual Edgework: The Logic of Extreme Ritual Performances'. *Journal for the Scientific Study of Religion* 46 (3): 287–303. https://doi.org/10.1111/j.1468-5906.2007.00359.x

Easton, Dossie and Janet Hardy. 2004. *Radical Ecstacy: SM Journeys to Transcendence,.* Oakland: Greenery Press.

Ezzy, Douglas. 2014. *Sex, Death and Witchcraft.* London, New Delhi, New York and Sydney: Bloomsbury.

Ferrell, Jeff. 2005. 'The Only Possible Adventure: Edgework and Anarchy'. In Stephen Lyng (ed.), *Edgework: The Sociology of Risk-Taking,* 177–202. New York and Abingdon: Routledge.

Harrington, Bridget. 2006. 'The Many Paths of Earthly Bondage: Bondage as a Tool Towards Spiritual Release'. In Raven Kaldera (ed.), *Dark Moon Rising: Pagan BDSM and the Ordeal Path,* 58–65. Hubbardston: Asphodel Press.

Kaldera, Raven. 2010. 'Blood Run Down'. In Lee Harrington (ed.), *Spirit of Desire: Personal Explorations of Sacred Kink,* 99–107. Lynnwood: Mystic Productions.

Khan, Ummni. 2014. *Vicarious Kinks: S/M in the Socio-Legal Imaginary.* Toronto, Buffalo and London: University of Toronto Press. https://doi.org/10.3138/9781442668096

Lindquist, Galina. 2005. 'Bringing the Soul Back to the Self- Soul Retrieval in Neo-shamanism'. In Don Handleman and Galina Lindquist (eds.), *Ritual in Its Own Right,* 157–173. Oxford and New York: Berghahn Books. https://doi.org/10.3167/015597704782352564

Lyng, Stephen. 1990. 'Edgework: A Social Psychological Analysis of Voluntary Risk Taking'. *American Journal of Sociology* 95 (4): 851–886. https://doi.org/10.1086/229379

Lyng, Stephen. 2012. 'Existential Transcendence in Late Modernity: Edgework and Hermeneutic Reflexivity'. *Human Studies* 35 (3): 401–411. https://doi.org/10.1007/s10746-012-9242-0

MacKendrick, Karmen. 1999. *Counterpleasures*. Albany: State University of New York Press.

Newmahr, Staci. 2010. 'Rethinking Kink: Sadomasochism as Serious Leisure'. *Qualitative Sociology* 33 (3): 313–331. https://doi.org/10.1007/s11133-010-9158-9

Newmahr, Staci. 2011a. 'Chaos, Order and Collaboration: Toward a Feminist Conceptualization of Edgework'. *Journal of Contemporary Ethnography* 40 (6): 682–712. https://doi.org/10.1177/0891241611425177

Newmahr, Staci. 2011b. *Playing on the Edge: Sadomaoschism, Risk and Intimacy*. Bloomington, IN: Indiana University Press.

Nye, Malory. 2000. 'Religion, Post-Religionism and Religioning: Religious Studies and Contemporary Cultural Debates'. *Method and Theory in the Study of Religion* 12 (4): 447–476. https://doi.org/10.1163/157006800X00300

Orsi, Robert. 1997. 'Everyday Miracles: The Study of Lived Religion'. In David Hall (ed.), *Lived Religion in America: Toward a History of Practice*, 3–21. Princeton, NJ: Princeton University Press. https://doi.org/10.2307/j.ctv143mdcw.4

Plante, Rebecca F. 2006. 'Sexual Spanking, the Self, and the Construction of Deviance'. *Journal of Homosexuality* 50 (2–3): 59–79. https://doi.org/10.1300/J082v50n02_04

R v Brown [1993] 2 ALL ER 75.

Robertson, Alison and Theo Wildcroft. 2016. 'Sacrifices at the Altar of Self-Knowledge'. *Body and Religion* 1: 88–109. https://doi.org/10.1558/bar.31763

Seligman, Adam B., Robert P. Weller, Michael J. Puett and Bennett Simon. 2008. *Ritual and its Consequences*. Oxford and New York: Oxford University Press. https://doi.org/10.1093/acprof:oso/9780195336009.001.0001

Sheets-Johnstone, Maxine. *The Corporeal Turn*. Exeter: Imprint Academic, 2009.

Tanos. 2003. 'BDSM'. In *Urban Dictionary* [online]. Accessed 4 June 2016. http://www.urbandictionary.com/define.php?term=BDSM

Taves, Ann. 2009. *Religious Experience Reconsidered*. Princeton, NJ and Oxford: Princeton University Press. https://doi.org/10.1515/9781400830978

Whitehouse, Harvey and Jonathan A. Lanman. 2014. 'The Ties That Bind Us: Ritual, Fusion and Identification'. *Current Anthropology* 55 (6): 674–695. https://doi.org/10.1086/678698

Alison Robertson is a research associate at the Open University, UK. She recently completed her doctorate exploring BDSM (Bondage, Domination, Sadism and Masochism) as a lived form of religion. She is interested in the places where the lines commonly drawn between categories (such as 'religious' and 'non-religious') become blurred or ambiguous and in how such blurring affects the ways people look at the world. Her research interests, other than kink, include lived and personal religion, edgework and self-inflicted or positive experiences of pain. She has published articles in these areas and is working on a monograph based on her doctoral thesis.

Chapter 10

Religion, Touch and Death: Ritual and the Human Corpse

CHRISTINA WELCH

Eve Sedgwick in her book *Touching Feeling* argues that 'touch is...to understand other people or natural forces' (2003: 14). In regard to death, touch can help us understand that a living person has become a lifeless corpse, and that this is a process of nature; although I hesitate to call it a natural process as death is not always understood as natural, often being perceived as the result of supernatural forces, and of course many people die unnaturally from accidents or from violence. Whatever the cause of death, though, the once warm body becomes cold soon after the blood stops pumping through the veins, it loses its suppleness as rigor mortis sets in, and as the processes of decomposition and putrefaction take hold, so too, argues Colin McGinn, does the human sense of revulsion (2011: 13–15). However, whilst touching the dead can be highly problematic in some cultures, it is not so in others, and I deliberately push at the notion that the corpse is innately repulsive (Quigley 2005: 15), taking a more culturally relative approach, to posit that a dead human body is ambiguous.

To cement the ambiguity of the corpse I have chosen a range of religious traditions and spiritual lifeways from a variety of time periods to explore how people deal with the dead. The chapter is arranged into three sections. The first section explores touch and the wet corpse in the context of a socially-good death (i.e. natural end of life), the second section explores touch and the wet corpse in the context of a socially-bad death (i.e. disease, suicide, murder) and the third section explores contact with the dry remains of the human body. Where a corpse is still enfleshed, regardless of how little soft-tissue persists, this is herein understood as the wet remains of the body; and where physical contact is made with skeletal or cremated human remains, this is herein designated as contact with the dry remains. This distinction draws on Hertz's anthropological exploration of death rituals in *Death and the Right Hand* (1960). Yet there are clear differences within the wet category; from a recently deceased cadaver through to a putrefied corpse. Attitudes to a fresh wet body typically differ from those to a rotting cadaver, and usually the recently-dead body tends to disgust less, or indeed disgust not at all. Interestingly, though, it is the recently-dead bodies that are most frequently subject to religious ritual.

In this chapter I deal predominantly with the recently-dead corpse, for before the fresh cadaver becomes insanitary via decomposition, the living have to make decisions as to what happens to the deceased body next; and this means that the corpse must be handled. Depending on when the corpse is dealt with, and what the person died of, the potential level of its insanitariness will differ. If someone dies from trauma, the corpse is 'very unlikely to cause outbreaks of diseases such as typhoid fever, cholera or plague...[but] they may transmit gastroenteritis...[should the corpse] contaminate streams, wells or other water sources' (WHO 2019). However, if the person dies from an infectious disease, even a fresh corpse will most likely be dangerous to the health of the living (notable examples here are Ebola and Covid-19). But regardless of how someone dies, concerns about corpses as a source of potential infection appear to be largely natural (Morgan 2004: 307), often with corpses eliciting feelings of disgust, and thus they require removal from the normative sphere of the living (Curtis and Biran 2001: 20). However, any generalised assertion that repugnance around a corpse is typical needs to be tempered against the normality of death, cultural relativity and the unremarkable need for someone to deal with the disposal of the corpse.

Working with the dead is customary for many people, and in contemporary industrialised society this would include members of the emergency services, health professionals, funeral workers and those who perform rituals to care for the deceased—this latter category is one that has doubtless existed throughout human history. Virtually all religions have some codified approaches to dealing with the dead and indeed Constance Classen, in her book *The Deepest Sense; A Cultural History of Touch*, has suggested that 'religious factors would seem to have played a large part in shaping [the] acceptance of dead bodies' (2012: 40). David Chidester maintains that religions have 'four basic ways in which religious beliefs and practices rise above or go beyond death' (2002: 35). These patterns of transcendence are, he states, found in religions globally for 'religious approaches to death are religious approaches to life' (ibid.: xii). As life in all its complexity is difficult and because 'religious resources are deployed under difficult conditions' (Chidester 2005: 62), it is no surprise to find religious resources intimately connected with death, as the finality of death is perhaps the biggest challenge the living have to come to terms with (Malinowski 1948: 86).

However, whilst Chidester's four patterns reflect how humans transcend the finality of physical existence, this chapter is concerned with the non-transcendent, and the time/s when the reality of death has to faced; when the physically lifeless corpse has to be dealt with. This means I explore here the many ways that the living put aside their possibly-innate feelings of horror, offence and disgust at the thought of biological death, and at the sight of the biologically dead (Bauman 1992: 13; Curtis and Biran 2001: 20), and get on with the act that removes the corpse from everyday life (McCorkle 2010: 375). In many ways the recently-dead are liminal beings, they are physically present but are not active in everyday life. The recently-dead are, at least in the contemporary industrialised world, an example of what Mary Douglas has termed 'matter out of place' as they transgress normative social boundaries (1966: 3), but this does not mean that the recently-dead are totally excluded from society. Indeed, for many working with the dead, touching the dead, just as touching the living, is 'the medium through which the intentions of the heart are conveyed' (Ferch 2011: 167); the dead are rarely understood as unworthy of dignity and often those touching a corpse do so with tenderness, even love.

Handling the recently-dead will involve some form of skin-on-skin connection, although since the advent of disposable medical gloves and other forms of Personal Protective Equipment (PPE) this may be mediated somewhat, and particularly during a pandemic such as Ebola or Covid-19. But regardless, dealing physically with the biologically dead can be difficult as confronting death so directly can be challenging. However, if, as many philosophers and historian of death suggest, we as individuals can only know about death through the death of others (Kristeva 1982: 4; Bauman 1992: 3; Quigley 2005: 9) then contact with the dead becomes imperative for us to understand the fullness of our lives. Further, as the dead can be considered sacred, as in set-aside and potent (Durkheim 1965: 301, 319, 410), and because 'religious tactility is ultimately the capacity to handle the challenges of the living world…' (Chidester 2005: 62), in effect we must to touch the dead to handle life.

RITES CONCERNING THE RECENTLY-DEAD

The most obvious connection that the living have with the dead is through the washing of a recently-deceased body. This common practice is usually rife with ritual. Green and Green in *Dealing with the Dead* (2006) note a number of religions where touching the corpse shortly after death is an important rite. In African and African-Caribbean communities typically the laying out of the cadaver and the ritual purification of the recently-deceased person is done by the extended family (Forde and Hume 2018). In Africa there is also huge variation, but for the Asanta of Ghana, the recently-dead body is decorated as well as ritually purified. Soon after death the body is washed, usually by female relatives of the deceased. It is then taken to a mortuary whilst funeral preparations are conducted. In the morgue the body is embalmed to allow time for elaborate funeral arrangements to be made, and it is decorated to provide an image of a good life: the hair is dyed, the lips painted and the body wrapped in traditional Kente cloth (*nwentoma*) (de Witte 2011: 186, 178). Following an effective lying-in-state, the body is laid in a coffin and then buried. In the past, the ritual washing of a body was typically carried out by an elderly female who used herbs to help slow down the decomposition process; she would then dress the deceased. Today this practice often still occurs before the corpse is taken to a mortuary for final preparations (Roberts 2011: 210–211). The importance of the correct preparation of the body in Ghana, regardless of the ethnic group, is evident from the perception that without a body, there can be no respectful burial. In Ghana, the dead person is the most important person in the funeral event, and elaborate funerals are a long-standing tradition. However, with modern embalming allowing for much greater body preservation, funerals can be delayed, allowing them to become sumptuous affairs (van der Geest 2000, 104–106; 2006: 487).

The ritual preparation of the corpse before disposal is, perhaps unsurprisingly, similar the world over. In Greece, as in Ghana, the role of laying out is traditionally done by female members of the community. In many traditional communities, women see to the birthing and dying rituals, their lives revolving around caregiving (Rundblad 1995: 175; Hera 1995: 226–227). What is different in Greece from Ghana, though, is that after the body is washed and dressed in new clothes, the corpse is laid out with feet tied together; this is to 'prevent the deceased from returning among the living' and becoming a vampire (Kovacheva 2013: 4; Sherman 2008: 486). The corpse's hands are then crossed over the body and tied with a candle placed between them, and an icon is placed on the legs (Danforth 1982:

39). In Greece the candle is believed to protect the corpse from ghosts (Kovacheva 2013: 2), whilst the icon symbolises the Christian faith.

Basic laying-out rituals vary according to cultural and religious mores, but rarely is the difference huge: typically a body is washed and dressed, and often the corpse's eyes are closed and the jaw tied shut. An interesting variance can be seen in the tribal death rituals of Kyrgyzstan where, as well as the above, the palms of the corpse's hands are massaged open to show they are empty. This symbolises that one can take nothing into the next world (Hardenberg 2010: 33); symbolism is rife in death rituals. The symbolism of closed or covered eyes to show the body is no longer part of this world appears to be ancient (Hachlili and Killebrew 1983; Grinder-Hansen 1991), but there is also a highly practical purpose to this rite. Unless closed soon after death, shutting the eyes of a deceased person can be tricky due to the process of decomposition, and as such often a coin or similar object is placed over each eye to keep it closed, or to hide the open eyes. This functional ritual speaks to traditional ways of marginalising the early stages of the decomposition process. In Japan, a handkerchief is placed over the corpse's face, whilst white socks and gloves are placed on their feet and hands respectively (Green & Green 2006: 304); these parts of the body turn blue very quickly after death and by covering them, the visible signs that the blood is no longer pumping through the veins (known as livor mortis) is disguised. Indeed, any covering of a dead body with clothing can be understood to provide the deceased with some final dignity but in practical terms it hides the physical signs of decomposition, notably the setting in of lividity (changes in skin colour). In a similar vein, the washing of the corpse is not only deemed respectful, but also washes away any bodily fluids that may leak out as the sphincter muscles lose their tension (for an overview of decomposition see Mulroy 2018). Arguably, the almost universal practice of washing and dressing a corpse speaks to both a human need to hide, maybe even deny, the signs of death, but also ensures the recently-dead are treated as a respected part of their community, and literally handled with great care.

Intimate contact with the recently-deceased is normative, although not universal. Zoroastrianism stands as example of a religion where there is minimal contact with the dead, and where the body is disposed of naked. But any form of contact must be culturally appropriate contact (necrophilia for instance is usually deemed inappropriate; see Rosman and Resnick 1989; Troyer 2008). Culturally appropriate contact with the recently-dead frequently relates to those who have died a socially-good death, that is, a death that is considered apposite within the community. For example, traditionally the Hidatsa Sioux peoples of North America would leave the dead on a scaffold to decompose naturally. The body would be wrapped in 'the blankets, robes etc. which belonged to them when alive.' Murderers, however, as people who lived and died outside the social norms of the community, would be buried face down in the ground as a mark of disrespect (Bushnell 1927: 24, 75). Traditionally in some Alaskan tribes, a corpse would normally be 'boiled with oil, moss, and driftwood', whereas the body of a criminal was left to rot, again as a public marker of disrespect (Chidester 2002: 22; for more information on mortuary rituals in Alaska see Garfield 1947–1951). Similarly, in medieval Europe, the bodies of criminals were routinely dumped in unconsecrated ground rather than buried in a set-aside sacred space (Ariès 1981: 42); although of course in unusual circumstances such as the plague, even the bodies of the socially-good could be abandoned or buried in mass pits with very little if any ceremony, and not necessarily in consecrated ground (Harding 1993: 62).

In many Asian-originating religious and spiritual traditions, washing and dressing the body for disposal is also normal even if the body is cremated rather than buried. Traditionally in Hinduism, usually within twenty-four hours of death, the body of the deceased is placed on the floor and the sacred items of Ganga water (from Mother Ganges) and a *tulsi* (sacred basil) leaf are placed in the mouth, often along with a silver or gold coin. The body is prepared by relatives and close friends of the same sex and caste, it is washed and dressed in new clothes and the toes tied to 'immobilise the ghost of the person' (Firth 1997: 73); as can be seen, the fear that the dead may return is a widespread concern mitigated against in various ways. In India, the prepared body is carried to the cremation ground where it is burned on an outdoor pyre, although electric crematoria exist in cities such as Varanasi and Delhi where the disposal process is more hidden from public gaze. However, since there are issues over whether electric cremation affects the sacrality/auspiciousness of the disposal process as actual fire is not involved, these facilities are less used by Hindus (Caixeiro 2016). The corpse in Hinduism has an ambiguous status as whilst it is understood as a source of pollution, it is also offered to the sacred fire, and in the home the deceased is treated like a deity with mourners circumambulating the body and touching the corpse's feet (Firth 1997: 73–74). Whilst there is considerable regional and caste variation relating to the details of the cremation itself, typically the face is left uncovered on the pyre and in some regions the skull is deliberately broken during the cremation process to allow the ritual breath to leave the corpse, thus letting the spirit escape (ibid.: 76–78). In India, the actual cremation itself is carried out by those in the lowest caste, the Doms. Like the corpse, these individuals occupy an ambiguous status, for the presence of a Dom is needed for the deceased to 'enter the gates of heaven' (Devi in Shanker 2017) but as low-caste people they are socially ostracised. Doms can be of either gender, and despite their low social status can often make a good living from handling the dead and dealing with the pollution that goes with the corpse (Mukherjee 2017).

Hindu Aghoris also have a very intimate relationship with the dead. These ascetic Shaivite sadhus (holy men) often live in charnel grounds, meditate upon corpses, use human skulls as alms bowls and sometimes eat deceased human flesh; the issue of human endo-cannibalism is not addressed in this chapter. It is important to note that the Aghoris' breaking of everyday Hindu norms through the ingestion of human remains as food, and the 'decoration' of their body with ash from the cremation fires that contain human remains (cremated remains), are rituals that place them as sacred. They engage in such unorthodox acts in an effort to liberate themselves from the cycle of reincarnation that is central to Hindu worldviews, and do so by removing the eight bonds that as Shaivites they understand to bind every person's soul; their intimate contact with the dead works to destroy the bond of fear (Barrett 2008; Suri and Pitchford 2010; Cresswell 2018).

For most Hindus in India, intimate contact with the physical remains of the human dead is central, but for Hindus in diaspora locations, such close and personal contact with the dead is generally not so accepted (Firth 2003: 28). This means that whilst the main mourners may have contact with the corpse in the family home before the coffin is sealed, the actual disposal of the body is private and also automated. Religions are usually inherently practical in terms of rituals, especially when it comes to religions in a diaspora context, and thus there is little vernacular issue over this adaptation of death rituals outside India.

A different religious community in India that has accepted electric cremation, is Zoroastrianism (AFP 2016). In Zoroastrianism, fire is a symbol of all that is sacred (Eduljee 2017), representing Ahura Mazda, the creator deity, whereas a corpse is believed to be the greatest pollutant; after death a body is attacked by the corpse-demon (Nasrušt) who comes in the form of a 'raging fly' (Zykov 2016: 288). As such cremation with fire is prohibited. The *Vidēvdād*, a section of the holy book, the *Avesta*, states that disposal of the corpse should take place in a high location where it can be devoured by either carrion-dogs or birds of prey; these creatures are considered to be unaffected by the pollutants of death but are considered unclean (Choksy 1987: 64). The exposure form of disposal causes as little pollution as possible to the earth, which is understood, like fire and water, to be sacred; as such there can be no earth or water burials in Zoroastrianism.

With a corpse understood as essentially polluting in Zoroastrianism, preparing the cadaver for disposal is problematic. There is a delicate balancing act in ritual preparations between the body of the deceased, which is believed to be contaminated and contaminating, and the personhood of the now-dead individual who must be respected. Further, with soil recognised as sacred, it is important that the corpse is kept off the ground whilst the post-mortem rituals take place; this is usually achieved by placing the cadaver on a large stone slab, although a plastered floor is acceptable as there is no physical contact with the earth. It is also important that the head of the corpse points away from the north where the corpse-demon is said to reside (Boyce 2011).

The Zoroastrian funerary rituals that are carried out when preparing the fresh corpse for disposal are complex. In brief, those who wash and dress the corpse (usually elderly same-sex relatives but not close family) under the direction of a priest, must work in pairs, connected by a piece of cloth or invalid *kusti* (a sacred cord worn by every Zoroastrian like a belt wrapped three times around the body under everyday clothing) to ensure protection against the forces of evil that are believed to be settling on the body now that the soul is unable to protect itself through regular purity rituals, and with the systematic implementation of good thoughts, good words and good deeds (Williams 1997: 157, 165).

Following the preparation of the corpse, a pair of professional corpse-handlers (*nasā-sālār*s), pick up the body from its place of ritual cleansing and position it on a metal bier (metal unlike soil is understood as unable to be contaminated by the forces of death and evil). Then the set of bier-handlers carry the corpse to the place of disposal, a *dakhma*, also known as a Tower of Silence, where the shroud and clothes are removed. In the *dakhma* the body moves from the wet stage to the dry stage as the flesh is picked off by carrion-birds, and the bones are then moved to an ossuary.[1] The job of bier-handler is considered meritorious and undertaken by male or female volunteers from the community (Zykov 2016: 290). Notably, the bier-bearers have very little contact with the corpse and, having transported the cadaver to where it will be disposed of, they withdraw allowing the *nasā-sālār*s (corpse-handlers) and priests to complete the final rituals; the priest cannot have any physical contact with the corpse throughout the entire process. The *nasā-sālār*s lay the corpse on its back, head to the

1 With the drastic population decline in species of vultures in India, the process of desiccation of the corpse is today achieved using solar concentrators.

west, and remove the shroud and clothes from the body, as according to scripture the corpse must be exposed fully naked (although usually women's body are left partly covered). The *nasā-sālārs* having been in contact with the corpse-demon, have to then undergo special purification rituals to rid themselves of the polluting effects of contact with the corpse; yet, even after undergoing these, they, like Hindu Doms, are excluded from the everyday community (Zykov 2016: 297). However, without these people who physically deal with the dead and take on the aspects of human life that most people deem socially unacceptable, societies would not be able to function appropriately.

Dealing with the corpse of someone who has died a socially-good death is, as noted previously, usually codified in religious doctrine or traditionalised through religious praxis, with acts of ritual purification after physical contact with the corpse not unusual. This is particularly the case in Islam where, after washing the body before burial, those engaged in caring for the corpse must undergo their own purification procedures (see for instance the Islamic laws on washing a dead body and then ritual purification after this: for Shi'a Islam see Al-Khu'i undated and Al-Sisyani undated; for Sunni Islam see *Fateha & Funeral Rites* 1999, and *Ashraf's Advice* 2001). However, the body of a Muslim who has died as a martyr (through Minor Jihad or Holy War) is neither washed nor shrouded before burial; their blood-stained body is considered a 'testimony to their great status and the sacrifices they made in the Islamic just war' (Al-Dawoody 2017).

Judaism too has codified rites regarding the washing of a corpse prior to its disposal (Diamant 1998). Washing the body in a ritual known as Taharah (see *Taharah Procedures* undated) is carried out by a specific same-sex group of volunteers known as the Chevra Kadisha. Although the dead must be respected, there are many texts in Judaism noting that people and utensils which have come into contact with a corpse might become ritually impure and as such the Chevra Kadisha, as ritual experts in dealing with the dead, ensure purity regulations are adhered to (Stadler 2006: 841). However, not all people die a natural death, and dealing with the bodies of those who have died a socially-bad death can be problematic.

SOCIALLY-BAD DEATHS

Socially-bad deaths can be understood as ones that do not conform to the social norms of the given society. Sometimes a socially-bad death in one society is understood as a socially-good death in another. In Aztec belief, a woman who died in childbirth was viewed as a warrior and her body would be guarded night and day until burial to ensure her now-potent remains were not stolen (James 2002: 341). Yet, for the rural Ghanaians living in Kwahu-Tafo, a woman who died in childbirth was considered a murderer for killing her child, and as such traditionally her body would be 'thrown in a bush where other pregnant women [would] come to hurl abuse...'. Today a minimal ceremony accompanies a perfunctory burial for such women (Bartle [1977] in van der Geest 2002: 12). Usually, however, socially-bad deaths are deaths from contagious disease, natural disasters or violence. Some violent deaths can mean that there is no intact corpse to ritually deal with, and this is often the case when the deceased died as a result of terrorism. A Jewish Haredi group of male volunteers called Zaka was established in Israel in 1995 to specifically deal with the remains of those who died through terrorism. The Zaka volunteer's task is to recover 'each and every fragment' of a body and pass them over to forensic scientists (Stadler 2006: 839). This job is understood as sacred, as in the Kabbalistic understandings of the Haredi, every person contains an aspect of the Divine. Further, as the Jewish body is a potent metaphor for the Sefer Torah, the Torah Scroll, once a soul has departed the body it is understood as a sacred vessel. However, working with body parts, and the associated blood and gore, means that members of Zaka are intimately in touch with things that are inherently polluting; they are touching matter out of place. Their work therefore is understood as a form of courageous martyrdom, or pious suffering in the cause of providing those who have died violently an appropriately respectful burial. But the members of Zaka must 'undergo purification rituals and onerous fasts' to mitigate against the contamination of those who have died such a violent death (Stadler 2006: 846–848, 850).

Socially-bad deaths come in many forms, and the Atlantic Slave Trade gave rise to body disposal methods far removed from the usual culturally-appropriate funerary rituals, often meaning that traditional African mortuary rites were replaced by the unceremonious dumping of bodies in pauper pits, or corpses being abandoned in fields (typically with the enslaved handling the corpses). With the plantation masters seeing their slaves only as commodities, once spent, their bodies were valueless (Soares 2011: 159–160). The same level of perceived worthlessness led, during World War Two, to the mass unceremonious burial and cremation of people murdered in concentration and extermination camps by the Nazis (Rhodes 2007); indeed, globally, the culturally-inappropriate disposal of the bodies and/or lack of post-mortem care for the dead adds further insult and injury to those who suffered, and the issues around socially-bad deaths can resonate strongly for generations.

In very recent times, mass burials have been the only option when coping with environmental disasters. Haiti is a case in point here, with earthquakes and hurricanes devastating the island between 2010 and 2014, killing up to 316,000 people in just four years (Kentish 2016). The usual Roman Catholic rites of preparing the corpse for individual burial in consecrated ground had to be put aside, and even traditional Vodoo rituals (where similarly the dead are given befitting burials) were abandoned to ensure the health and sanitation of the survivors (McEntire, Sadiq and Gupta 2012: 319). Haiti is a country wracked with poverty; even in normal times, if Haitian family members cannot afford to pay the rent on a grave plot, the corpse is dug up and disposed of in a mass outdoor cremation (MacFarland 2014). Social status matters even in death.

Deaths also come from disease, and these diseases can be highly contagious and the cause of socially-bad deaths that upset the natural rhythm of death rituals. Ebola is a highly infectious viral disease and the crisis in West Africa during 2014–2016 was the largest since the disease was discovered in 1976. Although a number of factors aid its spread, such as poor health facilities, traditional burial practices were linked to over 60% of the cases in Guinea (Manguvo and Mafuvadze 2015: 1). In a part of the world where ethno-medicines are culturally important and make up the majority of everyday healthcare, traditional healers were unwittingly passing Ebola from one patient to another through the transmission of contaminated bodily fluids. Further, until churches abolished the practice of Laying on of Hands, healing sessions with the sick, including those with Ebola, were commonplace and also aided transmission (ibid.: 2).

When a sick person is not able to be cured in West Africa, the importance of a culturally-appropriate burial ritual is crucial. Burial rituals assist the dead to make their transition to the world of the ancestors. Should the deceased not be able to make this transition then it is believed that their spirit will return and punish living relatives; the spirit will cause dis-ease and disease within the community and improper burial rites can be one of the reasons for such a return. An appropriate traditional burial ritual within West Africa has tribal and cultural variations, but typically includes the relatives washing and cleaning the body using a common bowl, and then touching the face of their lost loved one to cement the unity between themselves and their soon-to-be ancestor. If the deceased was a prominent healer, then it is not uncommon for people to lie on top of the corpse in the 'hope that some of [their] spiritual gift will be transferred over'

(Manguvo and Mafuvadze 2015: 2). These rituals increased the spread of Ebola; however, banning them created not only resentment in the communities, but in the case of Liberia also caused death certificates to be falsely validated so that traditional funeral practices could continue (ibid.: 3). In Sierra Leone, reports communicated to me highlighted additional issues. Traditionally, a paramount chief would not be buried with his head, as his skull would be used as the cup from which the new chief had to drink. This ritual meant that on the death of a previous chief from Ebola, the new chief would also contract the virus. Further, reports of ghosts in the community meant that the bodies of recently-buried Ebola victims were exhumed and mutilated, spreading the virus to all those who had direct contact with the contaminated corpse (personal correspondence from John Raine, Sierra Leone, 2013, via Elisa Kenton-Howells).

That a human corpse is appropriately disposed of, with the correct rituals carried out prior to disposal, is crucial to the normative workings of society. As previously noted, socially-bad people such as murderers typically receive/d socially-bad body disposal, while socially-bad body disposal for socially-good people was/is believed to cause disease and/or dis-ease within a community. As such, huge distress can occur for those who have no body to mourn over, and this is particularly the case for those who have had to abandon their dead loved ones. In a recent study of migrants attempting to cross the Sonoran Desert from Mexico into the USA, Jason de León (2015) has noted that, due to the norms of Roman Catholicism, leaving behind the body of a dead friend or relative has long-term consequences. It is usual for the corpse of a migrant just to be covered with rocks, and the migration continue on. Due to the heat, there is rapid skeletonisation, and carrion typically carry bones and clothing 'as far as twenty meters from the original death site' (2015: 80). This means that postmortem identification of deceased migrants is largely impossible and that no body is likely to be returned to the family back home. With no grave to visit, family members are unable to appropriately pray for the soul of their loved one, and worry that the scattered remains lying in the desert would prevent the resurrection of the deceased at the End of Days (ibid.: 81).

The case of Mexican migrant deaths and that of deaths through Ebola in West Africa both highlight that not being able to physically prepare the corpse for a socio-religiously appropriate burial affects both the dead and the living. The need to care for the dead, to touch the dead, to wash the body and lay it in the earth (or cremate it), appears to be a basic need; Covid-19 has further reinforced this, with those who have been unable to say a proper goodbye to someone they loved, and/or nurse them to the end, speaking openly about their distress (Newsnight 2020). There is efficacy in the rituals of connection with the corpse, and thus although Kristeva describes a corpse as abject (1982: 109), her feelings of horror are not universal, nor even universal within the Christian context in which she writes; for even in normal circumstances, across medieval Europe, corpses were being medically anatomised, eviscerated as a form of embalming (removing the internal organs which decompose quickest) or divided into parts so the soul in Purgatory could be prayed for in each of the numerous locations where the body bits were buried (Park 1995; Westerhof 2008). But such intimate contact with human remains extended beyond the wet into the dry, with the medical ingestion of human body parts as medical mummia being commonplace across Europe into the modern era (Sugg 2011). Meanwhile, in the Arabian world, after the death of Prophet Muhammad, the nail pairings and saliva were sometimes consumed by devotees as part of ritual observance (Flood 2014: 469). Whether wet or dry, human remains are central to the religious practice of a good many religious traditions.

CONTACT WITH DRY REMAINS

The use of human body parts in the form of relics is perhaps most associated with Roman Catholicism, where the dry (skeletal) and/or wet (enfleshed) remains of certain categories of the dead were/are commonly believed to possess supernatural powers, and were able perform miracles through divine intervention, notably in relation to healing (Ariès 1974: 15–16).[2] Typically, the special dead were saints (official or vernacular), and parts of their body, or sometimes even their entire body, as well as items associated with these people, were believed to be a conduit to God, able to permit powerful supernatural events to occur (Greary 1994: 200). The relics (bones and/or body parts) of these blessed individuals circulated widely throughout medieval Europe (Greary 1986: 181) and all who came into contact with relics hoped to witness for themselves the potency of the artefact. As saints, upon their earthly demise, were understood to go straight to Heaven to be with God, it was believed they could intercede for the pleader; as the relic of a saint demonstrated their continued presence on earth, they were both *reliquiae* (meaning left behind in Latin) and *pignora* (a pledge), and thus relics were hugely potent. Body parts were

---

2 Corporeal relics of venerated figures are also important for Buddhists, being enshrined within stupas or chortens that become places of worship and meditation.

usually displayed in reliquaries and included heads, limbs, blood, prepuce (foreskin), viscera and bone (Pittam 2015). The faithful would, and indeed still do, go on pilgrimage to see them and to touch the reliquary. However, some body parts were engaged with more intimately, particularly bones. The Wellcome Institute in London holds an amulet which would have been worn as a pendant. It contains, on a piece of cloth, a fragment of bone said to be from the body of St Geneviève, a French virgin whose relics are credited with ending an epidemic in Paris (Pitt Rivers 2012).

Interaction with the bones of saints is not the only intimate contact for some Roman Catholic communities. The annual Day of the Dead (Dia de las Muertos) in one Mexican village, Pomuch in the southeast of the country, includes a regular bone-cleaning ritual. Here, the body is exhumed two or three years after burial, and the skeleton moved to an individual ossuary. Each year 'in the last week of October', the bones are physically cleaned and the 'clothes' of the dead changed. Changing the clothes of the dead in this context means replacing the embroidered cloth in which the bones are laid; always with the skull on the top. This ritual has its origins in Mexico's Mayan past, and the Pomuch word for their annual bone-cleaning rite is Janal Pixan, meaning in Mayan, 'Food for the Soul' (Benitez and Chung 2015: 78–80). The Pomuch dead are integral to the living community, and their All Souls' Day Catholic-Mayan ceremony demonstrates this through its ongoing importance.

In Hawaiian traditional culture, the ancestors are also hugely important. Human bones (*iwi*) are believed to be the receptacle for the *mana* (spiritual energy) of the individual, and thus the bones of ancestors (*iwi kúpuna*) are cherished and revered. Considered sacred, historically they were hidden in 'secret burial caves or other well-protected locations'. Indeed, so important are the bones of ancestors that a self-designation for native Hawaiians is Kanaka 'Ōiwi, meaning 'People of the Bone' (Promey 2014: 628–629).

The need for an intimate connection with the deceased and the incorporation of the dead into the body of the living has, in contemporary society, gone beyond language links, metaphor and symbolism. It is now possible for a small portion of the cremated remains (known as cremains) of a loved one to be incorporated into tattoo ink used on the body of a relative. As a result, the bereaved are able to continue to have the physical presence of their loved ones, with 'the bodies of the deceased and the bereaved... literally interconnected'. In the words of a bereaved mother whose son's cremains were inked into her body as part of a memorial tattoo, 'it feels as if he is always with me' (Heessels, Poots and Venbrux 2012: 479). Here, the dead become part of the living organ that touches and feels, they are literally embedded into the skin and become integral to the self of the tattooed person.

CONCLUSION

In this chapter I have taken examples of physical contact with the dead from a variety of religious and spiritual lifeways across space and time. I have touched on the roles of gender, myth and especially ritual, in demonstrating that whilst many Western philosophers may understand the corpse as an object of horror, intimate contact with a cadaver in its wet and/or dry state is in fact socially normative; largely due to the practicality of needing to dispose of a cadaver. Indeed, I strongly suggest that Kristeva's notion of the corpse as inherently abject is incorrect, and that, as Chidester argues, to handle life, we must handle death, and as Sedgwick asserts, to touch is to understand. Comprehension of life in all its fullness must include physical contact with the dead.

In this piece I have noted how important it is to have a body to dispose of (as in the case of Mexican migrants dead in the desert), but also that there is huge importance to the socially appropriate disposal of human remains, even when these may be fragmentary (as with the Zaka). I have also demonstrated that the distinction between wet and dry remains is not clear-cut. My analysis here is not new, but perhaps is best expressed through noting that in Kyrgyzstan, the term for a body about to buried is *söök* which means bone (Hardenberg 2010: 33). The corpse is an ambiguous thing, and no single explanation of it can suffice. Whilst Hertz's dry remains usually mean a bony skeleton or fully cremated remains (cremains), the examples in this chapter complicate this. Hertz's wet remains are more complex still, signifying everything from a newly-dead cadaver to a skeleton with soft-tissue still attached, and how the living interact with all of these examples is culturally codified.

Further, the corpse itself is highly relative, for it can be everything from inherently potent (Hawaii) to ritually impure and only to be touched with extreme caution (Zoroastrianism), it can even be understood as somehow sentient (notably through Christian relics). Additionally, the same type of death in different societies can see the corpse perceived as crucially important (Aztec) or as a piece of trash (Kwahu-Tafo Ghanaian mothers who die in childbirth), while within a single spiritual tradition such as Hinduism the corpse can be highly ambiguous: the deceased body of a loved one is treated like a deity but also a source of pollution. Exposing a cadaver naturally to decompose can be understood as appropriate for a socially-good person (Hidatsa Sioux), but also the appropriate form of disposal for the socially-bad within a community (murderers in Alaska). The culturally-inappropriate disposal of human bodies has also sadly been a marker of disrespect for millions who died enslaved during the Transatlantic Slave Trade, or during World War Two under the Nazis. Whilst leaving a body exposed in any way, even through nakedness, is understood as highly disrespectful in most religious traditions and spiritual lifeways, it is the right thing to do according to Zoroastrianism scripture. Mass graves too can be seen as culturally important (Hidatsa), hugely disrespectful (WW2 Nazi Holocaust disposal) or as a necessity to protect the living in the wake of disasters and tragedy (earthquakes, hurricanes or widespread contagious disease). And this last category shows how, regardless of myth and ritual, there is a pragmatic, necessary element to dealing with the dead.

Many rituals followed in handling the dead are practical attempts to conceal the natural processes of decomposition. Placing coins over the eyes and tying the jaw closed hide the empty stare and gaping mouth of the dead; washing and dressing the body removes any post-mortem discharge and hides the signs of lividity; and there are several ways of preserving the body to stop or slow the decomposition process, such as evisceration. Dealing with a corpse requires action, and these actions have been, and continue to be, subject to socio-cultural norms, and religious myth and ritual.

BIBLIOGRAPHY

AFP. 2016. 'Why Parsis Chose Electric Crematoriums? Because Vultures are no More'. *HindustanTimes*, 7 June. Retrieved from https://www.hindustantimes.com/india-news/why-parsis-chose-electric-crematoriums-because-vultures-are-no-more/story-FMQrklH7h6N9IJMSukEJ1M.html

Al-Dawoody, Ahmed. 2017. 'Management of the Dead from the Islamic Humanitarian Law Perspectives: Considerations for Humanitarian Forensics'. *International Review of the Red Cross* 99 (2): 759–784. Retrieved from file:///H:/Docs/Downloads/irrc_99_905_15.pdf. https://doi.org/10.1017/S1816383118000486

Al-Khu'i, Ayatullah Abul Qasim. Undated. *Islamic Laws on Cleanliness, Prayers, Fasting, Hajj, Transactions, Marriage, & Other Topics*. Translated by Muhammas Fzal Haq. Retrieved from https://www.al-islam.org/printpdf/book/export/html/38594

Al-Sisyani, Al-Sayyid Ali Al-Husseini. Undated. 'Ghusl for Touching a Dead Body'. *Islamic Laws*. Retrieved from https://www.sistani.org/english/book/48/2179/

Ariès, Phillipe. 1974. *Western Attitudes towards Death from the Middle Ages to the Present*. Translated by O.M. Ranum. Baltimore: John Hopkins University Press.

Ariès, Phillipe. 1981. *The Hour of Our Death: The Classic History of Western Attitudes toward Death over the Last One Thousand Years*. New York; Alfred A. Knopf.

Ashraf's Advice upon the Death of a Muslim. 2001. Dewsbury, Yorkshire: Ashraf's Amānat.

Barrett, Ronald, L. 2008. *Aghor Medicine: Pollution, Death and Healing in Northern India*. Berkeley: University of California Press. https://doi.org/10.1525/9780520941014

Bauman, Zigmunt. 1992. *Mortality, Immortality and Other Life Strategies*. Cambridge: Polity.

Beliveau, Ralph. 2017. 'A Hunger for Dead Cakes: Visions of Abjection, Scapegoating, and the Sin-Eater'. In Cynthia J. Miller and A. Bowdoin van Riper, *What's Eating You? Food & Horror on Screen*, 169–186. New York: Bloomsbury. https://doi.org/10.5040/9781501322402_ch-010

Benitez, Eva L.B. and Heajoo Chung. 2015. 'Food for the Soul: Eternal Co-Existence in the Mayan-Catholic Traditions of Pomuch, Mexico'. *International Journal of Intangible Heritage* 10: 74–83. Retrieved from http://www.ijih.org/volumeMgr.ijih?cmd=volumeDtlView&volNo=10&lang=ENG&dVolId=565&manuType=02

Berger, Peter and Justin Kroesen (eds.). 2016. *Ultimate Ambiguities: Investigating Death and Liminality*. New York: Berghahn.

Boccaccio, Giovanni. 2003 [1353]. *The Decameron*. Translated by G.H. McWilliam. London: Penguin.

Boyce, Mary. 2011 [1993]. 'Corpse'. In Ehsan Yarshater (ed.), *Encyclopaedia Iranica* Vol. VI, Fasc. 3 (online), 279–286. Retrieved from http://www.iranicaonline.org/articles/corpse-disposal-of-in-zoroastrianism

Bushnell, David, I. 1927. 'Burials of the Algonquian, Siouan and Caddon Tribes West of the Mississippi'. *Smithsonian Institution Bureau of American Ethnology* 83: 1–103. Retrieved from https://repository.si.edu/handle/10088/15550

Caixeiro, Mariana. 2016. 'The Electric Crematorium (*vidyut shav dahh griha*) of Banaras (Varanasi)'. In Douglas J. Davies and Lewis H. Mates (eds.), *Encyclopedia of Cremation*, 236–238. Aldershot, Hants.: Ashgate.

Chidester, David. 2002. *Patterns of Transcendence: Religion, Death and Dying*. 2nd edition. Belmont, CA: Wadsworth.

Chidester, David. 2005. 'The American Touch: Tactile Imaginary in American Religion and Politics.' In Constance Classen (ed.), *The Book of Touch*. Oxford: Berg.

Choksy, Jamsheed, K. 1987. 'The Zoroastrian Nāhn Purification Rituals'. *Journal of Ritual Studies* 1 (2): 59–74. https://www.jstor.org/stable/44368342

Classen, Constance. 2012. *The Deepest Sense: A Cultural History of Touch*. Urbana and Chicago: University of Illinois Press. https://doi.org/10.5406/illinois/9780252034930.001.0001

Cresswell, Joanna. 2018. 'The Female Photographer Spent a Month within Indian's "Cannibal Cult"'. *Refinery* 21 (3 July). Retrieved from https://www.refinery29.com/en-gb/tamara-merino-aghor-cannibals

Curtis, Valerie and Adam Biran. 2001. 'Dirt, Disgust, and Disease: Is Hygiene in our Genes?' *Perspectives in Biology and Medicine* 44 (1): 17–31. https://doi.org/10.1353/pbm.2001.0001

Danforth, Loring, M. 1982. *The Death Rituals of Rural Greece*. Princeton, NJ: Princeton University Press. https://doi.org/10.1515/9780691218199

de León, Jason. 2015. *The Land of the Open Graves: Living & Dying on the Migrant Trail*. Oakland, CA: University of California Press. https://doi.org/10.1525/9780520958685

de Witte, Marleen. 2011. 'Of Corpses, Clay, & Photographs: Body Imagery & Changing Technologies of Remembrance in Asante Funeral Culture'. In Michael Jindra and Joël Noret (eds.), *Funerals in Africa: Explorations of a Social Phenomenon*, 177–206. New York: Berghahn.

Diamont, Anita. 1998. *Saying Kaddish: How to Comfort the Dying, Bury the Dead & Mourn as a Jew*. New York: Random House.

Douglas, Mary. 1966. *Purity and Danger: An Analysis of Concepts of Pollution and Taboo*. London: Routledge & Paul.

Durkheim, Emile. 1956 [1912]. *The Elementary Forms of the Religious Life*. Translated by Joseph W. Sawin. New York: George Allen & Unwin.

Eduljee, K.E. 2017. 'Fire Light'. *Zoroastrian Heritage*. Retrieved from https://www.heritageinstitute.com/zoroastrianism/worship/fire.htm

Fateha & Funeral Rites. 1999. Manchester: 'Sirat Ul Muslimin' & Shair-e-Rabbani Islamic Centre.

Ferch, Shann R. 2011. 'Meanings of Touch and Forgiveness: A Hermeneutic Phenomenological Inquiry'. *Counselling and Values* 44: 155–173. https://doi.org/10.1002/j.2161-007X.2000.tb00169.x

Ferrari, Giovanna. 1987. 'Public Anatomy Lessons and the Carnival: The Anatomy Theatre of Bologna'. *Past & Present* 117: 50–106. https://doi.org/10.1093/past/117.1.50

Firth, Shirley. 1997. *Dying, Death and Bereavement in a British Hindu Community*. Leuven: Peeters.

Firth, Shirley. 2003. 'Changing Attitudes to Cremation in the UK'. *Bereavement Care* 22 (2): 25–28. https://doi.org/10.1080/02682620308657571

Flood, Finbarr B. 2014. 'Bodies and Becoming: Mimesis, Meditations, and the Ingestion of the Sacred in Christianity and Islam'. In Sally M. Promey (ed.), *Sensational Religion: Sensory Cultures in Material Practice*, 459–493. New Haven, CT: Yale University Press.

Forde, Maarit and Yanique Hume (eds.). 2018. *Passages and Afterworlds: Anthropological Perspectives on Death in the Caribbean*. London: Duke University Press. https://doi.org/10.1515/9781478002130

Garfield, Viola E. 1947–1951. 'The Tinglit, Haida, and Eyak Indians of Southeastern Alaska'. In *The Indians. Encyclopedia Artica* (unpublished) 8: Anthropology and Archaeology. Retrieved from https://collections.dartmouth.edu/arctica-beta/html/EA08-11.html

Greary, Patrick J. 1986. 'Sacred Commodities: The Circulation of Medieval Relics'. In Arjun Appadurai (ed.), *The Social Life of Things: Commodities in Cultural Perspectives*, 169–191. Cambridge: Cambridge University Press. https://doi.org/10.1017/CBO9780511819582.008

Greary, Patrick J. 1994. *Living with the Dead in the Middle Ages*. Ithaca, NY: Cornell University Press.

Green Jennifer and Michael Green. 2006. *Dealing with the Dead: A Handbook of Practices, Procedures & Law*. 2nd edition. London: Jessica Kingsley Publishers.

Grinder-Hansen, Keld. 1991. 'Charon's Fee in Ancient Greece? Some Remarks on a Well-Known Death Rite'. In Tobia Fischer-Hanse, Pia Guldager, John Lund, Marjatta Neilson and Annette Rathje (eds.), *Recent Danish Research in Classical Archaeology: Tradition and Renewal*, 207–218. Copenhagen: University of Copenhagen Press.

Hachlili, Rachel and Ann Killebrew. 1983. 'Was the Coin-on-Eye Custom a Jewish Burial Practice in the Second Temple Period?' *Biblical Archaeologist* 46 (3): 147–153. https://doi.org/10.2307/3209825

Hardenberg, Roland. 2010. 'How to Overcome Death? The Efficacy of Funeral Rituals in Kyrgyzstan'. *Journal of Ritual Studies* 24 (1/1): 29–43. https://www.jstor.org/stable/44368819

Harding, Vanessa. 1993. 'Burial of the Plague Dead in Early Modern London'. In Justin Champion (ed.), *Epidemic Disease in London*, 55–63. London: Centre for Metropolitan History. Retrieved from https://archives.history.ac.uk/history-in-focus/Medical/epimenu.html

Heessels, Meike, Fluer Poots and Eric Venbrux. 2012. 'In Touch with the Deceased: Animate Objects and Human Ashes'. *Material Religion* 8 (4): 466–488. https://doi.org/10.2752/175183412X13522006994818

Hera, Jean. 1995. 'Reclaiming the Last Rites (Rights): Women and After-Death Policy, Practices and Beliefs in Aotearoa/New Zealand'. PhD thesis, Massey University. Retrieved from https://mro.massey.ac.nz/bitstream/handle/10179/3129/02_whole.pdf?sequence+1&isAllowed=y

Hertz, Robert. 1960. *Death and the Right Hand*. Aberdeen: Cohen & West.

James, Susan E. 2002. 'Mimetic Rituals of Child Sacrifice in the Hopi Kachina Cult'. *Journal of the Southwest* 44 (3): 337–356. https://www.jstor.org/stable/40170187

Jenkins, Tiffany. 2001. *Contesting Human Remains in Museum Collections: The Crisis of Cultural Authority*. New York: Routledge. https://doi.org/10.4324/9780203841310

Kentish, Benjamin. 2016. 'Haiti Forced to Bury its Dead in Mass Graves after Hurricane Matthew Death Toll Rises'. *The Independent*, 10 October. Retrieved from https://www.independent.co.uk/news/world/americas/haiti-hurricane-matthew-mass-graves-death-toll-rises-a7354006.html

Kovacheva, Lidija. 2013. 'The Funeral Customs in the Folk Traditions of Greece and the Territory of the Republic of Macedonia'. *SEEU Review Versita* 9 (1): 1–11. Retrieved from https://www.degruyter.com/downloadpdf/j/seeur.2013.9.issue-1/seeur-2013-0004/seeur-2013-0004.pdf

Kristeva, Julia. 1982. *Powers of Horror: An Essay in Abjection*. Translated by Leon Roudiez. New York: Columbia University Press.

Macfarland, Amanda. 2014. 'Death in Haiti'. *The Crudem Foundation*, October 10. Retrieved from http://crudem.org/death-haiti/

Malinowski, Bronislaw. 1948. *Magic, Science and Religion and Other Essays*. Boston: Beacon Press.

Manguvo, Angellar and Benford Mafuvadze. 2015. 'The Impact of Traditional & Religious Practices on the Spread of Ebola in West Africa: Time for Strategic Shift'. *The Pan African Medicine Journal* 22 Suppl. 199: 1–4. Retrieved from https://www.ncbi.nlm.nih.gov/pmc/articles/PMC4709130/. https://doi.org/10.11604/pamj.supp.2015.22.1.6190

McCorkle, William W. 2010. *Ritualizing the Disposal of the Deceased: From Corpse to Concept*. New York: Peter Lang. https://doi.org/10.3726/978-1-4539-0067-3

McEntire, David A., Abdul-Akeem Sadiq and Kailash Gupta. 2012. 'Unidentified Bodies & Mass Fatalities in Haiti: A Case Study of the January 2010 Earthquake with a

Cross-Cultural Comparison'. *International Journal of Mass Emergencies and Disasters* 30 (1): 301–327. Retrieved from https://scholarworks.iupui.edu/bitstream/handle/1805/3390/mcentire-2012-unidentified.pdf?sequence=1&isAllowed=y

McGinn, Colin. 2011. *The Meaning of Disgust*. Oxford; Oxford University Press. https://doi.org/10.1093/acprof:oso/9780199829538.001.0001

Metcalf, Alida C. 2005. *Go-Betweens & the Colonization of Brazil: 1500–1600*. Austin, TX: University of Texas Press.

Morgan, Oliver. 2004. 'Infectious Disease Risks from Dead Bodies following Natural Disasters'. *Revista Panamericana de Salud Pública* 15 (5): 307–12. Retrieved from https://www.scielosp.org/article/rpsp/2004.v15n5/307-312/en/. https://doi.org/10.1590/S1020-49892004000500004

Mukherjee, Sugato. 2017. 'India's Guardians of the Dead'. *The Diplomat*, 14 December. Retrieved from https://thediplomat.com/2017/12/indias-guardians-of-the-dead/

Mulroy, Zahra. 2018. 'What Happens to Your Body when you Die? Bit by Bit from the Moment Your Heart Stops'. *Daily Mirror*, 18 July. Retrieved from https://www.mirror.co.uk/lifestyle/health/what-happens-your-body-you-12940417

Newsnight. 15 April 2020. 'Coronavirus: How to Care for the Dying and the Terminally Ill'. Retrieved from https://www.youtube.com/watch?v=5prToYDTdns&feature=youtu.be

Park, Katherine. 1995. 'The Life of the Corpse: Division and Dissection in Late Medieval Europe'. *Journal of the History of Medicine and Allied Sciences* 50: 111–132. https://doi.org/10.1093/jhmas/50.1.111

Pitt Rivers. 2012. St Geneviève Reliquary, France'. *Pitt Rivers: Miracles & Offerings*. Retrieved from http://web.prm.ox.ac.uk/amulets/index.php/miracles-amulet2/index.html

Pittam, Matthew. 2015. 'Five Relics Whose Stories Have Gripped the World'. *CatholicHerald.co.uk*, 20 November. Retrieved from https://catholicherald.co.uk/commentandblogs/2015/11/20/five-relics-whose-stories-have-gripped-the-world/

Promey, Sally M. 2014. 'Spiritual Sensations and Material Transformations in Hawai'i Volcanoes National Park'. In Sally M. Promey (ed.), *Sensational Religion: Sensory Cultures in Material Practice*, 625–650. New Haven, CT: Yale University Press.

Quigley, Christine. 2005. *The Corpse: A History*. London: McFarland.

Rhodes, Richard. 2007. *Masters of Death: The SS-Einsatgruppen and the Invention of the Holocaust*. New York: Random House.

Roberts, Jonathan. 2011. 'Funerals & Fetish Internments in Accra, Ghana'. In Michael Jindra and Joël Noret (eds.), *Funerals in Africa: Explorations of a Social Phenomenon*, 207–226. New York: Berghahn.

Rosman, Jonathan, P. and Phillip J. Resnick. 1989. 'Sexual Attraction to Corpses: A Psychiatric Review of Necrophilia'. *The Bulletin of the American Academy of Psychiatry and the Law* 17 (2): 153–163. Retrieved from https://pdfs.semanticscholar.org/3bad/a70cf24c228572d522b3e32baed6b44761eb.pdf

Rundblad, Georganne. 1995. 'Exhuming Women's Premarket Duties in the Care of the Dead'. *Gender and Society* 9 (April): 173–192. https://doi.org/10.1177/089124395009002003

Salmon, William. 1685. *Pharmacopoeia Londinensis, or the New London Dispensatory*. 3rd edition. London: Dawks.

Sedgwick, Eve Kosofky. 2003. *Touching Feeling: Affect, Pedagogy, Performativity*. Durham, NC: Duke University Press. https://doi.org/10.1215/9780822384786

Shanker, Priyanka. 2017. 'Doms of Varanasi Make a Living among the Dead'. *Reuters*, 26 October. Retrieved from https://www.reuters.com/article/india-doms-varanasi-cremation/doms-of-varanasi-make-a-living-among-the-dead-idUSKBN1CV1K8

Sherman, Joseph (ed.). 2008. *Storytelling: An Encyclopedia of Mythology and Folklore*. London: Routledge. Retrieved from http://eindtijdinbeeld.nl/EiB-Bibliotheek/Boeken/Encyclopedia%20of%20Mythology%20and%20Folklore%20(2008)%20-%20Storytelling.pdf

Soares, Mariza de Carvalho. 2011. *People of Faith: Slavery & African Catholics in Eighteenth-Century Rio de Janeiro*. Translated by Jerry D. Metz. Durham, NC: Duke University Press. https://doi.org/10.1215/9780822394303

Stadler, Nurit. 2006. 'Corpse Symbolism, and Taboo Violation: The "Haredi Disaster Victim Identification Team in Israel"'. *Journal of the Royal Anthropological Institute* 12 (4): 837–858. https://doi.org/10.1111/j.1467-9655.2006.00366.x

Sugg, Richard. 2011. *Mummies, Cannibals and Vampires: The History of Corpse Medicine from the Renaissance to the Victorians*. New York: Routledge. https://doi.org/10.4324/9780203154182

Suri, Rochelle and Daniel B. Pitchford. 2010. 'The Gift of Life: Death as Teacher in the Aghori Sect'. *International Journal of Transpersonal Studies* 29 (1): 128–134. http://dx.doi.org/10.24972/ijts.2010.29.1.128

Taharah Procedures. Undated. Retrieved from https://kehillahsynagogue.org/wp-content/uploads/2012/05/TAHARA.pdf

Troyer, John. 2008. 'Abuse of a Corpse: A Brief History and Re-theorization of Necrophilia Laws in the USA'. *Mortality* 12 (2): 132–152. https://doi.org/10.1080/13576270801954518

van der Geest, Sjaak. 2000. 'Funerals for the Living: Conversations with Elderly People in Kwahu, Ghana'. *African Studies Review* 43 (3): 103–129. https://doi.org/10.2307/525071

van der Geest, Sjaak. 2002. '"I Want To Go!" How Older People in Ghana Look Forward to Death'. *Ageing and Society* 22: 7–28. https://doi.org/10.1017/S0144686X02008541

van der Geest, Sjaak. 2006. 'Between Death and Funeral: Mortuaries and the Exploitation of Liminality in Kwahu, Ghana'. *Africa: Journal of the International African Institute* 76 (4): 485–501. https://doi.org/10.3366/afr.2006.0061

Westerhof, Danielle. 2008. *Death & the Noble Body in Medieval England*. Woodbridge: Boydell & Brewer. https://doi.org/10.1017/UPO9781846156250

WHO. 2019. *World Health Organisation: Water Sanitation Hygiene*. https://www.who.int/water_sanitation_health/emergencies/qa/emergencies_qa8/en/

Williams, Alan. 1997. 'Zoroastrianism and the Body'. In Sarah Coakley (ed.), *Religion and the Body*, 155–166. Cambridge: Cambridge University Press.

Zykov, Anton. 2016. 'Zoroastrian Funeral Practices: Transition in Conduct'. In Shernaz Cama (ed.), *Threads of Continuity: Zoroastrian Life & Culture*, 287–305. New Delhi: Parzor Foundation.

Christina Welch, PhD, is an interdisciplinary neurodiverse scholar and Reader in Theology, Religion and Philosophy at the University of Winchester (UK), where she leads a Master's degree in Death, Religion and Culture. Her main research interests focus around the intersections between religion and visual and material culture and her work in this area includes late-medieval cadaver sculptures, religion and erotic death imagery, and the role of Christianity in colonial visual representations. She is currently co-authoring a book on the materialities of Caribbean religion.

Chapter 11

Immersive Hugging as a Ritual Act

MICHAEL HOUSEMAN

As the popular psychology and well-being literature attests, contemporary Westerners consider hugging to be both highly meaningful and intrinsically beneficial. The oft-touted (but seemingly apocryphal) quote from Family Therapy founder Virginia Satir says it all: 'We need four hugs a day for survival. We need eight hugs a day for maintenance. We need twelve hugs a day for growth.' Unsurprisingly, prolonged, intense hugging—between people, but also with trees, animals or visualised beings—is one of the hallmarks of ritualised practices associated with what have been called contemporary spiritualities: New Age-inspired movements, Contemporary Paganisms, Personal Development initiatives, etc. This chapter explores the interactive workings of such pointedly meaningful embracing which I will refer to as 'immersive' hugging. Drawing on ethnographic fieldwork and other illustrative material, I attempt to identify some of the recurrent features of immersive hugs in order to speculate about what is at stake in their performance.

HUGS GALORE

Hugging as a component of everyday interaction is both partially idiosyncratic and, like most everything else, governed by cultural codes. This has been made clear by the profusion of YouTube videos on hugging etiquette that has accompanied the recent upswing of hugging in the United States. Excluding the many videos on animal or tree hugging, as well as those on how to hug in a variety of online games, more than 150 such clips have been uploaded since 2007, the most popular of which, dating from May

2018, totals almost 15 million views. Consider, for example, the videos providing instructions on how to 'man hug' or 'bro hug'. Some with wacky humour, others in dead seriousness, advise men on how to avoid imbuing this same-sex embrace with homosexual undertones: keep your feet toes-to-toes, place one arm over and the other under your friend's arms, keep it short, don't talk while hugging, and no snuggling or stroking. Other videos specify the proprieties and pitfalls of heterosexual hugging (interestingly, there are no videos on hugging between women, which seems to be deemed unproblematic). In principle, such ordinary, mundane hugs, regardless of the conventions that guide them, are presumed to reflect the everyday relations between the huggers concerned. All else being equal, the more intimate people are, the more intense their hugging is likely to be.

Hugging may also be a canonical ceremonial practice. Examples include the solemn *accolade* that confers military and other honours in France, the consoling, *darshan*-bestowing embrace of the Hindu guru Mātā Amritānandamayī (Amma, the 'hugging saint'), the three-fold hug that ushers in the Muslim festival of Eid al-fitr, and the liturgical greeting known as the 'kiss of peace' or 'holy kiss' in many Eastern and Western Christian traditions. While such hugs may be inflected by interpersonal ties, they are above all indicative of a more impersonal, ritual relationship the hugging parties are held to enact: allegiance to a higher authority, the communication of blessedness to a disciple, reciprocal well-wishing between members of a devotional community.

There are also hugs that stand midway between commonplace and ceremonial hugging, such as the warm, public handshake-hug sometimes performed by male politicians and celebrities. This one-armed embrace Wikipedia describes as a 'pound hug' (also dude hug, cootie hug, homie hug, bro hug and thug hug) is often announced in a visible yet understated I-know-you-know-I-know fashion by leaning slightly back with arms extended downward at a 30-degree angle, and consists in a tight handshake inserted between the huggers' bodies, accompanied by several firm, open-handed taps on the back.

In all these cases, hugging assumes a form that, as a rule, is consonant with the relationship between those who hug. The formal qualities of the hug itself—how long it lasts, the emotions it exhibits, the positions adopted, the body parts involved, the degree of pressure exerted, the symmetries or asymmetries brought into play, etc.—articulate the nature of this relationship. Immersive hugging, however, seems to proceed from somewhat different premises.

BEING INTIMATE WITH CASUAL ACQUAINTANCES

Immersive hugs, sometimes called 'spiritual', 'therapeutic', 'heart-to-heart' or simply 'real', are embraces of exceptional intensity and duration presumed to have salutary effects in and of themselves. Known in some circles as the 'Findhorn full-frontal' in reference to the renowned British New Age 'colony of seekers' (Sutcliffe 2003: 164), immersive hugging is an inevitable feature of Pagan festivals, well-being workshops, spirituality training sessions and personal development practices of all sorts. In the wake of a mutually accepted invitation (a smile, an eyebrow flash, an opening of arms), people wrap their arms around each other and enter into a tight, face-to-face embrace. Eyes closed or unfocused, bodies still or gently rocking, participants appear to be fully absorbed in a blissful, self-contained whole. As their hug lengthens, they rearrange their grasp several times, repositioning their arms, moving their heads closer or further apart, pulling slightly back so as to fit their bodies together once again, as though exploring new ways of expressing their caring attentiveness and of savouring the sensations of safety and warmth their hugging provides. After a long while, they gently draw apart, wordlessly communicating feelings of gratitude and affection with a knowing smile, a kiss, a caress, a slow blink or a quick final hug.

What is remarkable about this way of hugging is that it acts out a heightened interpersonal familiarity between people who usually know each other only casually, if at all. Indeed, one of characteristic features of immersive hugging is the striking hiatus between the intense personal intimacy it displays and the lack of interpersonal commitment this display might ordinarily be expected to imply. In this regard, it is significant that immersive hugging typically occurs in the context of semi-public, structured events whose specialness is readily acknowledged. Speaking for example of personal growth-oriented dance practices like Biodanza or 5 Rhythms in which immersive hugs abound (Houseman and Mazzella di Bosco 2020), one participant explained that at such venues 'you can connect with [people] on another, higher level, [...] but then, outside, it's as if we suddenly don't speak the same language anymore'. Another said she feels 'moments of profound connection with other dancers, [...] but after the dance session, if I try to speak and socialize with them, it's as though everything has flattened out, the magic is lost'. The expectations that hold sway in such contexts diverge significantly from those of everyday interaction. I learnt this to my cost when, on the train platform going home from my first Pagan festival, my open-armed invitation to hug was violently rebuffed as an unwarranted aggression by someone I (wrongly) assumed had been at the festival as well. Inversely, as one person put it: 'If I go to a Pagan festival and encounter a few people I know well, I'll also hug them with a similar intensity to those strangers I hug at the same event.' Thus, partaking in an immersive hug with someone neither presupposes a close relationship with them, nor does it anticipate that such a relationship will follow. Immersive hugging tends to take place between those Karen Fingerman (2009) has called 'consequential strangers': people one may be familiar with, but with whom one feels free *not* to entertain a close relationship.

In light of this, one might be tempted to see the immersive hug as a ritual act. I will be arguing precisely along these lines. Specifically, in keeping with Véronique Altglas' analysis of contemporary religious exoticism (2014: Ch. 7), I see immersive hugging as a ritualised enactment of certain Euro-American middle-class aspirations and sensibilities closely linked with the emergent sociological category Pierre Bourdieu, writing at the end of the 1970s, identified as the 'new petty bourgeoisie' (1979: 409–431). However, because the 'spontaneous', 'heartfelt', qualities of immersive hugs are such a far cry from the distanced conventionality typical of ceremonial hugging generally, the idea that immersive hugging might be a ritual practice needs to be spelled out in detail. This will then allow me to envisage immersive hugging as a possible model for thinking about much contemporary Western ritual.

FEELING ONESELF WITH OTHERS

To get some idea of what immersive hugging as a ritual practice might be about, let us look at some of its formal features. Immersive hugs are voluntary and emphatic. Whether they are entered into gently or with force, they are enthusiastic and intense. Huggers hold each other tightly, and often tenderly caress each other's bodies (firm back-tapping almost never occurs). However, such hugs are also markedly undifferentiating. An immersive hug is a full-body, frontal embrace that emphasises participants' personal presence while being largely indifferent to individual-specific attributes like gender, age, size and physical condition. As was made clear to me during one Pagan festival, although huggers increasingly seek consent, it is because personal peculiarities are so earnestly disregarded in this way that some attendees make it known beforehand that they do not wish to be hugged.

Immersive hugs are deeply resonant with feeling and yet carelessly generic. They are performed to be highly expressive emotionally and intentionally, while being at the same time conspicuously depersonalised. Now, the depersonalised, generic nature of immersive hugging is fully congruent with the idea that the relationship it enacts is a conventional, ceremonial one. But what, then, are we to make of the intense intimacy and exacerbated affectivity its performance also displays? I suggest that the latter bears witness to the fact that unlike ceremonial hugging generally, immersive hugging is centred less on the acting out of a special (ritual) relationship, than on the acting out of special (ritual) selves. In other words, the value and meaning of an immersive hug pertain less to participants' shared experience of an extra-ordinary connection with one another, than to their respective experiences of becoming exceptional individuals capable of making such a connection.

To see how this might be so, consider another 'obvious aspect' (Rappaport 1979) of immersive hugging: it is inordinately long. In contrast to the three (plus or minus two) seconds of both everyday and ceremonial hugs (cf. Nagy 2011), twenty seconds is often presented as the minimum duration for a 'real' hug. According to popular renderings of some experimental work done between 2005 and 2015 (see Field 2019 for a review), this is the time needed for huggers' oxytocin (dubbed the 'love hormone') to be released. Now, several laboratory studies have demonstrated the comforting effects of touch before and during stressful situations (Field 2019: 375). However, it remains that a close embrace between adults, if prolonged, tends to make people anxious, as borne out by popular 'prank' videos documenting overly-long hugs between strangers (e.g. YouTube posts by Angrypicnic, BigDawsVlogs and The Daily Dropout). This is especially true in the absence of an intimate relationship that provides extended body contact with shared meaning. As a result, immersive huggers inevitably experience what marital and couple therapist David Schnarch calls 'the jolt' (1997: 166). This is the sudden dawning of a heightened self-awareness that occurs when a hug which normally would have broken off (after three to four seconds) keeps going. It gives rise to noticeable shifts in muscle tension, balance and breathing. Indeed, immersive hugs always have two phases: a short coming together part during which huggers grasp each other in a tight, fusional clinch, and a lengthy staying together part during which they self-consciously explore the sensations and feelings that accompany each other's bodily readjustments and gestured initiatives (changes of grip, caresses, eye-contact, etc.). When initiating an immersive hug, participants surrender to rushes of compassionate intention and to the diffuse pleasures of bodily touch. In doing so, they jointly aspire to the deeper connection their intense hugging is presumed to exhibit and/or bring about. However, because their hug is so long-lasting, their efforts are inescapably modulated by various complications—a flash of erotic excitement, a sense of disquiet, moments of physical discomfort, an unexpected smell, an awareness of possible observers, etc.—the handling of which prompts them to attend to their own personal sentiments and attitudes. Continually jolted in this manner, hugging partners are repeatedly thrown back upon themselves, moved to harken to and acknowledge their respective thoughts and feelings. In the case of prolonged hugging between intimate partners, Schnarch explains, making such 'a solid connection with *yourself*' is 'the key to [the] interdependence' that life as a couple entails (1997: 167). However, immersive hugging typically takes place between non-intimates who do not aspire to this type of open-ended interdependency. Instead, becoming aware of one's own feelings during sustained close contact with another takes on meaning and value in its own right as an intimation of one's capacity to successfully 'connect'.

Immersive hugging allows participants to demonstrate—to themselves, to each other, to onlooking parties—their respective capacities for 'really' hugging and for being 'really' hugged. It lets them experience themselves, and be experienced by others, as individuals endowed with certain exemplary if difficult-to-define qualities of thought and feeling deemed essential to the fulfilment of contemporary (middle-class) Western personhood: 'spontaneity', 'authenticity', 'deep feeling', 'self-awareness', 'openness to others', etc. In other words, those who partake in immersive hugs do not so much enter into intense, intimate relationships with others as they are afforded salient experiences of what current Euro-American understandings of personal identity invite them to construe as their 'potential' to do so. In this respect, purposeful, fervent hugging can be seen as a ritualised process of self-construction in which participants willingly act as resources for each other's development.

This reciprocally enabled, self-directed quality of immersive hugging comes out clearly, for example, in the 'Hugging meditation' video posted on YouTube in 2010 by journalist and writer Todd Aaron Jensen, author of *On Gratitude* (2010). This meditation, Jensen earnestly explains, is a 'simple' practice that 'works with everybody' to help us 'be [...] our higher selves'. It requires a partner, who 'can be a child, a parent, a friend, a lover, a complete stranger', and is made up of three successive hugs. The 'meditative thought' for the first embrace is 'I may not be here long, but I am here now', for the second 'This person may not be here long, but there're here now', and for the third 'there is a mutual acknowledgement: we may not be here long, but we're here now'. Jensen concludes: 'If we can practice our love with that level of mindfulness, and acceptance, and surrender, and gratitude, we are truly free, and our heart truly open to give and to receive.' There exist a number of other versions of this practice, such as that promoted as a mindfulness exercise by the Buddhist monk Thich Nhat Hanh and others. It entails bowing ('offering a lotus') to each other and then taking three deep, long breaths together while hugging 'heart-to-heart' (left sides touching). During the first breath participants think 'I am alive', during the second 'This person is alive', and during the third 'I feel happy' or 'I feel gratitude', before finishing with a closing bow. In 'absorptive' (Luhrmann, Nusbaum and Thisted 2010) practices such as these, as in immersive hugging generally, hugging partners' personal identities are plainly subordinate to the role each plays in affording the other with an intensified experience of whom they feel they can become.

Immersive hugging takes full advantage of the potential two-facedness of hugging as a close interaction in which participants do not meet each other's gaze. In the absence of eye-contact, sensations aroused by the prolonged pressing of another person's body against one's own easily take on a life of their own, with the other person being temporarily abstracted from the picture. In this light, it is tempting to take tree hugging, not to prevent logging but to promote well-being, as an exemplary model. As many Internet sites attest, this pleasurable display of embellished intimacy with an unfamiliar other involves consciously imbuing one's behaviour towards one's (other-than-human) partner with heart-felt, well-meaning intentions, all the while paying careful attention to one's own perceptions and feelings. And, in the course of tree hugging as it is usually construed (but not always, cf. Pike 2017), what personal agency this partner might have becomes sublimated into a source of 'energy' or 'connection' that allows the human hugger to knowingly raise their vibratory level, commune with Nature, recycle their worries and reduce their stress. There are virtual adaptations of this in which the tree is materially absent, such as the Qigong meditation exercise of 'hugging the tree' (also called 'standing like a tree'). Some Personal Development advocates recommend a still more radically self-serving form of immersive hugging in which one (physically or mentally) hugs oneself (see wikiHow staff 2019 for a simple illustrated example). Eye Movement Desensitization and Reprocessing (EMDR) therapy, for instance, promotes the self-administered 'butterfly hug' to alleviate the distress associated with traumatic memories (Shapiro

2013; Artigas and Jarero 2014). During the 2020 Covid-19 lockdown, British massage therapist Sally Morris provided a mindfulness-inspired 'self-hug meditation' YouTube video as a self-care support for those 'who are missing that physical contact with other people', and Becky Rosenthal posted a self-hugging meditation 'to soothe and take care of ourselves' on the UNION SA YouTube channel ('We empower positive transformation'). Finally, somewhere between another being such as a tree and one's own body are a variety of special vests and other electromechanical devices that generate heat and/or pressure to simulate hugging.

PERFORMING A TRANSCENDENT SOCIALITY

It would be a mistake, however, to understand immersive hugging as directed solely towards individual self-fulfilment. An immersive hug not only requires the presence of a consenting partner, whose reactions (and my reactions to their reactions) I am expected to be aware of, but like many spiritual practices, typically takes place in the company of still further attending others who are often similarly engaged. In short, another formal feature of immersive hugging is that it is exhibited. Now, to the extent that immersive hugs are presumed to be witnessed, their enactment becomes a performance. Participants' embodied representation of the ideal dispositions to which they aspire becomes addressed, and the participants themselves become both the wellsprings of desire that inspire hugging to happen, and the distanced, monitoring observers of their own feelings and behaviour. This assumption of an outside point of view underscores the conventional aspects of immersive hugging. It also forestalls possible abusive misconduct and acts as a hedge against the interpersonal alienation that prolonged bodily contact can easily bring about. The performative dimension of their embrace allows hugging parties to interact in a highly intimate, affectively engaged fashion while minimising the risks of the emotional commitment and interpersonal 'interdependency' (Schnarch 1997) or 'contamination' (Moisseeff 2020) such behaviour would naturally imply if they were on their own. To the degree to which an immersive hug is freed in this way from the sticky, endlessly negotiated entanglements of close interpersonal ties, it provides an exceptional—ritual—space in which participants' individual autonomy is preserved, allowing them to more fully explore, physically and emotionally, whom they feel they might *really* be. In this regard, the profuse picture-taking and video-recording that accompanies Free Hugs campaigns and other 'social experiments' involving pointedly meaningful hugging is a telling example of the attendant third-party perspective immersive hugging implies (see for instance ikizlerTV's 2014 'I Trust You, Do You Trust Me? Hug Me' video on YouTube).

Moreover, as previously mentioned, immersive hugging usually takes place as an expected feature of certain special venues or practices: festivals, self-development workshops, etc. It may occur in an impromptu fashion, or may be purposely initiated by others, such the Hug Patrols 'who wander around [Rainbow] Gatherings hugging people' (Niman 1997: 289). It is often provoked by those leading or facilitating these special activities or events. In this respect, immersive hugs, whether they are tacitly anticipated or explicitly encouraged, generally happen in response to incitements that are less directives than verbal or non-verbal 'invitations' whose authority-depreciating quality is characteristic of power relations in the context of alternative spiritualities (cf. Wood 2007). Archetypal in this respect is the paradoxical injunction that ended the closing ritual of a four-day English Druid Camp I took part in in 2015: 'Let the spontaneous hugging begin!'

Finally, a purely egocentric appreciation of immersive hugging is belied by another of its constitutive features which are the expressions of mutual recognition and gratitude it invariably occasions. Immersive hugs always end with participants looking deeply into each other's eyes and with some kind of concluding sign: a knowing look, a shared smile, a bow, a slow blink. By ratifying their common involvement in this way, participants acknowledge the part each willingly plays in allowing the other to experience the more accomplished self—spontaneous, authentic, emotionally expressive, open to others, etc.—they have momentarily become. More than the act of hugging itself, it is this shared awareness of oneself-with-another as the enabling environment of one's own self-discovery that underlies the sentiments of glad companionship and fortuitous like-mindedness that participants generally take away from a rewarding immersive hug. When immersive hugging occurs with multiple partners within the context of regular or extended activities—weekly dance sessions, weekend workshops, week or month-long festivals, etc.—such feelings of reciprocal recognition and demonstrative gratefulness easily reverberate outward to include the group as a whole, prompting invocations of 'family' or 'home' (cf. Pike 2001: 13, 29–37) as well as drawn-out group hugs ('cuddle puddles' in Rainbow parlance [Niman 1997: 285]). Inversely, as several long-time Pagans have pointed out to me, immersive hugging, as the embodiment of a shared worldview and set of attitudes, can also lose a measure of its ritual character to become a customary expression of community membership (cf. Prince and Riches 2000: 116). In such cases, the final mutual acknowledgement phase of immersive hugging tends to prevail over the warm but abbreviated embrace itself, the latter becoming an index of the antecedent hugs that are presumed to have taken place between the parties concerned.

Recall, however, that immersive hugging does not imply ongoing interpersonal intimacy. Mentions of 'home' and 'family' notwithstanding, those taking part in groups and/or networks in which immersive hugs regularly occur are rarely embroiled in the ambivalent co-dependencies and continually renegotiated accountabilities so characteristic of lasting emotional ties. Their interactions, undertaken in a spirit of affable complicity implying limited interpersonal liability, are upheld by a more ephemeral, freer sociality in which each is expected to pursue their personal fulfilment while acting as a willing resource for the personal fulfilment of others. Thus, while the social dimensions of immersive hugging are assuredly present, they pertain less to everyday relations than to this special, ritually circumscribed mode of relatedness in which the culturally constructed opposition between individual autonomy and collective solidarity is happily resolved. Indeed, in many respects immersive hugging is emblematic of this eminently Western utopic social model that one of Tavory and Goodman's (2009) informants, in reference to Rainbow gatherings, dubbed a 'collective of individuals' (cf. Houseman 2020 on 'collective individualism'). This is a situation, explain these two authors, in which 'both solidarity and individuality are constructed simultaneously—as an ongoing set of pragmatic achievements, mutually shaping each other in the field' (2009: 262–263; see also Pike 2001 on Pagan festivals generally, and Batchelor 2014 on New Age yoga and Sufi dance practices in England). In this perspective, it is perhaps no accident that intense, meaningful bodily contact between 'consequential strangers' so often occurs in contemporary spiritual practices that configure individual realisation and community fellowship as conjunct ideals. It may well be that such close dyadic interactions that accentuate feelings of personal presence while downplaying interpersonal commitment, notably when deployed in a round-robin pattern, are especially instrumental in mediating the connection between these two allegedly antagonistic poles (cf. Moisseeff and Houseman 2020). Exemplary in this regard, as far as new religious movements are concerned, is the YouTube video in which 'People from all over the world meet at Osho Humaniversity in the Netherlands celebrating the international Hugging Day 2009'. As several dozen people tenderly embrace one another, a deeply resonant voice, accompanied by soothing music, slowly explains:

> I know we can make Osho's dream into a reality, just by hugging you right now, exchanging warm vibrations of love and allowing our hearts to say yes. ... We are one, and God is happy. ... Hugging is only a [unintelligible] of love, of want, of gaiety. ... I know we can make Osho's dream into a reality. You see, together we can create a beautiful world to live in, filled with friends and lovers.

A POSSIBLE RITUAL MODEL?

Immersive hugging, then, is an (1) overly emphatic, (2) markedly undiscriminating (3) protracted embrace (4) between non-intimates that is (5) exhibited, (7) enjoined and (8) gratefully acknowledged. I have suggested that it is best understood as a ritual act. As such, it affords participants with memorable, conventional if somewhat hard to pin down experiences in which supposed opposites—close intimacy and interpersonal remove, absorptive bodily engagement and heightened self-consciousness, individual autonomy and mutual recognition in the service of collective solidarity—are made to go hand in hand. In the manner of rituals generally, to the extent that these special experiences remain difficult to account for in terms of everyday attitudes and patterns of behaviour, they are ill-suited to provide participants with viable models for their daily lives. What they do provide them with, however, are largely unassailable, lived-through touchstones in light of which their everyday interactions can be customarily appraised. Close contact with non-intimate others during immersive hugging can, for example, act as a privileged yardstick for appreciating what intimate contact with close others might and should be. Concomitantly, on a collective level, immersive hugging is one of the myriad ways whereby simply through the performance of certain acts, the axiomatic idea-values (Dumont 1979) of a particular cultural tradition—'spontaneity', 'authenticity', 'deep feeling', 'bodily pleasure', 'self-awareness', 'openness to others', etc.—are enshrined, embodied and passed on.

I would like to conclude by using the analysis offered here to think about ritualised practices linked with contemporary spiritualities in general. Immersive hugging displays on an easily accessible scale many of these practices' characteristic properties, the foremost of which is a kind of built-in reflexivity. As we have seen, because immersive hugs are so long-lasting, hugging parties are repeatedly jolted into becoming attentive to their own thoughts and feelings. This type of heightened self-consciousness is not a necessary component of ritual *per se*. Indeed, in many rituals in which certain ordained actions must be undertaken correctly, it is important that participants pay attention to what they are doing (Smith 1987: 103), but it is not necessary that they be knowingly aware of their own frame of mind while doing so. This is because the distinctive complexity of such rituals that gives their performance special potency pertains above all to the somewhat mysterious actions participants are expected to undertake. Take, for example, the case of a priest declaring 'This is my body' during a Catholic mass while displaying a wafer of bread. This construes what he is holding to be at once bread and the body of Christ, regardless of what his personal dispositions might be. He may be heedful of his own thoughts and feelings, but his vigilance in this regard is not constitutive of the ritual act he performs, which, as the reiteration of behaviour presumed to have been undertaken previously by more authoritative others, is deemed to have value and efficacy in and of itself.

In contrast to this, mindful reflexivity is an integral aspect of many ritual practices associated with contemporary spiritualities. This is often thought to be because these practices have yet to become part of established traditions. However, new rituals crop up all the time in many cultural contexts without self-attentiveness being emphasised. In light of this, it is tempting to link such an emphasis to Western modernity. Tanya Luhrmann (2012), for example, has argued that the 'self-conscious epistemological complexity' found not only in Contemporary Paganism and Neo-Shamanism, but also in evangelical Christianity, is strongly stimulated by participants' awareness of how much their practices and beliefs deviate from mainstream secular thinking. At the same time, from a historical perspective, the self-conscious epistemology she refers to can be understood as but the latest religious expression of a cultural tradition—what Colin Campbell (1987) has called 'the romantic ethic'—deriving from Pietistic Protestantism and dating back to the eighteenth century. All told, it would seem that the exacerbated self-awareness characteristic of many present-day spiritual practices, while perhaps not exclusive to Euro-American culture, is particularly well-developed in the contemporary West.

I understand this type of enhanced reflexivity to be an essential component of a specific mode of ritualisation that has gone largely unrecognised, at least by anthropologists. As I have suggested elsewhere (2007, 2016, 2020), the distinctive complexity of ceremonial activities organised according to this mode relates less to exceptional items of behaviour participants are supposed to undertake, than to special ways of thinking and feeling their behaviour is alleged to embody. For example, many ritual practices, ranging from Contemporary Pagan ceremonies to New Age inspired guided meditations, begin with acts of 'centring' or 'grounding'. Participants may be invited to form a circle holding hands, quiet their minds, take a deep breath, become fully present and feel their connection with the earth. While the actions involved—standing in a circle, holding hands, taking a deep breath—may be unusual, they are readily intelligible in and of themselves in a way that calling a piece of bread the body of Christ, for instance, is not. More puzzling, on the other hand, are the special dispositions these actions are taken to express and/or bring about: the ability to 'quiet one's mind', 'become fully present' and 'feel a connection with the earth'. Now, what bridges the gap between the participants' unremarkable actions and the remarkable things their performance of these actions allows them to accomplish are the participants themselves, construed as at once ordinary and extraordinary beings. Indeed, the mysterious, highly salient focus of rituals such as these—equivalent to the priest holding something that is both bread and the body of Christ—is the two-fold experience of self they engender and display.

Participants are induced both to experience certain special ways of thinking and feeling, and to consciously experience themselves as doing so. Immersive hugging incites huggers to appreciate themselves and each other as exceptional individuals able to 'connect' with others in a singular fashion, and also as regular men and women thankfully moved by their (more or less successful) attempts to do so. Similarly, by taking part in rituals structured in the manner of our centring/grounding example, participants are encouraged to feel themselves both as endowed with certain extraordinary aptitudes, and as ordinary persons affected by the performances in which they aspire to put these aptitudes into effect. In other words, rituals such as these give rise to refracted, dilated identities in which participants experience themselves as becoming more than what they seem (e.g. magical beings, higher selves, shamans, etc.) without ceasing to be whom they recognise themselves to be (e.g. members of a Western or Westernised middle-class). This happy uncertainty as to who exactly participants become within the context of the rituals they perform is upheld, for themselves and others, by a built-in reflexivity that these performances prompt them to entertain.

Under these conditions, what Caroline Humphrey and James Laidlaw (1994) have called the 'stipulated' quality of ritual takes on a specific form.

Thus, one of the hallmarks of much contemporary ceremonial is a tendency to replace appeals to prescriptive traditions (that require participants to do X, Y and Z) by appeals to regulatory auto-injunctions (that incite participants to ask themselves how they can best do X, Y and Z). What we might call a canonical 'action-centred' mode of ritualisation, posits, for example, that participants must light a white candle with their eyes closed to call upon the Goddess; if a candle of another colour is used, or if one opens one's eyes, the Goddess has not been properly called upon. On the other hand, in the 'actor-centred' ritual mode typical of many contemporary spiritual practices, having one's eyes open or closed can be left up to each of the participants who, having been informed that lighting a white candle is usually thought to be best, are invited to ponder what they feel the candle's colour should be in order for them to call upon the Goddess as properly as possible. This does not mean that anything goes. Nor is it simply a matter of acting according to what one thinks and feels. Rather, it is a question of acting according to what one thinks and feels one should be thinking and feeling. There is a correct, optimally effective way for each of us to call upon the Goddess and we need to draw on both others' knowhow and our own personal sensibilities to identify what it must be.

The reflexive dynamic built into immersive hugging and other 'actor-centred' rituals underlies the distinctive efficacy of these practices. The inherently unstable, two-fold sense of self it engenders allows participants to experience their potential to become extraordinary beings without deceiving themselves. Ritual experiences, however, are notoriously difficult to put into words, and the lived-through quality of this in-built reflexivity is no exception. One might be tempted to describe it as an inner dialogue or as an act of reasoned introspection. But such discourse-inspired or vision-based 'conceptual metaphors' (Lakoff and Johnson 1980), because they proceed from a clear distinction between interlocutors or between an observer and the observed, seem basically misleading. As is applying a relational vocabulary—to speak, for example, of 'a relationship with oneself'—to an experience that clearly lacks the latent uncertainties, shifting accountabilities and ongoing negotiations that any interaction with a genuine Other necessarily entails. The reflexivity involved here seems to be more a matter of enfolding oneself, of becoming one's own customarily sanctioned 'holding environment' (Winnicott 1960). In this light, conceptualisations based on hearing, touch or even proprioceptive sensation might be more appropriate to convey the process of intimate self-encompassment whereby those taking part in these practices can become newly present to themselves. It is more like listening to one's own breathing, or feeling one's weight—or giving oneself a hug.

ACKNOWLEDGEMENTS

I am very grateful to Laurent Gabail, Ron Grimes, Graham Harvey, Arnaud Halloy, Marie Mazzella di Bosco, Marika Moisseeff, Sarah Pike and Steven Sutcliffe for their helpful comments on earlier drafts.

BIBLIOGRAPHY

Altglas, Véronique. 2014. *From Yoga to Kabbalah: Religious Exoticism and the Logics of Bricolage*. Oxford and New York: Oxford University Press. https://doi.org/10.1093/acprof:oso/9780199997626.001.0001

Artigas, Lucina and Ignacio Jarero. 2014. 'The Butterfly Hug Method for Bilateral Stimulation'. Accessed 23 March 2020. https://emdrresearchfoundation.org/toolkit/butterfly-hug.pdf

Batchelor, Charlotte. 2014. 'Buying a Balance: The "Individual–Collective" and the Commercial New Age Practices of Yoga and Sufi Dance'. PhD dissertation, University of Oxford.

Beckford, James A. 1992. 'Religion, Modernity and Post-Modernity'. In Bryan Wilson (ed.), *Religion: Contemporary Issues. The All Souls Seminars in the Sociology of Religion*, 11–23. London: Bellew Publishing.

Bourdieu, Pierre. 1979. *La distinction. Critique sociale du jugement*. Paris: Editions de Minuit.

Campbell, Colin. 1987. *The Romantic Ethic and the Spirit of Modern Consumerism*. Oxford: Basil Blackwell.

Dumont, Louis. 1979. 'The Anthropological Community and Ideology'. *Social Science Information* 18 (6): 785–817. https://doi.org/10.1177/053901847901800601

Field, Tiffany. 2019. 'Social Touch, CT Touch and Massage Therapy: A Narrative Review'. *Developmental Review* 51: 123–145. https://doi.org/10.1016/j.dr.2019.01.002

Fingerman, Karen L. 2009. 'Consequential Strangers and Peripheral Partners: The Importance of Unimportant Relationships'. *Journal of Family Theory and Review* 1: 69–86. https://doi.org/10.1111/j.1756-2589.2009.00010.x

Houseman, Michael. 2007. 'Menstrual Slaps and First Blood Celebrations. Inference, Simulation and the Learning of Ritual'. In David Berliner and Ramon Sarró (eds.), *Learning Religion: Anthropological Approaches*, 31–48. Oxford and New York: Berghahn Books.

Houseman, Michael. 2016. 'Comment comprendre l'esthétique affectée des cérémonies New Age et néopaïennes?' *Archives des Sciences Sociales des Religions* 174: 213–237. https://doi.org/10.4000/assr.27807

Houseman Michael. 2020. 'Becoming Autonomous Together: Distanced Intimacy in Dances of Self-Development'. In Graham Harvey, Michael Houseman, Sarah M. Pike and Jone Salomonsen (eds.), *Reassembling Democracy: Ritual as Cultural Resource*, 87–104. London: Bloomsbury Publishing.
https://doi.org/10.5040/9781350123045.ch-005

Houseman, Michael and Marie Mazzella di Bosco. 2020. 'Dances of Self-development as a Resource for Participatory Democracy'. In Sarah M. Pike, Jone Salomonsen and Paul-François Tremlett (eds.), *Ritual and Democracy: Protests, Publics, and Performances*, 115–138. Sheffield: Equinox Publishing.

Humphrey, Caroline and James Laidlaw. 1994. *The Archetypal Actions of Ritual: A Theory of Ritual Illustrated by the Jain Rite of Worship*. Oxford: Clarendon Press.

Jensen, Todd Aaron. 2010. *On Gratitude*. Avon: Adams Media.

Lakoff, George and Mark Johnson. 1980. *Metaphors We Live By*. Chicago: University of Chicago Press.

Luhrmann, Tanya M. 2012. 'Touching the Divine: Recent Research on Neo-Paganism and Neo-Shamanism'. *Reviews in Anthropology* 41: 136–150.
https://doi.org/10.1080/00938157.2012.680425

Luhrmann, Tanya M., Howard Nusbaum and Ronald Thisted. 2010. 'The Absorption Hypothesis: Learning to Hear God in Evangelical Christianity'. *American Anthropologist* 112 (1): 66–78. https://doi.org/10.1111/j.1548-1433.2009.01197.x

Moisseeff, Marika. 2020. 'Dealing with Death in Contemporary Western Culture: A View from Afar'. In Graham Harvey, Michael Houseman, Sarah M. Pike and Jone Salomonsen (eds.), *Reassembling Democracy: Ritual as Cultural Resource*, 179–191. London: Bloomsbury Publishing.
https://doi.org/10.5040/9781350123045.ch-010

Moisseeff, Marika and Michael Houseman. 2020. 'L'orchestration rituelle du partage des émotions et ses ressorts interactionnels'. In Laurence Kaufmann and Louis Quéré (eds.), *Emotions Collectives*, 133–168. Paris: Ecole des Hautes Etudes en Sciences Sociales. https://doi.org/10.4000/books.editionsehess.29437

Nagy, Emese. 2011. 'Sharing the Moment: The Duration of Embraces in Humans'. *Journal of Ethology* 29 (2): 389–393. https://doi.org/10.1007/s10164-010-0260-y

Niman, Michael I. 1997. *People of the Rainbow: A Nomadic Utopia*. Knoxville, TN: University of Tennessee Press.

Pike, Sarah M. 2001. *Magical Selves, Earthly Bodies: Contemporary Pagans and the Search for Community*. Berkeley, CA: University of California Press.

Pike, Sarah M. 2017. *For the Wild: Ritual and Commitment in Radical Eco-Activism*. Oakland, CA: University of California Press.
https://doi.org/10.1525/california/9780520294950.001.0001

Prince, Ruth and David Riches. 2000. *The New Age in Glastonbury. The Construction of Religious Movements*. New York and Oxford: Berghahn Books.

Rappaport, Roy A. 1979. *Ecology, Meaning and Religion*. Berkeley, CA: North Atlantic Books.

Schnarch, David 1997. *Passionate Marriage: Sex, Love and Intimacy in Emotionally Committed Relationships*. New York and London: W.W. Norton.

Shapiro, Francine. 2013. *Getting Past Your Past: Take Control of Your Life With Self-Help Techniques from EMDR Therapy*. New York: Rodale Books.

Smith, Jonathan Z. 1987. *To Take Place*. Chicago: University of Chicago Press.

Sutcliffe, Steven J. 2003. *Children of the New Age: A History of Spiritual Practices*. London and New York: Routledge. https://doi.org/10.4324/9780203471227

Tavory, Iddo and Yehuda C. Goodman. 2009. '"A Collective of Individuals": Between Self and Solidarity in a Rainbow Gathering'. *Sociology of Religion* 70 (3): 262–284. https://doi.org/10.1093/socrel/srp038

wikiHow staff. 2019. 'How to Hug Yourself'. Last modified 14 October 2019. https://www.wikihow.com/Hug-Yourself

Winnicott, Donald. W. 1960. 'The Theory of the Parent-Infant Relationship'. *International Journal of Psycho-Analysis* 41: 585–595.

Wood, Matthew. 2007. *Possession, Power and the New Age: Ambiguities of Authority in Neoliberal Societies*. Aldershot: Ashgate.

Michael Houseman, anthropologist, is a Directeur d'études (chair of African religions) at the Ecole Pratique des Hautes Etudes, PSL Research University (France). He has undertaken field research among the Beti of Southern Cameroon, in Benin, in French Guyana and in France. He has published extensively on kinship and social organisation, and on initiation and ritual performance. His current areas of interest include ceremonial dance and emergent forms of ritual practice. His publications include *Naven or the Other Self: A Relational Approach to Ritual Action* (Brill, 1998, with C. Severi) and *Le rouge est le noir: Essais sur le ritual* (Presses Universitaires le Mirail, 2012).

Chapter 12

Handling Things Unseen: Tactile Aspects of the Christian Faith

GEORGE D. CHRYSSIDES

Religions typically emphasise seeing and hearing, possibly because they are the dominant senses: epistemologically most of our knowledge comes from sight and sound. Moreover, particularly in the Christian Protestant tradition, there is a preoccupation with 'the Word', and the Protestant Reformation endeavoured to ensure that the Bible was heard in reading and preaching. Augustine wrote, 'the objects we touch or taste or smell are less analogous to this truth [i.e. divine truth] than those we hear or discern' (Augustine 2010: 59). On a quick word count, the New International Version of the Bible reveals 1082 occurrences of 'see', with a further 600 of 'saw' and 957 of 'hear', in contrast with a mere 138 of 'touch' and 28 of 'feel'. Touch is sometimes regarded as an inferior substitute for the seemingly more dominant senses, for example Braille as a substitute for visually readable text.

Despite Augustine's disparagement of touch, the sense of touch can be claimed to have greater primordiality: there are fewer perceptual errors involving touch. People can claim to 'hear voices' or to 'have visions', the authenticity of which can be challenged, but tactile illusions are less common, although not completely non-existent. When Thomas doubts the evidence of his eyes that the risen Christ is present in front of him, Jesus invites him to touch his wounds (John 20:24–29). Although John does not record whether Thomas actually accepts this challenge, the sense of touch verifies the seemingly less reliable sense of sight.

TOUCH AND DEVOTION

Touch has various functions within the Christian faith. At its most obvious, it can convey friendship and greeting, for example when members of the congregation offer 'the sign of peace' to one another during the Eucharist by shaking hands. Touch can be made as a means of maintaining a tradition. Paul's recommendation, 'Greet one another with a holy kiss' (Romans 16:16) is sometimes regarded as the precedent for this more restrained handshake. Touching can be an act of devotion; it can be therapeutic; it can recapitulate actions relating to the Christian tradition; and it can be used at various stages of initiation. Tactile metaphors also acquire significance for the Christian. In what follows, I hope to demonstrate that, despite the tendency to privilege sight and hearing over the other three senses, the sense of touch is of fundamental importance in the practice of the Christian faith. I shall focus on those aspects of touch that are more usually found in present-day expressions of the Christian faith, which I shall classify into devotional, healing, initiatory and metaphorical. I shall also include brief discussion about whether emergent digital technology affords acceptable alternatives to physical touch.

Ritual touching can connote more than acceptance: certain religious forms of touch serve to personify religious objects. In an Eastern Orthodox church, the many icons that one typically sees surrounding the nave are not merely to be viewed; the worshipper is expected to kiss the icons, making direct tactile contact. The fact that the constant kissing usually damages the icon is considered unimportant: the icon is meant to be used, not preserved as if the building were an art gallery. Although the icon is not held to be 'alive' in the sense the Hindu would regard a *murti*, the devotional kiss is an act addressed to Christ, the Virgin Mary or one of the saints, with whom the devotee can experience some reciprocation. Similar devotion occurs in the Anglican liturgy, when it is customary for the priest physically to kiss the Gospel after it is read. Physical contact with the Bible underscores the proximity of and love for God's Word, and this devotional act simultaneously points beyond the written text to Jesus Christ, who is also described as God's Word (John 1:1). Less symbolically, it is customary in Roman Catholic and Anglican liturgies for the Bible to be carried in procession, acknowledging its importance, and also to indicate that it should be touched, and not just seen. Even in Protestant Churches, the service may commence with an office-bearer bringing in a large Bible and physically placing it on the pulpit to indicate that the Bible is central in Protestant Christianity.

BREAD AND WINE

Of all the substances that the believer handles, the most important are the sacramental bread and wine. The rite, variously known as the Mass, the Eucharist, Holy Communion, the Lord's Supper, among numerous other names, depending on the tradition, has of course aroused considerable controversy throughout Christian history. However one interprets the sacrament theologically, its significance transcends empirical experience. As Horatio Bonar's famous communion hymn puts it:

> Here, O my Lord, I see thee face to face;
> Here would I touch and handle things unseen.
> (*Hymns Ancient and Modern*, no. 274)

The obvious import of these words is that Christ is invisible, and one has not yet experienced the heavenly paradise that is promised, and which is frequently described as a banquet. The sacrament therefore makes the invisible visible, and the intangible tangible, the bread and the wine being visible and tactile tokens of Christ's presence and the believer's expectation of eternity. The elements are therefore to be handled somewhat differently from ordinary food and drink. Some readers may recall a comic sketch by Rowan Atkinson, in which he appears as a vicar addressing a wedding couple, and absentmindedly snacks on the communion wafers, dunking them in the wine (YouTube 2017). Depending on one's sense of humour, this is either funny or offensive, since it is totally inappropriate behaviour. A balance must be struck between acknowledging the ordinary nature of bread and wine, and their extraordinary significance. The Church of England's *Common Worship* describes the Eucharistic bread as that 'which earth has given and human hands have made', but which 'will become for us the bread of life' (Church of England 2000: 291).

The Eucharist is also maintenance of tradition, and an act of obedience to Christ's instruction, '…do this in remembrance of me' (Luke 22:19). It is a re-enactment of Jesus' last meal with his disciples, and since the Gospels are unclear as to whether or not this was a Passover meal, disagreement occurs as to the nature of the substances that the congregation handle and consume. The Orthodox tradition notes that the New Testament word used for 'bread' is *artos*, which means a loaf, and hence the element should be normal leavened bread. The Roman Catholic and Anglican traditions favour the use of unleavened wafers, partly because the use of leaven would be prohibited during the Passover season, but also because leaven symbolises impurity, and the host (the name for the Eucharistic wafer), representing the body of Christ, must be pure.

The theological interpretation of what happens at the Eucharist determines how the elements are handled. For the Roman Catholic, the protocols regarding the handling of the elements relate to the traditional doctrine of transubstantiation—the belief that a miracle occurs during the Mass, in which the bread and wine are in some real sense transformed into Christ's body and blood. The priest will elevate the chalice, signifying that in the Mass Christ is being offered to God the Father. If the Eucharistic elements have been transformed, care must be taken in their distribution. Since it is Christ's symbolic meal, he is the host (in both the liturgical and the lay sense), and hence, in the Catholic and Anglican traditions the celebrant is the first to partake, contrary to common conventions relating to dinner parties, where guests are served first, and the (human) host last. The priest has precise instructions about the conduct and relevant liturgical movements during the rite (Dearmer 1907: 302–431). As a ritual specialist, he or she must ensure that any remaining Eucharistic elements are suitably disposed of; it would be inappropriate to put them in a bin or a food recycling container, hence the officiating clergy consume what remains, and clean out the utensils, so that nothing is left.

By contrast, Protestant churches frequently tend to de-ritualise, in order to dissociate demonstrably from the Roman Catholic tradition. The elements are normally brought to the congregation by elders, the wine usually in individual small glasses, and ordinary baker's bread cut into small cubes. The celebrant often eats and drinks last, as a human host would do. If there is surplus bread, it is simply disposed of in the same way as ordinary food waste.

SACRAMENTALS, TALISMANS AND AMULETS

In addition to the vessels and substances that are used in the sacraments, Roman Catholic popular piety adds 'sacramentals'. These are objects that aid devotion, and which are typically blessed by a priest or appropriately ordained person. Examples of sacramentals include holy water, crosses and crucifixes, medallions, rosaries, scapulars and liturgical books. They differ from sacraments in that they are not believed to bestow grace through their own inherent properties, but rather to enhance devotion, and to give the believer power through the blessing that they have been given. They also differ from amulets and talismans. Not all amulets are associated with the Christian faith, while a sacramental is a distinctively Christian object. A talisman is often accredited with magical powers, particularly those of protection, and while popular piety may associate sacramentals with special powers—for example a Saint Christopher medallion in one's car offering greater protection against accidents—sacramentals are intended to offer spiritual help, and clergy are encouraged to draw on these forms of popular piety, directing them towards the spiritual life. The *Catechism of the Catholic Church* (1994) explains it thus:

> Sacramentals do not confer the grace of the Holy Spirit in the way that the sacraments do, but by the Church's prayer they prepare us to receive grace and dispose us to co-operate with it. (*Catechism*: 1670)

Some comment on some of these sacramentals may be appropriate. Holy water is frequently located at the entrance to a Roman Catholic church, and also in some Anglican churches. Worshippers may dip their fingers in the water, and place it on their forehead, making the sign of the cross. It is intended to be a reminder of the water of one's baptism, as well as symbolising cleansing, and the need to approach God with a clean heart. When found at sacred shrines, holy water is regarded as having healing properties.

The use of holy salt is not so widely known. Salt is sometimes used in baptismal water: the priest makes the sign of the cross as he sprinkles salt over the baptismal water. In the Roman Catholic tradition, a few grains of holy salt may be placed on a baby's tongue when he or she is eight days old: this is an ancient Roman custom, believed by some to expel evil spirits (Connaughton and Silcock 1997: 228). Salt is held to have purificatory properties, being associated with a story about the prophet Elisha. The people of Jericho complain to him that their water is bad, whereupon Elisha requests a bowl of salt, which he puts into the spring, miraculously making it pure (2 Kings 2:19–22). Salt was also a typical additive in priestly sacrifices (Exodus 30:35; Leviticus 2:13), which legitimises its liturgical use. Jesus' reference to his followers as 'the salt of the earth' (Matthew 5:13) indicates that they should be a purifying additive within the society in which they live.

Some Roman Catholics have associated salt with the power to drive out demons. It is sometimes added to holy water when used in exorcism. It can be scattered in one's bedroom for protection; it is occasionally sprinkled on thresholds to prevent burglary, and in cars to promote safety. Some Roman Catholics have affirmed that, added to water or food, it brings spiritual as well as physical benefits. However, without discouraging popular piety, the Church teaches that the proper use of sacramentals is to focus one's mind on Christ, just as a national flag focuses attention on one's country (Sacred Heart Holdings 2019).

Some sacramentals are garments. A scapular, as used in monastic orders, is worn from the shoulders, running down to one's back and in front to one's knees. Devotional scapulars, as used by the laity, are based on the monastic scapular, but are simpler and smaller. They consist of two small rectangular pieces of card, wood, wool or even plastic, worn on one's back and front, and connected by two pieces of cord running over one's shoulders. The card depicts objects of devotion, typically Jesus Christ and the Virgin Mary. Scapulars probably originated within confraternities—groups that supported monastic orders, and who undertook some of their vows. Some incorporate wording such as, 'Whoever dies wearing this scapular shall not suffer eternal fire.' This may seem to contradict the notion that sacramentals do not offer protection, but their benefits are not unconditional: to receive the scapular's benefits, one should, apart from having it blessed, become enrolled in the confraternity, using its sign as a vow of commitment to regular prayer, receiving the sacrament and undertaking devotional prayers using spiritual aids such as the Psalms or one's rosary (Morello 2000).

The objects mentioned above are particularly recommended by the Church as aids to devotion. However, ordinary mundane objects can be made into sacramentals by having them blessed. It is not uncommon for believers to request a blessing on their home, or on their car. Indeed, any material object that is not obviously inappropriate in the context of the Christian faith can be blessed; as the Vatican II Liturgy document states, 'there is hardly any proper use of material things which cannot thus be directed toward the sanctification of persons and the praise of God' (*Sacrosanctum Concilium*, article 61; quoted in Vatican 2012: 448).

One object that is particularly noteworthy is the monstrance. This is a kind of stand, used in the Roman Catholic, Old Catholic and some Anglican traditions, usually for holding a consecrated host. It is made of precious metal, with a base and a stem, and is usually highly decorated, with a cross superimposed with a large star-burst design, in the centre of which there is a circular glass receptacle, inside which the host is installed. The device can also be used to house relics rather than the sacrament. The monstrance can be displayed simply as an object of devotion, or it can be used liturgically. It is common practice for a priest to lead a Corpus Christi procession carrying a monstrance, to which the congregation will bow in reverence at an appropriate point in the ceremony. The monstrance can also be elevated by a priest pronouncing a benediction: this is a special blessing because it is Christ who is being held before the congregation, and the blessing is deemed to come from him, and not merely from a human priest.

Since sacramentals have been blessed and are therefore holy, they should be disposed of appropriately if they fall into disuse. They should be treated as one would treat a deceased person: they should be buried in a place over which no one is likely to walk or, if they are combustible, burnt, and the ashes disposed of by burial; a stone statue should be dismantled, and similarly buried (Kosloski 2017).

The desire to touch sacred objects admits of a variety of explanations. Some devotees may believe they can draw on their power, while others may feel that touching provides the greatest possible proximity to the sacred object or person. However, some objects are not available to be touched by ordinary believers for fear that constant tactile contact would cause deterioration. The famous Shroud of Turin cannot even be displayed for visitors to see, let alone touched, and it has only been handled by approved researchers and restorers. Other objects have simply been lost through the passage of time. No doubt many believers wish they could literally get their hands on the Holy Grail, and its absence has caused various futile quests, although it has given rise to numerous traditions and speculations. Some have averred that the Holy Grail lies buried underneath the Chalice Well in Glastonbury, England, and that this accounts for the reddish ochre in the water. Predictably, the water is regarded as sacred, and pilgrims are encouraged to drink it for its purportedly curative powers. Various other 'discoveries' have been made in recent times of Noah's Ark and the Ark of the Covenant (the two should not be confused), and—in the absence of authentic archaeological finds—one group of American creationists has set up 'Ark Encounter' in Kentucky, Texas, where visitors can enter a replica life-size ark, constructed in accordance with the instructions God gave to Noah (Genesis 6:14–16). There are no live animals in the ark itself, but there is a 'petting zoo' for those who want to touch directly some of the species believed to have been taken on board.

The most significant relic, undoubtedly, is Christ's cross, of which various churches claim to have fragments. According to tradition, the Empress Helena, mother of the Roman Emperor Constantine, visited the Holy Land in 326–328 CE, founding churches and almshouses. In the course of her journey she allegedly found three crosses, which she believed were those of Jesus and the two thieves who were crucified with him. Unsure which of these was the true Cross, she received a miraculous revelation, assuring her of the authenticity of the supposedly real one. According to legend, pilgrims removed part of the cross as trophies, and it underwent fragmentation at the hands of the Crusaders. Some Christians have claimed to have crafted crosses and crucifixes from the wood of the true cross, a small fragment of which is housed in a reliquary in the Church of the Holy Sepulchre, which is believed to be the site of Jesus' crucifixion and burial. Here tactile contact is encouraged, as pilgrims typically run their hands over the Stone of Anointing, where Joseph of Arimathea is believed to have prepared Jesus' body for burial.

The Protestant tradition has been particularly critical of the authenticity and the efficacy of such relics: the Protestant Reformer John Calvin (1509–1564) claimed that there were so many fragments of the cross in existence by the end of the Middle Ages, that they could provide the cargo for a large boat! (Calvin 1870 [1543]: 173). Within the Protestant tradition, a rival location for Jesus' crucifixion and burial is favoured: the Garden Tomb in East Jerusalem affords visitors the opportunity to climb inside the ancient tomb there, to touch its entrance and walls, and allow themselves mentally and spiritually to be transported back into the key happenings that are held to have brought about the world's salvation.

In the absence of the genuine true cross in its entirety, every Christian church houses a representational cross—plain in the Protestant tradition, and as a crucifix with the dying Jesus in Roman Catholic and Eastern Orthodox churches. While a church's central cross is not handled liturgically or devotionally, it is a common practice in some traditions during Holy Week to hold processions in which a large cross is carried. One practice in the Good Friday liturgy is for clergy to process bearing a large cross down the central aisle, which is then placed on the chancel. The congregation are then invited to come forward and to venerate the cross in whatever way they feel is appropriate. A common practice is to obtain a red ribbon, usually available at the front, and to place it reverently on the cross, thus placing themselves in the closest possible proximity to the heart of their faith.

RECAPITULATION AND THE LITURGICAL CALENDAR

Touching can be associated with the Church's liturgical calendar. The Christian liturgical year begins with Advent, when it is common practice to light an Advent candle successively for each of the four Sundays leading up to Christmas, when a fifth central candle is lit. Children are frequently assigned this task, under appropriate supervision, and the practice proves popular even among Protestants, despite their usual aversion to candle lighting.

The season of Lent and Holy Week provide opportunities for Christians to express their faith in a number of tangible and tactile ways, as they re-enact some of the key events that are believed to have taken place. In the Roman Catholic and Anglican tradition, Ash Wednesday affords the opportunity for the imposition of ash on one's forehead. The service is inevitably a solemn one, marking the start of the season of Lent, and the imposition involves worshippers going forward to the chancel, where a member of the clergy takes ash, which is made from burning the palm crosses from the previous Palm Sunday, mixed with chrism oil, and daubing the mixture on one's forehead, making the sign of the cross, and including the words, 'Dust thou art, and to dust thou shalt return.' This is a reminder of one's mortality, and the pronouncement comes from the book of Genesis, where God imposes death as a consequence for Adam and Eve's sin (Genesis 3:19).

On Palm Sunday (the Sunday before Easter) it is increasingly customary for a procession of palms to be organised, recreating Christ's entry into Jerusalem, when he was hailed as the messiah as he rode into the city on a donkey, with crowds waving palm branches to greet him. Congregations typically process around the church or around the streets, holding palm crosses. Some churches now ask a local farmer to provide a real donkey for the occasion; however, it is not normally ridden, since it would be cruel to require it to bear a grown adult's weight. Kindness to animals here outweighs considerations about maintaining tradition.

Chrism oil—mentioned above—is scented olive oil, which is normally consecrated at a special Chrism Mass, held on Maundy Thursday in Holy Week, and over which the Bishop presides. Representatives from the diocesan congregations—normally clergy—collect vials containing the oil, which they bring back to the congregations to be used for baptisms, and for anointing the sick. While believers would usually consider that ordinary oil would be just as efficacious, the practice of ensuring that the oil is prepared in the approved way, and handled by the Bishop, underlines the point that it comes from one common source, and that all those who use it are part of the one Church. Anointing is a practice that goes back to ancient times, when priests and kings (and possibly some prophets) were anointed as part of their initiation rites; indeed, it is customary practice for British monarchs to be anointed with holy oil as part of a coronation. Anointing serves to mark out the one who is chrismated as someone who is set apart from others. While candidates for baptism and confirmation, unlike priests and monarchs, do not have special public status, they are marked out as being separate from 'the world'. The officiant's words to each candidate are: 'Christ claims you for his own. Receive the sign of his cross.' Immediately before these words are pronounced the candidates affirm that they renounce the devil and his works, and the sins that separate them from God; the ceremony marks a transition from the world and its standards, to Christ and his redeeming work.

Maundy Thursday traditionally marks the anniversary of the Last Supper. Not only is this to be the event from which the sacrament of the Eucharist originated, but on arrival at the Upper Room in Jerusalem, Jesus is stated to have performed the humble act of washing the disciples' feet. Since feet are typically regarded as unclean, contact with people's feet was an act normally performed by servants; hence Jesus' action was a demonstration of humility. Foot washing was incorporated into worship in the Adventist and Pentecostal traditions, but has gained wider popularity in recent times. In many mainstream denominations twelve members—representing Jesus' twelve disciples—are selected for ritual foot washing, and a senior member of the clergy goes around their seats with a bowl and towel, washing and drying their feet.

At Easter it is common practice in Western churches, but not among Protestants, to light a Paschal candle. This is done either on Holy Saturday or at the commencement of the Easter Vigil. This is a large candle, into which the officiant presses five grains of incense in the form of a cross, and it is the first candle to be lit, representing the light of Christ. The candle is subsequently rekindled for baptisms, and its flame is passed on to the candles that are given to baptismal candidates.

TOUCH AND HEALING

Touch is also used in the Christian tradition as an agent of healing. In the Christian faith therapeutic touch assumes a ritualised form. Healing can sometimes form part of the Eucharist, when communicants can go to a priest after receiving the sacrament, and be anointed with chrism oil. The use of oil in healing is commended in the letter of James: 'Is anyone among you ill? Let them call the elders of the church to pray over them and anoint them with oil in the name of the Lord' (James 5:14). Oil itself was reckoned to have curative powers: the Good Samaritan pours oil and wine on the injured traveller's wounds (Luke 10:33). Anointing the sick is associated with assisting the dying. In the Roman Catholic Church this was formerly called the sacrament of 'extreme unction' ('unction' meaning anointing), popularly known as 'the last rites'. Although the sacrament is referred to as 'anointing the sick', anointing is only part of the rite, which also includes the opportunity for confession of sins and a final Eucharistic celebration. The use of the special chrism oil, rather than just any available oil, serves to link the sick person with the rest of the Church, since there has been a tactile continuity between the presiding officiant at the chrism Mass and the believer who is receiving anointing. Since theologically the Church is defined as consisting of the dead as well as the living, the final rite of passage has the function of connecting the dying person with the 'communion of saints'.

The use of touch is reminiscent of Jesus' healing ministry, in which touching the afflicted was a typical element. Jesus touched the eyes of the blind, and made physical contact with leprosy victims, and even touching his robe reputedly had miraculous healing powers (Mark 8:22–25; Matthew 8:2–3; Matthew 14:35–36). Touch indicates acceptance: it was a violation of Jewish law to come into physical contact with a leprosy victim. The Book of Acts recounts that the physical presence of the healer was not always needed: in Ephesus, people brought handkerchiefs and aprons that Paul had touched to the sick, who obtained extraordinary miracles (Acts 19:11–12). The practice of taking handkerchiefs to the sick and needy continues in a small number of—usually fundamentalist—congregations. A number of charismatic Christians today continue to express a belief in demon possession, and look to 'deliverance ministries' where a pastor will administer the laying on of hands (technically known as cheirotonia), commanding the evil spirit to depart, in the name of Jesus Christ.

Spiritual healing remains controversial among Christians. Many Christian fundamentalists would look to the Bible as legitimating modern-day miraculous healing, citing Jesus' parting instructions to his disciples, affirming that 'they will place their hands on people who are ill, and they will get well' (Mark 16:8). A small number of minor sects have gone so far as to implement Jesus' preceding words: 'they will pick up snakes with their hands; and when they drink deadly poison, it will not hurt them at all', and practised snake handling as a means of demonstrating their faith. Predictably, not all have survived!

INITIATION

(1) Baptism

A further role of touch is initiation, of which there are various stages. For most denominations, admission to the Christian faith is by baptism and, depending on the tradition, either involves the member of the clergy physically holding a baby and allowing the baptismal water to touch him or her—either by making the sign of the cross on the forehead with the consecrated water, or by sprinkling the water three times as the Trinitarian formula ('In the name of the Father, the Son, and the Holy Spirit') is pronounced. When an adult is baptised by sprinkling or 'affusion' (pouring), physical contact is normally confined to the administration of the water. In traditions where baptism is done by immersion, the baptismal candidate is held before being lowered into the font.

Some Christians continue to view baptism as causally efficacious, holding that it washes away sin, or brings good fortune, while others prefer to view the baptismal water as having a symbolic function, marking an initiation of the young child (or sometimes an adult) into the Christian fold. The rite acknowledges that children can be initiated into and become part of the Christian community, just as adults are members.

For those denominations who prefer children to wait until they have sufficient understanding of the Christian faith and commitment—mainly in the Baptist, Pentecostalist and Adventist traditions—baptism becomes an expression of commitment, and the contact with the water is typically compared with death and resurrection. Just as Jesus is believed to have gone down into the tomb and to have risen again, Paul compares baptism with this key salvific event: 'having been buried with him in baptism, in which you were also raised with him through your faith in the working of God, who raised him from the dead' (Colossians 2:12). Baptism thus signifies a new life of commitment—dead to sin, and alive in Christ.

Although baptism is a once-for-all event, there are occasions where some traditions provide reminders of one's baptism. In the liturgical calendar, the celebration of the Baptism of Jesus often includes the sprinkling of the congregation with water, adding a tactile element, reminding each member of his or her commitment to the Christian faith, which commenced at baptism.

(2) Confirmation and Admission to Membership

For those communities that practise infant baptism, a ritual to mark fuller commitment is considered necessary when the candidate comes of age; this also involves tactile elements. In the Roman Catholic and Anglican traditions, the rite is known as 'confirmation', since its purpose is to confirm the baptismal promises that have been made on one's behalf as an infant. The ceremony includes the laying on of hands by the bishop, who applies chrism oil to the candidates' forehead, and a further tactile element includes a confirmation candle, which symbolises, in the words of *Common Worship*, that they 'have received the light of Christ', and they are instructed to 'Shine as a light in the world to the glory of God the Father' (Church of England 2000: 363). The bishop may also give the candidates a suitably edifying gift, such as a book of prayers.

The term 'confirmation' is sometimes found in the Protestant tradition; more commonly the event is more prosaically known as 'admission to membership', and typically involves the minister offering the new members the 'right hand of fellowship'. Depending on local practice, the right hand of fellowship may also be offered by a number of elders. This is a simple handshake, and the term goes back to Paul, who recounts that 'James, Cephas [i.e. Peter] and John, those esteemed as pillars, gave me and Barnabas the right hand of fellowship when they recognised the grace given to me' (Galatians 2:9). The offering of the right hand of fellowship has a variety of functions. It is a commissioning: Paul and Barnabas were appointed as legitimate preachers of the gospel to the Gentile community, and were accepted and welcomed as such. Thus the offering of the right hand of fellowship signifies commissioning, acceptance and agreement, as well as the obvious function of welcoming.

(3) Ordination

A further rite of initiation, again involving haptic elements, is ordination. The laying on of hands, which is performed in the Orthodox, Roman Catholic and Anglican traditions by the Bishop, is regarded as important in assuring an unbroken line of apostolic succession. The practice also serves to highlight the oneness of the Church and the continuity between the ordinand and the rest of his or her tradition.

Various offices require ordination as a means of admission, depending on the tradition. In the Roman Catholic and Anglican traditions, one can be ordained as a deacon or a priest. In the case of becoming a bishop, the word 'ordination' tends not to be used; instead a bishop is described as being 'installed', 'enthroned' or 'consecrated'. One somewhat idiosyncratic detail in an Anglican bishop's installation is at the commencement of the ceremony, when the new bishop must knock three times on the Cathedral's Great West Door in order to gain entry. This signifies that the Bishop must seek the Dean's permission regarding the affairs of the Cathedral, over which the Dean—not the Bishop—has responsibility; the Bishop's sphere of responsibility is the diocese. Even bishops must know their place!

In many Protestant churches, the rite of admitting elders—office-bearers who have some pastoral responsibility and typically help with the distribution of the elements at holy communion—is described as an ordination. Because of the Protestant aversion to undue ceremony and ritual, laying on of hands is not carried out, but the initiatory form of touch is the right hand of fellowship from the presiding minister.

Ordination is a kind of initiatory rite, distinct from any specific church appointment that the candidate is given. If a priest or minister moves from one parish to another, he or she does not undergo a fresh ordination, but the new appointment is described variously as admission, induction, translation or installation. In the Church of England it is common practice for the Archdeacon to take the new appointee by the hand and lead him or her around the church building and to touch various key objects—the door, the baptismal font, the altar, the pulpit and the rope of the bell, which the new vicar then tolls. The candidate is then presented with a number of physical objects, which he or she handles. One such object is a key, signifying that the new incumbent is the church's custodian, and has the right of entry to the premises. Another typical gift is a Bible, signifying that the new priest is the proclaimer of God's word, and sometimes a prayer book is given. Sometimes the candidate is presented with water, wine and chrism oil—an obvious reference to the responsibility for administering the sacraments. I have seen a new vicar being presented with a wallet—perhaps as a wish for his material prosperity, but maybe with the deeper meaning that he or she is responsible for the congregation's material success.

DIGITAL TOUCH?

As we move into the digital age, where much is done online rather than through direct physical contact, there seems less scope for touch. When overhead projectors became popular, quite a few congregations took to projecting the words of hymns and songs on screen, in place of traditional hymn books that attendees could handle, and numerous congregations have now taken to using digital technology for this purpose, using CDs or PowerPoint packages. While this may have some merit in encouraging congregations to sing out by looking at the screen, rather than muffle their voices in a hymnal, such innovations militate against the tactile. With the traditional hymn book, members of the congregation could hold and peruse its contents; by being able to explore words that were not on the music list, as well as those that were scheduled for the service, they were able to familiarise themselves with the poetry of the hymn writers, rather than fleetingly view verses at the required moment.

A few religious communities have sought to replicate traditional devotional activities online. One early project was the Church of Fools, initiated by the Methodist Church in 2004, and which offered religious worship in cyberspace. (The reference to fools was an allusion to 1 Corinthians 4:10, where Paul says that he and his readers are 'fools for Christ'.) Early online innovations tended to offer spiritual social networking or, somewhat more ambitiously, tours of virtual quasi-physical church premises. One noteworthy cyber-church project is the London Internet Church, which is linked with a real traditional Christian congregation: when a visitor 'lights' a candle or makes a prayer request in cyberspace, St Stephen Walbrook's office-bearers undertake to light a physical candle on their premises, and to offer a prayer on the visitor's behalf with their own intercessions. This enables cyber-religion to retain the tradition visual, aural and tactile elements with online spirituality (St Stephen Walbrook 2019).

More difficult to offer online, however, are religious acts that involve physical tactile elements, such as baptismal water and Eucharistic bread and wine. In 2010 Methodist minister Tim Watts offered a communion service as a series of tweets, and participants were invited to bring bread and wine (or grape juice) to their computers to consume at the appropriate moment (Wynne-Jones 2010). However, although these substances were tangible, Eucharistic elements cannot be consecrated at a distance, thus calling into question the sacrament's validity.

The Open Episcopal Church, founded by Jonathan Blake, has attempted to surmount this problem. Blake was ordained as a priest in the Church of England, but signed a Deed of Relinquishment in 1994, and subsequently became ordained as a priest and bishop in the Liberal Catholic Church. Blake regarded the conventional forms of Church Christianity as limited, and he wanted to ensure that anyone—irrespective of their faith or lifestyle—could be allowed to handle the Eucharistic elements (Blake 2019).

On New Year's Eve 2000 Blake decided to borrow a table from a local restaurant in Leicester Square, which he set up as an altar to celebrate the Eucharist, to which all were invited to partake, irrespective of age, ethnicity, social status or even religion—a clear breach of protocol in the eyes of the Church of England.

More radically, Blake went on to offer the Eucharist over the Internet. Blake's solution to the problem of remote consecration is his 'Post the Host' service. The intending worshipper contacts Blake, who will consecrate the required amount of bread and wine, which is sent through the post to the recipient. Blake has physically handled the elements as an ordained priest; hence they are genuinely consecrated. The worshipper then visits the 'Post the Host' website, where he or she can find a video of Blake celebrating the sacrament. There are various styles of Eucharist to choose from, ranging from the traditional Roman Catholic Tridentine Mass to a modern trendy version in which Blake appears in a T-shirt, and addresses Jesus Christ throughout as 'J.C.' The worshipper consumes the elements at the appropriate point in the selected service (Blake 2007).

Predictably, this liturgical innovation has proved controversial. Both the celebrant and the worshipper handle the Eucharistic elements, but they are separated by physical distance, with no facilities for mutual physical contact—Blake cannot observe the worshipper, although the worshipper sees and hears Blake. The situation is very different from the traditional practice of bringing the reserve sacrament to the housebound, where there is physical continuity between those present at worship and the recipient of the sacrament. Further, there are issues about maintaining the safety of a sacred object. It is normal practice for clergy to ensure that worshippers do not secrete the Eucharistic elements and take them away. Being sacred objects, they are not to be handled outside the context of the Eucharist. If a host or a quantity of wine is sent through the post, it is handled by others who are not part of the worshipping community, and there is the additional risk of interception. Hosts that have been taken from worship have sometimes—although admittedly rarely—given rise to superstitions: their 'owners' have occasionally been known to allege their miraculous powers, or to claim that they have bled with Christ's blood. While the Church, for good reason, wishes to avoid these scenarios, such considerations do not worry Blake: in response to the question of whether the posted host might be intercepted by 'devil worshippers', he writes:

We believe that Jesus can take good care of himself. The Bible says that Jesus visited hell itself in order to redeem. We believe the more of Jesus that is spread around the world the better. (Open Episcopal Church 2019)

Another ambitious attempt at digital church is the VR Church, set up in 2016 by 'Bishop' D.J. Soto. The church exists entirely in cyberspace, and holds regular services, attended by members using VR headsets. Attendees adopt an avatar, and the technology enables them not only to listen to prayers and sermons, but to move in and around the congregation, enabling interactions between groups of people, who can perform quasi-tactile activities such as walking in, sitting down, shaking hands and hugging. More controversially, the VR Church has administered cyber-baptism (Carlton 2018). Obviously, in cyberspace one cannot use real water, but one can simulate the sound of water, accompanied by simulations of baptismal water being poured on the candidate. Evidently, baptismal candidates have found this a moving and inspiring experience, although such innovations raise the question of whether a 'valid' baptism has been administered, since physical water is not present (BBC 2019). In 2002 the Vatican, while acknowledging the possibility of religious experience through the Internet, declared that there cannot be online sacraments: 'Virtual reality is no substitute for the Real Presence of Christ in the Eucharist, the sacramental reality of the other sacraments, and shared worship in a flesh-and-blood human community' (Foley 2002). Cyber-religion involves emerging technology, and no doubt emergent theology, and at this point in its development it is unclear whether such innovations will gain acceptance, or whether the Church will continue to maintain the tradition of having its sacraments performed in ways that that allow physical contact among its members.

COVID-19 AND THE AVOIDANCE OF TOUCH

This book was about to go to press when the Covid-19 coronavirus broke out. First detected in Wuhan, China in December 2019, the virus quickly spread from Asia to Europe and the United States. Measures to control the virus included a prohibition on mass gatherings, introduced in the middle of Lent, when extra forms of devotion take place, such as Lent lectures and study groups, Palm Sunday processions and Holy Week gatherings, including the Maundy Thursday foot washing. Above all, the inability to receive the sacramental bread and wine was a source of particular regret.

Different congregations reacted in different ways. While most Christians found ways of continuing to practise their faith while complying with such difficult restrictions, a small handful of congregations, mainly in the Protestant fundamentalist tradition, regarded state policy as an infringement of religious freedom, and in the US as a violation of the First Amendment. Some pastors, such as Tony Spell of the Life Tabernacle Church, Baton Rouge, argued that public worship was even more essential than shopping and exercising, and that the right to worship, he contended, is given by God and not the State. A few evangelical US pastors encouraged their congregations to defy the ban, claiming that Covid-19 was Satan's attack on God's people, and that God would offer them physical protection from the virus. Pastor Rodney Howard-Brown of the River Church, Tampa, told his large congregation, all of whom were sitting in close proximity to each other, 'They don't want us to do this, but just turn around and greet two to three people, tell 'em you love 'em, Jesus loves 'em.... This has to be the safest place.' His congregation then shook hands and hugged each other (Now This News 2020). By contrast, Bishop Michael Curry, primate of the Episcopal Church in the US, insisted that loving one's neighbour was more important than physically attending church, and that the Church was not a physical edifice, but was the totality of God's people. He pointed out that, although it was a disappointment for Christians that churches were not open on Easter Sunday, there were no churches to attend on the first Easter morning (ABC News 2020). Accordingly, many congregations in the Roman Catholic, Lutheran, Anglican and Methodist traditions have made a point of streaming their services online, allowing many of the tactile components of worship to be seen, although not directly experienced. Since consecrated bread and wine are not permitted without the presence of an ordained minister, the practice of 'spiritual communion'—a rite that was little known until the epidemic—has been revived. In this rite it is acknowledged a Christian may receive the sacrament 'spiritually' if he or she cannot access the Eucharistic elements, but repents of sins and accepts the saving power of Christ's death.

The notion of receiving the sacrament by desire has a long pedigree, going back at least as far as Thomas Aquinas (1225–1274), who wrote '... one can be changed into Christ, and be incorporated in Him by mental desire, even without receiving this sacrament' (Aquinas 2017 [1920]: 73). Pope John Paul II endorsed the practice in his 2003 encyclical *Ecclesia de Eucharistia*; he quoted Saint Teresa of Ávila (1515–1582), who wrote, 'When you do not receive communion and you do not attend Mass, you can make a spiritual communion, which is a most beneficial practice; by it the love of God will be greatly impressed on you' (John Paul II 2003: 34). In the Reformed tradition, reference to the practice can be found in the 1549 *Book of Common Prayer*:

> But yf any man eyther by reason of extremitie of sickenesse, or for lacke of warnyng geven in due tyme, to the curate, or by any other just impedimente, doe not receyne the sacramente of Christes bodye and bloud then the curate shall instruct hym, that yf he doe truely repent hym of his sinnes and stedfastly beleve that Jesus Christ hath suffered death upon the crosse for hym, and shed his bloud for his redempcion, earnestly remembring the benefites he hath therby, and geving hym hertie thankes therfore; he doeth eate and drynke spiritually the bodye and bloud of our savioure Christe, profitably to his soules helth, although he doe not receyve the sacrament with his mouth. (Church of England 1549: 22)

Archbishop Thomas Cranmer principally had infirmity in mind when he compiled *The Book of Common Prayer*, but the circumstances and the language in which the invitation is expressed have been updated for 2020. At Lichfield Cathedral in England, worshippers are invited to open their hands, as if physically handling the elements, while the priest receives the sacrament in the conventional way on screen, and the following words are pronounced:

> Thanks be to you, Lord Jesus Christ, for all the benefits you have given me, for all the pains and insults you have borne for me. Since I cannot now receive you sacramentally, I ask you to come spiritually into my heart. O most merciful redeemer, friend and brother, may I know you more clearly, love you more dearly, and follow you more nearly, day by day. Amen. (Lichfield Cathedral 2020)

METAPHORICAL REFERENCES TO TOUCH

Finally, mention should be made of metaphorical uses of tactile imagery. Michelangelo's famous fresco in the Sistine Chapel of the Creation of Adam depicts God's finger nearly touching Adam's. God is frequently depicted anthropomorphically in the Bible, enabling him to be endowed with sensory attributes, including touch. The non-meeting fingers may indicate the need for humanity to take the initiative in reaching out to God—an idea that is reflected in a modern gospel chorus 'Reach out and touch the Lord as he goes by'. One YouTube rendering of the song depicts two near-meeting human hands in similar position to those depicted by

Michelangelo (YouTube 2011). There are numerous biblical injunctions to 'hold fast' to God, whose hand offers guidance and protection, and such descriptions are reflected in Christian hymnody, in hymns such as 'Leaning on the Everlasting Arms', inspired by the biblical verse, 'The eternal God is thy refuge, and underneath are the everlasting arms' (Deuteronomy 33:27, KJV), and popularised by the 1950s Billy Graham rallies. Jesus invites his followers to 'take my yoke upon you' (Matthew 11:28)—another tactile reference alluding to the coupling of oxen to pull a heavy load. The metaphor of yoking is frequently used in the Old Testament to signify political subservience, and Jesus' metaphor therefore suggests not only comfort for the 'weary and burdened', but may also allude to the burden of Mosaic legalism, which the Christian new covenant claims to remove.

Tactile allusions are not always positive and encouraging. The writer to the Ephesians describes the Christian life as a 'struggle', which he portrays as physical combat, for which one must 'put on the full armour of God'. It is a battle not merely against physical opponents but 'against the powers of this dark world and against the spiritual forces of evil in the heavenly realms' (Ephesians 6:10-12). Inspired by these words, the prayer attributed to Saint Patrick, and known as Saint Patrick's Breastplate, is sung as a hymn, which begins 'I bind unto myself today / The strong name of the Trinity.' The word 'bind' indicates the close proximity of this part of the warrior's armour, and was invoked by Saint Patrick for divine protection when converting the Irish people from Paganism to Christianity. The concept of 'binding' not only connotes the nearness of God, but the whole Church as a body that is bound together—an idea promoted in other Christian hymns, such as 'Blessed Be the Tie that Binds'. Indeed, as Durkheim pointed out, the root meaning of the word *religere* is 'to bind' (Durkheim 1971 [1915]: 47).

Finally, there is a sense in which any act performed with Christian piety can be reckoned to be touched by God, and transformed into a sacred act. The famous poem by George Herbert (1593-1632), which begins 'Teach me, my God and King, / In all things thee to see', frequently sung as a hymn, ends with the verse:

> This is the famous stone
> That turneth all to gold;
> For that which God doth touch and own
> Cannot for less be sold.
> (Herbert 1991: 174)

The allusion here is to alchemy. Just as the legendary philosopher's stone could turn base metal into gold, Herbert's hymn suggests that a humble task (he mentions a servant sweeping a floor) is transformed into something truly worthy when the worker makes it an act of devotion to God, allowing it to be—at least metaphorically—touched by him.

CONCLUSIONS

This discussion has shown first, and most obviously, that touch has a more important role within the Christian faith than is immediately apparent. Touch has an important role in making the intangible tangible, maintaining tradition and performing rites of passage and ceremonies of initiation. It is vital to the sacraments and to sacramentals and has an important role in guiding believers through the liturgical calendar, enabling them to re-enact key events pertaining to their tradition, identifying themselves with happenings in which they would have liked to have participated, if only they had lived in a previous era. Touch also serves as a channel through which healing and grace are channelled. Objects and places that can be touched and handled can be understood at different levels by different believers: some may believe that they have inherent potency and quasi-magical power, while others perceive them as aids to developing one's spiritual life. The use of physical aids that can be handled is more popular in the Orthodox and Catholic traditions, while within Protestantism there remains a fear that they could encourage superstition, and detract from true faith in Christ. Whether the tactile is a useful accompaniment to faith or a hindrance to it is an issue that continues to divide the various strands of Christianity.

BIBLIOGRAPHY

ABC News. 2020. 'Bishop who preached at Prince Harry, Meghan's wedding says "We are doing God's will by not going to church" during coronavirus pandemic'. 10 April. https://abcnews.go.com/GMA/News/bishop-preached-prince-harry-meghans-wedding-gods-church/story?id=70083083

Aquinas, Thomas. 2017 [1920]. *Summa Theologiae*. III, 73. http://www.newadvent.org/summa/4073.htm

Augustine. 2010. *On the Free Choice of the Will, On Grace and Free Choice, and Other Writings*. Cambridge: Cambridge University Press.

BBC. 2019. 'Sunday: Virtual Reality Baptisms'. Radio 4, 29 May. https://www.bbc.co.uk/sounds/play/m0005dxw

Blake, Jonathan. 2007. 'Post the Host Street Mass'.
https://www.youtube.com/watch?v=z7KCKNlJNIc.
Blake, Jonathan. 2019. 'About Bishop Jonathan Blake: Biographical Details'. www.bishopjonathanblake.com/about-jonathan-blake.htm
Calvin, John. 1870 [1543]. *A Treatise on Relics*. 2nd edition. Edinburgh: Johnstone, Hunter & Co.
Carlton, Bobby. 2018. 'Tech-Savvy Pastor Uses VR To Deliver Virtual Baptisms'. 27 May.
https://vrscout.com/news/pastor-delivers-vr-baptisms
Catechism of the Catholic Church. 1994. London: Geoffrey Chapman.
Church of England. 1549. 'The Order for the Visitacion of the Sicke, and the Communion of the Same'. In *The Book of Common Prayer*, chapter 22.
http://justus.anglican.org/resources/bcp/1549/Visitation_Sick_1549.htm.
Church of England. 1968 [1662]. *The Book of Common Prayer*. London: Collins.
Church of England. 2000. *Common Worship*. London: Church House Publishing.
Connaughton, Luke and Stannard Silcock. 1997. *A-Z of the Catholic Church: Its Doctrines, Teachings, Personalities and Controversies*. Bury St Edmunds, UK: Kevin Mayhew.
Dearmer, Percy. 1907. *The Parson's Handbook*. London: Henry Frowde.
Durkheim, E. 1971 [1915]. *The Elementary Forms of the Religious Life*. London: George Allen and Unwin.
Foley, John P. 2002. 'Pontifical Council for Social Communications: The Church and the Internet'. 22 February.
http://www.vatican.va/roman_curia/pontifical_councils/pccs/documents/rc_pc_pccs_doc_20020228_church-internet_en.html
Herbert, George. 1991. *The Complete English Poems*. Harmondsworth, UK: Penguin.
Hymns Ancient & Modern, Council of. 1983. *Hymns Ancient and Modern, New Standard*. Norwich UK: Hymns Ancient & Modern Ltd.
John Paul II. 2003. Encyclical Letter: *Ecclesia de Eucharistia*: The Eucharist in Its Relationship to the Church.
www.vatican.va/content/john-paul-ii/en/encyclicals/documents/hf_jp-ii_enc_20030417_eccl-de-euch.html
Kosloski, Philip. 2017. 'How Do You Dispose of Old Sacramentals?' *Aleteia*, 6 October.
https://aleteia.org/2017/10/06/how-do-you-dispose-of-old-sacramentals/
Lichfield Cathedral. 2020. Choral Eucharist for Easter Day 12 April 2020.
https://www.lichfield-cathedral.org/downloads/worship-at-home-resources/easter-day-2020.pdf
Morello, Sam Anthony. 2000. 'Scapular Catechesis: The Brown Scapular of Our Lady of Mount Carmel'.
https://www.meditationsfromcarmel.com/content/scapular-catechesis
Now This News. 2020. 'Conservative Pastors Encourage Congregants to Dismiss COVID-19'. www.youtube.com/watch?v=Z200D8dAWLM.
Open Episcopal Church. 2019. 'Post the Host'.
http://www.postthehost.net/5064.html?*session*id*key*=*session*id*val*
Sacred Heart Holdings. 2019. 'Catholic Sacramentals'.
https://www.catholicsacramentals.org/blessed-salt
St Stephen Walbrook. 2019. London Internet Church.
https://ststephenwalbrook.net/internet-church

Vatican. 2012. *The Liturgy Documents, Vol. 2.* Chicago: Liturgy Training Publications.
Wynne-Jones, Jonathan. 2010. 'Church Minister to Tweet Holy Communion to the Faithful'. *The Telegraph*, 24 July. https://www.telegraph.co.uk/technology/twitter/7908263/Church-minister-to-tweet-Holy-Communion-to-the-faithful.html
YouTube. 2011. 'Reach Out and Touch the Lord'. https://www.youtube.com/watch?v=yraR2oToREE.
YouTube. 2017. 'Rowan Atkinson, The Church Attitude towards Fellatio'. https://www.youtube.com/watch?v=mSwaqhwUOT4

George D. Chryssides is an Honorary Research Fellow at the University of Birmingham and York St John University (UK). He has taught at various British universities and was Head of Religious Studies at the University of Wolverhampton from 2001 until 2008. Having written extensively on Christianity and new religious movements, he has a particular interest in Jehovah's Witnesses. Recent publications include *Jehovah's Witnesses: Continuity and Change* (2016), *Historical Dictionary of Jehovah's Witnesses* (2nd edition 2019), *Minority Religions in Europe and the Middle East* (2019), *The Insider-Outsider Debate* (co-edited with Stephen E. Gregg, 2019) and *The Bloomsbury Handbook to Studying Christians* (co-edited with Stephen E. Gregg, 2020). George Chryssides is currently president of the International Society for the Study of New Religions, and a Governor of Inform (Information Network on Religious Movements), based at King's College London.

Index

abstinence 1
active touch 175
Adam (and Eve) 261, 271
Advent 260
Adventist 261, 264
affective senses 14, 175
Africa/African 2, 4, 10, 13, 28, 98, 100, 104, 106, 177, 192, 217, 223, 224, 225, 253
African Caribbean 217
agency x, 5, 25, 29, 38, 105, 168, 242
Aghoris 220
Aho, Marko 95, 98, 99
Alaska/Alaskan 219, 229
Alcala de los Gazules 67, 68, 79, 85, 86, 88, 90
alchemy 273
altar(s) 9, 11, 12, 53, 68, 70, 76, 86, 87, 90, 170, 266, 268
Amma (hugging saint) 237
amman 145
amulets 31, 256
Andalusia 28, 67, 68, 70, 73, 86
Anglican 18, 122, 124, 254–258, 261, 265, 266, 270
Anglo-Indian 11, 114, 116, 134, 119, 120
animals 96, 107, 139, 145, 236, 259, 261
animism xii, 10, 21, 73, 92, 97, 104–106, 109, 113
anointing 44, 162, 260, 261, 263
anxiety 155, 156, 160–162, 166
apprenticeship 34, 36, 39, 140, 183
Aquinas, Thomas 270
Aristotle 105, 184, 187

ash 18, 60, 97, 220, 261
Ash Wednesday 18, 261
Atkinson, Rowan 255
Atlantic Slave Trade 223
audition 175, 181
Augustine 95, 253
Ayahan 138–140
Aztec 222, 228

bagpipes 109
Bali 13, 138, 140, 142, 145, 147–151
baptism 18, 257, 262, 264, 265, 269
Baptist/Baptist church(es) 264
bard(ism) 101, 96
Barnabas 265
basket divination 14, 175, 177–185, 188
Basu, Paul 115, 116, 132
Bates, Eliot 93, 96, 104, 107, 108
BDSM 195, 196–201, 203–206, 208, 211, 212
bell ix, 15, 138, 266
benediction, 259
Benjamin, Walter 115, 117, 155
Bible 253, 254, 263, 266, 268, 271
binding 72, 272
bishop(s) 88, 123, 125, 261, 265–267, 269, 270
Blacking, John 93, 95, 106
Blake, Jonathan 97, 267, 268
blessing(s) 15, 42, 53, 54, 58–60, 62, 256, 258, 259
blind 177, 263
blood 32, 39, 40, 80, 139, 144, 146, 161, 162, 214, 218, 222, 223, 227, 256, 268

blood-letting 16, 32
bodily sensation 6
body fluids 56, 63
body knowledge(s) 2, 7
Bonar, Horatio 255
bone(s) 10, 93, 146, 164, 221, 225–228
Book of Common Prayer 271
boundaries 4, 7, 105, 201, 203, 211, 216
Braille 253
Bräunlein, Peter 2
Brown, Rodney Howard 270
burial 4, 17, 217, 222, 223, 225, 227, 228, 259, 260
Bwiti 10, 106, 107

Cadiz 68, 85
Calvin, John 3, 260
camarista(s) 70, 77, 81
candle(s) 18, 83, 217, 218, 249, 260, 261, 262, 265, 267
Catechism of the Catholic Church 257
cathedral(s) 12, 122, 123, 125, 129, 266, 271
CDs 94, 267
chancel 260, 261
Chevra Kadisha 17, 222
Chidester, David 3, 27, 182, 215, 216, 217, 219, 228
children xi, 15, 17, 51, 73, 82, 85, 116, 120, 122, 141, 158, 160, 174, 261, 264
chrism 18, 261, 262, 263, 265, 266
Christian/Christianity 3, 5, 11, 12, 18, 20, 27, 29, 43, 72, 97, 102, 105, 134, 218, 226, 228, 237, 247, 253–255, 257, 260, 262–264, 267, 270, 272, 273
Christopher (Saint) 257
Church of England 255, 265, 266, 267, 268, 271
Church of Fools 267
Church of the Holy Sepulchre 260
coffin club(s) 154, 163–171
communication 14, 26, 27, 73, 103, 144, 153, 157, 162–164, 166, 167, 168, 179, 188, 205, 207, 237
communion of saints 263

compassionate community 157, 173
confirmation 18, 262, 265
consent 157, 198, 201–203, 239
consumption 26, 55, 58, 59, 60, 62, 63, 93, 94, 180
corporeal ix, xi, 16, 27, 143, 145, 201
corpse-handler 221
Corpus Christi 258
Covid-19 6, 10, 17, 18, 67, 72, 79, 85, 90, 150, 215, 216, 225, 243, 269, 270
Cranmer, Thomas 271
cremation, 4, 14, 15, 146, 219, 220, 223, 224
cross(es) 18, 83
crucifixes/crucifixion 18, 256, 260
cult (of the Virgin) 87
Curry, Michael 270

darshan 13, 57, 58, 144, 145, 149, 237
death doulas 14, 154, 155, 157, 173, 174
decomposition 214, 215, 217, 218, 229
deity 8, 15, 51, 53–55, 57–62, 108, 137, 143–145, 148, 219, 220, 228
DeVale, Sue Carole 106–108
devotionals 9, 68, 69, 75, 76, 78, 87
De Witte, Marleen 3, 5, 27, 73, 155, 217
dialogue xi, 175, 181, 249
digital ix, 117, 122, 254, 266, 267, 269
disciples 255, 262, 263
disease 11, 17, 158, 160, 214, 215, 223–225, 229
divination basket 176, 183, 185
diviners 175, 176–181, 183–187
Douglas, Mary 60, 216
dress/ing 54, 55, 58, 59, 217–221, 229
dry 40, 140, 214, 215, 221, 226, 228
dying 14, 154–164, 169, 217, 260, 263

Easter 18, 83, 261, 262, 270
Eastern Orthodox 254, 260, 225
Ebola 215, 216, 224
Eck, Diana 57, 143
e-devotion(als) 86, 87
edgework 16, 201, 203, 211, 212
Elisha 257

embodiment x, xi, 5, 17, 79, 82, 146, 244
emotions 94, 108, 121, 160, 162, 164, 171, 196, 198, 204, 237
empirical (data) 115, 117, 121
end of life (see dying) 14, 154, 155, 157, 162, 163, 214
energies, transfer of 52, 54, 56
enhanced sight 180
Entwistle, Joanne 56, 63
ethical 157, 158
Eucharist 18, 254–256, 262, 263, 267–270
evil spirit 257, 263
extended touch 159, 181, 237
extreme unction 263
ex voto(s) 69, 75, 81, 86, 87
Ezzy, Douglas 202, 203

FaceBook 12, 86, 87, 108, 121, 123, 125, 126, 128, 132
fear 36, 143, 149, 150, 155, 156, 162, 166, 204, 209–211, 219, 220, 259, 273
feet 15, 37, 40, 54, 72, 90, 95, 98, 145, 158, 160, 162, 182, 217–219, 237, 262
festivals 13, 144, 145, 238, 244, 245
fingertips 7, 14, 15, 39, 74, 94, 99, 167, 169
flagellation (self) 16, 145
font 264, 266
Frazer, James 9, 56, 76
Fuller, C.J. 59, 60, 61, 143
fundamentalism/t 263, 270
funeral(s) 159, 161, 169, 170, 215, 217, 222, 225

garments, 1, 57, 58, 61, 258
Geertz, Clifford 89, 137, 138
Gell, Alfred 31–33, 57, 77, 144
genealogy 115
gentle touch/massage 155, 159, 166, 173
Ghana 217
ghost(s) xi, 218, 225
gift(s) xi, 44, 54–56, 58, 60, 62, 150, 177, 224, 265, 266
Glastonbury 259
Good Friday 18, 260
goses 161
Gospels 254, 265, 271

grace 60, 256, 257, 265, 273
Graham, Billy, 272
Greece 96, 98, 217, 218, 96, 98
grief 101, 156, 164, 165, 168, 169, 171
Guyanese Hinduism 8, 51–63

hair 7, 10, 161, 217
Haiti/Haitian 224
Hallowell, A. Irving 73, 109
handkerchiefs 218, 263
hands 1, 3, 7–9, 12, 13, 15, 16, 26, 28, 33, 37–40, 45, 46, 53, 55, 95, 96, 99, 100, 104, 106, 114, 131, 137, 140, 149, 155, 160, 162, 164, 165, 167, 168, 169, 170, 171, 176, 182, 185, 188, 198, 217, 218, 224, 248, 254, 255, 259, 260, 263, 265, 266, 269, 270, 271
haptic touch 175, 182
Harvey, Graham ix, xii, 5, 10, 13, 27, 73, 94, 105–107, 109, 137, 147, 149
Hawaii/Hawaiian 227, 228
healing 18, 32, 41, 72, 87, 165, 224, 226, 254, 257, 262, 263, 273
hearing ix, x, 3, 14, 175, 179–182, 184, 188, 249, 253, 254
hearpe 93, 98, 99, 108
Heathen/Heathenism 93, 96, 101, 102, 103
Helena (Empress) 259
Herbert, George 272, 273
Hermandad 72, 83, 84, 85, 87, 88
Hertz, Robert 215, 228
Hidatsa Sioux 219, 229
Hindu/Hinduism 8, 51–63, 137, 142, 149, 219, 228
holy communion 255, 266, 267, 270
Holy Grail 259
Holy Land 259
Holy Spirit 257, 264
holy water 18, 146, 219, 256, 257, 259, 264, 267, 269
Holy Week 86, 87, 260, 261, 269
Homo musicus 93
host 256, 258, 268
Howes, David 4, 9, 28, 57, 145, 149, 150, 166, 184

Hughes, Jessica 5
Huizinga, Johan 94
human corpse 17, 214, 225
human senses 175, 178, 180, 188
humility 262
hymns 255, 267, 272

icon(s) 27, 217, 218, 254
iconography 33
idol/idolatry 3, 77, 95, 144
images 3, 34, 54, 57, 60, 69, 73, 75, 76, 78, 83, 97, 108, 140, 141, 143, 176, 181, 184, 187
Ingold, Tim 4, 26, 45, 105–109, 168, 169, 178, 180, 186
initiation, 18, 35, 43, 177, 186, 252, 254, 261, 264, 265, 273
internet 18, 87, 115, 242, 268, 269
intersensory/intersensorality 14, 144, 176, 184
intimacy/intimate 8–11, 14, 17, 56, 59, 62, 63, 72, 77, 81, 83, 90, 93, 118, 128, 144, 147, 159, 200, 201, 202–205, 207, 208, 218, 220, 226, 227, 228, 237, 238, 240–243, 245, 246, 249
Islam(ic) 13, 15, 29, 222

James 262, 265
Jerusalem 260–262
Jesus Christ 254, 258, 263, 268, 271
Jewish/Judaism 12, 17, 116, 161, 222, 223, 263
John 265
Joseph of Arimathea 260
juthaa 8, 60, 61

Kant, Immanuel 184
kantele 98–100
Khan, Aisha 60, 198
kiss 13, 72, 156, 237, 238, 254
Kloß, Sinah 8, 51, 54, 55–57, 60, 61, 62

labour (ritual) 12, 139, 141, 149, 150
laying on of hands 224, 263, 265, 266
Lent 81, 261, 269
leprosy 263

Letcher, Andy 10, 93, 101, 102
Liberal Catholic Church 267
Lichfield Cathedral 271
Life Tabernacle Church 270
likeness (material) 19, 52, 56, 57
liminal 156, 157, 183, 201, 203, 216
liturgy/liturgical 18, 70, 77, 237, 254, 256, 257, 258, 260, 264, 268, 273
liturgical calendar 18, 260, 264, 273
lived religion x, xi, xii, 2, 6, 68
London Internet Church 267
Lord's Supper (see Eucharist) 255
Luther, Martin 3
Lutherans/ism 271
lyre 10, 93–110

magic/magical 9, 28, 30, 56, 103, 238, 248, 257
mantle 9, 13, 69–74, 78–82, 85, 88, 90
Marian shrine 9, 70, 143, 147
Marriott, McKim 53
mass 247, 255, 256, 261, 263, 268, 270
massage 41, 155, 158–160, 218, 243
material culture 20, 25, 26, 28, 66, 85, 235
material mediator 181
material oracles 176
material religion 2, 14, 27, 92, 176, 188
material symbol(s) 14, 60
materiality x, xii, 12, 21, 25, 28, 31, 68, 89, 92, 118, 128, 130
Matsunobu, Koji 102
Maundy Thursday 18, 261, 262, 269
Mauss, Marcel 26, 27
McDannell, Colleen 3
medallions 18, 81, 256
mediation 7, 28, 31, 33
Methodist 267, 270
Mexico/Mexican 225, 227, 228
Micronesia 43
Middle Ages 98, 106, 120, 260
migration 225, 52, 61, 63, 120, 134
Miller, Daniel 60
miracle(s) 68, 81, 86, 87, 227, 256, 263
monastic orders 258
monstrance 258, 259
mortality 14, 155, 156, 158, 261

movement xi, 15, 17, 42, 46, 71, 98, 99, 147, 148, 163, 167–169, 171, 182, 185, 187, 242
moving body 15, 175, 176, 188
murti 8, 51, 52, 54, 55, 58, 61, 62, 84, 143, 254
musical instrument 11, 12, 93, 95, 97, 98, 103, 104, 106–109
Muslim (see Islam) 16, 222, 237
Myer, Birgit 2, 5
myth 34, 105, 108, 228, 229

necrophilia 218
New Age 236, 238, 245, 248
New Testament 254
New York City 52, 55, 61
New Zealand (Aotearoa) 7, 14, 34, 114, 120, 121, 122, 126, 127, 129, 154, 163
ngombi 10, 106, 107
Nietzsche, Friedrich 95, 96
niskala 138, 145, 147–149
Noah 258, 259
Norris, Lucy 56

object(s) (religious) 3, 9, 12, 68, 254
objectivity 97, 178
offerings 11, 12, 15, 51, 54, 61, 69, 70, 73, 75, 78, 137, 138–142, 149
oil 18, 42, 43, 98, 143, 162, 219, 261–263, 265, 266
Old Catholic Church 259
Open Episcopal Church 267, 269
oracular centrism 178
ordination 18, 265, 266
orthopraxy 58, 137
Otto, Rudolph 94

Pagan/Paganism 94, 97, 100, 101–103, 202, 238, 239, 245, 247, 248, 272
Page, Christopher 99
Palm Sunday 261, 269
palms (of the hand) 7, 39, 204, 218, 261
Patrick (Saint) 272
Paul (Saint) 122–124, 263, 264, 265, 267
Pentecostal 107, 262

performance (ritual) 2, 9, 14, 18, 21, 36, 72, 95, 98, 101, 141, 182, 236, 240, 243, 246–248
physical comfort 159
physical touch 68, 74, 161, 254
pilgrim/pilgrimage 11, 15, 84, 105, 114–116, 122, 128, 132, 147, 227, 259, 260
Pinney, Christopher 57
Plate, Brent S. Rodriguez 4, 5, 7, 9, 19, 74
pleasure 16, 25, 94, 95, 132, 142, 197–200, 204, 206, 207, 246
Polanyi, Michael 27, 28
pollution 7, 13, 52, 58, 59, 60, 143, 146, 219, 220, 228
Polynesia/Polynesian 2, 27, 28, 31–34, 43, 46
polyrhythm 100, 106
Pope John Paul II 270
popular piety 18, 256–258
Positivism 177
Post the Host 268
prasadam 8, 59, 60, 61, 62
prayer 1, 11, 15, 42, 43, 79, 81, 87, 107, 123, 129, 156, 157, 162, 257, 258, 266, 267, 272
profane 3, 12, 26, 94, 163, 195
Protestant/Protestantism 3, 5, 105, 253, 254, 256, 260, 265, 266, 270
psalms 258
purity xii, 13, 52, 61, 138, 142, 143, 221, 223

reciprocity 6, 60, 74, 149, 204, 211
Red Power movement 17
relics 10, 226, 227, 228, 258, 260
religioning 16, 102, 105, 110, 195, 196, 212
reliquary 227, 260
repetition 95, 183
representation 1, 5, 7, 8, 25, 30, 32, 51, 74, 78, 169, 243
resurrection 225, 264
revelation 36, 45, 147, 188, 260
right hand of fellowship 265, 266
rites of passage 273
ritual economy 149

ritual efficacy 1, 14, 25, 26, 30, 38, 75
River Church, Tampa 270
Roman Catholic/Catholicism 18, 143, 162, 224, 225, 226, 227, 254–258, 260, 261, 263, 265, 268, 270
roots tourism 114–116, 118, 132
rosary/rosaries 11, 18, 69, 82, 86, 90, 256, 258

sacrament/sacramentals, 18, 162, 255, 256–259, 262, 263, 268, 270, 271, 273
sacred(ness) 3, 4, 7, 8, 10, 11, 13, 15, 18, 28, 30, 33, 43, 45, 57, 75, 89, 94, 127, 130, 137, 148, 163, 170, 195, 216, 219–221, 223, 227, 257–259, 268, 272
sacrifice(s) 105, 145
sadist(s) 198, 199
safe-word 203, 210
saints 226, 227, 263
salt 257
Samoa 8, 29, 32, 34, 43
Satan 270
saz 104, 107
scapulars 18, 257, 258
Schutz, Alfred 94
scop 99, 101, 108
séances 179, 181, 182, 188
seers 176, 177, 181
sekala 138, 145, 146, 148
Selvik, Einar 102, 103
sense of touch 1–4, 6, 7, 9, 10, 14, 19, 69, 154, 182, 184, 188, 196, 253, 254
sensorial modalities 175, 181
sensory orders 145, 149
sensotyping 178
sensual religion x, 2, 4, 5, 67
sex 1, 2, 11, 13, 41, 206, 208, 219, 221, 222
sexual abuse scandals 2, 11
shaking the basket 183
shakuhachi 102
shroud 221, 222
Shroud of Turin 259
sick 72, 162, 224, 261, 263
Sierra Leone 177, 225
sight ix, 14, 37, 142, 144, 149, 175–181, 187, 188, 216, 253, 254

sin 261, 264
Sistine Chapel 271
skill 7, 27, 28, 29, 37, 45, 149, 183, 201
skinscape 7, 8
smell 3, 15, 53, 138, 139, 142, 167, 184, 241, 253
snake handling 263
socially-bad/-good 214, 218, 219, 222–225, 229
somatic sense 182
songs 77, 106, 108, 267
Soto, D.J., 269
soul midwives 155
South America 2
Southeast Asia 2, 30, 227
souvenir 69, 75, 76
Spain 67, 72, 81, 83, 143
spanking 197, 201, 204, 206
Spell, Tony 270
spiritual communion 18, 72, 270
spiritual edgework 16, 203, 211, 212
spiritual knowledge 175, 180
Spock, Mr 96
Stallybrass, Peter 55
Star Trek 96
statue 9, 51, 54, 68, 70, 72, 74, 83, 144, 259
statue-person 73, 74, 75, 77, 78, 79
Stone of Anointing 260
storytelling 118, 163, 169, 170
Sun Dance 17
superstition(s) 148, 268, 273
sweat 15, 55–57, 62, 105
symbol(ism) 5, 7, 51, 60, 78, 183, 186, 220, 218, 227
symbolic 1, 5, 6, 26, 27, 32, 33, 36, 46, 67, 72, 73, 74, 77, 150, 175, 177, 181, 209, 256, 264
synergy 14, 176, 188

taboo 77
tactile knowledge 8
Taharah 222
talisman(s) 256, 257
Talmud 161
Tamil/Tamil Nadu 13, 140, 142, 143–145, 147, 149, 150

tapu 7, 32, 33
taste ix, 3, 17, 100, 138, 142, 143, 144, 184, 253
tattooing/tattoos 1, 2, 4, 7, 8, 25–46, 103
Taussig, Michael 56
therapeutic touch 14, 154, 262
Thomas 129, 253, 270
tools 8, 25, 26, 29, 164–169, 205
touch deprivation 167
touch therapy 159, 160
tradition 18, 26, 27, 30, 52, 69, 99, 102, 117, 195, 196, 217, 228, 246, 248, 253–257, 259–262, 264, 265, 267, 269–271, 273
transfer (touch as mode of transfer) 30, 52, 53, 54, 56, 59
transnational 8, 62, 63, 66
transubstantiation 199, 256
Tridentine Mass 268
Trossingen lyre 10, 97, 103, 108, 110
trust 59, 156, 201, 203, 208, 210–212, 244
truth (spiritual/divine) 14, 175–179, 181, 184, 187, 253
Turney, Jo 57

UK 68, 102, 121, 198, 201
USA 34, 225

Van Der Leeuw, Gerardus 94

Vatican 258, 269
veneration 12, 18, 52, 81, 83, 84
Verrips, Jojada 5
vigil 156, 157, 161, 262
Vikings 103
violation 201–203, 205, 207, 205, 211, 212, 263, 270
Virgin Mary 11, 68, 254, 258
Virgin of Alcalá 9, 10, 28, 67–90
Virgin of the Saints 70, 79, 81, 83–86, 89
visualism 178
VR Church 269

Wardruna 102, 103
washed/washing 18, 146, 217, 218, 219, 222, 224, 229, 262, 269
Watts, Tim 267
Weber, Max 94
wet 40, 139, 214, 215, 221, 226, 228
Whitehead, Amy, 40, 67, 73, 77, 78, 82, 139, 143, 144, 145, 149

Zaka 223, 228
Zambia 14, 175–177, 182, 183, 185, 187
Zoroastrian/Zoroastrianism 17, 218, 220, 221, 228, 229
Zwingli, Ulrich 3

www.ingramcontent.com/pod-product-compliance
Lightning Source LLC
Chambersburg PA
CBHW062003220426
43662CB00010B/1218